Charles Carleton Coffin

Redeeming the Republic

The Third period of the war of the rebellion, in the year 1864

Charles Carleton Coffin

Redeeming the Republic

The Third period of the war of the rebellion, in the year 1864

ISBN/EAN: 9783337118556

Printed in Europe, USA, Canada, Australia, Japan

Cover: Foto ©ninafisch / pixelio.de

More available books at **www.hansebooks.com**

REDEEMING THE REPUBLIC

THE THIRD PERIOD

OF

THE WAR OF THE REBELLION

IN THE YEAR 1864

BY

CHARLES CARLETON COFFIN

AUTHOR OF "THE BOYS OF '76" "THE STORY OF LIBERTY" "OLD TIMES IN THE COLONIES"
"BUILDING THE NATION" "DRUM-BEAT OF THE NATION"
"MARCHING TO VICTORY" &c.

Illustrated

NEW YORK
HARPER & BROTHERS, FRANKLIN SQUARE

Dedicated

TO

MRS. H. M. MILLER

FRIEND OF MANY YEARS, WHOSE LIFE WORK HAS BEEN THE IMPARTING
OF INSTRUCTION TO THOSE WHO WERE TO BE CITIZENS OF THE
REPUBLIC, AND THE INCULCATION OF A DEEP AND
REVERENT LOVE FOR OUR COUNTRY
AND ITS INSTITUTIONS

INTRODUCTION.

"REDEEMING THE REPUBLIC" is the third volume of the History of the War of the Rebellion. It is intended to present a concise but authentic narrative of the leading military operations and events during the third period of the war, from the opening of the year 1864 to the close of its summer months. When the war began, the one motive animating the people of the North was the preservation of the Union; but as the months rolled away, with clearing vision, it was seen that if the Union was to be preserved, slavery, which had caused the war, must be destroyed. Abraham Lincoln had issued a proclamation giving freedom to the slaves. It had been done as a war measure. Many men who at the outset had been earnest for the preservation of the Union questioned his right under the Constitution to promulgate such an edict, but the great majority of the people demanded that slavery should be exterminated. The issue, therefore, during the third period of the conflict, was not the preservation of the Union alone, but the redemption of the republic from the curse of slavery. This, quite as much as the maintenance of the Union, in 1864, was the motive which nerved the soldiers in battle, and prompted President Lincoln and the loyal people to reject all thought of peace till the last slave should be free and the flag of the Union waving throughout the country as the emblem of authority.

The midsummer of 1863 was distinguished by the victories of Vicksburg, the opening of the Mississippi River once more to peaceful commerce, and by the victory of Gettysburg, the turning-point in the war. The close of the year was characterized by the victories of Lookout Mountain, Missionary Ridge, and Knoxville, and the permanent occupation of the State of Tennessee by the soldiers of the Union. Up to that time there had been little unity of action by the commanders of the Union armies in the campaigns, which had been conducted in part by General Halleck, whose headquarters were in Washington. It was seen that for efficient and harmonious action there must be one commander who should have full control of military operations. To that end General Grant, who had won the victories of Donelson and Shiloh, who had planned the strategy of Vicksburg and Chattanooga, was created lieutenant-general by Congress and made commander of all the armies in the field. His appointment, in March, 1864, marked the beginning of a new period in the history of the war. This volume, therefore, is a narration of the leading events of the first months of the final struggle.

It will be seen that the conflict became more intense and sanguinary as the Army of the Potomac made its way, by successive flanking movements, from the Rapidan to the James, under General Grant, while the Army of the West, under Sherman, advanced similarly from Dalton to Atlanta.

On no European battle-field was there ever a loftier exhibition of bravery and valor—exhibited by Union and Confederate soldiers alike—than at the Wilderness, Spottsylvania, Cold Harbor, Petersburg, Resaca, Kenesaw, Marietta, and Atlanta; unbounded, aggressive energy on the one side, by the troops of the Union, and resolute determination on the other by the soldiers of the Confederacy.

Final victory is not determined alone by bravery, but by ability to endure. When the conspirators destroyed the Union, that they might establish an aristocratic government based on slavery, they were blind to the movements of the age, and ignorant of the material resources or physical power of a free people, endowed with all the industries and arts of a high civilization, to maintain millions of men in arms, supply every needful want, and construct a navy that should blockade every Confederate port. They did not see that instead of starving millions, ruin and desolation, the Northern States would become a great workshop; that every art and industry would thrive as never before. Neither, on the other hand, did they see that the time would come when there would be an utter exhaustion of supplies in the Confederacy; that slavery fostered no arts or industries; that in consequence there would come a fading away of all resources; and that there would come an hour when there would be utter inability on the part of the Confederacy to maintain the struggle.

It will be seen that the Confederate Government, in order to retrieve its waning fortunes, did not scruple to violate the laws of neutrality and hospitality by making preparations in Canada to organize a force for the release of Confederate prisoners, by gathering desperate men to make havoc, burn and destroy the great cities of the North, and inaugurate civil war throughout the country by an alliance with the secret and disloyal order known as the "Sons of Liberty." The plan, authorized by Jefferson Davis, failed through the vigilance and action of loyal men; but in its inception and attempted execution it will ever be a witness to the decadence of moral principle in those who could look with complacence upon a plan for letting loose a horde of ruffians upon an unprotected and unsuspecting people to burn, plunder, and destroy.

As in "Drum-beat of the Nation" and "Marching to Victory," I have endeavored to make an authentic record of events, divesting myself of prejudice as far as it is possible for one to do so who was in the conflict from the first month of the war to the closing scene. I cheerfully and unreservedly accord bravery, valor, and heroism to the Confederate soldiers as to those of the Union, great and distinguished ability to the generals commanding the Confederate armies, self-denial, patient suffering, privation, endurance, and sincere belief in the righteousness of their cause, to the people of the South; but on the other hand, after a quarter of a century has rolled away, and the passions and prejudices of the conflict are as ashes upon a hearth-stone, the conviction remains, and deepens with each passing year, illumined by the light of a loftier civilization than the world has ever seen, that the attempt to overthrow the benign government of the people, and the establishment of one based on slavery, will be regarded in the future not as a mistake, but as one of the gigantic crimes of all history. In writing the words, I am not conscious of any bitterness, but of pain and sorrow only. It was prompted by the aggressive spirit of the slave propagandists, who thought only of perpetuating their political power and the establishment of a nation in which the many should ever administer to the wants of the few.

As the artist gazing upon the landscape which he has attempted to portray sits down in despair over his inability to give adequate expression to its features, so I lay down my pen as I realize how feebly my words picture the valor, the love and devotion to the flag, manifested in the scenes of the Wilderness, Spottsylvania, Cold Harbor, Resaca, and Atlanta; but such as they are, I give them, that the sons and daughters of this fair land may know how much it has cost to Redeem the Republic.

I wish to express my obligations to Louis Prang & Co. for permission to use the spirited sketch of the scene on the *Kearsarge*, found on page 305, from their series of war pictures. Also for the illustration of General Sherman in the field, on page 217.

CHARLES CARLETON COFFIN.

BOSTON, *September*, 1889.

CONTENTS.

CHAPTER I.
OPENING OF THE YEAR 1864 1

CHAPTER II.
RED RIVER EXPEDITION 44

CHAPTER III.
THE GREAT COMMANDER 67

CHAPTER IV.
THE WILDERNESS 78

CHAPTER V.
SPOTTSYLVANIA 97

CHAPTER VI.
BERMUDA HUNDRED AND DREWRY'S BLUFF 133

CHAPTER VII.
FROM SPOTTSYLVANIA TO COLD HARBOR 153

CHAPTER VIII.
FROM CHATTANOOGA TO ALLATOONA 199

CHAPTER IX.
NEW HOPE AND KENESAW 228

CHAPTER X.
THE VALLEY OF THE SHENANDOAH 260

CONTENTS.

CHAPTER XI.
THE "ALABAMA" AND "KEARSARGE"................................... 288

CHAPTER XII.
FROM COLD HARBOR TO PETERSBURG 312

CHAPTER XIII.
APPROACHING ATLANTA 335

CHAPTER XIV.
THE SIEGE OF PETERSBURG 358

CHAPTER XV.
MOBILE BAY 377

CHAPTER XVI.
FALL OF ATLANTA 401

CHAPTER XVII.
CONFEDERATE RAIDS 427

CHAPTER XVIII.
POLITICAL AFFAIRS IN MIDSUMMER, 1864 439

CHAPTER XIX.
SILENT FORCES 454

INDEX 469

ILLUSTRATIONS.

	PAGE
Artillery going into Action	*Frontispiece*
Keeping Watch	7
Operations in the West	11
Washing up	15
Freedom	19
The Battle of Olustee	23
Return of the Union Army	27
Ulric Dahlgren	29
On the Way to Freedom	31
Destroying the Canal	35
Massacre at Fort Pillow	39
Union Refugees	45
Map of the Red River Expedition	49
Confederates under General Green	59
Passing the Dam	63
Lieutenant-general Grant receiving his Commission	69
Movement to the Wilderness	79
General Grant's Headquarters at Germania Ford	83
Major-gen. G. K. Warren	85
Wilderness Battle-field	87
In the Wilderness	89
Spottsylvania Court-house	98
House of Mr. Alsop	101
Map of Spottsylvania	103
Scene of Sedgwick's Death	105
General Sedgwick	107
"I propose to fight it out on this line, if it takes all summer"	113
The Field of the Bloody Angle	116
The House of Mr. McCool	123
Gen. Wesley Merritt	127
Sheridan and Stuart's Fight	129
From Cold Harbor to Petersburg	135

	PAGE
Pontoon-bridge, Point of Rocks, on the Appomatox. (From a Sketch made June, 1864.)	139
Engagement at Arrowfield Church	141
Laying Pontoons	143
Constructing Breastworks	145
Battle of Drewry's Bluff	147
From Spottsylvania to Hanover	155
Second Corps Batteries. (From a Sketch made at the time.)	158
Soldiers in Rifle-pits near Chesterfield Bridge, North Anna River. (From a war-time Photograph.)	159
Burning the Railway Bridge across the North Anna	160
Loading with Canister	161
Quarles's Mill, North Anna River. (From a Photograph taken in 1864.)	162
Pioneers constructing a Road at Ox Ford. (From a Sketch made at the time.)	163
Earthwork taken by the Second Corps. (From a Sketch made in 1864.)	164
Jericho Mill and Pontoon-bridge, North Anna River. (From a Photograph taken at the time.)	165
Map of the North Anna	166
Headquarters at Bethesda Church	169
The Fifth Corps at Totopotomoy Creek	175
Union Artillery at Cold Harbor	179
Attack of the Eighteenth Corps at Cold Harbor	183
Second Corps at Cold Harbor. (From a Sketch made at the time.)	185
Cold Harbor	187

ILLUSTRATIONS.

	PAGE
The Tavern at Cold Harbor. (From a Photograph taken in 1887 by the author.)	189
The Tenth Massachusetts Battery firing the Signal for the Assault. (From a Sketch made at the time.)	191
Officers' Quarters at the Front	194
Bomb-proof Shelter	195
Sharp-shooters, Eighteenth Corps	197
Sufferings of the Poor in Tennessee	201
From Ringgold to Resaca	205
Major-gen. George H. Thomas	208
Major-general McPherson	209
Buzzard's Roost	210
Cavalry Engagement, Snake Creek Gap	211
Engagement at Dug Gap	213
Railroad Depot at Resaca, Georgia	214
Gen. Leonidas Polk	215
General Sherman	217
Dragging out the Cannon	220
Burning Bridge at Resaca. (From a Sketch made on the morning of May 16, 1864.)	221
The Battle of Resaca. (From a Sketch made at the time.)	223
Battle of New Hope.—Attack of Hooker's Corps on the Right	229
Battle of New Hope.—Attack of Hooker's Corps on the Left	233
Ackworth Station. (From a Sketch made May, 1864.)	235
The Battle of Pickett's Mill. (From a Sketch made at the time.)	237
Battle of Dallas.—Logan Cheering his Troops	241
From Resaca to Kenesaw	243
Battle of Dallas.—Attack on Harrow's Division	245
Where General Polk Fell. (From a Sketch made in 1864.)	247
Deserters entering the Union Lines	249
Union Signal-station on Pine Mountain, looking towards Kenesaw	251
Kenesaw from Little Kenesaw	255
Marietta, 1864. (From a Sketch made at the time.)	257
Destroying the East Tennessee Railroad Bridge	261

	PAGE
Battle of New Market	263
Military Operations in the Shenandoah Valley	269
General Custer	271
Beginning of the Battle in the Woods	275
Early's Movement to Washington	279
Battle of Monocacy	282
The Defences of Washington	284
Confederates retreating across the Potomac with their Plunder	286
The *Alabama*	289
Raphael Semmes	292
Chart of the Cruise of the *Alabama*	297
The *Kearsarge*	299
Capt. John A. Winslow	303
Kearsarge and *Alabama*.—Hauling down the Flag	305
Movements of the *Alabama* and *Kearsarge*	309
The Second Corps, General Hancock, crossing the James. (From a Sketch made at the time.)	317
General Grant at City Point	321
Assault of Potter's Division, Ninth Corps	327
Attacking the Confederate Intrenchments at Petersburg. (From a war-time Sketch.)	329
Avery House, Headquarters of General Warren, in front of Petersburg. (From a war-time Sketch.)	332
Generals Hunt and Duane	333
The Fish-trap on the Chattahoochee where General Schofield crossed	336
Turner's Mill, Nickajack Creek	337
Major-general Schofield	339
General Howard's Corps crossing the Chattahoochee. (From a Sketch made at the time.)	341
Map of Atlanta and Vicinity	345
View of Atlanta, from the Union Signal-station east of the City. (From a Sketch made at the time.)	347
Where McPherson Fell	353
Return of the Cavalry	359
Tearing up the Rails	361
First Connecticut Artillery Siege Guns	363
Soldiers' Wells	365

ILLUSTRATIONS.

	PAGE
Behind the Breastworks	367
Capture of Guns by Miles's Brigade	371
Engineer's Lookout	375
Off Mobile Bay at Night	379
Admiral Farragut	381
Securing a Torpedo	383
The Opening of the Battle of Mobile Bay	387
The *Selma* surrendering to the *Metacomet*. (From a Sketch made at the time.)	392
The Battle of Mobile Bay	393
The Contest with the *Tennessee*. (From a Sketch made at the time.)	395
Capture of Fort Morgan. (From a Sketch made at the time.)	399
"I intend to place this army south of Atlanta"	403
Battle of Ezra Church. (From a war-time Sketch.)	407
Ezra Church	409
Gen. Judson Kilpatrick	411
Positions of the Union and Confederate Armies at Jonesborough	415
Battle of Jonesborough	417
Capture of Confederate Works at Jonesborough. (From a war-time Sketch.)	418
Confederate Prisoners taken at Jonesborough. (From a Sketch made at the time.)	419
Removing the People from Atlanta	423
General Sherman's Quarters	425
Gen. A. J. Smith	429
Forrest's Cavalry in Memphis	431
Ruins of Chambersburg	436
Agricultural Industry in the Confederacy	455
"Cotton is King!"—A Cotton Shed in New Orleans	458
Weaving in the Confederacy	460
Weaving in the North	461
The Power of Free Labor	463
"Sheep began to multiply upon the green mountains of Vermont"	465

REDEEMING THE REPUBLIC.

CHAPTER I.

OPENING OF THE YEAR 1864.

FOR two years and seven months the War of the Rebellion had gone on. The victories at Gettysburg, Vicksburg, Port Hudson, Lookout Mountain, Missionary Ridge, and Knoxville, won by the armies of the Union during the year, made the people of the North more than ever determined to carry on the war till the flag of the United States should be recognized everywhere throughout the country as the only rightful emblem of sovereignty.

Jan. 1, 1864.

Though the Confederate armies had suffered these defeats, they had won, during the year 1863, the victories of Chancellorsville and Chickamauga. Though the Mississippi had been opened and commerce was once more moving upon that river, though railroads had been torn up and locomotives destroyed, though the Army of the West had been forced out of Tennessee, the Confederate Government was as defiant as at the beginning. The newspapers of the Confederate States kept up the courage of the people by confident predictions of ultimate success. Far-seeing men, however, in the Confederate States saw that the resources of those States were rapidly wasting away, and that after a while there would be utter exhaustion. The soldiers might fight as bravely as ever, their courage on the battle-field and the *élan* of their charge upon opposing troops might be as noble as in the past, but they must be fed and clothed, and the waste of war made good if victory was to be won at last.

When the great conflict began the soldiers of the Confederacy were buoyant with hope. The victories won by them in 1862 had awakened a confident expectation of final triumph. Around their camp-fires they had sung of the "Bonnie Blue Flag," "Maryland, my Maryland." With the morning *reveille*, and at evening parade, the bands had played the tune of "Dixie." The soldiers had sung it on the march and by the bivouac fire. It had become the musical air of the Confederacy.

DIXIE.

Southrons, hear your country call you!
Up, lest worse than death befall you.
  To arms! to arms! to arms in Dixie!
Lo! all beacon fires are lighted,
Let our hearts be now united:
  To arms! to arms! to arms in Dixie!

  Advance the flag of Dixie!
    Hurrah! Hurrah!
  For Dixie's land we'll take our stand,
    To live or die for Dixie!
  To arms! To arms!
    And conquer peace for Dixie!
  To arms! To arms!
    And conquer peace for Dixie!

It was heard less frequently than at the opening of the strife. It is not easy for us to sing after defeat and disaster. More than this, the soldiers of the Confederate armies had begun to understand that the men opposing them were not the hirelings which the newspapers had represented them to be, but that they were fighting for the maintenance of the Union, and of the ideas upon which it had been established. They knew through sad reverses that the soldiers of the Union were as brave as themselves; still more, they knew that while they were suffering hunger and were in want of clothing, the men opposing them had abundant supplies. Many a Confederate soldier, with clearer insight than Jefferson Davis or the men composing the government, saw that the cause was waning, that the people of the United States were arousing themselves to prosecute the war with renewed energy.

The nations of Europe beheld with amazement the growing proportions of the mighty struggle—the marshalling of great armies by a people without military experience, and wholly unprepared at the beginning. Never before in the history of nations had there been such a voluntary uprising of a people to maintain a government. On April 15, 1861, President Lincoln called for seventy-five thousand militia to maintain the authority of the Government, and ninety-one thousand volunteers responded. On the 3d of May following he called for soldiers to serve for three years, and six hundred and fifty-seven thousand enlisted for three years, forty thousand for two years, and nearly ten thousand for one year. Again he called for volunteers in July and August, 1862, and four hundred and twenty-one thousand enlisted for three years, and eighty-seven thousand for nine months. From the beginning of the struggle to August, 1862, more than thirteen hundred thousand young men in the bloom of life left their farms and workshops and volunteered to maintain the authority of the Government.

But disease and death had decimated the ranks of the great armies. The Peace Democrats, a great political party, had declared that the Rebellion never could be put down, that the war was a failure, and demanded "peace at any price." No more volunteers came, and the President was obliged to issue, by authority of Congress, an order for a draft, under which, in 1863, three hundred and sixty-nine thousand soldiers were added to the ranks. It was seen that if the war was to be prosecuted vigorously the armies must be made still larger; and in March, 1864, the President issued another order for a draft, under which three hundred and eighty-six thousand were gathered into the ranks. During the three years ending April, 1864, two million three hundred and eighty thousand soldiers were marshalled, armed, and equipped, and furnished with all needful supplies.

The term of service of those who volunteered at the outbreak of the Rebellion had expired; but with unquenchable love for the flag of their country, many thousands re-enlisted, to serve till the last Confederate should lay down his arms. The veterans who re-enlisted are to be included in the twenty-three hundred and eighty thousand.

It never will be known just how many soldiers there were in the armies of the Confederacy, for there never were complete returns of those who volunteered or of those who were swept in by the conscription. When the war began, the young men, animated by military ardor, and by what to them was a lofty and ennobling idea—that they were called upon to maintain the sovereignty of the State, that their just rights had been invaded—hastened to enroll themselves as volunteers; but early in 1862 the enthusiasm began to wane, and the Confederate Congress passed an act giving Jefferson Davis authority to draft every able-bodied citizen between the age of eighteen and forty-five not specially exempted. There is no record of the numbers that were thus forced into the army. The first conscription called for those between eighteen and thirty-five years of age; but when the news of the defeat of General Lee at Get-

July, 1863. tysburg, of the surrender of Vicksburg and Port Hudson (see "Marching to Victory"), reached Richmond, the Confederate President called upon all men under forty-five years of age to repair at once to the camp in their several States. If they did not immediately do so they were to be regarded as deserters. When the Confederate Conscription act was passed it was estimated that there were between seven and eight hundred thousand men under thirty-five who could be brought into military service.([1]) The records of the Adjutant-general's office in Richmond were kept so loosely, and were in such confusion, that neither the Adjutant-general, the Secretary of War, nor Jefferson Davis could tell how many men were in the field.([2])

Mr. Seddon was Secretary of War and very friendly to Jefferson Davis, but he was incompetent to manage the multitudinous affairs of the Department. The muster-rolls in 1863 showed between four and five hundred thousand drafted and enlisted men in the field; but no one ever could tell how many had been gathered into the Confederate ranks, or how many had responded to the calls of the Governors of the several States. The conscription filled up the ranks thinned by death and disease, so that in the opening months of 1864 the Army of Northern Virginia, wintering on the banks of the Rapidan, was probably as strong as on the day when General Lee began his movement into Pennsylvania; while the army under General Johnston, at Dalton and vicinity, in Northern Georgia, was as powerful as those which fought the desperate battles of Shiloh and Chickamauga.

The Confederate Government passed a law to discontinue "the exemption from military service of those that had furnished substitutes." Only two votes were cast against it in the Senate. It was followed by the immediate disappearance from Richmond and other cities of a large number of men who had hired substitutes. Some of them made their way through the lines into the United States, others escaped on vessels running the blockade to Nassau, and from thence to Cuba or to England. A clerk in the Confederate War Department wrote this in his diary on the last day of December, 1863, the day following the passage of the law: "It rained the whole of this day; nevertheless, the Jews have been fleeing to the woods with their gold, resolved to take up their abode in the United States rather than fight for the Confederate States, where they leave in the ranks the substitutes hired by them."(')

Dec. 30, 1863.

We are not to understand that he had reference to the Israelites in the Confederacy, but to those men who had made money by speculation, and who had changed the Confederate paper-money into gold. We have a picture of the state of affairs in the capital of the Confederacy during the opening days of 1864. Flour was $150 per barrel; corn-meal $16 per bushel; guests at the hotels were paying $20 per day in Confederate paper-money; but an Englishman stopping at the best hotels, who had brought English shillings with him across the Atlantic, paid only seventy-five cents per day—of so little value was the paper-money. Colonel Preston gave a small dinner-party, which cost him $2000 in paper-money.(')

We are not to think that all the men in the United States who were liable to military service, between eighteen and thirty-five, were ready to take their places in the ranks when drafted; for when Abraham Lincoln issued his order for filling up the ranks, a great many men fled to Canada. A large number who called themselves Peace Democrats, who were opposed to the war, hastened at once beyond the reach of the draft officers, returning only when there was no longer any probability of their being called upon to enter the army.

The winter was cold and dreary and comfortless to the soldiers of the two great armies gathered on the banks of the Rapidan. Snow fell upon Union and Confederate alike, whirling around the huts which they had erected to shelter them from the blasts, blinding the eyes and chilling the sentries as they kept ward and watch against surprise. In the army

1*

of the Union there was abundant food, while the Confederate soldiers, through the inefficiency of the Commissary Department, through the wearing out of the railroads and locomotives, had scant supplies. The army under General Lee for many weeks had only one-half its daily allowance of food, and often during the winter had meat only two or three days in a week.

From the armies of the Union veteran soldiers were departing to their homes on furlough, to clasp loved ones once more in their arms—to hear the prattle of their little children—to look into loving eyes of parents, wife, or sister—to sit by the fire in the old kitchen and tell the story of the battles to listening neighbors; then bidding once more a tearful farewell, and returning to their comrades with their souls again on fire with love for the flag of their country.

In the ranks of the army under General Lee there was like constancy and devotion to the flag of the Confederacy. The Confederate soldier believed that he was fighting in a righteous cause, not comprehending that the war was inaugurated and maintained for the preservation of an institution which had become repugnant to the moral sense of men everywhere throughout the civilized world, and which, by attempting an overthrow of a government of the people, had doomed itself to destruction. That the soldiers of the Confederacy were mistaken as to the meaning of the war takes away nothing from their valor, courage, and endurance of hardship and privation. They believed that they were contending for their rights, yet it is quite probable very few of them would have been able to say just what their rights were. There were to be other weary marches, more battles, more outpouring of blood, before the fading away of the glamour which obscured their vision. Only by final defeat and exhaustion would they come to see that they had endured hardship and suffered defeat for the maintenance of slavery.

One of the newspapers of Richmond contained a long article upon the beneficence of slavery. "It is a system," it said, "in which the race enslaved has been brought to the highest condition of happiness and religious and social cultivation of which it is capable. It is an order of society, moreover, found to be peculiarly favorable to the development and permanency of republican institutions, relieving the State of all those dangers which have their birth in the passions of the mob."(⁴)

Jan. 2, 1864.

The Confederate Government was organized to maintain that institution. The Government of the United States, on the other hand, and the Union soldiers at the beginning of the war, had but one aim—the

KEEPING WATCH.

restoration of the authority of the United States; but in the progress of events the end in view had become the overthrow of the institution which was the corner-stone of the Confederacy.

When the war began, the few vessels composing the navy of the United States had been scattered far and wide by President Buchanan's Secretary of the Navy. (See "Drum-beat of the Nation," p. 29.) Through the three years of the struggle the Government had done what it could to create a navy which would effectually close by blockade every port of the Confederacy. So efficient had the navy become that at the beginning of 1864 the only ports which the blockade-runners of England could arrive at or depart from were Wilmington and Savannah, on the Atlantic coast, and Mobile, Galveston, and the mouth of the Rio Grande, on the Gulf of Mexico.

Only by taking advantage of nights when there was no moon, or when clouds shut out the stars, was there much chance for eluding the vessels lying off those ports, with crews ever on the watch. The growth of the navy had been very rapid. There were 75 iron-clad vessels, 393 steamers, and 112 sailing-vessels, numbering, in all, 588 vessels, carrying nearly 4500 guns, manned by 34,000 seamen. Nearly 1000 English vessels, valued at more than $20,000,000, had been captured and destroyed. So many vessels had been captured or sent to the bottom of the ocean, that the men in England whose sympathies were with the Confederacy, and who had been sending arms and ammunition across the Atlantic in exchange for cotton, began to find that their losses were more than their gains.

Jan. 1, 1864.

The vigilance and efficiency of the navy was having a marked effect upon the waning fortunes of the Confederacy. The Confederate Government, under the delusion that cotton was king, had established its financial system on that one agricultural product. When the conspirators brought about the war, they calculated that England would purchase three hundred million dollars' worth of cotton per annum; that the manufacturers, and the men and women who were spinning and weaving in the mills of Lancashire, would compel the British Government to break the blockade; but the brave-hearted men and women, who knew that the soldiers of the Union were fighting a great battle for freedom, though starvation had come to them and they were living on charity, gave their sympathies to the Union. (See "Marching to Victory," p. 114.) The blockade was not broken, nor was there any prospect that it would be. Very little cotton was finding its way from the Confederacy to England, and the Confederate financial system went down, through the vigilance of the men who, from the mast-heads of the blockading fleet, through the live-long nights scanned the horizon, while their vessels lay drifting upon the heaving sea or moving slowly between the headlands of the harbors. Planters in the heart of the cotton-growing States, whose sheds were piled with the harvests of three years, found themselves growing poorer, notwithstanding their accumulated crops of cotton. Their slaves were becoming burdensome, for they were no longer wealth producers but consumers. The Confederacy was ready to purchase corn and bacon from the planters, but the paper-notes of the Government were valueless. So slavery, the institution for the preservation of which the conspirators had inaugurated the war, was feeling the silent but effective work accomplished by the navy.

During the war, railroad junctions in the Confederate States were usually important places from the military point of view. Meridian, in eastern Mississippi, not far from the Alabama line, was a new town built in the pine woods, the junction of the railroad leading east from Vicksburg to Selma and Montgomery, in Alabama, and thence to Charleston and Savannah, and the road leading northward from Mobile to Corinth. The Confederate Government had selected Meridian as a convenient base for military supplies, had collected a large amount of provisions at that point, and established an arsenal and armory, where arms were repaired. It had thus become a place of great importance in connection with military operations. Lieutenant-general Polk was in command of the Confederate troops in Mississippi, with his headquarters at Meridian. He had two divisions of infantry, one commanded by General Loring, which was at Canton, on the railroad, a few miles north of Jackson, in the centre of the State, and the other commanded by General French, who was at Brandon, between Jackson and Meridian. The troops were stationed at these places because there was an abundance of food to be had from the surrounding plantations; and if they were needed at Mobile, or northward at Chattanooga, they could be sent by rail in either direction at short notice. More than this, they could be thrown forward to the Mississippi, and strike a blow in that direction should opportunity offer. The Confederate cavalry had become very bold, and steamboats on the Mississippi were frequently fired upon.

The Union troops at Vicksburg were under the command of General Sherman, who went to Nashville and asked permission of General Grant to organize an expedition with the special design of destroying the railroad junction and Confederate armory and stores at Meridian, which, if

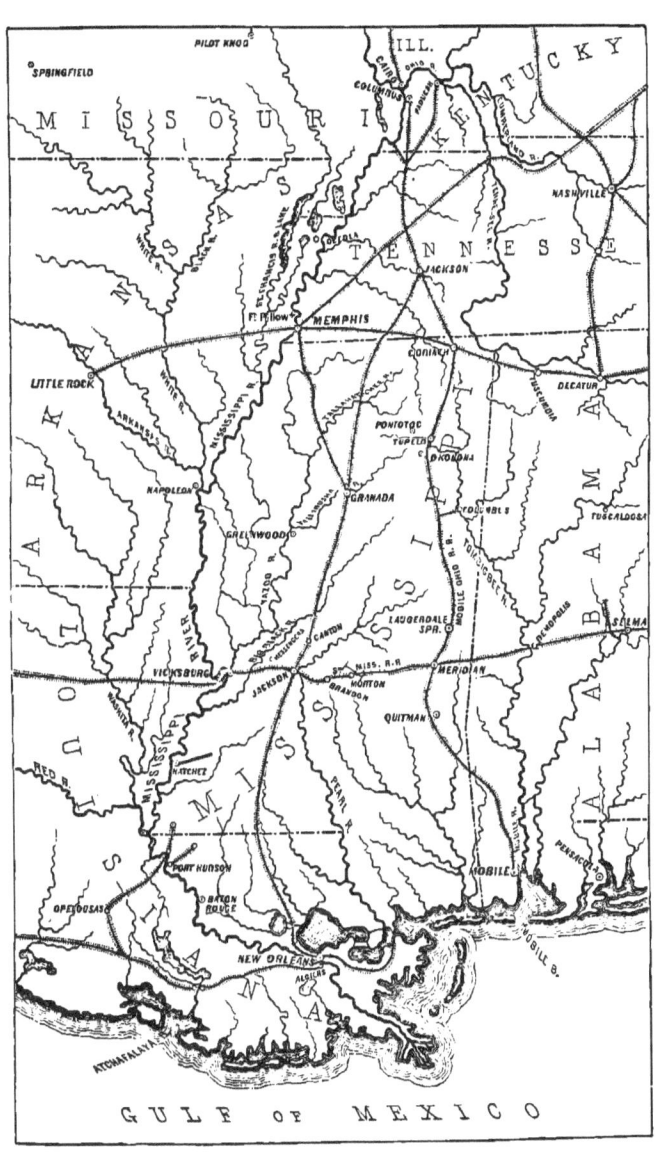

OPERATIONS IN THE WEST.

effectually done, would prevent the Confederate armies in Virginia and in front of Chattanooga from receiving supplies from the south-western section of the Confederacy. General Grant thought well of the plan. General Sherman's spies, who went out from Memphis and Vicksburg, informed him that besides the Confederate infantry at Canton and Brandon, there were between four and five thousand Confederate cavalry under General Forrest roaming through western Tennessee and northern Mississippi, moving rapidly, cutting off Union supply-trains and small bodies of troops, sending a few troops to fire upon steamboats, greatly annoying the Union commander. To put a stop to Forrest's operations, General Sherman directed Gen. William Sooy Smith to organize a large cavalry force, and to move from Memphis and scatter the Confederate cavalry. Smith was to start February 1st; Sherman, February 3d. Smith would march south-east; Sherman, due east.

"You will encounter Forrest. He is a good fighter, and you must always be prepared for him. After you have repulsed him you must attack and utterly rout him." Such the tenor of Sherman's instructions.(*)

It was a beautiful morning when the Sixteenth Army Corps, commanded by General McPherson, accompanied by the Seventeenth, commanded by General Hurlburt, marched eastward from their encampments at Vicksburg, preceded by a brigade of cavalry. There were forty-one regiments of infantry, three of cavalry, forty-two cannon; in all, nearly twenty thousand men. The roads were in excellent condition, and the soldiers, with life and spirit, after weeks of rest, marched rapidly, and at nightfall were seventeen miles on their way towards Meridian, kindling their bivouac fires at night on the eastern bank of the Big Black River. The next day they were marching past the battle-field on which they had won the notable victory of Champion Hills. (See "Marching to Victory," p. 70.) The succeeding day brought them to Jackson, where they had a skirmish with the Confederate troops sent out by General Loring.

Feb. 3, 1864.

At Decatur General Sherman narrowly escaped being captured. He rode up to a log-cabin, unsaddled his horse, threw himself upon a bed, and soon was sound asleep, but was awakened by the firing of pistols.

"The Rebel cavalry are all around us!" shouted Major Audenreid. General Sherman had himself posted a regiment at the junction of two roads as guard; but an officer, not knowing that he was in the house, had ordered the troops to move on. The Confederate cavalry had improved the opportunity to dash upon the wagon-train. Major Audenreid ran to bring back the troops, while General Sherman secreted himself in a corn-crib. The troops came upon the run, and the Confederates fled.(')

When the troops halted at night, they washed themselves at the village pump, kindled fires, cooked their coffee, and in the early morning again were on the march, making 160 miles in ten days. The advance was so rapid, the movement so unexpected, that the Confederates had not time to remove the locomotives and cars at Meridian. The railroad buildings and all the property belonging to the Confederate Government were burned, together with railroad bridges, and the tracks torn up eastward to Alabama, southward twenty miles, also westward and northward. Hearing nothing from the cavalry under General Smith, General Sherman began his return, reaching Vicksburg without a battle; having destroyed more than one hundred miles of railroad-track, burned sixty-seven bridges and seven thousand feet of trestle, destroyed twenty locomotives, twenty-eight cars, ten thousand bales of cotton, two million bushels of corn, owned by the Confederate Government, together with the arsenal and its machinery.

Swiftly from plantation to plantation spread the news of the movement of Sherman. The slaves knew of it before the information reached their masters; and when the sun went down, old and young, men, women, and children, were on the move, stealing noiselessly away from their cabins, with bundles in their hands or on their backs, on foot, on mules and horses, in rickety carts drawn by a single cow with rope harness—more than five thousand of them hastening to gain the freedom which had been given them by Abraham Lincoln, and which they knew would be theirs could they but go with the men who carried the Stars and Stripes.(*) They brought chickens, turkeys, and sucking-pigs to the soldiers, carried their knapsacks for them, waited upon them, thus expressing their gratitude. The movement was a blow which greatly crippled the operations of the Confederate army for the remainder of the year. It gave General Sherman an insight of the true condition of the country: that there were abundant supplies of food in the Confederacy, and that a Union army might cut loose from its base of operations without fear of starvation. What came of this observation we shall see in due time.

Where was the force of cavalry which started from Memphis on the 1st of February, and was to co-operate with the infantry? A military commander may lay his plans wisely, may think out a strategic movement which promises great results, but which may fail through the inefficiency of a subordinate officer. General Sherman had planned the

WASHING UP.

OPENING OF THE YEAR 1864. 17

movement not only to destroy Meridian, but to scatter Forrest's cavalry to the winds. He had given General Smith a strong force, had directed him to start on the 1st of February, but not till the 11th of the month was he in motion. He waited for a brigade which was on steamboats descending the Mississippi, and which was ice-bound at Columbus.(°) When at last he began his movement, Sherman was at Meridian, too far away to co-operate with him. General Forrest confronted him near Okalona, on the Mobile and Ohio Railroad. After destroying a portion of the railroad-track and a large quantity of corn and cotton, General Smith, finding Forrest so strong, returned to Memphis, accompanied by more than one thousand negroes, many of whom, a few weeks later, were enlisted as soldiers in the service of the Union. The cavalry movement had been inefficiently conducted, and General Forrest's forces, instead of being dispersed, became bolder than ever in their operations.

The Union and the Confederate armies west of the Alleghanies, at the beginning of 1864, were like men upon a chess-board. The Union Army of the Cumberland, under General Thomas, was at Chattanooga, confronted by a Confederate army at Dalton, Georgia, under Gen. Joseph E. Johnston, who had succeeded General Bragg. General Thomas had lost so many horses, and had such a scant supply of provisions, that he could not make any offensive movement, except a demonstration towards Dalton to prevent General Johnston from sending troops to General Polk.

It is twenty-four miles from Chattanooga to Ringgold, thirty-one to Tunnel Hill, the dividing line between the waters of the Tennessee northward and the streams which run southward to the Gulf of Mexico, and forty miles to Dalton. The advanced troops of General Johnston held Tunnel Hill, where the railroad from Chattanooga to Dalton passes through a tunnel. The Union troops held the battle-field of Chickamauga and the town of Ringgold.

General Palmer commanded the Union troops nearest to Ringgold. Deserters from Johnston's army came into his lines and said that Cleburne's and Cheatham's divisions of the Confederate army were hastening southward on the railroad to join General Polk. General Palmer thereupon sent word to General Thomas, who ordered an advance of all available troops towards Tunnel Hill. There was skirmishing between the Union and Confederate cavalry, cannonading by the artillery, the advance of Davis's, Cruft's, and Baird's divisions, which had the effect of bringing back the two Confederate divisions that had started to join General Polk.

Feb. 22, 1864.

2

General Thomas found that the Confederates occupied a very strong position, and that Johnston's army was larger than his own, and so returned to Ringgold and Chattanooga, having lost in the several skirmishes and in the attack of General Turchin's brigade at Tunnel Hill between three and four hundred men. But he gained valuable information. He saw that the position of General Johnston was very strong; that there were hills and mountain ranges rising sharp and steep, with white ledges of limestone crowning their summits; that there were natural fortifications which were being made impregnable by the Confederate soldiers; that westward of Tunnel Hill there was a valley, called Snake Creek Gap; that if an army could make its way through that pass, all of the strong positions could be flanked and made of no account. We shall see by-and-by how valuable was the knowledge gained by this movement.

Going to East Tennessee, we see a Union army under General Schofield at Knoxville, and a Confederate force under General Longstreet, who in November, 1863, had been repulsed with heavy losses in his attack upon Knoxville. (See "Marching to Victory," chap. xxiii.) General Longstreet's troops were at Bristol and Abingdon, subsisting upon the surrounding country. The army under General Schofield could make no aggressive movement, for want of horses and supplies. The country was becoming very poor, and the people of East Tennessee were suffering terrible hardships.

During the months of January and February there were numerous bands of guerillas in Tennessee—men who sympathized with the Confederates, who would be working on their farms one day as quiet, peaceable, unoffending citizens, who the next day would be miles away from their homes, burning bridges on the railroad, drawing spikes from the ties, rolling stones upon the track, or pouncing upon a Union army-train or an outpost guarded by half a dozen soldiers. There were frequent skirmishes and small engagements. General Thomas organized a force of loyal Tennesseans who were thoroughly acquainted with the country, who guarded the railroads and bridges, thus relieving the troops. The one line of railroad leading from Chattanooga to Nashville was repaired, but not till the month of March could there be any preparation for the great campaign of the year. Steamboats were built to ply upon the Tennessee, a great storehouse was erected at Chattanooga, blockhouses were built at the crossings of rivers, together with fortifications, so that a few troops would be able to protect the bridges. By such arrangements the Union cavalry, which had been guarding the railroads

FREEDOM.

and holding the country in rear of the armies, were relieved and placed in positions to take part in the approaching campaign.

President Lincoln was informed that there were a large number of Union men in Florida, and that if a military force were sent to that section a State government that would be loyal to the Union could be organized. He therefore directed General Gillmore, in command of the troops on the south Atlantic coast, who had captured Fort Wagner, and who had reduced Sumter to a shapeless ruin (see "Marching to Victory"), to send an expedition to Jacksonville. So it came about that on February 7th twenty steamers, several gunboats, and a fleet of schooners appeared off the mouth of St. John's River with five thousand troops, which landed at Jacksonville, and marched into the country along the line of the Central Railroad leading westward, dispersing small bodies of Confederate troops, capturing eight cannon, several wagons, a large amount of supplies, and several thousand bales of cotton. The object of the expedition was not only to establish a loyal government, but to procure an outlet for cotton and lumber. A great many slaves had made their way out to the blockading vessels along the coast, leaving their cabins and entering boats with a bundle of clothes, hoecake or chicken for food, and it was supposed that recruits might be obtained for the colored regiments.

Feb. 7, 1864.

The troops were under the command of Gen. Truman Seymour. Having scattered the Confederates and captured their cannon, General Seymour pushed on twenty miles to Baldwin, where he was directed by General Gillmore to concentrate his force.([10])

General Seymour, having accomplished so much, ardently desired to do more—to destroy the railroad bridge across the Suwanee River, twenty-five miles farther on; and so, without supplies, with a small quantity of ammunition, disregarding General Gillmore's orders, he ordered an advance from Baldwin.([11])

It was a wearying march along a sandy road, through pine woods and groves of live-oak, where long festoons of moss hung trailing from the trees. The troops made their way across marshes and through palmetto thickets. They had a scant supply of food. Herds of pigs were running wild in the woods, but General Seymour issued stringent orders that none should be killed. He was entering Florida on a mission of reconciliation, to re-establish the authority of the Government, and expected that the people would welcome his coming. An officer who disregarded the order, and who allowed his hungry men to kill a pig, was severely reprimanded.([12])

"You will come back faster than you advance," said the citizens who lived along the route, and who knew that the Confederates were concentrating for a battle. General Colquitt, with his brigade of Georgia troops, had arrived on the cars, sent by General Beauregard, in command of the Department, to Lake City to join General Finnegan. Instead of waiting for the Union troops to reach that place, General Finnegan ordered his army forward to a strong position in the woods, near the hamlet of Olustee, posting them along the railroad embankment. The Confederates outnumbered the Union troops and had twelve cannon. They had the advantage of position, and were acquainted with all the roads and winding paths, the marshes, ponds, and streams.

It was two o'clock in the afternoon; the Union troops had marched sixteen miles without halting, when the cavalry came upon the Confederate pickets. The troops were in three columns; Colonel Barton's brigade was on the right, consisting of three regiments, the cavalry and mounted infantry in the centre, with two regiments of infantry; the brigade of Colonel Hawley occupied the left, with three regiments of colored troops under Colonel Montgomery.

Feb. 20, 1864.

The flanks of the Confederate troops were protected by swamps. They had thrown up breastworks, and were quietly waiting for the advance of the Union troops. The thickets were so dense that the Confederate position could not be discerned. The advancing troops heard no commotion in front of them; only their own tramping and the sighing of the wind through the foliage of the lofty pines broke the silence. The Seventh Connecticut was in the advance; it passed a swamp and came out into a field, when suddenly from right to left there burst forth a deadly fusillade. Quickly the Union troops came into position and opened fire. In a very few minutes the battle was fiercely raging. There was brave fighting. The Union troops were veterans who had been in the terrible storm of Wagner. (See "Marching to Victory," chap. xvi.) The Confederates, behind their breastworks, and screened by the thickets, had greatly the advantage; but for three hours the contest went on, till the ammunition of Union and Confederate alike was nearly exhausted. Under the fierce fire it is not strange that the Union soldiers gave way, but they were rallied by their officers.

The Confederates bided their time, the sharp-shooters picking off the Union officers, shooting the horses of the artillery—so many of them that when the Union troops retreated they were obliged to leave five cannon on the field.

The battle ended with the coming on of night. The Union troops, dis-

THE BATTLE OF OLUSTEE.

comfited, having lost more than fifteen hundred men in killed, wounded, and prisoners, without provisions, began their weary march towards Jacksonville. Thus, through disobedience of orders by General Seymour, the attempt to re-establish a loyal government in Florida had ended in disaster. The time had not come for the restoration of the authority of the United States in that State.

In the old tobacco warehouse known as Libby Prison, in Richmond, and on Belle Isle, on James River, were several thousand Union prisoners. Some of the officers of the Army of the Potomac believed that a large body of cavalry, moving swiftly, might make its way into Richmond and release them. General Meade consented that the attempt might be made, and it was intrusted to General Kilpatrick, who selected General Gregg's and General Merritt's divisions, and who intended first to get between General Lee's army and Richmond, destroy the railroads, so that no trains loaded with troops could come thundering down upon him. He had about five thousand men, who took rations for three days in their haversacks and three feedings of oats in bags for their horses. General Kilpatrick believed that he would find grain in the corn-bins to supply his horses with food. It was an enterprise which enlisted the sympathies of every soldier. The thought of releasing their comrades in prison fired their enthusiasm.

One of the officers who ardently desired to serve in the expedition was Ulric Dahlgren, whose father was an admiral in the navy. He was but twenty-two years old, but had rendered signal service in West Virginia at the beginning of the war, and also on General Hooker's staff. He had lost a leg in a skirmish just after the battle of Gettysburg, but the wound had healed, and he had returned to the army and was commander of a brigade.

It was three o'clock Sunday morning when the column left Stevensburg, moved south-east, came to the Rapidan at Ely's Ford, captured the Confederate pickets, and moved on to Spottsylvania Courthouse. From that point we see Colonel Dahlgren moving south-west with five hundred men, with the intention of reaching James River above Richmond, destroying the James River Canal, and then moving upon the city from the west. General Kilpatrick with the main body moved south to destroy the railroads, one leading to Fredericksburg, the other to Gordonsville, and by which General Lee received his supplies.

Feb. 28, 1864.

While this large force of Union cavalry is in motion towards the Confederate capital, another division under General Custer is moving from

Madison Court-house south-west towards the left flank of General Lee's army, to attract the attention of the Confederates in that direction while Kilpatrick executes his movement.

Early Monday morning General Kilpatrick reached the Virginia Central road, and the soldiers quickly tore up the track. At Frederickshall the troops came so suddenly upon a Confederate court-martial in session that the officers composing it—a colonel, five captains, and two lieutenants —were captured. A few hours later General Kilpatrick was at Ashland, seventeen miles from Richmond, burning bridges and tearing up the track. On Tuesday noon he was within five miles of the Confederate capital.

Just before noon the Confederate authorities in the city learned that a large body of Union cavalry was rapidly approaching, and there was a quick mustering of men—clerks in the Departments, invalid soldiers, and guards—some hastening north and north-east, and others north-west, manning the fortifications. It was one o'clock when the citizens heard the booming of cannon in the north. General Kilpatrick had only one battery of light artillery, six guns, and could do very little against the heavy cannon in the fortifications, but for two hours the cannonade went on with the expectation on the part of the Union commander of hearing from Dahlgren, but no uproar of battle could be heard, and he withdrew his troops towards the White House, at the head of York River. An hour later a roll of musketry was heard north-west of the city, in the direction of Goochland, the beginning of a short engagement between Dahlgren's men and the Confederates. Colonel Dahlgren had marked out a route, had calculated the time it would take him to reach James River and destroy the canal, burn bridges, and reach Richmond. It was a well-considered plan, but the man who guided him, either designedly as a traitor or ignorantly, took a road which led him nine miles out of the direct course. It was four o'clock in the afternoon when he reached the Confederate earthworks north-west of the city, to find them occupied by the hastily gathered force from Richmond. He saw what Kilpatrick had already seen, that there could be no sudden rush through the streets and opening of the doors of Libby Prison, and moved east to join Kilpatrick. He crossed the Mattapony River, and went on towards Williamsburg. On Wednesday night he thought himself so far away that he was beyond all possibility of attack, but a body of Confederates followed him, discovered his bivouac fires, placed themselves by the road-side in ambush, and fired a volley. Colonel Dahlgren quickly formed his troops to charge upon them, but fell mortally wounded. His troops dispersed, some to make their way to Kilpatrick, others to be taken prisoners. Colonel Dahlgren's body was

RETURN OF THE UNION ARMY.

taken to Richmond, exposed to public view, and then buried. His father, by flag of truce, asked that it might be sent to him, but it was not given up. The Richmond papers published, with many bitter comments, what purported to be an address of Colonel Dahlgren to his soldiers, which, it was stated, was found upon his body. The address, as read to the troops before they started, set forth the dangers and difficulties and objects of the expedition, together with directions for the good behavior of the troops, and also spoke of the honor which would come to them if they were successful in releasing their comrades from prison. The address as published contained a sentence setting forth that they were "to destroy the hateful city and not allow the Rebel leader Davis and his traitorous crew to escape."

General Lee sent a flag of truce to General Meade, asking if he, or General Kilpatrick, or the authorities at Washington, had authorized a course of action so contrary to the rules of war. General Meade replied that no such order had been authorized, and General Kilpatrick said that he had read the address before Colonel Dahlgren started, and that it contained no such language, but that the obnoxious words had been interpolated. Notwithstanding this disavowal, photographs of the address were sent to the Confederate agents in England, who stirred up the English newspapers to write editorials to make the people of England believe that Abraham Lincoln and the officers of the Union army were little better than savages.

ULRICH DAHLGREN.

The cavalry under General Custer, moving from Madison Court-house, reached the Rivanna River near Charlottesville, and came upon some Confederate artillery so suddenly that they captured several caissons which the Confederates could not take away in their swift retreat. The caissons were blown up and the battery wagons destroyed. A train of cars loaded with Confederate infantry came from General Lee's army at Gordonsville, and General Custer found it necessary to retreat. He recrossed the Rivanna, burned the bridge, and a large mill which was grinding corn for the Confederate army. He recrossed the Rapidan without having lost a man, accompanied by a large number of colored people, some of whom had been ploughing, but who, the moment they saw the Union troops, unharnessed the horses from the ploughs, mounted them, and without stopping to say good-bye to their masters, improved the opportunity to gain their freedom under the proclamation of Abraham Lincoln.

The expedition had failed, but officers and men had obtained information in regard to the country which would be valuable in the great campaign soon to begin. It is quite probable that had General Kilpatrick moved with all his force in the direction taken by General Dahlgren he would have entered Richmond, for the fortifications on that side were not so strong as on the north and east. If Dahlgren had not been taken out of his direct course by the guide, it would seem that he might have entered the city, for the force that confronted him reached the fortifications only a few minutes before he made his appearance.

In narrating the events in chronological order, we turn once more to the west.

The Confederate cavalry commander, General Forrest, planned a movement which he intended should offset what Sherman had been doing—a movement from northern Mississippi, northward through West Tennessee and Kentucky to the Ohio River. Three regiments of Kentuckians, which had been serving as infantry, joined him. They were young men who, though the people of the State refused to secede from the Union, had cast in their lot with the Confederacy. They were good horsemen, accustomed to the saddle. General Forrest's troops were from Kentucky, Tennessee, Mississippi, Missouri, Arkansas, and Texas. Many of the volunteers in his ranks were ruffians, who delighted in the freedom of the cavalry over the infantry, the opportunities for plunder. They were reckless of their own lives, and ready to shoot men upon the least provocation. They hated the negroes who had enlisted under the Stars and Stripes.

The Confederate cavalry commander was born on the banks of Duck River, in Tennessee. He began life as a poor boy. Before the war he sold slaves in Memphis, had accumulated money rapidly, owned a great cotton plantation and many slaves. His yearly cotton crop was more than one thousand bales. He had advocated secession, and when the war began enlisted as a private; but he was known to be a man of inflexible will, with great energy and force. He was tall, had a dark, swarthy countenance, dark, searching eyes, and black hair. Governor Harris, of Ten-

ON THE WAY TO FREEDOM.

nessee, sent for him in July, 1861, and commissioned him as colonel of cavalry. He went to Kentucky, where he was well known, and gathered the hot-blooded young men into the Confederate service. He was in command of the cavalry at Fort Donelson, in 1862, when that fortification was invested by General Grant, and escaped with his command by fording a creek. He had rendered great service to the Confederacy, and had been commissioned as lieutenant-general by Jefferson Davis. He was bold, brave, and self-reliant. His acquaintance with the country, the roads, and fording-places in the rivers gave him great advantage over the Union commanders. He moved rapidly, made long marches, pouncing suddenly upon small detachments of Union troops, capturing wagon-trains loaded with supplies, living upon the country. He was harsh in discipline. When the Conscription law was passed by the Confederate Congress, sweeping into the army all between the ages of eighteen and forty-five, he sent out bodies of troops and gathered in a large number of men, who, if unwilling to enter the Confederate service, were handcuffed and compelled to leave their homes. Thousands of men were ruthlessly torn from their families and driven into the ranks. It is not strange that some of them improved the first opportunity to desert. Nineteen deserted in a body, but were pursued, captured, brought back in chains to Forrest's headquarters at Oxford, Mississippi. This the scene as pictured by General Forrest's eulogist: "Their coffins were made ready, their graves dug, and the men advised to make their peace with their Maker and the world. The women of Oxford and the ministers, hearing that the men were to be shot, pleaded that they might be spared. Some of the officers remonstrated, and said that they feared a mutiny if he persisted. The men were blindfolded and seated upon their coffins, and the soldiers who were to shoot them stood waiting for the command to fire." The command was not given. "On another occasion," writes Forrest's eulogist, "if the spirit of desertion had not been stayed, Forrest would have been inexorable, however disagreeable might be the duty to him."([13])

Such was the despotism of the Confederacy. Tennessee never had seceded from the Union by vote of the people. (See "Marching to Victory," p. 366.) The Governor, Isham G. Harris, without authority, had made a league with the Confederate Government, by which the State had been given over to the Confederacy. The despotic Government at Richmond had extended its power over the helpless people. Under the remorseless conscription, Forrest filled up his ranks and prepared for his movement. In a Southern paper we have this report of a speech made to his troops:

3

"He was much annoyed at Tupelo by the inconsiderate habit his men had of capturing the enemy by wholesale, and on one occasion, when he was going out on a tear, he delivered a short lecture on the art of war. 'Now, boys, war means fight, and fight means kill. What's the use of taking prisoners, to eat your rations?' From that time there was a material falling off in the number of prisoners taken by Forrest's men."([14])

Forrest was in Mississippi, but moved to Corinth, and pushed rapidly from that point northward, sending a portion of his troops, under Colonel Duckworth, to Union City, in the north-western county of Tennessee, where there was a fortification held by between four and five hundred Union troops, commanded by Colonel Hawkins. The Confederates sent out a messenger with a white flag, demanding the immediate surrender of the fort. The Union commander pleaded for delay, but at eleven o'clock in the forenoon complied with the demand. His force was nearly as large as that of the Confederates, and had he held out a short time he would have been reinforced by two thousand men on their way from Columbus. It was an ignominious surrender.([15])

General Forrest, with the main body of his command, appeared before Paducah, on the bank of the Ohio, at the junction of the Tennessee with that stream. The place was seized by General Grant in 1861, and had been held by the Union forces. A fortification had been erected, and named Fort Anderson, in honor of Maj. Robert Anderson, of Kentucky, who had gallantly defended Fort Sumter at the outbreak of the Rebellion. The Union troops, numbering 646, one-third of whom were colored, were commanded by Col. S. G. Hicks, who had been in the thick of the fight at Shiloh, and who was wounded in that battle. He was a veteran of a temper far different from that of the officers who had surrendered at Union City. Two small gunboats, the *Pawpaw* and *Piosta*, commanded by Lieutenants Shirk and O'Neil, were lying in the river.

March 24, 1864.

Most of the people of Paducah, from the outbreak of the war, had sympathized with the Secessionists. In 1861, and the spring of 1862, they had heard far away the thunder of heavy cannon at Fort Henry and at Columbus, but the tide of battle till that hour never had surged around their homes. Now, like the sudden coming on of the summer rain, rifles were cracking in the streets, as Forrest's three brigades, between four and five thousand cavalrymen, dashed into the town. One of his brigade commanders was Gen. N. P. Thompson, who, when the war began, was practising law in Paducah, and whose home was there, the citizens were his friends and old-time acquaintances. Kentucky had not seceded from the

DESTROYING THE CANAL.

Union, but he had cast aside all allegiance to his State and to the Stars and Stripes, to assist in establishing a Confederacy based on slavery. The battle began, the Confederates dismounting from their horses and sheltering themselves in the houses. There was a lull for a few moments as a Confederate officer, with a white flag, bore this message towards Fort Anderson:

"COLONEL,—Having a force amply sufficient to carry your works and reduce the place, in order to avoid unnecessary effusion of blood, I demand the surrender of the fort and troops, with all public property. If you surrender you shall be treated as prisoners of war; but if I have to storm your works you may expect no quarter.(")

"N. B. FORREST."

No other Confederate commander, during the war, appended such a threat to a summons to surrender—a threat common in by-gone days, but not under the civilization of the nineteenth century.

This the reply of Colonel Hicks: "If you want the fort take it."

While the flag of truce was flying, the Confederate sharp-shooters made their way along the streets to a position whence they could fire upon the gunboats and upon the fort.

When it was known that the Confederates were approaching the town, and that a battle would be fought, the church bells had been tolled, and the women and children hurried down to the river-bank, and thence were ferried to the Ohio shore. The Confederates took possession of the houses and fired from the chamber windows which overlooked the fortification, whereupon the gunboats sent shells crashing through the houses, setting them on fire.

General Thompson, who had come to his old home to fight for the Confederacy, was torn to pieces by a cannon-shot. The Union cannon swept the streets with grape and canister; several times the Confederates charged upon the fort, but were repulsed with great loss. Through the afternoon the contest went on; when night came, the Confederates, under cover of the darkness, helped themselves to whatever suited their fancy in the deserted houses. They set the buildings containing Government supplies on fire. Other buildings were burned by the order of Colonel Hicks —those near the fort which had furnished shelter to the sharp-shooters. Many of the best houses were thus destroyed.

Morning dawned, and General Forrest sent out a flag of truce, asking for an exchange of prisoners; he wished to give up those captured at

Union City in exchange for Confederates. Colonel Hicks replied that he had no authority to make an exchange. A steamboat arrived from Cairo, bringing reinforcements. The attempt to capture the place had failed. During the night the Confederates disappeared, leaving the dead where they had fallen.

It is sad to know that men in all ages have hated, despised, and oppressed those who were weaker than themselves. We respect those who are our equals in physical strength and in intellect; but, to our dishonor, we sometimes look down upon those who occupy a less exalted position. Through by-gone centuries the white race has robbed and oppressed the negro and Indian. We are to keep ever in mind the fact that the war was begun by the Secessionists for the perpetuation of slavery; that slavery, as declared by Mr. Stephens, of Georgia, was the corner-stone of the Confederacy. Every soldier in the service of the Confederacy was fighting to maintain slavery as an institution. Before the war learned men, lawyers, ministers of the gospel, doctors of divinity, presidents of colleges, had maintained that it was a beneficent institution, ordained by Almighty God for the mutual welfare of the Anglo-American and African races. We need not wonder, therefore, that the enrolling of negroes who had been slaves, emancipated by Abraham Lincoln, as soldiers of the Republic, aroused the hatred of the slave-holders to the race whom they had oppressed; or that out of it came a terrible tragedy, which I do not like to write about; but were I to omit it, this story of the war would be incomplete—a scene so horrible and ghastly that I am sure every one who supported the Confederacy wishes it could be obliterated forever from the memory of men. What I am about to write is the truth of history.

On the east bank of the Mississippi, in Tennessee, stood Fort Pillow, erected by the Confederates in 1861, and greatly strengthened by General Beauregard in 1862, but abandoned when that commander evacuated Corinth, after the battle of Shiloh. In the fortifications were 557 men, of whom 262 were negroes. Maj. L. F. Booth commanded.

It was the anniversary of the beginning of the war at Fort Sumter. Through the night rain had fallen. Daylight was dawning when the pickets in the woods east of the fortification saw a Confederate force approaching. Forrest's command, Captain Smith's company, of Missouri cavalry was in advance, guided by a citizen who lived near by, and who knew just where the pickets were stationed. The Confederates stole softly through the woods, and came so suddenly upon the pickets that all, except one, were captured.(") The one who escaped gave the alarm. The drums began to beat the long roll, and the soldiers

April 12, 1864.

MASSACRE AT FORT PILLOW.

sprang from their tents and log-huts, quickly formed, and rushed to the breastworks. There were two 10-pounder Parrott-guns, two 12-pounder howitzers, and two 6-pounder rifled cannon. The Confederates dismounted from their jaded horses and advanced; McCulloch's brigade from the south, Bell's brigade from the north. The artillery on both sides opened fire together with the Confederate sharp-shooters. The Confederates numbered several thousand. At nine o'clock Forrest arrived. He had ridden seventy-two miles during twenty-four hours. Soon after his arrival the Union commander, Major Booth, was killed, and the command devolved upon Major Bradford. The gunboat *New Era* was lying in the Mississippi, and sent its shells up the ravine south of the fort, firing, during the forenoon, two hundred and eighty-two rounds of shell, shrapnel, and canister, which, with the fire from the fortifications, kept the Confederates at bay.

It was three o'clock in the afternoon. Forrest had failed in his attempt to surprise the fort, and sent out Captain Goodman with a flag of truce, bearing a letter. This the communication:

"As your gallant defence of the fort has entitled you to the treatment of brave men, I now demand an unconditional surrender of your force; at the same time assuring you that they will be treated as prisoners of war. I have received a fresh supply of ammunition, and can easily take your position.

"N. B. FORREST."(¹⁰)

Major Bradford asked for an hour's delay to consult with the captain of the gunboat. "Twenty minutes will be given you," was the reply of the Confederate commander. "I will not surrender," was the answer sent by Major Bradford.

These are brief sentences, but while the parleying was going on, had we been there we should have seen, as the Union troops saw, a body of Confederates from McCulloch's brigade advancing through a ravine south of the fort, and taking possession of the Government buildings, in which were quartermaster's and commissary stores, and firing upon the steamboat *Olive Branch* in the river, on board of which were some unarmed Union soldiers on their way from New Orleans to Cairo, together with passengers, among whom was General Shepley. The *Olive Branch* could render no assistance to the garrison, and passed on towards Cairo.

While the flag of truce was flying there was bantering and jeering between the Confederates and those within the fort, the Confederates making their calculations the while for assaulting the fortifications. We see a bugler riding to the top of a knoll, whence he can look over all the field, and where every Confederate along the lines can see him.([19]) He raises the bugle to his lips, and a blast long and loud rings out upon the air. In an instant the Confederate carbines and muskets flame, some of them within thirty feet of the ditch outside the fort. The sharp-shooters aimed at the Union officers, nearly all of whom were shot down in a few minutes, when the Confederates on the south side, who, under cover of the flag of truce, had selected their positions, rushed over the embankment. The Union troops fought desperately a few moments, but, outnumbered ten to one, with no officer to direct them, threw down their guns in token of surrender, or else fled towards the river. The butchery began. This the report of the committee of Congress, gathered from the sworn testimony of those who survived the massacre:

"The Rebels commenced an indiscriminate slaughter, sparing neither age nor sex, white nor black, soldiers nor civilians. . . . Men, women, and children, wherever found, were deliberately shot down, beaten, and hacked with sabres; some of the children, not more than ten years old, were forced to stand up and face their murderers while being shot. The sick and wounded were butchered without mercy, the Rebels even entering the hospital building, dragging them out to be shot, killing them as they lay there unable to offer the least resistance. . . . Some were shot while in the river; others on the bank were shot and their bodies kicked into the water, many of them still living but unable to make any exertions to save themselves from drowning. Some of the Rebels stood on the hillside, called the Union soldiers to them, and as they approached shot them in cold blood. . . . All who asked for mercy were answered by the most cruel taunts and sneers. . . . The huts and tents in which many of the wounded had sought shelter were set on fire both that night and the next morning while the wounded were still in them. . . . Some of those seeking to escape the flames were brutally shot or had their brains beaten out. . . . The deeds of cruelty ceased at night only to be renewed the next morning; any of the wounded yet alive were deliberately shot. . . . Some of the living were buried, but succeeded in digging themselves out. . . . Three hundred were murdered in cold blood."([20])

Major Bradford, who succeeded to the command of Fort Pillow after the death of Major Booth, was from Tennessee. From the beginning of the war he had been loyal to the flag of his country. While the small body of white prisoners were on the march towards Jackson, after the fort had been captured, an officer and five soldiers took him a short distance into the woods. He begged for his life, but they gave no heed to his pleading, and he fell pierced by three balls.(²¹) It is said that when General Forrest saw that the Union men were being shot down, he issued orders against it; but if such orders were given, they were not heeded by his soldiers.

Nearly all of the white Union soldiers were from Tennessee, as were many of the Confederates. Men who had been friends before the war were now enemies. The animosity of the Confederates towards the Union men had been intensified by the events of the war; and when they found themselves masters of the fort, they lost all sense of mercy and humanity, and became brutal, cruel, and relentless. I drop the curtain upon the ghastly scene.

NOTES TO CHAPTER I.

(¹) E. A. Pollard, "Lost Cause," p. 478.
(²) J. W. Avery, "History of Georgia," p. 658.
(³) J. B. Jones, "A Rebel War Clerk's Diary," vol. ii., p. 122.
(⁴) Idem, p. 125.
(⁵) *Richmond Examiner*, January 2, 1864.
(⁶) "Memoirs of Gen. W. T. Sherman," vol. i., p. 419.
(⁷) Idem.
(⁸) "Rebellion Record," vol. viii., p. 470.
(⁹) "Memoirs of Gen. W. T. Sherman," vol. i., p. 422.
(¹⁰) Gen. Q. A. Gillmore's Order, "Rebellion Record," vol. viii., p. 403.
(¹¹) Gen. Truman Seymour's Letter, "Rebellion Record," vol. viii., p. 409.
(¹²) "Rebellion Record," vol. viii. p. 409.
(¹³) "Campaigns of Lieut.-gens. Forrest, Jordon, and Pryor," p. 384.
(¹⁴) *Charleston Mercury*, April 14, 1864.
(¹⁵) "Rebellion Record," vol. viii., p. 49.
(¹⁶) "Campaigns of Lieut.-gens. Forrest, Jordon, and Pryor," p. 411.
(¹⁷) Idem, p. 425.
(¹⁸) Idem, p. 433.
(¹⁹) Idem, p. 436.
(²⁰) Congressional Report—Conduct of the War.
(²¹) "Rebellion Record," vol. viii., p. 4.

CHAPTER II.

RED RIVER EXPEDITION.

THE southern half of Louisiana is unlike any other section of the United States; you can traverse a very large portion of it in boats along rivers, creeks, bayous, and lakes, amid groves of oak and palmetto and thickets of cane, with here and there large reaches of open fields. One of the great tributaries of the Mississippi is the Red River, which rises in the far-off mountains of New Mexico, runs east till it touches Arkansas, then turns south-east, and with many windings runs past Shreveport, then the landing-place of Grand Ecore, four miles from Alexandria, and makes its way to the Mississippi, between Port Hudson and Natchez.

Were we to take a steamer at New Orleans and go down-stream and out on the ocean westward, we should come to the Atchafalaya River, up which we might go when the spring floods were on, and emerge into the Mississippi just below the mouth of the Red River. Passing still farther west, to the Sabine, which forms the western boundary of the State, we might go up almost to Shreveport. The country is fertile. There are great sugar plantations along the coast, the cane changing to cotton farther inland, and the oak giving place to the pine.

During the first two years of the war the Confederate armies east of the Mississippi received large supplies of food from the Red River region. The capture of Vicksburg, however, put an end to that. The gunboats patrolled the river. Troops could cross in small parties, but corn and sugar were bulky, and could not be readily ferried across the stream. After the opening of the Mississippi the Union troops west of it might have been withdrawn and used otherwheres, but the authorities at Washington acted on the idea that a section of country once occupied must be held.

It was in this region in the spring of 1864 that what is known as the Red River Expedition was undertaken. In most histories of the war it is claimed that the expedition was necessary to re-establish the authority of the United States in north-western Texas. At the beginning of the war

UNION REFUGEES.

and through the first months the authorities at Washington were anxious to have the old flag waving in every State of the Union. They thought that it would show to England and France that the North was in earnest, and that the Union people still remaining in the South would rally around it. Hence the desire to have it waving in Texas.

General Halleck, at Washington, believed that the true policy for the Government to pursue, was to occupy all the territory wrested from the Confederates, and re-establish the authority of the United States. By adopting that plan a large number of soldiers must needs be employed in holding the important towns in Arkansas.

The Government at Washington was desirous of occupying the whole country west of the Mississippi for several reasons. When the full history of the war shall be written, it will be seen that Louis Napoleon, Emperor of France, who had established Maximilian of Austria on the throne of the Montezumas in Mexico, was very anxious for the success of the Confederates; that he desired to overthrow republican institutions. Not only that, but while he hoped to see the Confederate Government established, he wished also to see the State of Texas secede from the Confederacy and establish a government of its own.(¹) If the great Republic could be broken to pieces it would be all the easier for him to carry out his plans in Mexico. The Government of the United States therefore wished to see the Stars and Stripes waving once more in Texas. It was known that there were many Union people in Texas and Louisiana who had been driven from their homes, and who were hiding in swamps to save themselves from conscription.

There were commercial reasons for a military movement west of the Mississippi. We are to remember that cotton was worth sixty cents a pound in Boston and Liverpool. Never before had it been worth so much. The cotton-mills of New England—of Lowell, Manchester, and Fall River—were for the most part idle. Across the Atlantic, in Old England, the wheels had ceased to whirl, and a silence like that of Sunday had settled over the manufactories of Oldham and Rochdale. Thousands of spinners and weavers were begging bread, or were fed by the magistrates. In the Red River region there was stored three years' crops of cotton worth sixty cents in Boston—not worth a cent where it was.

The Confederate Government had obtained a large amount of money in England for the purchase of arms, ammunition, and military supplies, and for the construction of the *Alabama* war-ship, and for the building of iron-clad war-vessels, which was to be paid for in cotton. By getting possession of the cotton all the mills in the North would be set to work, and the needs of the country supplied. There was much correspondence between General Halleck in Washington, Generals Banks, Sherman, and Grant, and Steele, who was at Little Rock, in Arkansas. Arrangements were made by which Sherman, who was at Memphis, was to lend Banks Gen. A. J. Smith's division of ten thousand men. General Steele was to march south-west and join Banks at Shreveport, or at least was to co-operate by a demonstration in that direction. Admiral Porter was to co-operate with a fleet of gunboats up the Red River. It would not be quite correct to say that the expedition was planned solely to obtain cotton. That was what the speculators particularly had in view, but they were loud in their advocacy of the re-establishment of the old flag once more in that section. They knew that if that were done there would be a rich harvest for somebody, and they would take good care to be the somebody.

Before the expedition started, two men (Mr. Butler, of Illinois, and Mr. Casey, of Kentucky) came to Admiral Porter and General Banks with an order from President Lincoln, directing all persons in authority, military or naval, to grant them all facilities in going where they pleased. Admiral Porter indorsed the order, as did General Banks. Other speculators had been bringing out cotton from the country west of the Mississippi before the starting of the expedition, carrying on a surreptitious trade, as we learn from Captain Breeze, of the navy, who says: "These cotton speculators had charts of the country, with every parish and township in the State marked off, with the amount of cotton in each, where it was stored, the marks upon it, and everything about it. Many of the speculators would come and give information concerning these things, in the hope that we would take some that they claimed as their own, so that they could present their claims in court. The cotton taken by the navy was sent to the court, and if they could present their claims they stood a fair chance of having them allowed. A large number of speculators came on the steamer *Black Hawk*, with a large quantity of bagging and roping, which was landed and hauled to Alexandria, where they purchased a large number of bales." What became of the cotton purchased there we shall see by-and-by.

A great deal of cotton was seized along the river by the officers of the navy, which was sent up the Mississippi to Cairo, where a judge decided as to its value and what should be done with it. We are to remember that the Confederate Government was dealing in cotton, receiving it for taxes, sending it to England—the English blockade-runners slipping past the Union fleets at night, and returning with arms and supplies. All through the Southern States there were piles of cotton gathered by the tax collectors, and labelled "C. S. A." Such cotton when captured was known as prize cotton, and the officers of the navy, under the laws, were entitled to a share in it, which naturally made them very vigilant.

It was an easy matter for a speculator to get word to an officer where cotton might be found, which would be seized and sent to Cairo; but when the matter came before the judge it was just as easy for the speculator to appear and testify that it was his own property, and that the Confederate Government never owned it. No one will ever know the true history of the cotton business; but this much may be said, that the administration of affairs in the Department west of the Mississippi was very loose. There was a great deal of trading between the people on both sides, and it is possible that some of the Union officers improved the opportunity to make money in ways not wholly legitimate.

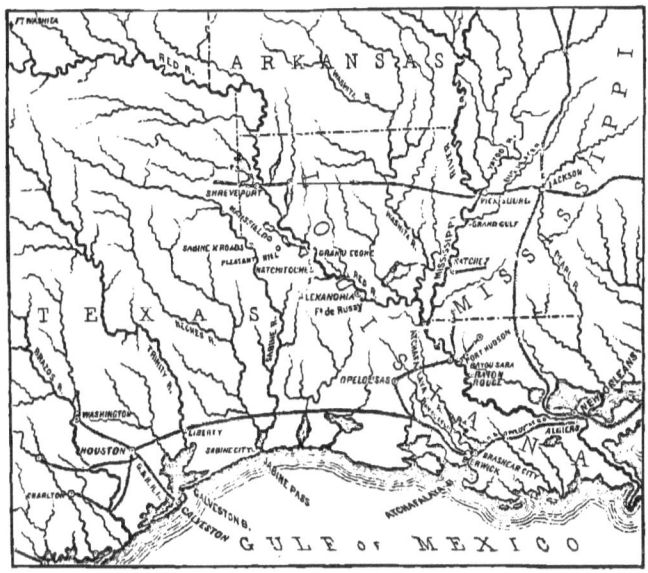

MAP OF THE RED RIVER EXPEDITION.

The troops under General Banks were in lower Louisiana. General Franklin, who had been under McClellan and Burnside in the Army of the Potomac, was in immediate command, with orders to march from Opelousas northward to Alexandria, which was to be the rendezvous. Usually in winter the Red River has a flood pouring into the Mississippi, but now it was very low; there had been no great rains; the snow had not

4

melted on the far-away mountains. Not till there was a rise could the large gunboats go beyond Grand Ecore, just above Alexandria; nor could the river steamers transporting the supplies go beyond that point. There were ten gunboats and more than thirty river steamers. The Marine Brigade, under General Ellet, numbering three thousand, was needed at Memphis, and returned. It had no wagons, and General Banks had none to give it.

General Banks intended to move along the south bank of the river to Shreveport, while the fleet made its way up the stream. The water being so low, he was obliged to change his plan and establish his base of supplies at Alexandria. He was obliged to leave Grover's division of three thousand at Alexandria to guard the supplies, so that when the army was ready to march the force was much less than that which General Banks expected to have. But he did not expect to encounter the Confederates till after reaching Shreveport. General Franklin, next in command, was very positive that the Confederates would not show themselves, forgetting the wise saying, "Never underrate your enemy." Many a battle has been lost by not heeding the maxim, "Eternal vigilance is the price of liberty." One never can tell in military matters just what an opponent will do. It is not like a game of chess. There are more factors, more points to be kept in mind. In war one must exercise common-sense, and just because General Franklin did not exercise it the expedition met with disaster, as we shall see.

Gen. E. Kirby Smith was commander of the Confederate troops west of the Mississippi. His forces were widely scattered. A portion were with him confronting General Steele, near Little Rock. General Taylor was on the Red River, General Polignac, a French officer, who had crossed the Atlantic to fight for the Confederates, was on the west bank of the Mississippi, between Vicksburg and Natchez. General Walker's division was in Texas. General Smith knew from his spies, who kept him informed of all that was going on at Little Rock and Vicksburg, that a movement was to be made by the Union army.

These spies were acquainted with every creek and bayou, and could make their way through the lines at night without detection. When General Taylor learned that the expedition was fitting out, he sent in every direction for troops, gathering all the isolated bodies, concentrating them at Shreveport. They came from Texas and Arkansas. In a short time he had an army as large as that under Banks advancing from Alexandria. He sent his cavalry out to skirmish with the Union cavalry, with instructions to fall back towards Shreveport. He determined to make a stand in Louisiana, for the reason that if he were to retreat to Texas the Louisiana troops would leave him in disgust.

General Banks had five brigades of cavalry and mounted infantry under General Lee, with the Second Massachusetts Battery (Captain Nims), and Battery G, Fifth United States. The infantry consisted of the Thirteenth Corps, commanded by General Ransom; Cameron's and Landram's divisions, Emory's division of the Nineteenth Corps, and detachments of the Sixteenth and Seventeenth corps, under Gen. A. J. Smith; also a brigade of colored troops.

On the morning of March 12th the gunboats, followed by transports, entered the Red River. On the 13th the troops landed at Simsport, and the next morning moved towards Fort De Russy. General Walker, commanding the Texas troops, left three hundred men to hold it, with eight heavy guns and two field-pieces; but General Smith's troops charged upon the fortifications, swarmed over the breastworks, and captured the entire garrison. The gunboats found lines of piles driven across the channel of the river, with trees piled against them by the force of the current, but they soon removed the obstructions and reached the town of Alexandria on March 15th. The gunboats had been up to Alexandria in 1863; but they were still three hundred and forty miles from Shreveport, by river, the point which they desired to reach.

The water of the Red River is colored by the red ochre of the soil. The country between Alexandria and Shreveport is very fertile, and in 1864 was regarded as the wealthiest and best-settled section of the State. The river is seven or eight hundred feet in width, flowing between high banks. Just above Alexandria are rapids, which cannot be passed by steamboats when the water is low, and it was very low for the season in the spring of 1864.

On April 3d the troops by land and the gunboats in the river reached Grand Ecore. These words are used by the Normans in northern France, and mean "high ground." Grand Ecore is four miles from Natchitoches, which is on the great road used by emigrants before the war when moving to the plains of Texas. This road leads through the town of Mansfield, where General Taylor was concentrating the Confederate troops.

The road along which General Banks was marching runs north-west. Just south of the town of Mansfield another road leading from the Red River to the Sabine crosses it, running south-west. General Franklin was intrusted with the command during the march. He placed the cavalry and mounted infantry, about five thousand, in advance, with their supply-train of about three hundred and fifty wagons. This body of cavalry, with such a train, reached five miles. Then came the infantry and artillery, each brigade with its wagons, all on a single road through a dense forest. There were other roads farther north and south not so good, but which might have been used.

The Union cavalry, under General Lee, during the forenoon came to an elevation of land which is known as Pleasant Hill. Passing over the ridge and going on five miles, the skirmishers were fired upon by the Confederate cavalry under General Major. General Lee ordered up a regiment. The fire grew more brisk, and Lee put in a brigade. He ordered up the artillery, and finally drove the Confederates, losing seventy-five men and capturing twenty-five prisoners.

April 7, 1864.

Passing over now to the Confederate side, we see General Green arriving on the ground with a portion of his troops. General Taylor was at Mansfield, five miles away, when the skirmish opened, and he rode to the field. He met a party of demoralized soldiers and began to curse them.

"General, if you won't curse us we will go back with you," said one.(*) There was a rebuke in the words which won his respect, and instead of swearing, he smiled and bowed to the man, who, with his comrades, turned about and went back to the field. General Taylor examined the ground around the house of Mr. Wilson, selecting it as a strong position for a battle. There was an open field half a mile long and three-fourths of a mile wide. The road ran through it. On the eastern side of the field there were a forest of pines and a rail-fence. The road from the Red River to the Sabine crossed the Pleasant Hill road near the house of Mr. Wilson. It is three miles from Mansfield, where Taylor had concentrated his army. At nine o'clock in the evening he ordered his troops to be on the march at daylight.

General Taylor knew that the Union army was strung out for a distance of thirty miles on one road, and resolved to strike a staggering blow before it could be concentrated.

Going back now to the Union side, we hear General Lee protesting to General Franklin against the presence of so many wagons at the front. General Franklin, on the other hand, says that they belong to the cavalry, and that Lee must keep them out of the way of the infantry. Lee asks Franklin for an infantry support, but not till General Banks is informed of the situation is any infantry ordered forward. This was the situation on the evening of the 7th: The Confederates concentrated and advancing; the Union troops, a string thirty miles long, in a dense forest, with the cavalry and its wagons five miles in advance of the infantry.

In the morning the Confederate troops under General Taylor were coming into line on the plantation of Mr. Wilson, at Sabine Cross-roads. He stationed Walker's division of three brigades on the south side of the road leading to Pleasant Hill, with two batteries, and Mouton's division of two brigades on the north side, with two batteries. The cavalry under Green swung out on Mouton's left, and De Bray's cavalry, with McMahon's battery, was placed in reserve.

April 8, 1864.

General Taylor says: "I had on the field 5300 infantry, 3000 horse, and 500 artillerymen; in all, 8800 men—a full estimate. But the vicious dispositions of the enemy made me confident of beating all the force he could concentrate during the day, and on the morrow Churchill would be up with 4400 muskets."(³)

General Lee, with the Union cavalry, moved on, but found himself confronted by the Confederate cavalry. He had seen enough to make him cautious, and waited for the brigade of infantry ordered up by General Banks. General Ransom had already sent Landram's, and followed with Vance's. Franklin, with the Nineteenth Corps, was at Carroll's Mills, five miles in rear of General Lee and the position chosen by the Confederates. He reached the mills, and at eleven o'clock halted his troops to build a bridge. As the cavalry, artillery, and Ransom's division had already crossed, one does not see the necessity of a halt at that hour or the need of a bridge. General Banks arrived. The booming of cannon five miles distant broke the stillness of the noontide hour.

General Ransom, before the arrival of General Banks, had made disposition of the troops. He was an able officer, and placed them judiciously, but was greatly outnumbered. He had only two brigades of infantry—two thousand five hundred in all. Landram, with the Forty-eighth, Eighty-third, Ninety-sixth Ohio, and Nineteenth Kentucky, was on the right. Nims's battery was on a low elevation, supported by the Twenty-third Wisconsin. The Sixty-seventh Indiana supported the battery on the left. The infantry on the left were the Seventy-seventh Illinois, Nineteenth Kentucky, Forty-eighth, Eighty-third, and Ninety-sixth Ohio. When the Chicago Mercantile battery and Klaus's Indiana battery arrived they were placed on the ridge at the right of the road.

General Ransom did not wish to bring on a battle, but waited for the coming up of Franklin to support him. Franklin, the while, was resting five miles away. The Confederate commander was getting impatient. He was waiting to be attacked. It did not suit his plan to rest quietly till Banks's troops were in position. The afternoon was wearing away, and he resolved to attack Ransom.

4*

General Banks does not seem to have comprehended the situation of affairs. He directed General Lee to move on towards Mansfield. "You cannot move without bringing on a battle," was the reply of Lee, and the order is countermanded.

Four o'clock. Taylor will wait no longer. Looking now across the field on the east side of the road, the Union troops behold the Confederates of Mouton's division advancing. First there is the rattling fire of the skirmishers, then the thunder of the cannon, the screaming of the shells, and the yell of the troops. They are in two lines, and advance with confident expectations of sweeping all before them. It is a withering fire that bursts upon them from Landram's lines. A "murderous fire," Taylor calls it. Mouton is killed. There is a fearful slaughter of Confederate officers. Colonel Armand, of the Eighteenth Louisiana; Colonel Beard, of the Crescent Regiment, and Walker, of the Twenty-eighth Louisiana, are killed; also Colonel Noble, of the Seventeenth Texas. There are several company officers killed and wounded at the first volley. The front line melts like lead in a crucible in the glowing flame and white-heat of battle. It gives way and rolls back on the second line. Rallied by the officers, the troops advance once more, throw themselves upon the ground, and open fire.

Going now across the road, we see the right of the Confederate line advancing upon the mounted infantry, extending far beyond it, and curling round the flank.

"The mounted infantry are falling back," is the word which comes to Ransom. He gallops across the field, confident that Landram will hold the right. The Chicago and Indiana batteries are just coming up. They come into position by Banks's headquarters and open fire upon the exultant Confederates, who are sweeping all before them on the west side of the road. The Eighty-third Ohio comes upon the run to support the artillery, but the left of the line is already turned; the mounted infantry cannot stand against the force so greatly outnumbering them. Before the gunners of Nims's battery can bring up their limbers, the Confederates rush upon them, seizing the guns and pouring a destructive fire into the flank of Vance's brigade. Ransom sees that he must fall back, and orders Vance to take a new position, and sends word to Landram to retire. Captain Dickey carries the order, informing the colonels of the regiments as he passes them, but before all are informed he is struck with a bullet. Some of the regiments retire; others remain. There is increasing confusion. Going back to the edge of the timber, we see Ransom, Landram, Lee, Stone, and other officers trying to rally the men. A shell explodes among them, severely wounding Ransom, who is carried to the rear.

General Banks rides along the lines, swinging his cap and trying to rally the disordered regiments, but the stampede has begun. There is only the one road. The line has been pressed back to the wagons. The teamsters are panic-stricken: many of them are negroes. Some cut the horses loose, mount them, and ride away; others abandon them and take to their heels; some try to turn the teams, and thus block the road. Wagons tip over, and then there is kicking and rearing of mules. The mounted infantry try to make their way through the woods, and become mingled with the infantry, artillery, and wagons; while crowding on, pouring in their fire, come the Confederates. It is an indescribable scene of confusion. Colonel Vance is killed and a large number of officers wounded. General Cameron assumes command of the Thirteenth Corps.

It would be unjust to convey the idea that all the soldiers on the field were panic-stricken, or were going upon the run to the rear. On the contrary, the veterans of the Thirteenth Corps rallied deliberately three-quarters of a mile in the rear, and for half an hour held the Confederates in check; but the regiments were only skeletons now, and were obliged to fall back. It was a rich harvest of plunder which dropped into the hands of the Confederates—nearly all the wagons and supplies, and eight hundred mules and ten cannon. It had been a complete rout.

The Confederates had swept all before them. It has been said by military commanders that nothing, after a defeat, so demoralizes an army as a decisive victory where there is a great amount of plunder; and the disorganization of the Confederates began. The loss in killed and wounded on their part had been very large. In the movement through the woods the lines had become disordered; soldiers had left the ranks to secure plunder. Night was coming on, but Taylor, having got the Union men upon the run, determined to follow on and finish the victory.

Through the closing hours of the day the thunder of battle had rolled over the forest to the ears of the men of Emory's division of the Nineteenth Corps, and Franklin, in obedience to the order from Banks, had started. He had said there would be no fighting, but the battle, with disaster, had come. The troops were on the march, meeting the growing stream of fugitives. Franklin selected a position in the woods on the eastern edge of the field, with Dwight's brigade on the road, Benedict's on the left, and McMillan's in reserve. A line of skirmishers was thrown out. Down the road and through the woods streamed the troops of the Thirteenth Corps and the mounted infantry. Before the line was complete the battle began once more. The skirmishers were driven in. They fell back upon the main line, behind which the Thirteenth Corps was rallying.

The last rays of the sun fell upon the two armies as the Confederates advanced. "Reserve your fire till they are close up!" was the order. On came the men in gray, but the whole line burst into flame and they staggered beneath it. Again and again they attempted to break the line, but in vain.

General Banks saw that the battle would be renewed in the morning, and fell back to Pleasant Hill, selected a favorable position, brought up General Wright's troops, and prepared for the assault of the Confederates. Pleasant Hill is fifteen miles south of the Red River, on the road leading from Alexandria to Shreveport. There is a cluster of houses on the hill, which slopes gently towards the west. While the thunder of battle was dying on the evening of the 8th of April, General Wright, with his troops, and Col. William H. Dickey, with a brigade of colored troops, arrived at the little village. During the night, the Thirteenth Corps, the wounded, and what was left of the wagon-train, arrived, followed by the Nineteenth Corps.

Were we to go out north of the town we should follow a ravine, on which the right wing of the army rested—Dwight's brigade of the Nineteenth Corps. Then came McMillan's in the centre, with Benedict's on the left, in a ditch, the extreme left being in an open field. This was the first formation; but before the battle began, McMillan was placed on the right and rear of Dwight, while Shaw's brigade was thrown into the place before occupied by McMillan, and a little in advance of the main line. The Twenty-fifth New York Battery was placed between Dwight and McMillan, on a hill, so as to sweep the open field with its fire. The line turned an angle, with Mower's brigade joining Benedict's facing south-west. At the angle were the Ninth Indiana Battery and Battery B, First United States, in position to cover the field in front. On the left of the line was the First Vermont Battery. The Thirteenth Corps was placed in reserve. That the wagons might not be in the way, the trains were all sent towards Natchitoches, several miles in rear.

During the night Taylor was reinforced by the arrival of Churchill's and Parsons's Arkansas and Missouri troops, about five thousand. He had the cannon captured at the battle of yesterday. It was four o'clock before the Confederates were in position. Taylor, flushed by his victory, made his dispositions quickly, sending Churchill round to attack from the south. The cavalry were to fall upon the Union left flank, double up Mower, and cut off Banks's retreat. General Walker was next in line, with Green's, Buchell's, and De Bray's cavalry on the left. Mouton's division, now commanded by Polignac, was held in reserve.

April 9, 1864.

Taylor intended to have Churchill's and Walker's divisions do the heavy work. His plan was to turn the left of the Union line, which, as we shall see, obstinately refused to be turned. He intended to conceal his plan by opening the battle on the Union right, and then make a terrific onslaught on the other wing.

The battle began by a shot from the Confederate battery, the Valverde, on the east side of the road, in front of Shaw's brigade. The Twenty-fifth New York Battery replied, but in a feeble way. The commander of the battery seems to have been scared at the outset, for he suddenly limbered up his guns and started for the rear, leaving one gun and caisson in the road.

General Buchell, commanding a brigade of Confederate cavalry, dashed on to secure it, but a volley burst from the muskets of the Fourteenth Iowa and Twenty-fourth Missouri, from men who had no thought of taking to their heels. Horses and riders went down in a heap. Buchell was mortally wounded. The attack was repulsed.

A moment later and Walker's division falls on Benedict's brigade to the left and partially in rear of Shaw, and at the same moment the Confederates attack the extreme right of the Union line. Shaw is obliged to fall back, and so is Benedict, but there is no panic. Every movement is in order except in Benedict's brigade, where some of the regiments are thrown into confusion.

General Mower holds the left of the Union line. His troops are veterans who have fought on many fields; they are fresh and vigorous. The Confederates advancing to attack them are Churchill's, who have made a long and wearisome march. Taylor expects them to turn the Union left flank, but his expectations are doomed to failure. Every attack is repulsed. Churchill can make no impression upon that solid line. His men are too weary and the line too compact and determined to be moved an inch from their chosen position. General Mower says: "The enemy advanced rapidly on my line, as though confident of success, but were repulsed by our troops, who withstood the charge with great firmness and repulsed them with great slaughter. The enemy made a stand at a ditch, which was about three-fourths of the width of the field from my original position. They lost largely in killed and prisoners here, and were, after a desperate resistance, driven back into the woods."([4])

Mower, having repulsed the attack, advanced and drove Churchill. In the charge the Forty-ninth Indiana recaptured two of the cannon of Nims's battery lost on the preceding day.

Night closes in with the Confederates repulsed and defeated, lines broken, regiments disordered. General Taylor says: "After order was restored, I ordered the infantry to fall back some six miles to water, as there was none to be found nearer. All the cavalry, except De Bray's division, was sent to Mansfield to feed and rest."

During the night we have the spectacle of both armies retreating. General Taylor had been defeated and was out of ammunition. His army, at eight o'clock in the evening, was sadly demoralized. The Union army had won a signal victory. The troops were not demoralized, but General Banks seemingly had only one thought—to get back to Alexandria. He ordered the troops to be silently withdrawn, the wounded to be gathered, and the surgeons to remain and care for them. At midnight the troops were moving towards Alexandria. The reasons for the retreat were that no water could be had; that the provisions were nearly gone; that it was necessary to communicate with the fleet to obtain ammunition.

General Smith protested against retreating. He believed that the Confederates had been so thoroughly defeated that they would make no stand this side of Shreveport. It seems probable that a commander of nerve and energy could have made his way to Shreveport without difficulty after the battle of Pleasant Hill. This is to be said—nothing in particular was to be gained by going there. The only object of the expedition, so far as the Government was concerned, was to establish the old flag once more in that section of the country. The other part of the expedition was to get hold of the immense stores of cotton. But it would have been far better for Banks to have gone on than to have made an inglorious retreat. The defeat of Taylor at Pleasant Hill would have disheartened the Confederates and put him on the defensive. He would have lost prestige as a commander and been forced back into Texas. The retreat of Banks made Taylor the lion of the hour, brought reinforcements to his ranks, and otherwise strengthened the Confederate cause.

The Union army reached Grand Ecore and threw up fortifications. The water in the river was beginning to fall, and Admiral Porter saw that he must make haste or the fleet would be left upon the sand-bars or snags thickly strewn along the streams.

The Confederates, instead of marching to Grand Ecore to attack the army, gave their attention to the gunboats, a portion of the troops, under General Liddell, crossing to the north bank, to fire from behind trees upon every person exposed upon the boats. Several of the transports, with horses and supplies on board, were accompanied by the gunboats *Osage* and *Lexington*. The *Osage* and one of the transports were aground, when the Confederates brought four cannon into position and

CONFEDERATES UNDER GENERAL GREEN.

opened fire, and a large body of Texans under General Green opened a musketry fire. The heavy cannon of the gunboats sent a storm of shells upon them which did great execution. General Green was killed and his troops repulsed. The boats reached Grand Ecore, and thence began one by one to descend the river to Alexandria. The Confederates placed a torpedo in the river, which exploded under the *Eastport*, opening a leak which stranded the boat. By great exertions the water was pumped out, and the vessel floated but again grounded. Again and again the water was pumped out, and the vessel moved down-stream fifty miles. Admiral Porter, finding it so difficult to keep the *Eastport* afloat, ordered her to be blown up.

Just as the match was lighted, a large body of Confederates appeared upon the bank of the river and opened fire upon the gunboat *Cricket*, which was tied by a cable to a tree. Captain Gorringe, who was in command, replied with grape and canister.

It was an easy matter for the Confederates to move from one bend in the river to another, and place themselves in position to fire upon the boats, which, on account of the low water, could not move very rapidly. Just above the mouth of Cane River, the Confederates placed eighteen guns in position, to open fire upon the *Cricket*, the *Juliet*, and the *Hindman*. All the other boats had passed the point. The Confederate cannon were well aimed. At the first round nearly all the gunners of the *Cricket* were killed or wounded, the chief engineer wounded, also all but one of the men in the fire-room. One gun was dismounted. The *Juliet* was disabled by a shot crashing into the engine. This gunboat was lashed to the pump-boat which had been used in pumping out the *Eastport*. A shot passed through its boiler, and nearly all the two hundred men on board were scalded by the escaping steam. The *Juliet* was being towed by another boat, the pilot of which in his fright abandoned the wheel, whereupon the junior pilot, Mr. Maitland, took his place and headed the boats up-stream till out of range. The *Cricket*, making ready once more, putting on steam, in charge of the admiral, swept past the Confederate guns under a terrific fire, being struck thirty-eight times in five minutes, and losing twenty-five killed and wounded—half her crew. Through the night the crew of the *Juliet* repaired that vessel, but not till the next afternoon were they ready to run the gantlet. When within five hundred yards, the Confederate cannon opened fire. A shot passed through the pilot-house of the *Hindman*, cutting the wheel-ropes, rendering the vessel unmanageable. The brave pilot, Maitland, was on the pump-boat, and had both legs mangled by a shell. A third shell cut away the bell-rope and speaking-tube leading to the engineer; but though both legs were crushed, he reached out his hand to the other bell-cord, and gave a signal which took the vessel to the other side of the river. The captain had been killed. The crew leaped ashore and attempted to escape, but were captured. The *Juliet* and *Hindman* both passed the batteries, but lost between twenty and thirty men.

Just above Alexandria are the rapids of Red River, and two rocky formations, upon which there was only three feet four inches of water, whereas the gunboats needed seven feet to float safely over the bowlders in the bed of the stream. Ten gunboats and two tugs were thus imprisoned at a season of the year when it was expected that all the low lands would be flooded by the water pouring down from the snows melting on the far-off mountain. What should be done?

It may be safely asserted that no armies ever marshalled surpassed in intelligence those which fought in the War of the Rebellion. In every regiment of volunteers were men who, though they never had received education in military engineering, were competent to accomplish great undertakings. In the army of General Banks there was a volunteer who, before the war, was building dams for the erection of mills upon the rivers in the State of Wisconsin, Col. Joseph Bailey, of the Fourth Regiment of Volunteers, from that State. He was acting as chief engineer under General Franklin, and informed that officer that he saw no great difficulty in getting the boats past the rapids. He would build a dam across the river, leaving only a narrow opening in the channel, thus deepening the water sufficiently to permit the passage of the boats. Those who knew nothing about building dams laughed at Colonel Bailey; but Admiral Porter and General Banks and General Franklin thought it wise to make the attempt. Colonel Bailey was accordingly placed in charge, and given all the men he needed to carry on the work.

In the army were two regiments from Maine. Before the war the men were employed on the waters of the Kennebec and Penobscot "driving" logs from the forests to the mills near the sea. They understood rivers, the sweep and swirl of currents and eddies. They were woodchoppers as well, and laid aside their guns and knapsacks to become lumbermen and rivermen once more.

It is a mile and a quarter from the lower rapids to the upper, and in that distance there is a fall of thirteen feet. There was a forest of tall trees upon the northern bank, and there the wood-choppers began felling the trees into the stream, floating them to the head of the rapids. The first tree, with its branches, was laid against the bank, brush made into bun-

PASSING THE DAM.

dles was placed upon it and weighted with stones, and earth shovelled in. Houses were torn down, trunks of trees were locked together in cribs as boys in the country build houses of corn-cobs, the cribs floated into position, filled with stones, and the dam extended to them. Boats and barges were brought into requisition. Three thousand men and two hundred teams were kept at work night and day. The negro troops on the south bank were employed in constructing a dam from that side of the stream. The men from Maine made little noise while at work; each man understood just what to do, and did it quietly. Very different the scene on the southern bank, where the enthusiasm of the men, who a few months before were slaves, broke out in plantation song and chorus.

When Colonel Bailey set forth his plan, very few men in the army believed its execution possible; but when the doubting ones saw the dams gradually growing from each bank into the stream their doubts gave place to enthusiasm, and the army watched with increasing interest the progress of the work. The Confederates learned of what was going on, and the pickets, with taunt and jeer, shouted to the Union men and asked, "How's your dam?" The Confederates did not believe that the undertaking would succeed, and looked gleefully forward to the day when the imprisoned fleet would fall into their hands. At night great fires were kindled upon the banks to enable the men to go on with the work. On the eighth day there remained an opening of only one hundred and fifty feet. The water was rushing through with increasing velocity. While the dam was under construction the crews of the iron-clads were lightening their vessels, removing the guns, ammunition, cables, anchors, and drawing them round the rapids. The iron plating was taken from portions of the vessels and tossed into the river where the water was deep, and where the shifting sands soon covered it. This was done to prevent the Confederates from recovering it after the departure of the army. Some of the old 32-pounder cannon which were considered of little account were loaded to the muzzle, burst, and sunk in the river.

At last all was ready for closing the sluice-way of the dam. To accomplish this, several coal-boats weighted with brick and stone were floated into the opening and sunk. Quickly the water began to rise. Those who watched the river saw the rocks of the upper rapids a mile distant disappear beneath the rising flood, and then several of the vessels, one by one, passed safely over them. Not all had passed when those who stood by the dam saw that two of the barges were being swept out by the rising flood. Admiral Porter issues orders to the captain of the *Lexington* to run the rapids and drive on through the opening. The engineer's bell tinkles, his hand touches the throttle, the wheels turn, and the boat, moved by current and steam, sweeps on. The vessel plunges into the rushing torrent, masses of foam are tossed upon her deck. For a moment the rocks hold her; then with majesty she moves on into the calm waters below, while the whole army rends the air with cheers. The *Neosho*, *Hindman*, and *Osage* follow, but the water falls, the rocks reappear, before the others can pass, and they must bide their time.

Stimulated by what has already been done, Colonel Bailey set himself to complete his task. The dam was at the lower rapids, and he saw that by building wing dams at the upper rapids he could bring all the water into one channel. Three days, and the work was done, the dams raising the water nearly seven feet, and allowing the boats, one by one, to pass safely to Alexandria, where guns and anchors were reshipped. In thirteen days from the beginning of the undertaking the entire fleet was on its way down the river, and the army keeping pace with the vessels in its return. Thus, by the experience, good-sense, and energy of Colonel Bailey was accomplished one of the most brilliant feats of engineering in modern times. The President, recognizing the value of what he had done, sent him a general's commission. Military engineers in Europe expressed their admiration at the success of the undertaking.

A good deal of cotton had been gathered at Alexandria and at other points along the river, but much of it was burned by the soldiers; and so the speculators, who had done much to bring about the movement, reaped little benefit from the campaign.

NOTES TO CHAPTER II.

([1]) Unpublished Documents of the Confederate Department of State.
([2]) Gen. Richard Taylor, "Destruction and Reconstruction," p. 160.
([3]) Idem, p. 162.
([4]) General Mower's Report.

CHAPTER III.

THE GREAT COMMANDER.

WHEN the war began in 1861, Gen. Winfield Scott was lieutenant-general, and in command of all the troops of the United States; but he was an old man, too far advanced in life and too feeble to have the direction of all the great armies which had been organized to put down the Rebellion. So, after the battle of Bull Run, in 1861, when the country called for a leader ("Drum-beat of the Nation," chap. v.), General McClellan was placed in command of all the troops; but when he began the movement to Richmond in 1862, President Lincoln relieved him from the general command, and called Gen. Henry W. Halleck to Washington to have direction of military movements. There had been so many failures of enterprises through contradictory orders sent from Washington by General Halleck and the Secretary of War, Mr. Stanton, that the people and President Lincoln alike were dissatisfied with the state of affairs. Mr. Stanton assumed the right to issue orders. Those transmitted by telegraph were sent in cipher. Mr. Stanton controlled the telegraph and appointed operators, who alone could read the ciphers, which made them independent of the generals commanding a department.

It was seen that there must be one directing mind—one man in authority to plan the movements, to issue orders, so that the troops in different sections of the country should move concertedly for the carrying out of his plans. There was one commander who, by the victories he had won, commended himself to the people as endowed with the qualities needful to direct military affairs—Ulysses S. Grant, who never had lost a battle, but who had won the victory at Belmont, Missouri, in 1861, Fort Donelson and Shiloh, in 1862 ("Drum-beat of the Nation," chaps. vii. and ix.), who had opened the Mississippi by his strategy and siege operations, who had directed affairs at Lookout Mountain and Missionary Ridge ("Marching to Victory," chap. xxii.). When the war began he was a clerk in a store at Galena, Illinois, so quiet and unobtrusive that he had made the acquaintance of very few people in the town. He had been appointed major-general by President Lincoln, but other major-generals outranked him. That he might have supreme command, Congress, on February 26, 1864, passed a law reviving the grade of lieutenant-general. President Lincoln never had seen General Grant, but he had great faith in him, and appointed him to the position formerly held by General Scott, which the Senate, on March 1st, confirmed, and the telegraph the next day informed General Grant that the President wished to see him in Washington. He was at Nashville, Tennessee. The people who rode with him in the cars little dreamed of what he was thinking—that he was laying a grand plan for the prosecution of the war. He saw that the country was divided into nineteen military departments, each with its independent commander receiving orders from Washington; that thus far the movements had not been made simultaneously; that the different armies are like the balky horses of a team—not pulling together. Now that he is to have supreme command, he determined to have the armies move at the same moment. The troops were widely scattered; he would have them consolidated. The theory of General Halleck and the War Department had been to hold all the conquered territory, and re-establish the authority of the United States. General Grant believed that the best way to re-establish the authority of President Lincoln was to crush out the authority of Jefferson Davis by force of arms; that when the Confederate armies were wholly defeated there would be no difficulty in re-establishing the civil government. He saw that in Washington the uppermost idea had been to capture Richmond, the capital of the Confederacy. When the war began the cry throughout the country was "On to Richmond!" General McClellan moved down the Potomac and up to Yorktown and the Peninsula to lay siege to the city. In the estimation of General Grant, Richmond was of small account. He would plan his campaigns to strike the Confederate armies east and west at the same time.

General Grant entered the Cabinet-room in the White House, and for the first time in his life met President Lincoln. The members of the Cabinet had assembled. General Halleck, to whom Grant had been a subordinate, was there; also Mr. E. B. Washburne, of Galena, member of Congress, who had been instrumental in securing General Grant's appointment as lieutenant-general. Two of his staff and his eldest son accompanied him. It was a memorable scene, during the War of the Revolution, when President Washington received his commission as Commander of the Continental Army; and equally impressive this, in which the President of the people, born in a slave State, uneducated in the schools, who had issued the proclamation abolishing slavery,

March 9, 1864.

LIEUTENANT-GENERAL GRANT RECEIVING HIS COMMISSION.

presented to this man, who when the war began was an obscure clerk selling leather, his commission as commander of a million men in arms. These the words of the President: "General Grant, the nation's appreciation of what you have done, and its reliance upon you for what remains to be done in the existing struggle, are now presented with this commission constituting you lieutenant-general in the army of the United States. With this high honor devolves upon you also a corresponding responsibility. As the country herein trusts you, so, under God, it will sustain you. I scarcely need add that with what I here speak for the nation goes my own hearty personal concurrence." The words fell from trembling lips, so deep the feeling of the President.

This the reply: "Mr. President, I accept the commission, with gratitude for the high honor conferred. With the aid of the noble armies that have fought in so many fields for our common country, it will be my earnest endeavor not to disappoint your expectations. I feel the full responsibilities now devolving on me; and I know that if they are met it will be due to those armies, and, above all, to the favor of that Providence which leads nations and men."(¹)

"You will have entire control of the armies," said the President. It was a trust which had been conferred upon no other commander, and he assured General Grant that everything possible should be done to add to the efficiency of the armies. The Secretary of War, Mr. Stanton, said the same.

"I do not wish to know your plans," said Mr. Lincoln, who believed that the man who had won Donelson, rolled back the enemy at Shiloh, captured Vicksburg, and won the great victory at Chattanooga, would make wise plans for the future.(²)

The next day General Grant was at Brandy Station, fifty miles from Washington, looking for the first time into the faces of the soldiers of the Army of the Potomac. He had seen what the Eleventh and Twelfth corps of that grand army could do, as they swept up the sides of Lookout Mountain, and he had the same confidence in the men of the East that he had in those of the West.

Rain was falling, the mud deep, but General Meade was at the station to receive his old friend, whom he had last met on the battle-fields of Mexico, when they were lieutenants.

The rumor was abroad that General Meade was to be removed; that Grant intended to appoint a more active commander.

General Meade was a true patriot. He took command of the army of the Potomac at Frederick three days before Gettysburg. Under him the army fought the great, decisive battle of the war, evermore a turning-point in history. He had rendered efficient service. He had not struck a blow which he might have given after that battle, but he had built up the army. He had foiled Lee in a movement upon Washington. He withdrew the troops from Mine Run, south of the Rapidan, when he saw that it would result in disaster. He was wise and prudent; more than this, he was intensely loyal.

"The emergency of the country is above all other considerations. Remove me at once without any delicacy, if it suits your plans," were the words of Meade.

"I see no reason for displacing you," was the quiet reply.(²)

Alone the two commanders talked about the army, the country, roads, rivers, Lee's force, and the situation of the Union and Confederate armies.

In the morning General Grant was on his way to Washington. President Lincoln had arranged a dinner in his honor, but he could not stay to eat. He had no time for the reception of honor. He was thinking out a great plan. Were he to sit an hour or two at the presidential table to listen to the stories that would be told he would lose time, and it might break into his line of thought. He sent his respects to President Lincoln, stepped into the cars, and was whirling westward over the Alleghanies. While he was flying on the express train the lightning was bearing a despatch from him to General Sherman, who was at Memphis: "Meet me at Nashville."

A man to be a great military commander must understand men. The country did not know much about General Sherman. He had commanded a brigade in the first Bull Run battle, but won no particular distinction. Because he had seen the need for an army of two hundred thousand men in Kentucky at the beginning of the war, the idea was abroad that he was crazy. It was said that he was surprised at Shiloh; that he failed at Chickasaw Bluffs. He had done efficient service under Grant at Jackson, Vicksburg, and Chattanooga. General Grant had seen that he was the man who could be trusted to command in the West. General Halleck doubted if Sherman was the right man; but President Lincoln desired that Grant should have his own way, and the order which assigned him to command all the armies made Sherman commander of the military division of the Mississippi.

Sherman arrived at Nashville. He wanted Grant to remain in the West and direct affairs. "You are at home here; the soldiers know you; you are acquainted with the ground and with your officers," he said.

March 17, 1864.

THE GREAT COMMANDER. 73

General Grant saw differently—that the army under Lee was the strongest of the Confederate armies; that Lee was the ablest Confederate commander; that the Confederate Government would sacrifice everything else to sustain the army which was to hold Richmond. The army under Lee must be crushed before the war could end.

We are not to think that the fighting men of the Confederacy had all been gathered in before 1864. On the contrary, the remorseless conscription enforced during the winter months, which swept in everybody between eighteen and forty-five had filled up the Confederate ranks. The army under Lee never was more powerful than at that moment. Through the months the Tredegar Works at Richmond had been running night and day, casting cannon, shot, and shell. Every vessel running the blockade brought arms and supplies from England. The Confederate Government was straining every nerve to make the armies as powerful East and West as when Lee moved to Gettysburg and Bragg to Chattanooga.

The army which had been routed from Chattanooga was at Dalton, in northern Georgia, commanded by Joseph E. Johnston. Bragg was at Richmond, advising the Secretary of War what to do.

Grant's plan was for Sherman to move against Johnston; for Banks to turn back from the Red River, make all haste to New Orleans, join General Canby, who was commanding there, sail to Mobile, get in rear of the city, capture the forts, which were garrisoned by less than four thousand men, and then march north, or steam up the Alabama River and threaten Johnston in the rear, while Sherman pressed on from Chattanooga.

He had a plan for the Army of the Potomac to strike at Lee's army; while General Butler, who was at Fortress Monroe, was to make a quick move towards Richmond.

The Ninth Corps was under General Burnside. It had returned from Tennessee, and was at Annapolis, in Maryland. No one could tell where it was going. Vessels in the harbor were supposed to be waiting to take the troops on board. General Burnside did not know whither he was going. Secretary Stanton did not know. The newspaper correspondents said he was to sail for North Carolina.

"I want an officer of fire and nerve, to command the cavalry," was Grant's remark to Halleck.

"How would Sheridan do?"

"Just the man."

The country had not heard of General Sheridan. Very few people knew that there was such an officer. The correspondents in their narratives of the battles of Stone River and Missionary Ridge had given glowing accounts of the effective part taken by Sheridan's troops. From the beginning of the war he had been commanding infantry. Now Grant proposed to put him at the head of all the cavalry. During the years 1861 and 1862 the Union cavalry had accomplished very little. It had been in driblets until Hooker consolidated it. The Confederates, at the beginning of the war, laughed at the awkward riding of the Union cavalry. "The people of the North do not know how to ride horses," they said. But they discovered at Brandy Station, in May, 1863, and at Gettysburg in June, and when Grierson rode through the length of the State of Mississippi, coming out at Baton Rouge, that the cavalrymen of the North were becoming very efficient.

Grant intended to make the cavalry a powerful arm of the service, and he wanted a commander, bold, fearless, quick to see and execute. He had seen Sheridan's division sweep the slopes of Missionary Ridge as an ocean-wave rolls up the pebbled beach, and Sheridan was the man to command the eleven thousand horsemen who were to protect his flanks and trains, and be the eyes, ears, and wings of the army.

Before the week was out General Grant was at Fortress Monroe, talking with General Butler.

"All the forces that can be spared from points along the coast will report to you. You are to move up the James, and seize City Point, making Richmond your objective point," were his orders to Butler. "Secure a footing as far up the river as possible."

To General Halleck he wrote, "The army will start with fifteen days' rations."

He was going to cut loose from Washington. He knew that if he attempted to keep the railroad open it would require several thousand men to protect it. He would reopen communication whenever necessary.

I was in Washington on the last days of April, I heard the drum beat and beheld a long column of troops passing down Pennsylvania Avenue. Unheralded, the Ninth Corps had marched from Annapolis. The veteran regiments which had seen service in North Carolina and Tennessee had full ranks once more. There was a division of colored troops. It was an army of nearly thirty thousand men. So well had General Grant kept his own counsel that even General Burnside knew nothing positively as to his destination till the order came for him to break camp and make a rapid march through Washington and join the Army of the Potomac.

I copy from my note-book the words written as I saw them pass:

"The bright sunshine gleams from their bayonets. Above them wave their standards tattered by the winds, torn by cannon-ball and rifle-shot, stained by the blood of dying heroes. They are priceless treasures, more beloved than houses, or lands, riches, honors, ease, comfort, or wife, or children. Ask the battle-scarred soldier what he loves best on earth, and he will have but one answer—'The flag! the dear old flag!' It is his pillar of fire by night and cloud by day; the symbol of everything worth living for, worth dying for.

"I see upon those banners as they flutter in the breeze, 'Bull Run, Ball's Bluff, Roanoke, Newbern, Gainesville, Mechanicsville, Seven Pines, Savage's Station, Malvern Hill, Fredericksburg, Chancellorsville, Antietam, South Mountain, Knoxville, Vicksburg, Port Hudson, Gettysburg'—all those names are there in golden letters, and others so torn and defaced that I cannot read them.

"The streets are lined with men, women, and children. The grave Senators have left their chamber, and the members of the House of Representatives have taken a recess to gaze upon the defenders of their country once more, as they pass through the city, many of them, alas! never to return. There is the steady tramping of the thousands, the deep, heavy jar of the gun-carriages on the pavement, the clattering of hoofs, the clanking of sabres, the drum-beat, the bugle-call, and the music of the military bands. Pavement, sidewalk, windows, and roofs are occupied by the people. Upon the balcony of the hotel is their corps-commander, General Burnside, and by his side the President of the United States, pale, careworn, returning the salutes of the officers and acknowledging those of the soldiers.

"A division of veterans pass. And now, with full ranks, platoons extending from sidewalk to sidewalk, are brigades which never have been in battle; but at the call of their country, they are going forth to crush the Rebellion. *Their country!* They never had a country till the tall man on the balcony, so pale and worn, gave them one.

"For the first time they behold their benefactor. They are darker hued than their veteran comrades who have gone before; but they can cheer as heartily as they. 'Hurrah for Uncle Abe! Hurrah for Massa Linkun! Three cheers for the President! Hurrah! hurrah! hurrah!' There is a swinging of caps, a clapping of hands, a waving of handkerchiefs and banners. There are no cheers more lusty than those given by the redeemed sons of Africa; there are no responses more hearty than those in return from the admiring multitude. Regiment after regiment of stalwart men, slaves once, but freemen now, with steady step, closed-up file, and even rank, pass down the street, moving on to Old Virginia to certain victory or certain death."

By this movement of the Ninth Corps General Grant brought his troops into a compact body. During the winter, the Army of the Potomac had been consolidated into three corps. The Second commanded by General Hancock, the Fifth by General Warren, the Sixth by General Sedgwick. Military authorities are of the opinion that it was a mistake—that it would have been better if there had been more corps organizations; but General Meade had made the consolidation, and General Grant did not change it. Out of deference to the feelings of General Burnside, General Grant did not, at the beginning of the campaign, regard the Ninth Corps as a part of the Army of the Potomac, but as a distinct army.

General Burnside had commanded the Army of the Potomac in 1862, and General Meade was the commander of a division under him, and General Grant thought it to be not quite consistent with military etiquette for a former commander to be placed under one who had been a subordinate. At the beginning of the campaign, General Grant, as lieutenant-general commanding all the armies, only issued general orders to General Meade and General Burnside, allowing them to exercise their own discretion in the execution of the orders. With two subordinate commanders, independent of each other, the efficiency of the great army was much impaired.

The entire army numbered about 125,000 men, with 306 cannon.

The Confederate army under General Lee was encamped south of the Rapidan. General Longstreet's corps, which had passed the winter in Eastern Tennessee, had received a large number of recruits, and was encamped at Gordonsville. From no returns of the Confederate War Department is it possible to know just how many soldiers there were under General Lee. Conscripts were constantly arriving—not new regiments, but individuals from the different States, who were put into regiments already organized. It was far better than the plan adopted by the Union authorities—the organization of new regiments. The raw Confederate recruit, standing side by side with men who had seen three years of service, in a very short time himself becomes a veteran. The Confederate army, as near as can be ascertained, numbered between sixty and seventy thousand, with two hundred and twenty-four cannon, and was composed of three corps, commanded by General Longstreet, Gen. A. P. Hill, and General Ewell.(¹) Notwithstanding the defeat at Gettysburg, the soldiers of the Confederacy believed that the Army of Northern Virginia was invincible; that General Grant, the moment he attempted to advance, would be hurled back, as McClellan, Burnside, and Hooker had been.

The disasters in the West, at Vicksburg, Port Hudson, Chattanooga, and Knoxville, had disheartened many Confederate soldiers in the Southwest as to the success of the Confederacy in establishing its independence; not so the soldiers in the Army of Northern Virginia, who had won many battles, and who had unbounded faith in the ability of General Lee to win victories, and who loved him as children a fond father devoted to their welfare.

From Clark's Mountain, which overlooks the plains upon which the two great armies were encamped, the Confederate signal-officers looked down upon the white tents of the Union troops. With their telescopes they could sweep the horizon ten miles away, and note every movement. General Lee's spies within the Union lines kept him informed of all that was going on. Yet there was not much going on during the last week in April, except the removal of superfluous baggage — the unmistakable sign that ere long the army would move in some direction; but by no change that took place could General Lee discover in which direction the Army of the Potomac would move.

General Grant had planned not only his own movement against Lee's army, but one from Fortress Monroe by an army under Gen. B. F. Butler, which he hoped would either make its way into Richmond, or secure the lines of railway communication leading south and west from that city, which would cripple the Confederate army. In addition, General Sigel was to move from Winchester up the Shenandoah Valley to threaten Lee's communication in that direction, while General Crook was to advance eastward up the Great Kanawha Valley. It would have been better if the troops under Crook and Sigel had been united in the Shenandoah.

Simultaneously with these movements in the East, General Sherman was to advance against General Johnston's Confederate army at Dalton, in northern Georgia.

By the concerted movements of the several armies, the Confederate Government could not again send, as it had done the year before, Longstreet to reinforce the western army, nor could troops from the west be hurried east to assist Lee in confronting the Army of the Potomac. Such the strategy thought out by General Grant.

NOTES TO CHAPTER III.

([1]) Gen. U. S. Grant, "Personal Memoirs," vol. ii., p. 115.
([2]) Idem.
([3]) Idem, p. 117.
([4]) Gen. A. A. Humphreys, "Virginia Campaigns of 1864 and 1865," p. 17.

CHAPTER IV.

THE WILDERNESS.

ON the evening of May 3d orderlies were riding through the great army with sealed packages—the orders for the army to move. At midnight I looked upon the scene, beholding glimmering camp-fires, long lines of men. There was no drum-beat, but a quiet mustering of troops, a folding of tents, and then the column of men and long lines of white-topped wagons disappeared, moving south-east towards the fords of the Rapidan.

The cavalry, under Sheridan, were in the advance, then a long train of wagons with pontoons—the Engineer Corps, hastening to Germania Ford, where they quickly constructed two bridges of boats, and two more at Ely's, and one at Culpeper Mine.

If there had been ten bridges instead of five—if a pioneer brigade of two thousand men had been organized, with axes and shovels—there probably would have been no battle in the Wilderness. The most difficult part of Grant's plan was the movement of the four thousand wagons. A wagon-train, at the best, cannot get on very fast. An obstinate mule, the breaking of a trace or strap, stops the whole train. The trains must be protected by the troops. It would not have been very difficult to construct a new road between the Germania and Ely's Ford road. It could have been accomplished in a few hours. A year later such a road was opened in rear of the works at Petersburg for the last grand movement. It was the delay of the trains, moving on two roads, which compelled General Grant to fight the first battle in the Wilderness.

At midnight the whole army was on the march—Wilson's cavalry and the Fifth and Sixth corps towards Germania Ford; Gregg's cavalry and the Second Corps to Ely's, six miles down-stream. At 10 o'clock the next morning the Second Corps was at Chancellorsville, resting on the field where they fought a year before. The Fifth Corps was at Wilderness Tavern, five miles south of Germania Ford; the

May 4, 1864.

MOVEMENT TO THE WILDERNESS.

Sixth at the ford; the Ninth moving from Manassas, where it had halted after passing through Washington.

I had last seen General Grant at Corinth, in June, 1862. During the spring campaign of that year he had treated me with great kindness, and though so many months had passed, though he had been chief actor in one of the greatest wars in the history of the human race, his wonderful memory had not failed him as to my name and occupation—that of a newspaper correspondent, and I was cordially welcomed to his headquarters. I rode with his staff to Germania Ford. Upon the south bank stood a deserted Virginia farm-house. Although soldiers of the Confederacy and of the Union had passed and repassed it many times, the windows had not been broken. The departing family had left a few articles of furniture behind—a table and some chairs.

The frugal supper of the lieutenant-general—cold ham and tongue and army bread—was spread upon the table, and I had the honor of being his guest, in company with my friend Hon. E. B. Washburne, Member of Congress. When supper was finished, General Grant sat on a camp-stool by the door-way, smoking his cigar, silent, absorbed in thought, looking out upon the gleaming camp-fires of a division of the Sixth Corps, forming the right wing of the army in this movement.

The great religious interest manifest in the army during the winter had not lost its force. The soldiers of an entire brigade were holding a prayer-meeting. The sky was without a cloud, and the gleaming stars looked down upon them while the glimmering bivouac fires brought out in bold relief the kneeling throng. This was to be their last meeting before the beginning of the terrific struggle. Before another sunset the lips of many of that congregation would be silent evermore. The prayers finished, they stood erect, and then joined in their parting hymn, the mighty chorus of manly voices mingling with the tattoo of the evening drum-beat, swelling out in the melody and harmony of Old Hundred, the music of Martin Luther, the great apostle of Liberty.

> "Eternal are thy mercies, Lord,
> Eternal truth attends thy word;
> Thy praise shall sound from shore to shore
> Till suns shall rise and set no more."(¹)

General Lee did not believe that General Grant was marching towards Spottsylvania, but that it was a movement to attack his right flank.(²) The Union signal-officers were reading his despatches, for they had discovered the key to the Confederate code of signals. It was past one in the afternoon, and the Fifth Corps had reached the Wilderness Tavern, when Lee directed Ewell and Hill to occupy their old line of intrenchments at Mine Run ("Marching to Victory," p. 466). He sent orders to Longstreet, who was at Gordonsville, to move up the plank road. General Lee was familiar with the country. Many times he had ridden along the roads. His military secretary says:

"Its intricacies, which were familiar to him and his generals, were unknown ground to Grant. In them he had already vanquished a large army with half its force. The natural hope of success in baffling his new opponent which this gave him he did not fail to avail himself of, and Grant found himself unexpectedly arrested in his march by the presence of the Confederate army in the wilds in which, just a year before, Hooker's confident army had been hurled back in defeat."(³)

That General Lee confidently expected to overwhelm General Grant, and send him back across the Rapidan and Rappahannock as Hooker and Burnside had been sent, will be seen by this narrative as given by his military secretary, who spent the night and breakfasted with him, and who has given this picture of the Confederate commander:

"The general displayed the cheerfulness which he usually exhibited at meals, and indulged in a few pleasant jests at the expense of his staff-officers, as was his custom on such occasions. He expressed himself surprised that his new adversary had placed himself in the predicament as 'Fighting Joe' had done the previous spring. He hoped the result would be even more disastrous to Grant than that which Hooker had experienced. He was in the best of spirits and expressed much confidence of the result; a confidence which was well founded, for there was much reason to believe that his antagonist would be at his mercy while entangled in the pathless thicket."(⁴)

The country had been settled many years, but it was still a wilderness—dense woods, tangled thickets, here and there a clearing, a tumble-down farm-house. The land was once almost wholly owned by a rich old man, who leased farms to tenants. He had many slaves and lived in grand style, raising tobacco and slaves. Roads were laid out before the Revolutionary War. The tide of travel then was east and west, between the mountains and the sea-coast, to Williamsburg and Fredericksburg.

To accommodate this, two roads were laid out—the Orange turnpike, five miles south of Germania Ford, and one and a half miles farther south the Orange plank road. The road from Germania Ford runs south-east, the other south-west. The Wilderness Tavern is on the turnpike near its junction with the Germania road. The house of Mr. Lacy is south-west

GENERAL GRANT'S HEADQUARTERS AT GERMANIA FORD.

from the tavern a short distance. It was here that Stonewall Jackson had his arm amputated during the battle of Chancellorsville.

Early in the morning General Grant was in the saddle. It was between seven and eight o'clock when he reached General Meade, near Wilderness Tavern. The cavalry pickets had been out on the turnpike and plank road, and had exchanged shots with the Confederates. The troops of the Fifth Corps were in the fields and woods west of Lacy's house.

May 5, 1864.

"General Warren says that Lee intends to fight us here," General Meade remarked.

"Very well," the reply.

The two commanders entered the edge of the woods west of the road and dismounted. General Humphreys, chief of General Meade's staff, took out his order-book and wrote a few lines. Aides on fast horses carried the messages to Warren, Sedgwick, Hancock, and Sheridan.(*)

Riding out to the front line I saw across a field the Confederates under Hill coming into position, the sunlight gleaming from barrel and bayonet. The skirmishers were exchanging shots; soldiers were at work with axes felling trees, constructing rude intrenchments.

MAJ.-GEN. G. K. WARREN.

With great promptness, and confident of victory, Lee moved to strike a staggering blow.

It was a sublime confidence which animated the Confederate troops on that bright May morning. I could see it in their marching, coming out squarely into the open field, and taking deliberate position to hurl themselves upon Warren's corps. They had unbounded faith in Lee.

The soldiers of the Union army knew General Grant only by reputation. They had read about Donelson, Vicksburg, and Chattanooga, but he had not reviewed them, never had ridden along the lines with a grand staff. It can hardly be said that General Grant on that morning possessed the confidence of the army; he was yet to win it.

6*

While the troops under Meade were deploying for battle in the Wilderness, those under Burnside were moving from Manassas Junction, forty miles north of Germania Ford, where they had been holding the railroad. They marched all night, and in the morning were crossing at Germania Ford and filing in rear of the Sixth Corps. One division of cavalry was retained north of the Rapidan to guard against any movement to strike Grant's line of communication.

The Union army was marching south, the Confederate east, and Grant saw that instead of reaching, as he had hoped, the cleared fields around Spottsylvania, the first battle must be fought in the Wilderness.

His plan was to take the initiative whenever he could draw the enemy from his intrenchments. He did not wait till all his troops were up, but ordered Warren to attack as soon as he could get his troops into position.

General Getty's division of the Sixth Corps filed in rear of the Fifth Corps and came into line on the right, to hold the ground in that direction till Hancock could make the march from Chancellorsville. The Union line at the beginning of the struggle was formed with Rickett's division of the Sixth Corps nearest the Rapidan, forming the right wing, then Wright's division, then the Fifth Corps, with Getty's division of the Sixth.

The Second Corps, upon its arrival, formed on the left of Getty, reaching southward in the direction of Todd's Tavern, occupied by the cavalry under Sheridan. The Ninth Corps was moving south from Germania Ford and coming into position in rear of the Fifth.

On the Confederate side Ewell confronted the Sixth Corps, A. P. Hill the Fifth, while Longstreet was advancing to meet Hancock, and Stuart to attack Sheridan. The wagons of General Grant, more than four thousand, were at Chancellorsville. The last eastward railroad train had left Culpeper Court-house. The Union army had cut loose from Washington by that line.

General Crawford's division of the Fifth Corps at eight o'clock was out on Mr. Chewing's farm, on the plank road; General Wadsworth's was close behind, also General Robinson's. There were cavalry pickets at Parker's store, which were being driven in, but Crawford advanced and held the ground.

Going from the Wilderness Tavern south we ride along the Brock road, which, before railroads were built, was a great highway between Spottsylvania and the Germania Ford. A mile and a half down this road brings us to the plank road. If we turn west and ride a mile and

THE WILDERNESS. 87

a half we come to Parker's store. Keeping these roads and places in mind, we shall be able to understand the great battle which was fought almost wholly in the woods, where the trees—scrub-oaks, pines, cedars,

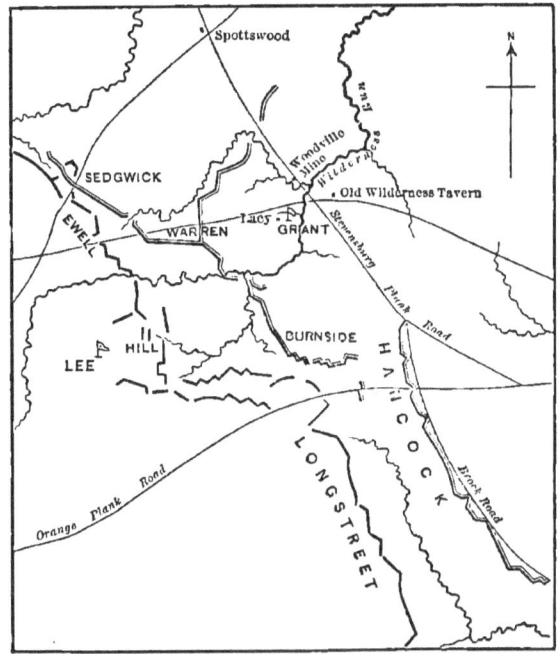

WILDERNESS BATTLE-FIELD.

and sassafras—were so thick that the contending armies could not see each other.

General Lee did not care to bring on the battle until Longstreet was in position.

Three o'clock. We see Wright's division of the Sixth Corps moving south-west through the woods, the Fifth Corps in position from the right of the turnpike, across it, down to the plank road.

The battle begins along Warren's line. It is not long before Wright's division of the Sixth Corps strikes Ewell's flank and drives it in disorder. Ewell brings up reinforcements, and Wright is driven in turn. It is five o'clock before Hancock comes up.

I shall not attempt to describe the movements of the Union and Confederate brigades backward and forward through the thickets, because I could not make it intelligible. We may think of men in blue and men in gray surging to and fro, neither side advancing very far, neither retreating any great distance. The ground is a succession of hills and hollows, knolls and ravines, covered with thick bushes, scrub-oak, sassafras, chincapin, and hazel. Two columns of smoke rise above the trees. Men fire into the thickets, aiming only at flashes and lines of smoke. The twigs of trees are cut into shreds by the leaden rain. The woods are so thick that cannon are of little use. Till the sun goes down the mighty uproar goes on, little advantage being gained by either party, each holding its ground. The woods are thick with killed and wounded. The last year's dead leaves are like tinder. They take fire, and the flames sweep over the ground between the lines. The wounded cry for help. Some are snatched from the flames, but for others there is no relief.

Night came on with each army preparing for the morrow's struggle, throwing up intrenchments, both preparing for the attack at daylight. On the Confederate side Longstreet was bringing up his division by Parker's store. On the Union side the Ninth Corps was coming into position between Warren and Hancock.

I spread my blanket for the night beneath a shed, once occupied by a gold-mining company, near General Grant's headquarters. I was astir at daybreak, for I knew that General Grant intended to renew the attack as soon as day dawned. I do not know why General Meade wished him to postpone it till six o'clock; but in deference to his wishes the order was modified to five.(*) General Grant knew from his spies that Longstreet was hastening on, and wished to strike a blow before his arrival. General Lee, wishing to delay, if possible, any attack upon his right by Hancock, directed Ewell to open fire upon the Sixth Corps.

It was a little past five when I heard a ripple of musketry in front of the Sixth Corps, then a longer roll. The spring birds were singing their morning songs in the trees around me, the air was fragrant with the perfume of opening flowers, army wagons were rumbling along the roads, when the uproar of battle began. A moment later I heard the outburst of the tempest, where Hancock was falling upon the left of A. P. Hill's command. If General Lee thought to delay the expected stroke, if he thought that Grant would order Hancock to wait, he was mistaken. Wadsworth's division of the Fifth Corps, north of the Orange plank road, and Hancock with the Second Corps south of it, moved upon Hill. The assault of Hancock first fell upon Heth's and Wilcox's divisions. A Confederate historian says: "Hill was assailed with

May 6, 1864.

IN THE WILDERNESS.

increased vigor, so heavy a pressure being brought to bear upon Heth and Wilcox that they were driven back, and owing to the difficulties of the country, were thrown into confusion. The failure of Longstreet to appear came near causing a serious disaster to the army." (⁷)

There was confusion in rear of the Confederate army. General Lee sent his adjutant-general to Parker's store, ordering the trains to be ready to move. Messengers rode in haste with an order to Longstreet to hasten the march of his troops. Had we been there we should have seen General Longstreet ordering his men to go upon the run, and himself putting spurs to his horse and galloping towards the line of battle, each moment coming nearer as Hancock's troops pressed on. General Lee and Hill were endeavoring to rally the retreating Confederates. It was a critical moment for General Lee. Hill's troops were breaking when Gregg's brigade of Texans appeared, the foremost of Longstreet's command. They, with the other troops of Longstreet, went west before the battle of Chickamauga, and had not for several months seen their beloved commander; but beholding him rallying Hill's troops, with the bullets falling around him, broke into a cheer. This the account of the scene by a Confederate :(⁸)

"The Texans cheered lustily as their line of battle, coming up in splendid style, passed by Wilcox's disordered columns, and swept across our artillery pit and its adjacent breastwork. Much moved by the greeting of these brave men and their magnificent behavior, General Lee spurred his horse through an opening in the trenches, and followed close on their line as it moved rapidly forward. The men did not perceive that he was going with them until they had advanced some distance in the charge. When they did recognize him, there came from the entire line as it rushed on, the cry, 'Go back, General Lee! go back!' A sergeant seized his bridle-rein and turned his horse." (⁹)

In the charge upon Hancock more than one-half of Gregg's brigade were killed or wounded; but their assault, together with Benning's division, was so vigorous that the advance of Birney's and Mott's divisions was checked. General Grant has this to say regarding the attack by Hancock:

"I believed then, and see no reason to change that opinion, that if the country had been such that Hancock and his command could have seen the confusion and panic in the lines of the enemy, it would have taken advantage so effectually that Lee would not have made another stand outside of his Richmond defences." (¹⁰)

Both Union and Confederate lines were broken up—regiments separated from their brigades and disorganized. This before 6.30 in the morning. There came a lull while the line reformed.

South of the plank road was an unfinished line of railroad, and later in the day Longstreet swung his troops in that direction, struck Hancock's left flank and drove the Union troops back to their intrenchments. The woods were on fire, and the logs of the breastworks were burning, but amid the crackle of the flames the battle went on. I have heard the uproar of many battles, but never so heavy a fire of musketry as rolled up along Hancock's line during the afternoon, when almost the whole of his corps and two divisions of Burnside's corps were engaged with Longstreet's and Hill's. I think that thirty thousand men were firing at the same moment.

At five o'clock Longstreet's troops fell back. They had forced the Second Corps back from the advance made in the morning, but could not drive Hancock from his chosen position.

At sunset the battle died away. I was at General Grant's headquarters in the grove of pines north of the Lacy house.

Suddenly, far up on the right, rose the Confederate war-whoop, then volleys of musketry and the thunder of cannon. The Confederate generals Gordon and Johnston had formed their brigades in the woods in front of Shaler's brigade of the Sixth Corps. A portion of Shaler's men laid down their guns and were using axes and shovels, when the Confederates rushed upon them, taking Shaler and nearly all his men prisoners. It was an attack as sudden as the swoop of an eagle. They rushed on and struck Seymour's brigade. Pegram's Confederate brigade came upon Wright's division. The battle became fierce and bloody. Looking across the fields I could see fugitives streaming towards Chancellorsville. Teamsters were harnessing their horses; wagons were in motion; there was a quick packing up. An officer greatly excited came riding to headquarters.

"The Rebels have massed their whole force on our right; got between us and the river; turned our flank. They have captured Shaler's and Seymour's brigades, and are sweeping all before them!" he shouted.(")

General Grant was sitting with his back against a tree, whittling a stick. He did not rise, nor was he disturbed. General Meade, hearing the report and seeing evident signs of disaster, with quick, nervous energy, said, "Shall I order in supports, general?" "Yes, if you think best," the reply. But troops were already on their way, which General Humphreys had taken the responsibility of ordering to support the Sixth Corps. He says: "Staff-officers of the Sixth Corps rode into General Meade's headquarters and informed me (General Meade was at General Grant's headquarters) that the right of the line had been broken and rolled up, that the enemy occupied the position, and that a part of them were advancing down the Germania plank road, on our right and rear, following the fugitives from Shaler's and Seymour's brigades, and that probably both Sedgwick and Wright were captured. I at once made dispositions to meet this with the provost guard and some troops that General Warren sent me."([12])

Had we been within the Confederate lines we should have seen in the afternoon Johnston's brigade of Rodes's division arriving from Hanover Junction, and the troops marching up to the left of the line to join General Early. The Confederates discovered that the right of the Sixth Corps had no troops near at hand in support. As the sun went down Gordon's and Johnston's brigades marched north, then east, and then south-east, to gain the flank and rear of the Union troops, while Early with his remaining brigades attacked in front. The Union troops, under General Shaler, were building breastworks. The pickets were not very far out from the main line. Gordon's and Johnston's men came upon them, capturing a large number of Shaler's men before they could throw down their axes and shovels and seize their guns. The brigade was thrown into confusion, some of the men fleeing across the fields. The wave next struck Seymour's brigade, which also was thrown into confusion, but the men quickly rallied and poured in such destructive volleys that the Confederate ranks in turn were broken and thrown into disorder. Night was fast settling over the forest, illuminated by the flashing of thousands of muskets. The Confederate officers were unable to rally the men in the darkness, and the struggle ended almost as quickly as it began. "It was fortunate," writes the Confederate General Early, "that darkness came to close this affair, as the enemy, if he had been able to discover the disorder on our side, might have brought up fresh troops and availed himself of our condition."([13])

Minutes seem hours at such a time, for the uproar increased and came nearer. In the field north of the Wilderness Tavern, the reserve artillery, the provost guards, and a division of the Fifth Corps were coming into position for a new line. The coolest person in that group beneath the pines was the man who never lost a battle. At last the silent man spoke:

"Washburn, I do not believe that story. The Rebels can have no great force on our right. Through the afternoon Longstreet and Hancock have been at it. Warren has had all he could do with Hill. Lee has not had time to change his troops and mass them on the right."([14])

He had thought it out, and was not concerned. It was a disaster to lose several hundred prisoners, but that was not going to force him from his position.

An officer came riding in, giving a clear account of what had happened. "We have a new line established, and can hold them," he said.

During the two days' struggle General Grant had lost about fifteen thousand killed and wounded and taken prisoners. There are no returns of the losses of the Confederates, but as General Grant was the assailant, it is probable that the number of killed and wounded was not so great as on the Union side. The biographer of General Lee admits that the loss was seven thousand;([18]) the probabilities are that, including prisoners taken, the Confederate loss exceeded ten thousand. A great many statements have been made by writers in regard to the war that are not true. A Confederate writer states that the Union loss in this battle was forty thousand.([19])

General Grant did not intend to have his troops slaughtered by an attack upon the Confederate intrenchments. He had no idea of retreating. The one thought in his mind was how best to get at Lee's army. He would move by his left flank to Spottsylvania. The first great conflict of the campaign had been fought. Lee possibly thought he could compel Grant to follow the example of Hooker, and recross the Rapidan, but he was mistaken. Lee had not won a victory. General Grant did not desire to fight in the Wilderness, but accepted battle while waiting for his trains. He had held his ground, and proposed to go on.

Through the night long lines of ambulances were moving towards Fredericksburg with the wounded, who had to be cared for before the army could be moved on. All but one of the bridges across the Rapidan had been taken up; that one was used to reopen communication with Washington, and a large number of the wounded were sent by that route.

Through Saturday there was a strange quietness along the lines, in contrast to the turmoil of Thursday and Friday. General Lee was sending his wounded southward, to be transported to Richmond or to Gordonsville. All the farm-houses in rear of his lines were filled with wounded. Of the battle of the Wilderness General Grant has left this record:

May 7, 1864.

"More desperate fighting has not been witnessed on this continent than that of the 5th and 6th of May. Our victory consisted in having successfully crossed a formidable stream almost in the face of an enemy, and in getting the army together as a unit. We gained an advantage on the morning of the 6th, which, if it had been followed up, must have proved decisive. In the evening the enemy gained an advantage but was speedily repulsed. As we stood at the close, the two armies were relatively about in the same condition to meet each other as when the river divided them; but the fact of having safely crossed was a victory."(¹⁷)

In this battle the electric telegraph was used for the transmission of orders. The moment General Grant had selected a place for his headquarters a man riding a mule started upon a trot, reeling off lines of insulated wire, to the headquarters of generals Sedgwick, Warren, Hancock, and Burnside. A wagon followed dropping poles ten feet long, with an iron spike at one end and a fork at the other, by which the wire was lifted from the ground, so that the troops could march and countermarch without tripping. Being insulated, it worked just as well in rain as in sunshine. Each brigade unrolled its own length of wire; so in a very few minutes there was a line of telegraph in operation and the instruments clicking at the headquarters of each general. To the close of the war the field telegraph was used by General Grant.

For two days the contest had raged. When General Grant rose from his camp-bed on the morning of Saturday he had formed his plan for future action. He would not renew the struggle in the Wilderness, but would make a movement to get between General Lee and Richmond; but he must remain where he was till he could remove the wounded.

Before he sat down to breakfast he issued the order for the corps commanders to be ready to make a night march towards Spottsylvania. So through the day the long line of ambulances was moving towards Fredericksburg, and the four thousand wagons southward towards the Ny River.

In making the movement, the Fifth Corps at sunset was to quietly withdraw from its intrenchments and march down the Brook road, the great highway of former days leading from Germania Ford to Richmond. The Sixth and Ninth corps were to move by other routes, while Hancock with the Second Corps was to remain in position till the others had passed. General Grant thought it likely that General Lee would fall upon Hancock, but he did not. The Confederate commander instead telegraphed to Richmond that the Union army was once more defeated, and was retreating to Fredericksburg.(¹⁸)

But he soon discovered his mistake, and ordered Anderson, placed in command of the First Corps after the wounding of Longstreet, to hasten to Spottsylvania, for if General Grant were to reach that point in advance and retain possession, he would be compelled to attack him, with the advantage of position on the side of the Union troops. He was too wary to do that after the two days' conflict in the tangled thickets of the Wilderness.

NOTES TO CHAPTER IV.

([1]) Author's Note-book, May, 1864.
([2]) Gen. U. S. Grant, "Personal Memoirs," vol. ii., p. 191.
([3]) Gen. A. L. Long, "Memoirs of Robert E. Lee," p. 326.
([4]) Idem.
([5]) Author's Note-book, May, 1864.
([6]) Gen. U. S. Grant, "Personal Memoirs," vol. ii., p. 195.
([7]) Gen. A. L. Long, "Memoirs of Robert E. Lee," p. 329.
([8]) Idem, p. 331.
([9]) C. S. Venable, of Lee's staff, Address before Southern Historical Society.
([10]) Gen. U. S. Grant, "Personal Memoirs," vol. ii., p. 197.
([11]) Author's Note-book, May, 1864.
([12]) Gen. A. A. Humphreys, "Virginia Campaigns of 1864 and 1865," p. 50.
([13]) Gen. J. A. Early, "Memoirs of the Last Year of the War," p. 20.
([14]) Author's Note-book, May, 1864.
([15]) Gen. A. L. Long, "Memoirs of Robert E. Lee," p. 324.
([16]) Gen. C. M. Wilcox, quoted by Gen. A. A. Humphreys, in "Virginia Campaigns of 1864 and 1865," p. 424.
([17]) Gen. U. S. Grant, "Personal Memoirs," vol. ii., p. 204.
([18]) Idem, p. 211.

CHAPTER V.

SPOTTSYLVANIA.

SPOTTSYLVANIA COURT-HOUSE is a little hamlet, consisting of the court-house and jail, a large two-story brick tavern, a grocery, and a few houses. It is upon the Brook road leading from Richmond to Culpeper north-west. From the tavern a road leads north-east to Fredericksburg, fifteen miles distant. The river Ny rises amid the woods south of Chancellorsville, and crosses the road leading to Fredericksburg one mile from the court-house. The river Po, which rises amid the woods south-west of the Wilderness battle-field, with many windings between rugged banks, runs south-east. If we go west from the court-house upon a road leading to Shady Grove Church, we may cross the Po by Block House Bridge, or by Snell's Bridge, near the farm of Mr. Chewnig. If we travel up the Brook road, one mile and a half will bring us to the farm of Mr. Spindler, and another mile will take us to the house of Mr. Alsop; still another mile will bring us to Todd's Tavern. The road runs along the high land between the Ny and the Po. It was about fifteen miles from General Grant's headquarters on the Wilderness battle-field to the court-house.

The sun was setting when the troops of the Fifth Corps of the Army of the Potomac left their intrenchments and moved down the Brook road towards Spottsylvania. The daylight faded away, and then the regiments of the Sixth Corps moved noiselessly across the fields by the old Wilderness Tavern in the same direction. The Ninth Corps turned eastward, going down the road leading to the field of Chancellorsville, passing in the depths of the forest the graves of those who a year before gave up their lives for their country. The Second Corps remained where it had fought during the battle of the Wilderness.

May 7, 1864.

It was past nine o'clock when I mounted my horse at General Grant's headquarters, and rode with the commander-in-chief to the headquarters of General Hancock. General Meade was there. The men of the Second Corps, who had confronted Longstreet in the terrible struggle, were

7

in line behind their breastworks along the Brook road. The woods were on fire between them and the Confederates, the flames throwing a lurid light upon the tall forest-trees. Some soldiers were asleep, others smoking their pipes, others on the watch for any advance of the Confederates. Few of the men of the Second Corps had ever seen General Grant, but when they saw him, and knew that instead of retreating he was moving to strike Lee, they swung their hats and made the forest ring with their cheers.

SPOTTSYLVANIA COURT-HOUSE.

The Confederates knew not what to make of it. A moment later there came an answering cheer, and then a volley of musketry and artillery. They thought that Hancock was going to attack them. The bullets were singing in the air above us, and we could hear them spinning amid the foliage, but little harm was done, and the firing soon ceased. I was weary and worn, and threw myself upon the ground in the thicket, and was soon asleep, but was awakened by the stir around me as General Grant and General Meade again mounted their horses. A moment later we were riding down a narrow road in a dense forest. Suddenly a musket flashed before us. There was a quick drawing of our bridle-reins. We had taken the wrong road, and were close upon the Confederate pickets. A few rods farther and General Grant, with his staff and he who writes these lines, would have encountered General Anderson's Confederate troops, which were on the march to throw themselves in front of the Fifth Corps, and prevent General Grant from reaching Spottsylvania.([1]) Quickly we turned about. Colonel Comstock, engineer-in-chief, discovered the right road, and we rode swiftly on. Day was breaking in the east when we reached Todd's Tavern, a two-storied building with a chimney at each end, where, in by-gone days travellers had found lodgings and refreshment.

SPOTTSYLVANIA.   99

The landlord and his wife were old and feeble. Little had they dreamed that two great armies would suddenly struggle for the mastery in the surrounding fields and woods.

The Union and Confederate cavalry were fighting, the cannon flashing, as I tied my horse to the palings of the fence by the tavern, placed my saddle upon the ground for a pillow, and dropped off to sleep, undisturbed by the tramping of passing troops, the thunder of the cannon, or the rumbling of ammunition-wagons.

During the preceding day important news had come to General Grant, that General Butler moved from Fortress Monroe according to orders, and had landed his whole force at City Point, surprising the Confederates and threatening Richmond. It was this information which led General Grant to endeavor to get between Lee's army and the Confederate capital, for he thought it possible that an order might have been sent by Jefferson Davis to Lee, withdrawing him to Richmond.(²) We shall see in another chapter just what General Butler had accomplished.

May 5, 1864.

During the battle of the Wilderness the cavalry under Sheridan had been holding all the country from Todd's Tavern to Fredericksburg against any surprise from the Confederate cavalry under Stuart. At Todd's Tavern, Gregg's and Merritt's divisions of Union cavalry, all through May 7th, were confronted by Fitz-Hugh Lee's Confederate division, holding the Cathargin road, which runs south-west to Shady Grove Church. It crosses the Po at Corbyn's Bridge, two miles west of Todd's Tavern. General Wilson's division of cavalry was on the road leading from Spottsylvania to the court-house, and was ordered by Sheridan to move to the court-house, and thence west to Shady Grove Church, to be joined by Gregg and Merritt, to drive the Confederate cavalry beyond Corbyn's Bridge. All three divisions were to move at daylight on Sunday morning.

General Meade arrived at Todd's Tavern at midnight. The orders which Sheridan had issued had not reached Gregg and Merritt, and General Meade directed Gregg to move out towards Corbyn's and watch the roads, while Merritt was to go down the Brook road to Spottsylvania. This was done without consulting General Sheridan.

May 8, 1864.

Wilson moved as he had been directed by Sheridan, and at daylight drove in the Confederate pickets, advanced to the court-house, and was in possession of the all-important point, when there came the thunder of the cannonade from the north-west near Corbyn's Bridge, and from the farm of Mr. Spindler. Going up the Brook road towards the battle,

Wilson found himself stopped by two divisions of Anderson's troops, which had just arrived and were throwing up intrenchments. He was in an isolated position, and orders soon came for him to fall back along the Fredericksburg road. So it came about that Spottsylvania was lost at the outset, because the small body of cavalry could not hold it against infantry.

I was awakened from sleep by the sudden roar of cannon near at hand, and in the dawning light could see across the field the Union artillerymen loading their pieces. Shells from the Confederate guns were whirring through the air. The Fifth Corps was passing the Tavern, Robertson's division in advance, filing from the road into a field by the house of Mr. Alsop—a small building with a porch at one end. The Brook road along which the troops were marching forks near the house, the two roads coming together a mile farther on. The Union troops moved to the right.

General Lee had discovered that General Grant was inaugurating a movement, but had misinterpreted it, thinking that he was retreating. This was the despatch which he sent to Richmond: "The enemy has abandoned his position, and is moving towards Fredericksburg."(²) When he discovered his mistake he directed Anderson to move to Spottsylvania in the morning; but the woods were on fire, and Anderson, finding no good place where he could go into bivouac, began his march at once. So it came about that the Confederates under Anderson and the Fifth Corps had marched on parallel roads, scarcely more than one mile apart, towards Spottsylvania. More than this, General Lee directed General Early, who had been placed temporarily in command of Ewell's corps, to march to Todd's Tavern by the very road on which we have seen the Second and Fifth corps. When General Anderson reached the main road, between Todd's Tavern and Spottsylvania, he saw the error which General Lee had made, and quickly prepared for battle. So, through a mistake on the part of General Lee, and not by any correct comprehension of the situation of the Union army or the intention of General Grant, the great struggle at Spottsylvania began. If General Anderson had obeyed the order of General Lee, the probabilities are that General Grant would have succeeded in placing his army between Lee's army and Richmond; or if not that, he would have chosen his own ground, and General Lee would have been compelled to attack at a disadvantage or make a rapid retreat. Such the strange complications of the moment.

General Lee had a large number of spies—men who knew all the roads, and who had a general acquaintance with all the features of the

country. Since the war, I have talked with a Confederate who was thus employed to find out what the Union army was doing. This his story:
"I rode through the Union corps, keeping my eyes and ears open. When with the Fifth Corps I asked where I should find the Sixth, or Ninth, or Second. I said that I had despatches in my hand for Hancock, or Sedgwick, or Burnside. When I wanted to gain the Confederate lines I rode boldly past the Union pickets. If they stopped me, I was an engineer officer ordered to examine the ground. Of course I had no difficulty in getting inside the Confederate lines."(¹)

HOUSE OF MR. ALSOP.

The sun was several hours up before the Fifth Corps was prepared for battle. The headquarters of General Grant were established at Piney Grove Church. No bell called the worshippers to its portal on that Sunday morning; the thunder of the cannonade and rolls of musketry, instead, vibrated the air.

The day was intensely hot, and I sat beneath the apple-trees, fragrant with blossoms, and listened to the strange Sabbath symphony—the humming of bees, the songs of birds, the roll of musketry, and the cannonade.

I saw Tyler's brigade—Sixteenth Maine, Thirteenth and Thirty-ninth Massachusetts, and One Hundred and Fourth New York—advancing on the left; Denison's brigade of Maryland troops, four regiments, on the right; Coulter's brigade—Twelfth Massachusetts, Eighty-third and Ninety-seventh New York, Eleventh, Eighty-eighth, and Ninetieth Pennsylvania—in rear of Tyler. The skirmishers move across the field. The lines reached Alsop's house, when there came a roll of musketry from the woods beyond, with solid shot and shell from the Confederate artillery. The great battle of Spottsylvania, which was to go on day after day, had begun.

The Confederates were behind intrenchments. They were Kershaw's and Humphreys's brigades. Kershaw had six regiments and a battalion of South Carolina troops; Humphreys had four Mississippi regiments.

The Confederate army was organized mainly with regiments from a State brigaded together. It was carrying out the idea of State exclusiveness—of State rights. The State was more than the Confederacy.

The brigades in the Union army were usually made up of regiments from different States. It was carrying out the idea of Union. Massachusetts and Wisconsin, New York and Ohio, fought side by side.

As far as practicable, the Confederate divisions were also made up of troops from a single State. Pickett's division—four brigades—were all from Virginia; of Johnson's four brigades, three were from Virginia; of Rodes's division of five brigades, three were from North Carolina.

Almost at the first fire General Robinson was wounded. The Confederates were in the woods, behind intrenchments, under cover, while the Union troops were in the field and suffered severely.

While Robinson's division was moving across the field, Griffin's division advanced south of Alsop's house, Bartlett's brigade in advance—Twentieth Maine, Eighteenth Massachusetts, Forty-fourth New York, Eighty-third and One Hundred and Eighteenth Pennsylvania, First and Sixteenth Michigan.

These troops were in the middle of the field when the hot blast from the Confederates struck them. Robinson's and Griffin's troops recoiled under the fierce fire. Ayres's and Sweitzer's brigades were in rear of Bartlett's, whose lines reformed. Crawford's division—the Pennsylvania Reserves—came up on Griffin's left, and the Confederates were driven from their position.

At this moment Field's division of Longstreet's corps came into line, striking Griffin's right flank; but help was at hand for Griffin—Cutler's division, commanded by Wadsworth at the Wilderness till his death. The men of this division have been resting, and they moved into battle with resistless force and energy, folding back the Confederate right, obtaining an advantageous position and throwing up intrenchments. It was one o'clock. The soldiers of the Fifth Corps had marched all night, had had no breakfast; nature was exhausted.

General Meade directed Sedgwick, with the Sixth Corps, to come up on the left of the Fifth, and the two corps together to push on towards the court-house, but the afternoon wore away before the Sixth Corps was

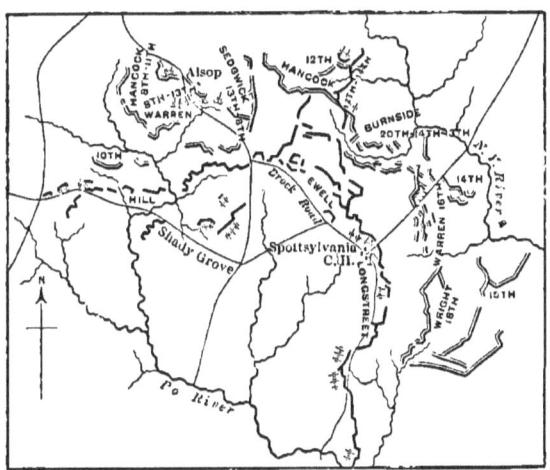

MAP OF SPOTTSYLVANIA.

in position. It was too late to begin a great struggle. Crawford's division advanced, but fell back again, and the troops, with axes and shovels, threw up intrenchments.

Monday morning opened with the cannon of both armies in action. General Grant discovered a movement of the Confederates eastward, as if Lee intended to advance upon Fredericksburg. He changed his headquarters from Piney Grove Church to a position immediately in rear of the Fifth Corps. At daylight a large portion of the cavalry under Sheridan was riding south, with orders to strike the railroads leading to Richmond, tear up the tracks, do all the damage possible, and obtain new supplies from General Butler on the banks of the James. Such a movement would compel Lee to abandon all thoughts of marching upon Fredericksburg. It is not known that Lee intended any such movement. He had only transferred Early, in command of Hill's corps, over to the extreme right of his line, to prevent any attempt Grant

May 9, 1864.

might make to cut him off from Richmond, for Wilcox's division of the Ninth Corps had crossed the Ny River and was intrenching.

At one o'clock in the afternoon Grant sent this despatch to Halleck: "The enemy are now moving either to interpose between us and Fredericksburg, or to get the inside road to Richmond."(*)

I rode through the woods and came to an open field. I could see Confederate wagon-trains headed towards Spottsylvania on the Shady Grove road. Generals Grant and Meade and Hancock were in consultation near me. I do not know whether either of them directed the Union artillery to open fire upon the baggage-wagons; probably the artillery captains could not resist the opportunity to fire upon the train, which created a sudden stampede of the horses and the disappearance of the wagons. Hancock thought it would be well to send Brooks's brigade across the Po to capture the wagons. General Grant directed him to send not only a brigade, but to use three divisions and swing them towards Spottsylvania.

Riding across the open fields beyond Alsop's house, I could see the Confederate columns moving towards the court-house. Shells were screaming across the open space, and there was a brisk fire along the picket line. General Grant had been reconnoitring through the morning. He talked with General Sedgwick, who was directing the placing of the batteries along his line, upon the northern bank of a ravine, when a Confederate sharp-shooter singled him out and aimed a minie-bullet, which passed through his brain, and he fell dead beside a cannon. His body was brought to the rear and laid upon the porch of Mr. Alsop's house. The army had lost a noble commander, who had the love and confidence of his troops, who was ever calm and brave in battle.

Gen. Horatio G. Wright was appointed to succeed him in command of the Sixth Corps.

When General Grant saw that Lee had taken the troops under Early from the extreme left of his line and transferred them to his right, he did not hurry the Second Corps eastward to confront Lee's movement, but directed Hancock to move down to the River Po, leaving Mott's division to hold Todd's Tavern. I followed Hancock's troops as they went across the farm of Mr. Hart. Birney's division was on the extreme right, Gibbon's in the centre, and Barlow's on the left, occupying in part the ground held by Robinson's division of the Fifth Corps on Sunday. It was nearly night, and the sun going down through leaden clouds. The day had been very hot, but a delicious coolness was wafted across the advancing lines by a gentle breeze. Barlow's men were leading, pressing steadily on over un-

SCENE OF SEDGWICK'S DEATH.

dulating pasture-lands, through fringes of forest, into a meadow, across it into a thicket of pines. Shells were exploding above them, solid shot were ploughing furrows in the earth, and the muskets of the skirmishers flashing. General Hancock was seated upon his horse, with his staff around him. The Confederate artillerymen sent a shell towards the group. Two or three of the horses were uneasy as it came spinning past them, but no officer paid any attention to it. Riding forward and mounting a breastwork thrown up by the Fifth Corps, I had a view of what was going on. The Second Corps batteries, to my right—thirty guns—were sending shells over the heads of the advancing troops upon a line of Confederates in an orchard on the south bank of the Po. Barlow's men were close upon the Confederates, and the muskets on both sides were flaming as the sun went down. Gradually the uproar died away as night came on. The engineers of the Second Corps hastened down to the Po, and before morning three bridges had been constructed, the three divisions of the Second Corps had crossed, and were in position to move towards Spottsylvania. It was General Grant's intention to gain the rear of General Lee. Had we been at the court-house during the night, we should have seen General Lee's tent with his flag beside it, pitched beneath the trees in the court-house grounds. The Confederate commander, as has been said, had moved Early from the left of his line round to its extreme right. The biographer of General Lee says that he did so to place his army squarely across the path of General Grant in his movement to Richmond;(*) but Lee's army, and not Richmond, was what General Grant was after, and Hancock's movement threatened Lee's rear and the loss of his trains, which were on another road a short distance south. So it came about that the tired troops of General Early were quickly brought back past the court-house, up the Shady Grove road, to Glady Run. The moment they arrived upon the

GENERAL SEDGWICK.

ground they threw down their guns, and went to work with axes and shovels, building breastworks along the southern bank of the little stream. The main body of the troops did not stop there, but crossed Glady Run, and came into position on the farm of Mr. Chewnig. General Mahone's division was on the right, and Heth's on the left, towards Mr. Waite's shop.(') General Hampton, with a division of cavalry, was holding the roads.

The river Po is a very crooked stream. Where Hancock had laid his bridges it runs east, then it turns south, and south-west. Although the troops of the Second Corps had crossed it, they were only in a great bend of the stream, and must cross it again at Block House Bridge to gain the rear of Lee. The Confederates under Early were placed in position to hold the bridge.

The forenoon witnessed the troops of Hancock on the one side, and Early on the other, preparing for a conflict; but just as General Hancock was ready to begin his attack he received an order from General Meade to withdraw his troops and move eastward; that three Confederate lines in the centre were to be assaulted, and that he was to have charge of the troops in the attack. So we see Gibbon's division followed by Birney's recrossing the Po, and marching eastward, leaving Barlow's division alone on the farm of Mr. Chewnig. The skirmishers of Barlow were hotly engaged at two o'clock, when he received orders to recross the stream. His men did not want to retire: nor could they without a battle, for the Confederates under Early, thinking that a great opportunity was before them of annihilating Barlow's division, pressed eagerly forward. The Union artillery had been withdrawn across the bridges, but the batteries came into position on the north bank of the stream. There were only two Union brigades, Brooks's and Barlow's, against Early's two divisions. General Hancock has given this account of the battle:

May 10, 1864.

"The combat became close and bloody; the enemy in vastly superior numbers, flushed with the anticipation of an easy victory, appeared determined to crush the small force opposing them, and pressing forward with loud yells, forced their way close up to our line, delivering a terrible musketry fire as they advanced. Our brave troops again resisted their onset with undaunted resolution. Their fire along the whole line was so continuous and deadly that the enemy found it impossible to withstand it, but broke again and retreated in the wildest disorder, leaving the ground in our front strewed with their dead and wounded. During the heat of this contest the woods on the right and rear of our troops took fire. The flames had now approached close to our line, rendering it almost impossible to retain the position longer. The last bloody repulse of the enemy had quieted him for a time, and during this lull in the fight General Barlow directed Brooks and Brown to abandon their position and retire across the Po."(*)

Two guns of Arnold's battery had been retained south of the river, and the horses, frightened by the fire and exploding shells, became unmanageable, ran away, dragging a cannon between two trees, where it became so firmly wedged that it could not be removed. The artillerymen were obliged to leave it. It was the first gun ever lost by the Second Corps. Miles's and Smythe's brigades, farther west, were the last to retire. When the Confederates attempted to advance they were met by a destructive fire from the Union artillery."

Nothing had been gained by the movement across the Po, and the withdrawal of the Second Corps is generally regarded as a mistake, for had Hancock's three divisions moved on, it would have undoubtedly compelled General Lee to take a new position; besides, there was not time for Hancock to join Warren and Wright and assault the Confederate centre before night set in.

The uproar of battle was growing louder, and drawing nearer as the troops changed position. The air was thick with smoke from cannon and musket, and the cloud hung low; the western wind drifted the sulphurous fumes across the field, where the negroes had established their hospital tent, and where upon the ground lay hundreds of wounded. I beheld men with bandaged heads and limbs; those who had lost an arm or foot; those with ghastly wounds, from which their life-blood was flowing with every heart-beat. I had been so long with the army that the soldiers recognized me as a correspondent, and were eager for news.

"How is the battle going? Are they driving us? Will the boys hold them?"

Such the questions; natural questions they were, and there was solicitude in them, for if the Confederates were to sweep back their comrades, the hundreds of wounded would become prisoners of war.

"I do not think that the enemy can drive us; our position is a strong one," was my reply. It was a cheery word spoken for their comfort. A soldier who had just lost his left arm, who was weak and faint from the amputation, with his heart all aglow for the old flag, broke into the song which through the war had been sung by the bivouac fire and on the march:

"We are marching to the field, boys; we're going to the fight,
　Shouting the battle-cry of Freedom.
And we bear the glorious Stars for the Union and the Right,
　Shouting the battle-cry of Freedom."

It was like the quaffing of wine to weak and fainting men who heard it, and all around I saw them lift themselves—some to stand erect, others half reclining, swinging their caps as they joined in the chorus:

"The Union forever, hurrah, boys, hurrah!
　Down with the traitor, up with the Stars,
While we rally round the flag, boys, rally once again,
　Shouting the battle-cry of Freedom."(⁹)

Let us now see what was being done in the centre during the afternoon. It was six o'clock before Cutler's and Crawford's divisions of the Fifth, and Webb's and Carroll's brigades of the Second Corps, under Gibbon, were in position. They were in a thicket of young pines and cedars. So close and compact the trees that the troops could make their way only by crouching. They passed through the thicket, came into an open field to be cut to pieces by a terrific fire, but on across the field up to the Confederate breastworks they rushed, to find themselves amid the interlaced branches of fallen trees. Some of Carroll's men reached the breastworks, but only to yield their lives.(¹⁰)

The troops were swept back in disorder. General Hancock arrived and attacked again, with Birney's and Gibbon's divisions, and a portion of the troops of the Fifth Corps, just as the sun was sinking in the west; but the remorseless fire of the Confederates again swept them back.

As we go north from this position we come to the Sixth Corps, behind its intrenchments west of the house of Mr. McCool. General Wright has been out to the skirmish line and looked at the Confederate position held by Rodes's and Johnson's divisions. Dole's brigade was behind intrenchments in the open ground two hundred yards from a thicket of pines. The Confederate soldiers had made an abatis in front of their breastwork, and, seemingly fearful that they might not be able to hold the position, had constructed a second line in rear of the first. General Wright believed that the front line could be captured, and selected Upton's and Russell's brigades and four regiments of Neill's to make the attack. An assault was to be made farther up the line, north, by Mott's division. It was to be at the point where the Confederate breastworks turned a right angle eastward, on the farm of Mr. Landron. Upton formed his men in four lines. Quietly they picked their way in the cedar thicket. Through the afternoon the Union cannon had been raining shells upon the Confederate works. The Union artillerymen see a signal, and instead of ramming home the cartridges, stand beside their pieces. They hear a hurrah—the voices of the men who upon the instant break from the thicket into the open ground, and rush across the field towards the house of Mr. McCool. The Confederate breastworks are fringed with fire, but in an instant the Union men are upon them; there is a hand-to-hand struggle. Five minutes—in this brief space more than one thousand Union men have fallen; but the line of works has been carried, and more than one thousand prisoners, with several stands of colors, have been captured.([11]) The Confederates brought up reinforcements and assaulted in turn, but were repulsed, and the sun went down with the Union troops holding the intrenchments. Mott's attack up at the angle had resulted in failure. His troops had been repulsed, and Upton and Russell were left in such an exposed position that when night came on, after the removal of the wounded, the troops who had won the breastworks by such a heroic charge were ordered back. Reluctantly they obeyed the command.

Among the wounded was Gen. James C. Rice, who, when the war began, enlisted as a private in the Garibaldi Regiment of New York. He had lived for nine years as a school-teacher in Natchez, Mississippi. He had seen what slavery was. He was deeply religious, and enlisted to fight for his country from a deep consciousness of duty and obligation. It does not take long for such a man as he was to find his true place. He was selected to be lieutenant-colonel of the Forty-fourth New York, and so distinguished himself in the battle of Gettysburg that President Lincoln commissioned him a brigadier-general. In the rush upon the intrenchments he received a mortal wound. I was in the woods behind the assaulting troops when those appointed to care for the wounded came back with him upon a stretcher. He was in great pain, and wished to be turned over.

"How will you lie?" asked the surgeon. "Let me lie with my face to the enemy."([12]) They were his last words. A few moments and the heaving heart was still forever.

It was nearly eleven o'clock in the evening when I dismounted from my horse at the headquarters of General Grant. He was sitting on a camp-chair smoking a cigar. The only person present was Hon. E. B. Washburne, member of Congress, his most intimate friend from Galena, his old home in Illinois, who had been instrumental in bringing about General Grant's appointment as lieutenant-general. There were times when the commander-in-chief was reticent upon all subjects. He has been called, like William of the Netherlands, the Silent Commander; but there were times also when General Grant gave free expression to his thoughts. I asked for information in regard to the events of the day, that I might communicate it to readers far away, which was kindly given; and then, not in response to any question, he said: "We have had hard fighting to-day, and I am sorry to say we have not accomplished much. We have lost a good many men, and I suppose that I shall be blamed for it." He was silent a moment, and then added: "I do not know any way to put down this rebellion and restore the authority of the Government except by fighting, and fighting means that men must be killed. If the people of this country expect that the war can be conducted to a successful issue in any other way than by fighting, they must get somebody other than myself to command the army."

Again he was silent; but after a brief pause, resumed the conversation, and unfolded the great plan of the campaign which had been inaugurated in the West under General Sherman. "We are having a hard time here, because my orders have not been complied with in the West. When I became commander of all the troops, General Banks was on his way up the Red River. I sent directions for his return. Whether or not the orders ever reached him I do not know.(¹³) I intended that he should hasten with his force to New Orleans, join General Canby in command there, and that the united force should hasten to Mobile, capture that place, and move northward, which would compel the Confederates under General Johnston to give way before Sherman, who is having almost as hard a time as I have here." At this moment there was the tramping of hoofs, and General Meade rode up in the darkness and dismounted, and the correspondent comprehending that they would wish to be alone departed to his quarters.(¹⁴)

The following morning saw Hon. E. B. Washburne and myself sitting on our horses in front of General Grant's headquarters. We were about to start for Washington *via* Fredericksburg and Acquia Creek on horseback, and thence by special steamer.

May 11, 1864.

"Have you any word to send to the President or the Secretary of War?" asked Mr. Washburne. "I will send a brief note," was the reply. A few moments later General Grant appeared with a letter addressed to General Halleck, which Mr. Washburne placed in his pocket. We did not know that a single sentence in that note would electrify the world. This the sentence: "I am now sending back to Belle Plain all my wagons for a fresh supply of provisions, and *I propose to fight it out on this line, if it takes all summer.*"(¹⁵)

"I PROPOSE TO FIGHT IT OUT ON THIS LINE, IF IT TAKES ALL SUMMER."

There was no fighting through the day except in front of General Mott's division, who drove back the Confederate picket line that the engineers might get a little nearer to the Confederate works, and that they might peer through their field-glasses from behind trees, to find out how the breastworks were constructed. They reported to General Grant that the angle, shaped somewhat like the letter V, between the house of Mr. Landron and Mr. McCool, was a point which, in their opinion, might be successfully attacked. General Grant thereupon determined to attack along the entire line, while the Second Corps, under Hancock, supported by the Sixth, was to carry the works at the angle. If an attack were to be made everywhere at the same moment, General Lee would not be able to withdraw troops from any part of the line to assist those defending that portion of the line.

It was three o'clock in the afternoon when General Grant wrote an order to Hancock to move his corps in rear of the Fifth and Sixth, and come into position between the Sixth and Ninth. The march was not to be made till after dark. He wrote an order to Burnside to be ready at four o'clock the next morning with his entire force, and to attack with all possible vigor. He was to make his preparations with the utmost secrecy. Two members of Grant's staff were sent to impress upon Burnside the importance of a most energetic assault.(¹⁰) The Fifth and Sixth corps were to be under arms and in line to improve any advantage that might be gained.

The night was dark and cloudy, rain was falling, but the men of the Second Corps were making their way along a narrow path through the woods. The heavy rain turned the earth to a mortar-bed. For a week the soldiers had been on the march or in battle. Through all the days there has not been an hour when one could not hear either the boom of cannon, the volleys of musketry, or the rattling fire of the pickets. The soldiers were weary, but on through the deep mire, their clothes drenched with the falling rain, they marched without a murmur. At midnight they came into position in the woods between the houses of Brown and Landron, throwing themselves on the ground just in rear of the picket line. No word was spoken. There had been no rattling of canteens, no clanking of swords. In silence, like spectres, they had marched through the mire and gloom of the night, and now they were waiting for the dawn.

With their compasses the engineers during the day had taken from Landron's the position of the breastworks, and now they set them, examining them by striking a match to get the right direction.

Birney's division was on the right. The men must cross a marsh, creep through a dense thicket of young pines, growing where the plough once turned its furrows, where slaves had once hoed tobacco—land worn-out for cultivation and turned to wood.

May 12, 1864.

Barlow's division was on the left, with a clear field before him. Gibbon's division and Mott's were in reserve.

THE FIELD OF THE BLOODY ANGLE.

The Confederate breastworks are dimly seen along the edge of the woods at the right. They were held by Gen. Edward Johnson's division. The Second Corps of the Union army, under Hancock, charged from the woods at the left. The Sixth Corps came to the assistance of the Second across the foreground. Upton's troops were to the right, upon ground not included in the view.

The division commanders have timed their watches. Day is breaking. The fog hangs low. It is a half-mile to the Confederate intrenchments.

Barlow has four brigades—Brooks's, with the Second Delaware, Sixty-fourth and Sixty-sixth New York, Fifty-third, One Hundred and Forty-fifth, One Hundred and Forty-eighth Pennsylvania; Miles's—the Twenty-sixth Michigan, Sixty-first New York, Eighty-first, One Hundred and Fortieth, One Hundred and Eighty-third Pennsylvania: these in the front line, with Smythe's and Brown's brigades in the second line.

On through the low shrubbery, out into the open fields they move, keeping even step till, in the gray of the morning, they see the dim outline of the works, and then with a cheer they rush on in solid mass. A single volley flames in their faces as they run up the slope. The next moment they are over the works, charging with the bayonet.

Between three and four thousand confederates surrender themselves; nearly the whole of General Johnson's division—twenty cannon, caissons, and horses, several thousand muskets, and thirty colors—are taken.

With the killed and wounded, Lee has lost in a moment nearly five thousand troops. Those not captured flee through the woods towards the second line of intrenchments, nearer the court-house. Hancock's men rush after them. Barlow's advance is at the east angle, held by Stuart's and York's Confederate brigades.

Owen's and Carroll's brigades of Gibbon's division are close behind Barlow, and at the decisive moment come pouring over the intrenchments, capturing two of Stuart's cannon, wheeling them round and sending shells into the fleeing Confederates. Birney's division, followed by Mott's, carry the west angle held by Terry's, Walker's, and Battle's brigades.

It was not wholly a surprise to the Confederates. Their pickets had been sending in word that the Union troops were moving on Brown's and Landron's farms. General Lee thought that Grant was endeavoring to turn his flank, and withdrew a portion of the artillery along the intrenchments to move the batteries to the court-house; but at daylight it was on its way back. Johnson had sent word to Lee that he was to be attacked. His own troops were ready, and Gordon's division was also ready to support him. Gordon had placed Evans's brigade by the McCool house, and Pegram's and R. D. Johnston's to support Rodes's division.

The success of the charge threw Birney and Barlow into confusion. The men were in a mass, the regiments disorganized. In their enthusiasm they rushed after the retreating Confederates. A Confederate officer gives this account of the state of affairs behind the breastworks:

"After the artillery had been withdrawn on the night of the 11th, General Johnson discovered that the enemy was concentrating on his front, and convinced that he would be attacked, requested the return of the artillery that had been taken away. The men in the trenches were kept on the alert all night and were ready for the attack, when at dawn on the morning of the 12th a dense column emerged from the pines half a mile in front of the salient, and rushed to the attack. They came on, to use General Johnson's words, in great disorder, with a narrow front, but extending back as far as I could see. Page's battalion of artillery, which had been ordered back at four o'clock, were just arriving, and were not in position to fire upon the attacking column; the guns came just in time to be captured. The infantry fought as long as fighting was of any use, but they could do little to check the onward rush of the Federal column, which soon overran the salient, capturing General Johnson himself, twenty pieces of artillery, and twenty-eight hundred men—almost his entire division. . . . Lane's brigade of Hill's corps, which was immediately on the right of the captured works, rapidly drew back to the unfinished line in rear, and poured a galling fire upon their left wing, which checked its advance, and threw it back with severe loss. General Gordon, whose division was in reserve, and under orders to support any part of the line about the salient, hastened to throw it in front of the advancing Federal column. As the division was about to charge, General Lee rode up and joined General Gordon, evidently intending to go forward with him. Gordon remonstrated, and the men, seeing his intention, cried out, 'General Lee to the rear!' which was taken up all along the line. One of the men respectfully but firmly took hold of the bridle and led his horse to the rear, and the charge went on. The two moving lines met in the rear of the captured works, and after a fierce struggle in the woods, the Federals were forced back to the base of the salient. On the left, where Rodes's division had connected with Johnson's, the attack was pressed with great determination. General Rodes drew out Ramseur's brigade from the left of his front line, a portion of Kershaw's division taking its place, and sent it to relieve the pressure on his right and restore the line between himself and Gordon. Ramseur did not fill the gap, and his right was exposed to a terrible fire from the works held by the enemy. Three brigades from Hill's corps were ordered up. Perrin's, which was the first to arrive, rushed forward through a fearful fire, and recovered a part of the line on Gordon's left. General Perrin fell dead from his horse just as he reached the works. General Daniel had been killed, and Ramseur, though painfully wounded, remained in the trenches with his men. Rodes's right being hard pressed, Harris's Mississippi and McGowan's South Carolina brigades were ordered forward, and rushed through the blinding storm into the works on Ramseur's right." (")

"Go to Hancock's assistance," was the order from Meade to Wright, commanding the Sixth Corps.

Russell's and Wheaton's divisions, accompanied by Wright, came in upon Hancock's right near the McCool house.

Wright was wounded at the outset, but did not leave the field. And now began one of the most stubborn contests recorded in history. The Confederates were on one side of the intrenchments, the Union troops on the other. It was six o'clock when A. P. Hill's troops come pouring through the woods to Gordon's assistance, capturing a few Union soldiers.

General Hancock plants his artillery on a knoll on Brown's farm, sending shells over the heads of the men in blue. Upton's brigade, composed of the Fifth Maine, One Hundred and Twenty-first New York, Ninety-fifth and Ninety-sixth Pennsylvania, crossed the north-western angle of the salient, to support the troops of the Second Corps, which were falling back towards the breastworks before the advance of Hill's troops. Colonel Upton determined to hold the angle at all hazards. Equally determined were the Confederates to regain it. The smoke was dense, the clouds hanging low, and rain falling. Through the woods came the Confederates, firing their guns and charging up to the breastworks, and the fierce hand-to-hand struggle begun.

In rear of Upton's men is Metcalf's Battery C, Fifth United States Artillery. General Wright is watching the struggle, and rides to Metcalf, points towards the angle, and the artillerymen hear this order:([18]) "Limber the guns! Drivers, mount! Cannoneers, mount! Caissons to the rear!" The drivers lash their horses, and they leap forward towards the thickening cloud and into the pitiless tempest of leaden rain. The staff-officer leading them tumbles from his horse. The guns wheel into position, and send round after round of canister into the Confederate ranks with terrible effect. How rapidly the battery-men went down is thus told by one of them:

"Our section went into action with twenty-three men and one officer— Lieutenant Metcalf. The only ones who came out sound were the lieutenant and myself; every horse was killed outright, seven of the men killed, sixteen wounded. The gun-carriages were so cut with bullets as to be of no further service. . . . Twenty-seven balls passed through the lid of the limber-chest while Number Six was getting out ammunition, and he was wounded in the face and neck by the fragments of wood and lead. The sponge-bucket on my gun had thirty-nine holes in it, being perforated like a sieve."([19])

Capt. John D. Fish, of Colonel Upton's staff, rode through the storm, carrying the cartridges from the caissons to the guns. "Give it to them, boys! I'll bring you the canister!" he shouted; but the next moment reeled from his saddle mortally wounded. The guns were up to the breastworks, their muzzles almost projecting over the logs. Immediately in rear were the dead and dying horses and men. Within three feet of one another, separated only by the breastworks, were Union and Confederate, crouching in the mud, loading, raising their guns, and firing at random; their tattered, bullet-riddled colors hanging limp against their staves in the falling rain. Pack-mules with boxes of ammunition, three thousand rounds in each box, were brought as near as possible to the troops, dropped upon the ground, and the soldiers crept out on their hands and knees and brought them in. A Union soldier thus pictures the struggle:

"Sometimes the enemy's fire would slacken, and the moments would become so monotonous that something had to be done to stir them up. Then some resolute fellow would seize a fence-rail or piece of abatis, and throw it over among the enemy, and then drop upon the ground to avoid the volley that was sure to follow. A daring lieutenant in one of our left companies leaped upon the breastworks, took a rifle that was handed him, and discharged it. In like manner he discharged a second, and was in the act of firing a third shot when his cap flew in the air, and his body pitched headlong among the enemy. On several occasions squads of disheartened Confederates raised pieces of shelter-tents above the works as a flag of truce; upon our slacking fire and calling them to come in, they would immediately jump upon the breastworks and surrender. One party of twenty or thirty thus signified their willingness to submit, but owing to the fact that their comrades occasionally took advantage to get a volley into us, it was some time before we concluded to give them a chance. With levelled pieces we called upon them to come in. Springing upon the breastworks in a body, they stood for an instant panic-stricken at the terrible array before them; that momentary delay was a signal for their destruction. While, with our fingers pressing the trigger, we shouted to them to jump, their troops massed in the rear poured a volley into them, killing or wounding all but a few, who dropped with the rest and crawled in under our pieces, while we instantly began firing. . . . So heavy was our fire that the head-logs of the breastworks were cut and torn until they resembled hickory brooms. Several large oak-trees, which grew just in rear of the works, were completely gnawed off by our converging fire."([20]) One tree, twenty-two inches in diameter, was gradually eaten off, and fell with a crash upon the Confederates.

It was half-past nine when the troops of the Fifth Corps advanced, but were received by so destructive a fire that they were withdrawn by General Humphreys, chief of staff to General Meade. The Ninth Corps was ordered forward, and General Potter's division rushed upon the intrenchments held by Lane's Confederate division of Hill's corps, and captured two cannon; but Scales's and Thomas's brigades came to Lane's assistance, and Potter was obliged to retire without being able to carry off the guns.

At nine o'clock there was another struggle. Wilcox's division of the Ninth Corps held the left of the Union line south of the Fredericksburg road. Heth's (Confederate) division was behind the intrenchments. General Wilcox's men crept up through a pine thicket, but when they came into the open ground were met by a heavy fire. The Confederates moved

SPOTTSYLVANIA.

to strike his flank, and the *mêlée* began. The struggle was fierce and desperate. The uproar all along the lines in both armies aroused in Union and Confederate alike a resolute determination to carry on the struggle to the bitter end.

A hundred cannon were thundering; there were continuous rolls of musketry from McCool's, north-west of the court-house, all the way round to Wilcox's division, south-east of it. The woods were smoking like a furnace.

This the account of a brigade commander in the Second Corps:

"It was not only a desperate struggle, but it was literally a hand-to-hand fight. Nothing but the piled-up logs, or breastworks, separated the combatants. Our men would reach over the logs and fire into the faces of the enemy; would stab over with their bayonets; many were shot and stabbed through the crevices and holes between the logs; men mounted the works, and with muskets rapidly handed them, kept up a continuous fire until they were shot down, when others would take their places and continue the deadly work. . . . Several times during the day the Rebels would show a white flag about the works, and when our fire slackened, jump over and surrender, and others were crowded down to fill their places. . . . It was there that the somewhat celebrated tree was cut off by bullets; there that the brush and logs were cut to pieces and whipped into basket-stuff; . . . there that the Rebel ditches and cross-sections were filled with dead men several deep. . . . I was at the angle the next day. The sight was terrible and sickening, much worse than at Bloody Lane (Antietam). There a great many dead men were lying in the road and across the rails of the torn-down fences, and out in the cornfield; but they were not piled up several deep, and their flesh was not so torn and mangled as at the angle."([21])

Why such a struggle for a position which had no special military value? It was not for position, but a pounding to see which would stand it the longer. General Grant had attacked because he believed in crushing the Confederate army. Through the day the terrible contest went on. At midnight it ceased in front of Burnside, but up by McCool's the muskets rattled till past midnight, when Lee withdrew his troops to his second line of intrenchments, leaving the first line in the possession of the Sixth and Second corps. General Grant had lost seven thousand in killed, wounded, and prisoners. It will never be known how many Lee lost; but, with the prisoners, not less than ten thousand.

The Confederate generals Daniel and Perrin were killed; Walker, Ramseur, R. D. Johnston, and McGowan wounded; Major-gen. Edward

Johnson and Brigadier Stuart taken prisoners. Three Union generals were wounded—Wright, Webb, and Carroll.

After such a struggle there must of necessity be a lulling of the storm; but General Grant was everywhere along the lines, unmindful of the rain which fell through the day. He was laying new plans, and during the night moved the Fifth and Sixth corps past the Ninth, directing them to come into position south-east of Spottsylvania. The first battles were fought three miles north-west of the court-house, but this movement carried them half-way round a circle. So deep was the mire that the soldiers were obliged to cut trees and corduroy the roads. It was daylight before they came into position.

May 13, 1864.

General Upton's division charged upon the Confederates, who were intrenched upon a knoll, driving them, but was driven in turn. General Ayres's brigade of the Fifth Corps came to Upton's assistance, and the Confederates were compelled to abandon their position.

May 14, 1864.

General Lee, seeing that their movement threatened his right flank, abandoned the intrenchments in front of the Second Corps, moved the troops which had held them down past the court-house, whereupon Grant directed Hancock to leave his intrenchments by Landron's and McCool's, and to march in rear of the other corps, to be ready for action whenever the moment was opportune.

Like chess-players the two great commanders carried on the terrible game of war. Rain was falling the while, the mire becoming deeper, rendering the roads impassable, compelling General Grant to give up the plans which he had contemplated.

The army needed rest. Reinforcements came—the heavy artillery, eight thousand, which had been guarding the forts around Washington. They were no longer needed there.

General Lee no doubt desired to strike a blow in turn which would be as effective as that which Grant had given on Landron's farm. From his scouts he learned the position of the several corps of the Union army, and decided to send General Ewell from his extreme left, from the ground where the first battle was fought, past the house of Mr. Alsop, to gain the rear of General Grant's right flank.

May 19, 1864.

A farmer who knew every foot went through the woods as his guide. It was five o'clock in the afternoon when the head of Ewell's column appeared west of the road leading to Fredericksburg, and west of Mr. Harris's house, near which were General Grant's headquarters. Colonel Kitching's brigade and General Tyler's division of heavy artillery were near the road.

THE HOUSE OF MR. McCOOL.

Colonel Kitching's pickets discovered Ewell's advance, and came running up with the news.

I was at General Grant's headquarters.

"Pack up those wagons; harness the horses; quick!" It was the order of the provost marshal General Patrick. Ten minutes and the trains were packed ready to move.(²⁹)

There came a ripple of musketry from the woods, and then volley upon volley. It was the first engagement for the soldiers of the heavy artillery, and though they had been practising with heavy cannon they were at home with the musket, and sent their volleys upon Ewell's advancing line.

The Fifth Corps was nearer than either of the others, and the Maryland brigade came up on the run, followed by Birney's division of the Second Corps.

If Ewell had any thought of creating a stampede, he did not have an opportunity to carry out his plan. He was held at bay by Kitching and Tyler, and when Birney arrived was driven step by step. The sun went down, with flashes of light gleaming in the thickets. At nine o'clock Ewell gave up the struggle, having lost nearly one thousand men. He had found out where a portion of Grant's troops were, but had accomplished nothing more.

Nearly three weeks had gone by, with continuous stubborn fighting; scarcely an hour of silence the while, but a ceaseless cannonade or musketry, either the firing of pickets or roll of volleys by brigades and divisions. Never before had there been such a struggle in this Western World.

More than twenty-eight thousand men had been killed or wounded in the Union army, and nearly five thousand had been taken prisoners or were missing, making a loss of thirty-three thousand. Many were only slightly wounded, and in a few weeks were out of the hospital and once more with their regiments. There are no returns of Confederate losses, but it is supposed that the killed, wounded, and missing from General Lee's army were from twenty to twenty-five thousand.

Leaving now the infantry of the Army of the Potomac, let us see what the cavalry under General Sheridan was doing. We have seen (p. 99) that

May 8, 1864. General Meade, at Todd's Tavern, issued orders to the cavalry, interfering with orders issued by General Sheridan, who remonstrated. There was a wide difference of opinion in regard to the cavalry between the two commanders, and on Sunday forenoon, while the fight was going on at Alsop's farm, high words passed between them. General Meade said that the cavalry, by occupying the Brook road, prevented the troops from marching, to which General Sheridan replied that if that was the case, General Meade himself had ordered the troops to occupy the road, without notifying him; and he further said that General Meade had broken up his plans, and had needlessly exposed General Wilson's division, while Gregg's was kept idle. The two commanders were greatly irritated. Said Sheridan: "I can whip Stuart, if you will let me; but since you insist on giving the cavalry directions without consulting or even notifying me, hereafter you may command the cavalry yourself; I will not issue another order." Saying this, he left General Meade's tent. We do not know just what General Meade thought of this man from the West, who, at Stone River, under Rosecrans, when the exultant Confederates were sweeping all before them, stood with his division like a rock upon the shore of the sea, hurling back the billows, and who swept like a whirlwind up the slope of Missionary Ridge. Whatever were General Meade's thoughts and feelings, he could not keep them to himself, but went at once to General Grant and repeated the conversation.

"Did he say that he could whip Stuart?"

"Yes."

"Very well. Then let him go and do it." ([23])

It was not an order in peremptory language to General Meade; but nevertheless it was an order which must be obeyed, and so we see General Meade's chief of staff, General Humphreys, at one o'clock on that Sunday afternoon, issuing an order to Sheridan "to proceed against the enemy's cavalry, and when his supplies are exhausted, proceed *via* New Market and Green Bay to Haxall's Landing, on the James River, there communicating with General Butler, procure supplies, and returning to this army." ([24])

While the sun is going down on that Sunday afternoon we see Sheridan giving his instructions to his three division commanders, Gregg, Merritt, and Wilson.

"We are going to fight Stuart's cavalry in consequence of a suggestion from me. We will give him a fair square fight. We are strong, and I know we can beat him. I shall expect nothing but success." ([25])

With alacrity the three commanders prepared for the movement.

Early in the morning the cavalry was in motion, moving as if to go to Fredericksburg; going east nearly to Hamilton's Crossing, where General Meade's division fought Stonewall Jackson in the battle of Fredericksburg, then turning south, the entire column being thirteen miles in length and moving towards the North Anna River.

May 9, 1864.

The scouts of the Confederates, looking towards the east, saw a long cloud of dust rising above the tree-tops, and sent word to General Stuart, who directed Fitz-Hugh Lee to attack Sheridan's rear, while Stuart himself, with his other divisions, moved also towards the North Anna, to get between Sheridan and Richmond. General Stuart was a very able commander, but he made a mistake at the outset. He knew that Sheridan had a force larger than his own. By dividing his command he greatly weakened it. General Sheridan detailed Davies's brigade to guard his rear. Fitz-Hugh Lee came up with Davies just after the last of the column crossed the Po River, but it was very easy for to resist the attack, and then move on. Just as the sun was going down, Merritt's division reached the North Anna, and crossed it. The three divisions watered their horses in the stream. There had been no hard riding, but an easy gait, which did not break down the horses. Custer's brigade pressed on to Beaver Dam Station, on the Central Railroad, came upon a body of Confederates and scattered them, recaptured four hundred Union prisoners who had been taken in the Wilderness, destroyed two locomotives, three trains of cars and ninety wagons, and more than two hundred thousand pounds of bacon, and nearly all the medical stores of General Lee's army. The soldiers rode along the railroad, and in a short time tore up six miles of the track.

General Stuart was concentrating his troops at Beaver Dam Station, but Sheridan, instead of stopping to fight him there, was moving south along the Negro-foot road towards Richmond; and the Confederate commander, seeing what a mistake he had made, endeavored once more to get between Sheridan and the Confederate capital by urging his troops on at a speed which soon broke down many of the horses; but by hard riding Stuart, on Wednesday morning, reached a famous old hotel known as Yellow Tavern, seven miles north of Richmond, in advance of Sheridan.

May 10, 1864.

There in the woods and fields, early in the morning, Stuart posted his brigades for a battle. The Union troops were at Ashland, where a train of cars were captured and a locomotive destroyed. In the march to Yellow Tavern General Merritt's division was in advance, Wilson's came next, followed by Gregg's. They were upon the Brook road—the same on which the battles of the Wilderness and Spottsylvania had been fought, and now again the cavalry was upon it, for a battle near the Confederate capital. General Merritt was quick to attack, and he soon drove the Confederates eastward of the turnpike.

May 11, 1864.

General Sheridan gives this brief account of what followed: "I quickly brought up Wilson's and one of Gregg's brigades, to take advantage of the situation by forming a line of battle on that side of the road. Meanwhile the enemy, desperate but still confident, poured in a heavy fire from his line, and from a battery which enfiladed the Brock road, and made Yellow Tavern an uncomfortably hot place. Gibbs's and Devin's brigades, however, held fast there, while Custer, supported by Chap-

SPOTTSYLVANIA. 127

GEN. WESLEY MERRITT.

man's brigade, attacked the enemy's left and battery in a mounted charge. Beginning at a walk, the troops increased their gait to a trot, and then at full speed rushed towards the enemy. At the same moment the dismounted troops along my whole front moved forward, and as Custer went through the battery, capturing two of the guns, with their cannoneers, and breaking up the enemy's left, Gibbs and Devin broke his centre and right from the field. Gregg meanwhile charged the force in his rear—Gordon's brigade—and the engagement ended by giving us complete control of the road to Richmond. We captured a number of prisoners, and the casualties on both sides were quite severe, General Stuart himself falling mortally wounded, and Gen. James B. Gordon, one of his brigade commanders, being killed."([26])

General Sheridan was inside the outer intrenchments around Richmond, but all the clerks in the Departments, and all the troops that could be gathered up, had been hurried out to hold the inner line of defence, and General Sheridan made no attempt to enter the city. The Confederates planted torpedoes along the road which they supposed he would take, and laid along the ground wires which, when tripped by the horses' feet, exploded the torpedoes; but General Sheridan compelled the prisoners he had taken to go in advance and remove the wires, so no one was injured. The Confederates had destroyed the bridges across the Chickahominy, and thought that they had him in a trap, but he rebuilt one under a good deal of difficulty. Once more he accepted battle, the Confederate cavalry being reinforced by the infantry from Richmond, but repulsed all attacks, crossed the Chickahominy, and went on to General Butler, reaching James River on the 14th, recruiting his horses, leaving his wounded, and returning to the Army of the Potomac on the 24th.

May 24, 1864.

There was commotion in Richmond during these days—the ringing of church bells calling the able-bodied men and boys to the Capitol Square, to be armed and hurried to the trenches for the defence of the city. A clerk in the Confederate War Department recorded the scenes in his diary, May 11th :

"At midnight the Departmental Battalion was marched from the south-side of the river back to the city, but at 9 A.M. they were marched hurriedly to Meadow Bridge. They came past our house. Custis and his brother Thomas ran in, remaining but a moment. Custis exclaimed : 'Let me have some money, mother, or we will starve. The Government don't feed us, and we are almost famished. . . . The Secretary issued this morning a new edition of his hand-bills calling the people to arms. Mr. Mallory's usual red face turned purple. He has not yet got out the iron-clad, *Richmond*, which might have sunk Butler's transports. . . . The Governor has issued a notification that the enemy will be here to-day. All classes not in the army were gathered up and marched to the defences. Mr. Memminger (Secretary of Treasury) is said to have been frightened terribly, and arrangements were made for flight. . . . **May 12.** The

SHERIDAN AND STUART'S FIGHT.

report of General Lee's victory was premature, and Butler has not gone, nor the raiders vanished. On the contrary, the latter were engaged in battle with Stuart's division late in the afternoon, and recommenced it this morning at three o'clock, the enemy remaining on the ground, and still remain some five miles from where I write. Major-gen. J. E. B. Stuart was wounded last evening through the kidney, and now lies in the city in a dying condition. The battle raged furiously; every gun distinctly heard at our house until 1 P.M., the enemy being intrenched between our middle and onter line of works. Meantime our ambulances are arriving every hour with the wounded, coming in by the Brook turnpike. . . . It is said that preparations have been made for the flight of the President and Cabinet up the Danville road in the event of the fall of the city. The enemy disappeared in the night. We suffered most in the several engagements near the city. But the joy of many and the chagrin of some at his escape so easily was soon followed by the startling intelligence that a raid from General Butler's army had cut the Danville road. (A force of cavalry sent out under General Kautz.) All communication with the country, from which provisions are derived, is now completely at an end! Colonel Northrop told me to-day that unless the railroads were retaken and repaired he could not feed the troops ten days longer."([27])

Those were sad days in Richmond which witnessed the death and burial of General Stuart. He had shown great ability as a cavalry commander, and was greatly beloved. This the closing scene of his life, as recorded by the editor of one of the newspapers.

May 13, 1864.

" His worldly matters closed, the eternal interests of his soul engaged his mind. Turning to the Rev. Mr. Peterkin, of the Episcopal Church, and of which he was an exemplary member, he asked him to sing the hymn,

"'Rock of ages cleft for me,
Let me hide myself in thee,'

he joining in with all the voice his strength would permit. He then joined in prayer with the minister. To the doctor he said: 'I am going fast now. I am resigned. God's will be done.' Thus died General Stuart."([28])

General Lee was deeply affected when he learned of his death. " When the news reached him," writes General Lee's biographer, "he retired from those around him and remained for some time communing with his own heart and memory. He said, 'I can scarcely think of him without weeping.'"([29])

So the terrible harvest of death went on, cutting down brave and noble men alike in the Union and Confederate armies. Let it ever be kept in mind that the sacrifice came from the attempt of a few men to establish a government based on slavery.

NOTES TO CHAPTER V.

([1]) Gen. U. S. Grant, "Personal Memoirs," vol. ii., p. 210.
([2]) Adam Badeau, "Military History of General Grant," vol. ii., p. 133.
([3]) Gen. J. A. Early, "Memoirs of Last Year of the War," p. 33.
([4]) Confederate Soldier to Author.
([5]) General Grant's Despatch.
([6]) Gen. A. L. Long, "Memoirs of Robert E. Lee," p. 336.
([7]) Gen. J. A. Early, "Memoirs of Last Year of the War," p. 23
([8]) General Hancock's Report.
([9]) Author's Note-book, May, 1864.
([10]) General Longstreet's Official Diary, quoted by Gen. F. A. Walker, "History of the Second Army Corps," p. 458.
([11]) Gen. Emory Upton's Report.
([12]) Author's Note-book, May, 1864
([13]) Gen. U. S. Grant, "Personal Memoirs," vol. ii., p. 559.
([14]) Author's Note-book, May, 1864.
([15]) Gen. U. S. Grant to Halleck, May 11, 1864.
([16]) Gen. U. S. Grant, "Personal Memoirs," vol. ii., p. 229.
([17]) Gen. C. M. Law, *Century Magazine*, June, 1887, p. 289.
([18]) G. N. Galloway, *Century Magazine*, June, 1887, p. 305.
([19]) Idem.
([20]) Idem, p 306.
([21]) General Lewis, Grant's Report.
([22]) Author's Note-book, May, 1864.
([23]) Gen. Philip H. Sheridan, "Personal Memoirs," vol. i., p. 205.
([24]) Idem.
([25]) Idem.
([26]) J. B. Jones, "Rebel War Clerk's Diary," vol. ii., p. 205.
([27]) Idem.
([28]) *Richmond Examiner*, May 14, 1864.
([29]) Gen. A. L. Long, "Memoirs of Robert E. Lee," p. 343.

CHAPTER VI.

BERMUDA HUNDRED AND DREWRY'S BLUFF.

BEFORE the Army of the Potomac began its movement from Culpeper to the Wilderness, General Grant went to Fortress Monroe, to give General Butler instructions in regard to the part he was to perform in the great drama. General Butler was in command of the Tenth and Eighteenth Army Corps, commanded respectively by Gen. Quincy A. Gillmore, who had been ordered to that point from Morris Island (see "Marching to Victory," chap. xvi.), and William F. Smith, who had been ordered east from Chattanooga (see "Marching to Victory," chap. xxi.). General Butler was to go up the James with a fleet of gunboats, land at City Point, cut the railroads leading south from Richmond, and do all the damage possible. While General Grant, with the Army of the Potomac, was to thunder at the front door, General Butler, with the Army of the James, was to take possession of the back door of the Confederate capital. The troops were at Yorktown and Gloucester, as if about to go up York River. Their presence at that point mystified the Confederate Government as to what Butler intended to do.

April, 1864.

Let us think of ourselves as being in Richmond the last week in April. We see General Bragg, who has been recalled from the West in consequence of his disastrous defeat at Chattanooga, but who had been appointed chief of staff and military adviser to Jefferson Davis, issuing orders for the President of the Confederacy. General Beauregard was in command of all the troops between Richmond and South Carolina, with his headquarters at Weldon, in North Carolina. General Pickett was in command, under Beauregard, of the troops manning the fortifications at Drewry's Bluff, on the banks of the James, and at Petersburg. Ever since 1862 the Union troops have held Newberne, North Carolina, where, in the last week of April, there were about six thousand, so widely scattered that Jefferson Davis believed that they could be easily captured, and had personally planned an expedition for that purpose. General Beauregard believed that a movement was to be made by the troops of Butler up the James, but in obedience to Jefferson Davis's orders, gave instruction to General Hoke to move against Newberne. The movement, however, was suddenly abandoned when a despatch was received in Richmond that General Grant's army was crossing the Rapidan at Germania Ford.

The telegraph operators were busy in Richmond. Messages were coming from the North and from the South. Jefferson Davis sent this to Beauregard: "Unless Newberne can be captured by *coup de main* the attempt must be abandoned, and the troops returned with all possible despatch to unite in operations in northern Virginia. There is not an hour to lose."(¹)

May 5, 1864.

General Beauregard sent this despatch to General Whitney, in command at Wilmington: "Hurry Hagood's brigade through to Petersburg without delay. Use passenger trains and all others."(²)

If we had been in the telegraph office at Petersburg, we should have heard this despatch from Beauregard to General Pickett: "Concentrate your forces towards Petersburg."

This despatch went from Richmond to Weldon: "Order General Pickett not to stop Hagood's brigade: send it immediately here."

The train bearing Hagood's troops was going north from Weldon, and had just crossed Stony Creek, one of the streams that make up Nottaway River, when a body of Union cavalry came through the pine woods and burned the bridge. Had the train been a few minutes late, or had the cavalry arrived a few minutes earlier, in all probability the history of what happened at Petersburg in 1864 would have been far different from what it is. Who were these troopers? Had we been at Suffolk on the morning of the 4th we should have seen them—two brigades under General Kautz, moving north-west, and then west, to cut the railroad leading from Petersburg to Weldon. They burned the bridge, tore up the track, moved on to Rowanty River, to find the bridge there defended by a regiment of infantry. Not being able to destroy it, they turned north, burned one or two small bridges, but did so little damage that the Confederates soon had the cars running again. General Kautz might have destroyed the road all the way to Petersburg without molestation, but for some reason not stated by him did not do so.

There was much running to and fro in Richmond in the evening when this message flashed over the wires: "There are two single-turreted monitors, one double-turreted, three gunboats, and about forty transports in the fleet, coming up the James. Two gunboats have gone up the Appomattox. Each transport will average five hundred men. Some of the transports have horses on board. White and negro troops are in the expedition.

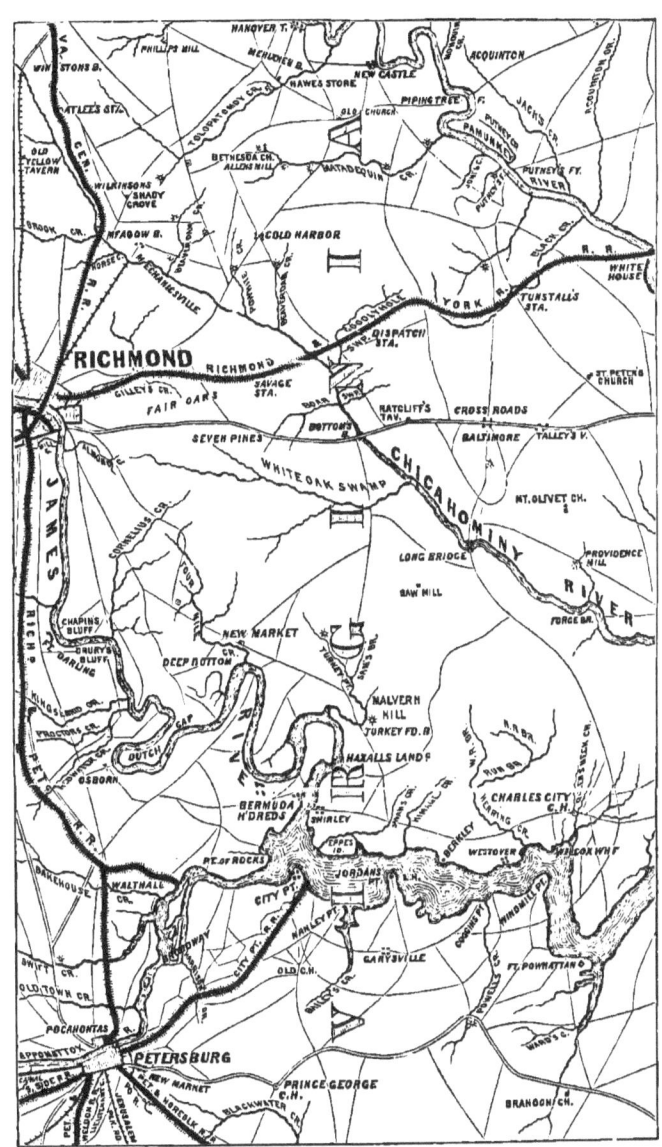

FROM COLD HARBOR TO PETERSBURG.

They are landing at City Point, and have hauled down the Confederate flag, and raised the Yankee flag." (¹)

It was the force under General Butler which had left Yorktown and Gloucester twenty-four hours before.

At that hour General Pickett had only six hundred men in Petersburg. He had not more than one thousand men to hold that city and the railroad north to Port Walthall Junction. General Butler had about twenty thousand, and was getting ready to march to Petersburg on the south side of the Appomattox, and to push out a force to seize the railroad leading to Richmond on the north side. At that moment the three railroad trains with Hagood's brigade came rolling into Petersburg to be welcomed by the citizens, who in their gratitude gave them all the food they wanted.

What narrow turning-points there are in history! Had Kautz, as we have seen, arrived at Stony Creek a few minutes sooner, or had the troops under General Butler started from Yorktown, Newport News, and Gloucester a little earlier, Petersburg would have been occupied by the Union troops in the first week in May, 1864.

It was four o'clock in the afternoon when one of the transports ran alongside the bank three miles below City Point, and two regiments leaped on shore and took possession of Fort Powhatan, erected by the Confederates in 1862. A division of colored soldiers of the Eighteenth Corps, under General Hinks, landed at City Point. The other two divisions, with the Tenth Corps, pushed on to Bermuda Hundred, and landed on the farm of Dr. Epps. Bermuda Hundred is the point of land included in the bend of the James just above the Appomattox. Going westward along the banks of the last-named stream, three miles brings us to Point of Rocks, above which, in the Appomattox, are several long and narrow islands, fringed with willow-trees which droop their branches into the sluggish stream. Port Walthall is a landing-place on the north bank of the river, whence a railroad runs west two miles to its junction with the Petersburg and Richmond Railroad. It is only two miles from the junction north-east to the James, so that General Butler, by holding the land from Port Walthall to the bend of the river, would be able to protect his supplies. The monitors and gunboats could prevent the Confederate iron-clad vessels which were lying in the stream below Richmond from coming down to make havoc of the fleet of transports.

A mistake was made at the outset. There are times when celerity of movement is everything. The troops went into bivouac for the night, when they should have been thrown forward to seize the railroad at the junction, tear it up, and erect fortifications.

It was six o'clock in the morning when Heckman's brigade moved westward from Bermuda Hundred. At noon the troops were at Cobb's Hill, a knoll on the north bank of the Appomattox. No Confederate troops opposed them. The soldiers here and there had caught a glimpse of a Confederate cavalryman riding across the fields at a safe distance. Heckman was ordered to wait till the other brigades of General Smith's corps arrived. General Gillmore, with the Tenth Corps, was also moving, but at a snail's pace, westward farther north. Neither Generals Butler, Smith, nor Gillmore, seemingly, had any comprehension of the need of a rapid movement. Every consideration demanded a quick seizing of the railroad, tearing up the track, and erecting fortifications to hold it. Why such slowness never has been explained. Butler's movement to Bermuda Hundred had not been anticipated by the Confederates; it was such a surprise that a signal-officer who was fishing in the James when the fleet came in sight fled as fast as he could run, leaving his fishing-lines and fish behind him. The Union troops were much obliged to him for having supplied them with fish. From noon till four o'clock in the afternoon Heckman's brigade rested at Cobb's Hill, waiting for General Smith to give the order for their advance; and then the brigade, accompanied by Howard's Fourth United States Battery, started upon a reconnoissance, descending the hill, passing a mill, and moving on to a farm-house. Looking across a field, they could see a cloud of dust raised by a body of Confederates going upon the run to hold the railroad at the junction of the Port Walthall branch with the main line of railroad. Howard wheeled his battery into position, and sent a shot which struck the rails of a fence and tossed them into the air. Heckman advanced his skirmishers, and a line of Confederate skirmishers came forward at the same moment. Stealthily the men in blue and the men in gray crept towards each other, crouching in the grass and grasping their rifles. It was a remarkable scene. They were so near that either party could toss a stone across the space between them, and yet they did not fire. For fifteen minutes they glared at each other—not two men, but two entire lines of men—and then the Confederates slowly backed themselves towards the fence. When the Union men discovered the movement, they sprang to their feet, fired, and instantly dropped into the grass. Then there was a volley from the fence, followed by a louder volley from Heckman's main line. For a few minutes the contest went on, the Confederate fire slackening. Heckman sent an aide to General Smith, asking for reinforcements, but instead of supports he received an order to fall back, and so, as the sun went

May 6, 1864.

down, this brigade turned about and retired towards Bermuda Hundred.

It was Hagood's brigade—the one which passed over Stony Creek just before Kautz reached that stream—that had thus confronted Heckman. The Confederate troops came across the Appomattox on the same platform cars that brought them from North Carolina. They could see Heckman's troops before the cars reached the junction, leap from them, and hurry down to the rail-fence. It was not the fault of General Heckman, or any remissness on the part of his troops, that the railroad was not seized and held. It went sorely against the wishes of this commander

PONTOON-BRIDGE, POINT OF ROCKS, ON THE APPOMATTOX.
From a Sketch made June, 1864.

and of his troops that they were ordered back, thus allowing the Confederates to have the prestige of victory when there had been really no battle, only the firing of a few volleys; but back to Cobb's Hill marched the grumbling soldiers, who wanted to rush upon Hagood and seize the railroad and build intrenchments.

Morning dawned. The two divisions of the Eighteenth Corps advanced, but only to find a stronger force of Confederates holding the railroad—Hagood's and Bushrod Johnson's brigades. It was ten o'clock before the Union artillery opened fire. Brooks's division swung round upon the Confederate left flank north of the junction, reached the track of the main line, and tore it up, also cutting the telegraph line. In the afternoon there was a sharp engagement near the house of Mr. Cragie, where the railroad crossed the turnpike; but the Union troops went into bivouac on the railroad, the Confederates retreat-

May 7, 1864.

ing across a little stream towards Petersburg. Brooks's division of the Eighteenth Corps of the Army of the James bivouacked on the railroad, and destroyed the track. This occupation of the railroad by the Union troops created great consternation in Richmond. Church bells rang, calling out all the home troops—the citizen soldiers organized for the defence of the city. We have this insight of affairs at the Confederate capital from a clerk in the War Department:

"There is more anxiety manifested to-day. Senator Hunter and Mr. Ould, the agent of the Exchange, have been in the office next to mine once or twice to drink some good whiskey kept by the disbursing clerk of the department: Mr. H.'s face is quite red. Six P.M. the tocsin sounded for the militia; I suppose all others being in the field. It is reported that the attack on Drewry's Bluff, or rather on our forces posted there for its defence, has begun. Barton's brigade marched thither to-day. There is now some excitement and trepidation among the shopkeepers and extortioners, who are compelled by State law to shoulder the musket for the defence of the city, and there is some running to and fro preliminary to the rendezvous in front of the City Hall. The Nineteenth Militia Regiment will have the pleasure of sleeping in the open air to-night, and dreaming of their past gains."(¹)

The Army of the James had not made any long marches. It had been transported by steamers to Bermuda Hundred, had fought no battle, had been resting through the day, when it might have been in motion. In contrast to this inaction, the Confederates were hard at work. The bridges destroyed by Kautz had been rebuilt, and cars loaded with troops were on their way from the south to Petersburg.

May 8, 1864.

On Monday morning Heckman's brigade began to march towards Petersburg, while all the other troops under General Butler started northward towards Richmond. A mile, and Heckman was at Arrowfield Church, on the turnpike, where a road comes in from the right and another from the left. A little stream winds down from the west—Swift Creek—crossing the turnpike and going on to the Appomattox. The Confederates made it their line of defence, three Tennessee regiments being posted by the railroad bridge. General Heckman placed the Twenty-seventh Massachusetts and Ninth New Jersey west of the turnpike to advance by the church, and his other two regiments east of the turnpike to secure the railroad bridge. The church bells in Petersburg had struck the hour of noon when the Confederates began the battle by moving forward; but they were quickly repulsed, and retreated across Swift Creek. Butler had detailed another

May 9, 1864.

brigade to support Heckman. It is quite probable that he could have made his way into Petersburg, or at least compelled the withdrawal of the Confederate troops south of the Appomattox. If General Butler had turned his attention first in that direction, in all probability he would have easily taken possession of the city. Having done that, he could have destroyed the bridges across the Appomattox. A small force then could have held the line of the Appomattox, and left him free for a movement towards Richmond. Had that been done, it would have seriously affected the Confederate capital and the operations of the army under General Lee.

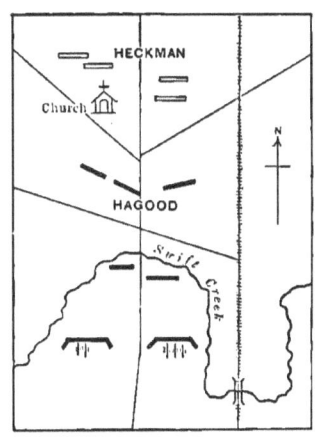

ENGAGEMENT AT ARROWFIELD CHURCH.

The Army of the James had possession of the railroad, and had torn up six miles of track between Richmond and Petersburg. Having done this, General Butler ordered the troops to fall back towards Bermuda Hundred. Quite likely he thought that with so much track torn up, the Confederates would not be able to repair it, but in a few days the cars were running once more.

General Smith and General Gillmore both proposed to General Butler a plan for the laying of pontoons across the Appomattox at Bermuda Hundred, to leave enough troops to hold the intrenchments, and to march with the rest during the night to Petersburg and capture that city. It would be a short march of about six miles. Had the plan been carried out on the evening of the 9th or 10th, the chances are that it would have resulted in failure, for Beauregard was in or near Petersburg, with nearly all his troops, till the 12th. Had it been entered upon on the evening of the 13th, in all probability it would have been a complete success. Butler declined to accept the plan. He informed them that Kautz had destroyed the railroad leading to Weldon; that with the six miles gone between Petersburg and Richmond, he thought it would not be possible for the Confederates to repair the breaks.

May 10, 1864.

Let us see the situation from the Confederate side. Gen. Robert Ransom, in command of the troops at Drewry's Bluff, moved out to reconnoitre the Union army with Barton's and Gracie's brigades, on the morning of the 10th, just as the pickets of the Tenth Corps were being withdrawn. There was a little skirmishing, but no battle. The falling back of the

Union troops, which outnumbered the Confederates, gave encouragement to Ransom's men. Going down towards Petersburg, we find Beauregard's troops along Swift Creek, by Arrowfield Church. There were eight brigades and eight batteries. There were two brigades in Petersburg and more troops on the way. The damage done by Kautz at Stony Creek had been repaired, and the cars were running before he had reached City Point. Telegrams were flying thick and fast. This from General Whiting, who had just arrived at Weldon from Wilmington: "Am here on my way; coming as fast as I can." On the morning of the 13th Beauregard sent this to Jefferson Davis: "Propose leaving to-day about noon with Colquitt's and Corse's brigades. which arrived yesterday. Martin's and Wise's remain here. Light batteries will follow as soon as possible after arriving."(*) So on the afternoon of the 13th we see the Confederate troops leaving the cars at Swift Creek, turning north-west, marching up the road leading to Chesterfield Court-house, and joining Ransom at Drewry's Bluff. On the 14th Beauregard had his army, with the exception of Whiting's division, concentrated near that point. On that evening Whiting was whirled through Petersburg and up to Arrowfield Church, where he was informed by a messenger that Beauregard was about to attack the Union army, and that he was to march towards the sound of the guns. Jefferson Davis had come down from Richmond to look after affairs. Beauregard, on the morning of May 16th, had an army of twenty-two thousand, with two thousand cavalry. The Confederates had acted with great energy, Butler with great deliberation. Through the 10th and 11th the Union commander did not move at all. On the next day he advanced slowly towards Drewry's Bluff.

Let us begin with the 13th. The cavalry under Kautz had arrived, and pontoons had been laid across the Appomattox. Kautz crossed to the northern shore, and was to move west to strike the Richmond and Danville Railroad. The colored troops under Hinks were still at City Point. General Ames's division of the Tenth Corps was stationed near Walthall Junction to prevent any attack from the direction of Petersburg, while the other brigades of both corps started north towards Richmond. The object was not to attack the Confederates, but to cover the movement of Kautz. A small stream comes down from the west and empties into the James, called Proctor's Creek, along which was a line of breastworks occupied by the Confederates. General Smith examined them and reported to Butler that if held in force they could not be carried. General Gillmore was on the left of the Eighteenth Corps,

May 13, 1864.

LAYING PONTOONS.

and marched towards the north-west. It was well on in the afternoon when Terry's division advanced to the attack. The artillery on both sides began the battle. The Confederate right was half a mile west of the railroad, on Woolridge Hill. Terry found it difficult to advance under the heavy fire which swept the open field, and was preparing for a second attack when the Confederates left the hill and retreated to the second

CONSTRUCTING BREASTWORKS.

and much stronger line of fortifications, which had been thrown up by the slaves, extending from James River along Kingsland Creek to the railroad. The intrenchments faced south.

Fort Darling, with heavy cannon, crowned the summit of Drewry's Bluff, which rises more than one hundred feet above the James. From that altitude the Confederates could send rifled shot and shell down upon the gunboats were they to approach the fort. Being so high, the gunboats might fire all day and do little damage in return. It was along the line of Kingsland Creek that the strongest breastworks had been thrown up, and there Beauregard, with great energy, had concentrated his troops, though on the afternoon of the 13th not half of his soldiers had reached the position, but were on the march from Chesterfield Court-house.

General Weitzel's division of Union troops was on the right of the turnpike, half a mile from the Confederate intrenchments, occupying those which had been abandoned the previous evening. Brooks's division was next in line, and then Turner's, of the Tenth Corps, with Terry on the left, on Woolridge Hill. Heckman's brigade was on the extreme right of the line. Weitzel had constructed a line of log breastworks along the edge of a piece of woods, and out a short distance in front stretched a telegraph wire from tree to tree. General Smith saw that it would be easy for the Confederates to come out from their intrenchments between the right of the line and the James, and that he must have more troops; and three regiments of Ames's division came up the turnpike and halted at the Half-way House, which is just half-way between Richmond and Petersburg, and near which Butler had his headquarters. When General Butler landed he outnumbered the Confederates three to one, but now that he was in position to attack they were as strong as himself. He had divided his force. Hinks was at City Point doing nothing other than to guard it with five thousand men. The gunboats and a regiment would have been sufficient to hold that position. Three thousand had been left at Bermuda Hundred to hold the intrenchments. Ames was at Walthall Junction with five thousand, to protect his rear. Kautz was on his way west to strike the Danville road. The troops in position along Kingsland Creek were holding a line two and a half miles long, with a gap of more than two miles between the right of the line and the James—ground over which it would be easy for the Confederates to make a flank movement, get between Butler and the river, and move to shut him off from Bermuda Hundred.

That was just what Beauregard, after looking over the situation from the ramparts of Fort Darling, proposed to do. He had the divisions of Ransom, Hoke, and Colquitt, with plenty of field artillery. Whiting was at Swift Creek with Wise's and Martin's brigades, four thousand six hundred strong, besides two thousand cavalry under General Dearing. In addition, there was a brigade under Hunton at Chapin's Bluff, besides the heavy artillery in the forts. Butler intended to attack on the afternoon of the 15th, but could not get the troops into position. Beauregard at the same time was making his plans to move out from Fort Darling and attack, with all possible force, the right of the Eighteenth Corps at daylight on the 16th.

The Confederates marched to their positions during the night—Ran-

May 14, 1864.

BERMUDA HUNDRED AND DREWRY'S BLUFF.

som's division along the base of the hill down towards the James, Gracie's Alabama brigade on the left of the line. This was the force which was to come round Butler's right flank, gain his rear, and cut him off from Bermuda Hundred. General Hoke was to advance and throw out a strong skirmish line, as if to attack Smith directly in front. When Ransom's

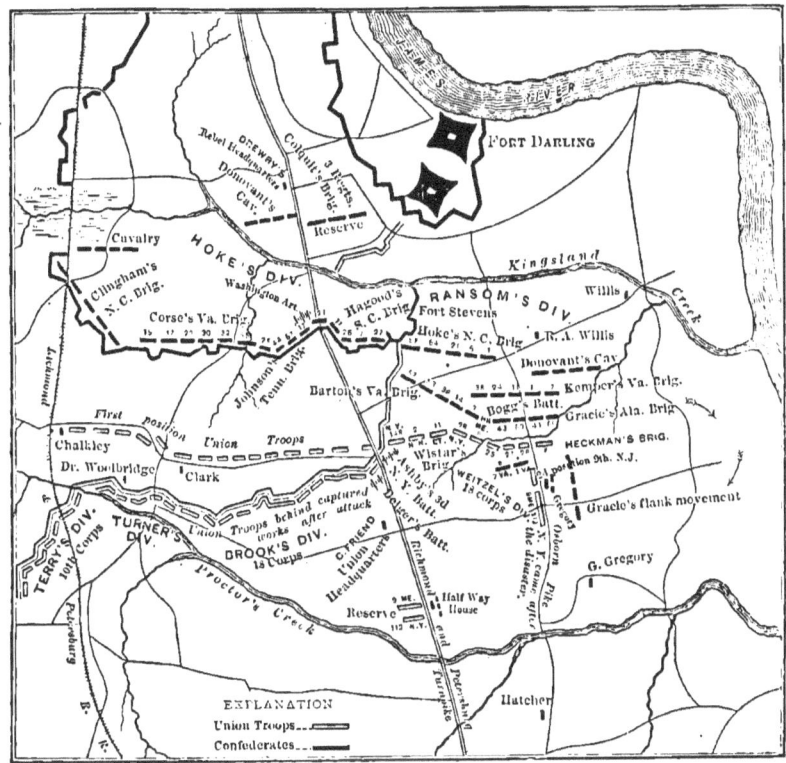

BATTLE OF DREWRY'S BLUFF.

guns opened in Butler's rear, Hoke was to make a real attack. Colquitt was in reserve, to be ready for attack wherever he might be needed. Whiting, with his 4600 muskets, twenty pieces of artillery, and 2000 cavalry, was to march towards the sound of the heaviest firing immediately after the opening of the battle.

It was a moonlight night. Weitzel's sentinels could see that something was going on in the Confederate line. There were musket-shots between the pickets. The officer at the front did not report to Weitzel, as he ought to have done. Ransom's troops at two o'clock moved east, towards the James. The moon went down in the west, and then a thick fog hung over the land, so dense that it was difficult to see an object ten feet distant. Ransom expected to have been in position by four o'clock, but it was nearly five before his skirmishers came upon Heckman's pickets, who in an instant were in line. They were veterans, and were called the "Star Brigade." General Heckman says: "Shortly after dawn a dense fog enveloped us, completely concealing the enemy from view. Five picked brigades in column debouched from the enemy's works, and rapidly advancing, drove in our pickets, pressing up on a run to our main line. Hearing their approach, my brigade swept instantly into line and steadily awaited their coming. When only five paces intervened between the Rebel bayonets and our inflexible line, a simultaneous scorching volley swept into the faces of the foe, smiting hundreds to earth, and hurling the whole column back in confusion. Five times encouraged and rallied by their officers, that magnificent Rebel infantry advanced to the attack, but only to be met and driven by those relentless volleys of musketry. Finding it impossible to succeed by direct attack, they now changed front and attempted to crush my right, held by the Ninth New Jersey; but here, the right wing having been reserved, they were met by a galling fire, and again for a moment faltered. But soon they advanced in column by brigade, and the Star Brigade being without artillery, and withal vastly outnumbered, was, for the first time in its history, compelled to fall back and take a new position."(*)

May 16, 1864.

After taking a new position, General Heckman, going through the fog from the Ninth New Jersey to a point which he supposed to be occupied by the Twenty-third Massachusetts, and dimly seeing an advancing line, ordered them to wheel to the right. The next moment he was a prisoner. The advancing troops were the Confederates of Gracie's brigade.

It takes but a minute to read this, but for more than an hour the men of the Star Brigade held the right of the line, till, outflanked, they were compelled to retreat, leaving a large number upon the ground, but a vastly greater number of Confederates killed and wounded.

The Confederate attack was along the right of the Union line, upon Weitzel's and Brooks's divisions; but the Union troops, with the exception of Heckman's, were behind breastworks, and the Confederates advancing in the fog found themselves confronted by gleaming lines of light, and were cut down by the incessant volleys. Every attack was repulsed. General Smith, finding that the assault was upon his right, sent word for the batteries which were at the front, near the turnpike, to withdraw, as they were useless in the dense fog. The messenger to one of the batteries was struck down by a bullet, and the captain of the battery was left so far in advance that five guns were lost. Smith sent two regiments which were at the Half-way House—the Ninth Maine and the One Hundred and Twelfth New York—to the right, to prevent the Confederates from completely turning his flank. They arrived too late to prevent the falling back of Heckman, but were in position to hold in check the Confederates moving rapidly and in force to assault the rear.

The battle had been going on for more than an hour on the right of the Union line before it begun on the left. Hoke's Confederate division came upon Gillmore, between the turnpike and railroad. The Washington Artillery, of New Orleans, was on the turnpike, sending its shells straight down towards the Half-way House. Johnson's brigade stood next in line, then Corse's, with Clingman's extending west to the railroad, and a short distance beyond it.

On the Union side the troops of the Tenth Corps reached across the railroad. Terry's division faced north-west, while Turner's fronted north. The angle was at the point where the line crosses Proctor's Creek. Brooks's division of the Eighteenth Corps was next in line towards the right, on the turnpike. The Confederate onset was against Weitzel, Brooks, and Turner; but every assault was repulsed. At half-past six o'clock the whole line was heavily engaged. The assault of the Confederates on the Union right was successful, and General Smith was obliged to reform his line to prevent the Confederates from gaining his rear. In the fog his regiments became confused, not from any lack of courage, but because they could not see which way to face or move. There was like confusion in the Confederate ranks. The two brigades which gained the flank of Heckman were in disorder. Some soldiers were picking up Union prisoners lost in the fog, and some in turn were being gathered up by Union soldiers. We have already seen how General Heckman himself had given an order to a body of Confederates, supposing them to be his own troops, and the next moment finding himself a prisoner.

Let us think of ourselves as being in the Twenty-third Massachusetts on this morning, with the fog so thick that we cannot see twenty paces. We are firing towards a dim outline of men in front of us, holding them at bay, when suddenly there is a rattling of musketry in our rear.

"Face to rear! Fall back!" the order. What is the matter? Before we can think what has happened, there comes a volley, and men drop all around us. We run through brambles and bushes, each one bent on getting to the rear. Sergeant Wallace carries the national flag. He wraps it round the staff grasps the lance end, and trails it behind him as he runs. The bullets sing around him, two passing through his clothing; but he saves the flag. Corporal Fernald carries the regimental flag. He is very sure that the line of men out yonder in the fog are friends, and refuses to retreat. The line comes nearer. "Surrender! surrender!" is the shout. The men of the Twenty-third are not there to surrender. They lift their muskets and send a volley into the advancing troops. The next moment ten of them are reeling earthward, with blood streaming from ghastly wounds, seven killed and three wounded. Only four men are left out of the squad. William D. Cole has been wounded in the arm. His son Edwin is lying at his feet, wounded in the leg. The father has fired so rapidly that the rifle all but burns his hands. Once more he fires at the advancing Confederates, and then goes down with twelve wounds, lying beside his son. The flag falls, to be picked up by the Confederates as a trophy.([7])

Captain Raymond, in the retreat, stops to help one of the wounded men of his company, Benjamin Bray, but sees that his life is swiftly ebbing. The Confederates are close upon him. "Surrender!" they shout. His answer is a shot into their faces with his revolver. Then comes a volley, riddling his clothes, carrying away his sword-belt; but he is unharmed, and escapes in the fog. He comes, a moment later, upon three of his men, who are carrying an officer to the rear, Lieutenant Wheeler, aide to General Heckman. "You may as well leave me; I cannot live. Please take my watch and diary. If you attempt to carry me you may endanger yourselves and the regiment." Captain Raymond will not leave him, but sees him safely to an ambulance, then comes upon another group, and finds that they have the lieutenant-colonel of the regiment, John C. Chambers, upon a stretcher, and that they have lost their way in the fog. He sets them right, and the officer reaches the hospital only to die of his wounds.([8])

I, who am writing this story, used to sit by the side of Lieutenant-colonel Chambers in a newspaper office in Boston. He was of noble spirit; he served in the Mexican War. Everybody loved him. Such were some of the scenes dimly discerned in the enveloping fog.

The fog lifted at last, with both armies in some measure disorganized. General Butler was moving his troops to hold the ground on his right, that Beauregard might not cut him off from Bermuda Hundred. At the same time Beauregard was rearranging his own lines, which had been thrown into confusion. He had brought every regiment into action.

Johnson's brigade had lost nearly one-third of its men. Clingman and Corse had been obliged to fall back before the stubborn resistance of the troops of Gillmore.

Private Sidney Atkinson, of the Twenty-fifth Massachusetts Regiment, was taken prisoner in the fog. He carried a small hatchet, which was very useful when he wished to kindle a fire or prepare his bed for the night. "Well, Yank, I will take that nice little hatchet," said one of his captors. "I s'pose you will, Johnny." The half-dozen men who had captured him soon lost their way. "Look here, Johnnies, I was over this ground this morning, and know where we are. I'll show you the way." The Confederates went as he directed, and soon found themselves prisoners. "I guess I'll take that hatchet, Johnny," said Atkinson, and the Confederates began to comprehend that they had foolishly allowed themselves to be outwitted by their prisoner.(*)

The Confederate commander was greatly disappointed in not hearing the roar of Whiting's cannon and rolls of musketry in the rear of Butler. Whiting had been ordered to march towards the sound of the heaviest firing, but though not more than five miles distant he had heard no firing. The Union and Confederate cannon had been thundering all the morning; the air had been still, but no sound of conflict had been heard at Walthall Junction, where Whiting had come against the pickets of Ames's division of Union troops. No messenger reached him from Beauregard. If he advanced in a direct line towards Drewry's Bluff he must fight his way. While waiting for the sound of battle word came that the division of colored troops under Hinks, at City Point, was advancing towards Petersburg. It was a false report, but Whiting marched to Arrowfield Church before he learned that it was not true. There was but little motion of the air on that morning of dense fog, and though more than threescore cannon were in action nothing of the battle was heard by Whiting, who could not be held responsible for not marching according to orders. Had he attempted to obey instructions he would have been held in check by Ames, so that Beauregard would not have derived any particular benefit.

Night came, and with it the withdrawal of Butler to his intrenchments at Bermuda Hundred, followed by Beauregard in the morning, who also threw up a line of works, making any further attempt by Butler in that direction impossible. The auspicious opening of Butler's movement had ended in complete failure. In a few days the cars were once more running into Richmond. General Kautz had gone west to the Danville Railroad, torn up the track in several places, burned stations and supplies, crossed to the south side of the Appomattox, turned east, came once more to the bridge on the Weldon Railroad across the Nottaway, which he had burned a few days before, and found that it had been rebuilt. On the 17th he was once more at City Point. His work of destruction was not sufficiently thorough, for in a short time all the railroads were mended and the cars running. In the battle of Drewry's Bluff the Union loss in killed and wounded was about two thousand, and the Confederate about the same; but nearly fourteen hundred Union soldiers had been captured, and five cannon lost.

On the 20th the Confederates assaulted Terry's and Ames's divisions, and took possession of a line of rifle-pits, but lost seven hundred men, with nothing in particular gained. Beauregard could do no more. Lee was in need of reinforcements, and all except nine thousand were sent north of Richmond to the North Anna, to hold Grant in check. Butler could make no aggressive movement, and about half of his troops went on steamboats down the James and up York River, to join the Army of the Potomac at Cold Harbor, where we shall see them.

NOTES TO CHAPTER VI.

(¹) "Military Operations of General Beauregard," vol. ii., p. 547.
(²) Idem, p. 548.
(³) Idem, p. 549.
(⁴) "A Rebel War Clerk's Diary," vol. ii., p. 201.
(⁵) "Military Operations of General Beauregard," vol. ii., p. 557.
(⁶) General Heckman's Report.
(⁷) "History of Massachusetts Twenty-fifth Regiment," Battle of Drewry's Bluff.
(⁸) Idem.
(⁹) "History of Company A, Twenty-fifth Massachusetts Regiment," p. 281.

CHAPTER VII.

FROM SPOTTSYLVANIA TO COLD HARBOR.

HOW to get at General Lee's army was still the great question with General Grant, for General Lee had erected formidable intrenchments covering Spottsylvania. To continue to attack there was simply a waste of life. General Grant did not desire to push Lee back upon Richmond, but to meet him in the open field, and planned a movement to induce Lee to make an attack. It was to send the Second Corps under Hancock by a roundabout way south towards the North Anna River, hoping that the Confederates would move to attack Hancock, and then before they could throw up intrenchments Grant would fall upon them.

There are four small streams which rise north-west of Spottsylvania, which the Indians named the Mat, the Ta, the Po, the Ny. Coming together, they make the Mattapony, which runs south-east to the Chesapeake.

The next stream south towards Richmond is the North Anna. General Grant intended that the Second Corps, followed by the Fifth, should get between Lee and that river. It was a dividing of the Union army, and might be attended with disaster, but General Grant calculated that Hancock and Warren would hold their own against any force that Lee might send, and he would be quick to move to their assistance.

At eleven o'clock on the night of May 20th, the soldiers of the Second Corps were on the march. When the morning dawned they were at
May 20, 1864. Guiney's Station, on the railroad leading from Fredericksburg to Richmond. A number of Confederate cavalrymen were there who quickly informed General Lee of the movement. At sunset General Hancock was at Milford, having marched twenty miles. The skirmishers suddenly came upon a brigade of Confederates, under General Kemper, who was going north to join General Lee. In the skirmish that followed, seventy Confederates were captured.

The march from Spottsylvania to Cold Harbor was through a section never before visited by Union troops. At the crossing of the Ny I found quarters at a farm-house owned by a feeble, forceless, gray-bearded, black-eyed man. He owned eighty acres of land, two negroes, an old horse, and a rickety cart. His house was mean, but it was charmingly located, overlooking the broad valley of the Mattapony, and surrounded by locusts and magnolias. Nature had done a great deal towards making it a paradise, but the owner had been an indifferent steward. Lying upon the grass beneath the trees, I fell into conversation with the proprietor.

May 22, 1864.

" This is Caroline County, I believe."

" Yes, sir, this is old Caroline—a county which has sold more negroes down South than any other in Virginia."

" I was not aware of that; but I remember now a negro song which I used to hear. The burden of it was,

"'I wish I was back in old Caroline.'"

" Quite likely, for the great business of the county has been nigger-raising, and it has been our curse. I never owned only old Peter and his wife. I wish I didn't own them, for they are old and I have got to support them; but how in the world I am to do it I don't know, for the soldiers have stripped me of everything."

" Do you mean the Union soldiers ?"

" Yes, and ours also. First, my boys were conscripted. I kept them out as long as I could, but they were obliged to go. Then they took my horses. Then your cavalry came and took all my corn and stole my meat, ransacked the house, seized my flour, killed my pigs and chickens, and here I am, stripped of everything."

" It is pretty hard, but your leaders would have it so."

" I know it, sir, and we are getting our pay for it."[1]

It was frankly spoken, and was the first admission I had heard from Southern lips that the South was suffering retribution for the crime of Secession. It probably did not enter his head that the selling of slaves, the breaking up of families, the sundering of heartstrings, the cries and tears and prayers of fathers and mothers, the outrages, the whippings, scourgings, were also crimes in the sight of Heaven. Broken hearts were nothing to him—not that he was naturally worse than other men, but because slavery had blunted sensibility.

During the march the next day towards the North Anna, I halted at a farm-house. The owner had fled to Richmond in advance of the army, leaving his overseer, a stout, burly, red-faced, tobacco-chewing man. There were a score of old buildings on the premises. It had been a notable

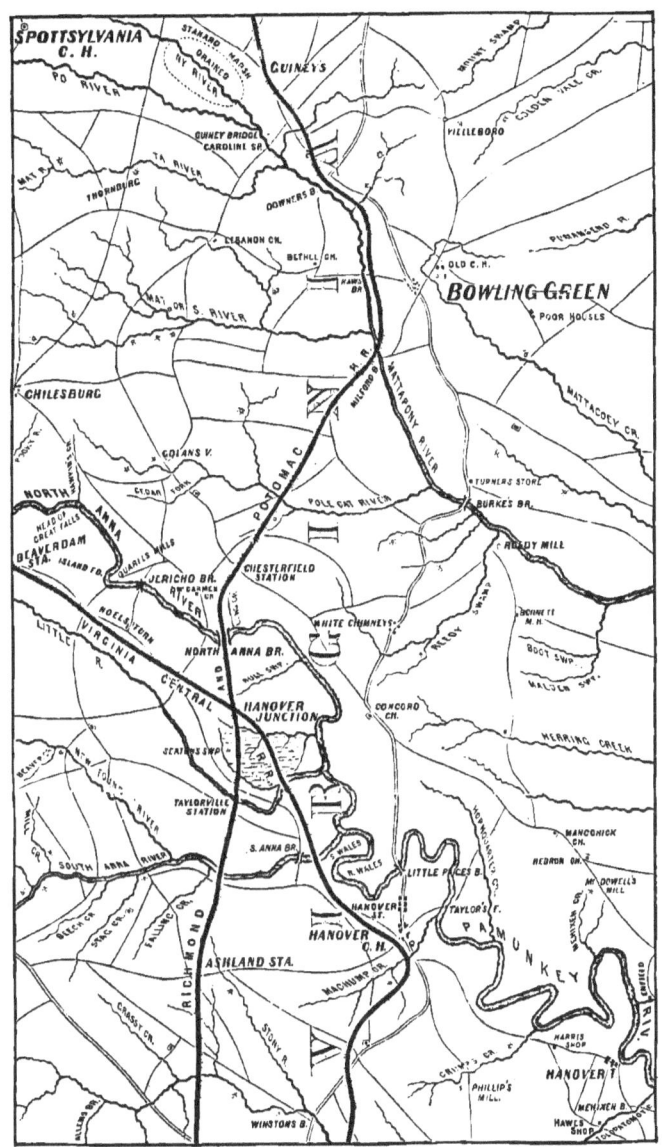

FROM SPOTTSYLVANIA TO HANOVER.

plantation, yielding luxuriant harvests of wheat, but the proprietor had turned his attention to the culture of tobacco and the breeding of negroes. He sold annually a crop of human beings for the Southern market. The day before our arrival, hearing that the Yankees were coming, he hurried forty or fifty souls to Richmond. He intended to take all—forty or fifty more—but the negroes fled to the woods. The overseer did his best to collect them, but in vain. The proprietor raved and stormed and became violent in his language and behavior, threatening terrible punishment on all the runaways, but the appearance of a body of Union cavalry put an end to maledictions. He had a gang of men and women chained together, and hurried them towards Richmond.

The runaways came out from their hiding-places when they saw the Yankees, and advanced fearlessly with happy countenances. The first pleasure of the negroes was to smile from ear to ear, the second to give everybody a drink of water or a piece of hoe-cake, the third to pack up their bundles and be in readiness to join the army.

"Are you not afraid of us?" I asked.

"Afraid! Why, boss, I'se been praying for yer to come; and now yer is here, t'ank de Lord."

"Are you not afraid that we shall sell you?"

"No, boss, I isn't. The overseer said you would sell us off to Cuba, to work in the sugar-mill, but we didn't believe him."(²)

Among the servants was a bright mulatto girl, who was dancing, singing, and manifesting her joy in violent demonstration.

"What makes you so happy?" I asked.

"Because you Yankees have come. I can go home now."

"Is not this your home?"

"No. I come from Williamsport in Maryland."

"When did you come from there?"

"Last year. Master sold me. I 'spect my brother is 'long with the army. He ran away last year. Master was afraid that I should run away, and he sold me."

General Lee saw that the movement which Grant was making would cut him off from Richmond, and at once began a march to get across the North Anna River, a rapid stream with steep, high banks. The railroad from Fredericksburg to Richmond crosses it. The Virginia Central Railroad crosses the former road at Hanover Junction, making it a very important point. Hancock's movement was towards that locality, but Lee, having the shortest road, was able to reach it before the troops of the Second Corps came to the North Anna.

Reinforcements were coming to General Lee. General Breckinridge came down the Virginia Central road in the cars with three thousand; May 23, 1864. Pickett's division of five thousand, which charged at Gettysburg, hastened up from the fortifications below Richmond, also Hoke's brigade of twelve hundred.

General Hancock reached the river at the railroad and Chesterfield bridges, which span the stream, the latter on the Telegraph road—the main thoroughfare. The Fifth Corps, under General Warren, was farther up-

SECOND CORPS BATTERIES.
From a Sketch at the Time.

stream, at Jericho Mill, with the Ninth between, at Ox Ford. The water was waist-deep, but the skirmishers of the Fifth Corps waded across, and drove the Confederate pickets from the other bank. The bridge-builders were quickly at work, and in a short time the divisions of the Fifth Corps were filing across the stream, Cutler's on the right, Griffin's in the centre, and Crawford's on the left.

The afternoon was hot, the atmosphere murky. Away in the west, dark clouds with golden fringes were rising, and muttering thunder rent the air. It was past three o'clock when General Hancock directed his batteries to open fire upon a fortification held by Kershaw's brigade of Confederates, on the north bank of the river, near Chesterfield Bridge. The earthwork was constructed in 1862. Why the Confederates chose to attempt holding this one isolated work on the north side, when the rest of the army was upon the south bank, is not known. Certainly nothing could be gained by attempting to hold it. Five Union batteries wheeled into position and sent a storm of shot and shell into the work. The Confederates had two cannon, which could make but feeble reply; but there were brave men in the fort. While the fire was hottest, while the missiles were streaming across the yellow bank of earth every second, an officer on horseback rode up from the bridge and handed a paper to the officer commanding the Confederates, and walked his horse leisurely back again. For more than an hour the artillery rained its missiles. Then there was sudden silence, followed by a loud ringing cheer, as the soldiers of Egan's and Pierce's brigades rose from the ground where they had been lying, and rushed upon the fortification. Puffs of blue smoke spurted from the embankment, but only for an instant, and then some of the Confederates threw down their arms and ran for the bridge. Others remained where

SOLDIERS IN RIFLE-PITS NEAR CHESTERFIELD BRIDGE, NORTH ANNA RIVER.
From a War-time Photograph.

they were, preferring to surrender rather than be mowed down by a volley fired into their backs. With a wild cheer the Stars and Stripes were planted on the fortification. The Confederates had set fire to the railroad bridge a mile below, and a column of smoke arose from its burning timbers. Going now up to Jericho Mill, we see the divisions of the Fifth Corps moving out over the plain, into wooded thickets, coming into line, the soldiers stacking their arms, kindling fires, making coffee, and frying bits of ham. Suddenly there came a rattle of musketry on the right, where Cutler's division was in line, and then the uproar of cannon.

The troops of Hill's corps were falling upon Cutler. The attack was so sudden and fierce that the Union troops soon came pouring out of the

BURNING THE RAILWAY BRIDGE ACROSS THE NORTH ANNA.

woods, running through Hoffman's brigade in the second line. It had been commanded by General Rice, who was killed at Spottsylvania. The soldiers were veterans who had been in many battles. Captain Mink, commanding a battery, was in position near Colonel Hoffman, and directed his gunners to ram three charges of canister into the guns. Out from the woods came the Confederates in pursuit. They saw the battery and rushed to capture it, but the pieces flamed and the Confederates fell headlong, torn in pieces by the storm of bullets from the cannon and from Hoffman's line.

The Confederates having been repulsed, the Union troops seized axes and shovels and began the construction of breastworks. The sun set with the lightning flashing and thunder rolling through the heavens. The battle was over, but the ground where Cutler had fought was thickly strewn with killed and wounded, the Confederate loss being greater than the Union. Five hundred Confederates surrendered rather than to attempt to retire under so destructive a fire.(³)

Night shut down with the Fifth Corps south of the river, at Jericho Mill, six miles up-stream from the Second Corps, while Hancock was on the

FROM SPOTTSYLVANIA TO COLD HARBOR.

LOADING WITH CANISTER.

north bank. Now was Lee's opportunity to give Grant a staggering blow; the moment when he should have hurled his whole force upon Warren and swept him into the river. The position of Warren was indeed critical. The tactics of General Grant in this movement have been much criticised. General Lee's hesitation to attack Warren with overwhelming force, as he might have done, has been also criticised by Confederate officers. Lee had received fifteen thousand reinforcements, and his army was nearly as large as it was on May 3d, when he took his stand to compel

May 24, 1864.

Grant to attack him in the Wilderness. In the morning the troops of the Second Corps crossed the Chesterfield Bridge, and formed on the southern bank. Lee had stationed his lines along the railroad to protect the junction, and had thrown up formidable breastworks. The Union troops reached a portion of the railroad and destroyed it. The Sixth Corps arrived, crossed

QUARLES'S MILL, NORTH ANNA RIVER.
From a Photograph taken in 1864.

the river at Jericho Mill, and came into position to support Warren, reaching the Virginia Central Railroad, tearing up the track, and burning the ties. Burnside, with the Ninth Corps, came to the North Anna at Ox Ford, but could not cross. The Confederates held the south bank, and were so strongly posted that General Grant saw it would be impossible to dislodge them. A third ford was discovered near Quarles's Mill, between Ox Ford and Jericho Mill, and Burnside sent over Crittenden's division, which joined Crawford's. The Confederates tried to prevent the crossing, and Crittenden lost many men. Potter's division of the Ninth Corps went down to Chesterfield Bridge, and joined Hancock. Grant had thus divided his army. Lee had the advantage of position, and his troops were behind strong fortifications. His army was concentrated, while Grant's was divided. His lines extended from the river at Ox Ford in an acute angle like the letter V. With a comparatively small force he could have held one side of the angle against either wing of Grant's, while hurling the bulk of his troops upon the other; but he made no attack. The opportunity went by never to return, for, to the close of the war, the Union army never was again divided so temptingly to the Confederate commander. General Grant has this to say of the position: "Lee now

PIONEERS CONSTRUCTING A ROAD AT OX FORD.
From a Sketch made at the Time.

had his entire army south of the North Anna. Our lines covered his front with the six miles separating the two wings, guarded by but a single division. To get from one wing to the other the river would have to be crossed twice. Lee could reinforce any part of his line from all points of it in a very short time; or could concentrate the whole of it wherever he might choose to assault. We were for the time practically two armies besieging. Lee had been and was being reinforced. Pickett, with a full division, had arrived from Richmond; Hoke, from North Carolina, had come with a brigade, and Breckinridge was there: in all probability not less than fifteen thousand men. But he did not attempt to drive us from the field."(¹)

The Ninth Corps, which up to this time had been regarded as an army by itself, was now incorporated into the army of the Potomac, General Burnside voluntarily putting himself under his junior officer, General Meade. The Sixth Corps moved towards the Confederate lines, which were found to be so strong that General Grant determined not to sacrifice his men by charging them. Through the day the skirmishers and sharp-shooters were engaged, but General Lee, with all the advantage of position in his favor, did not want to sacrifice his men by advancing upon the breastworks thrown up by the Union troops.

May 25, 1864.

EARTHWORK TAKEN BY THE SECOND CORPS.
From a Sketch made in 1864.

General Grant, having decided to make another movement, directed General Wilson's division of cavalry to make a demonstration upon Lee's left flank. We see the cavalry turning westward, crossing the North Anna above Jericho Mill, turning south, reaching the Virginia Central road, and destroying another section of the track. During the day General Grant sent this despatch to General Halleck in Washington:

May 26, 1864.

"To make a direct attack from either wing would cause a slaughter of our men that even success would not justify. To turn the enemy by his right between the two Annas, is impossible on account of the swamp upon which his right rests. To turn him by the left leaves Little River, New Found River, and South Anna River, all streams presenting considerable obstacles, to be crossed. I have determined, therefore, to turn the enemy's right by crossing at or near Hanover Town. This crosses all three streams at once, and leaves us still where we can draw supplies. . . . Lee's army is really whipped. The prisoners we now take show it, and the action of his

army shows it unmistakably. A battle with them outside of intrenchments cannot be had. Our men feel that they have gained the *morale*
over the enemy, and attack him with confidence." (*)

Up to this time General Grant had been receiving his supplies from
Fredericksburg, but he must open a new base and receive them from
White House, at the head of York River, whence McClellan had received his in 1862. Orders were sent to Washington and preparations
made accordingly.

General Sheridan arrived with the cavalry from James River in the
afternoon. The North and South Anna rivers, together with Little River,
after uniting, form the Pamunkey, a wide, deep, winding stream flowing
south-east to York River. When the sun disappeared at night, two divis-

JERICHO MILL AND PONTOON-BRIDGE, NORTH ANNA RIVER.
From a Photograph taken at the Time.

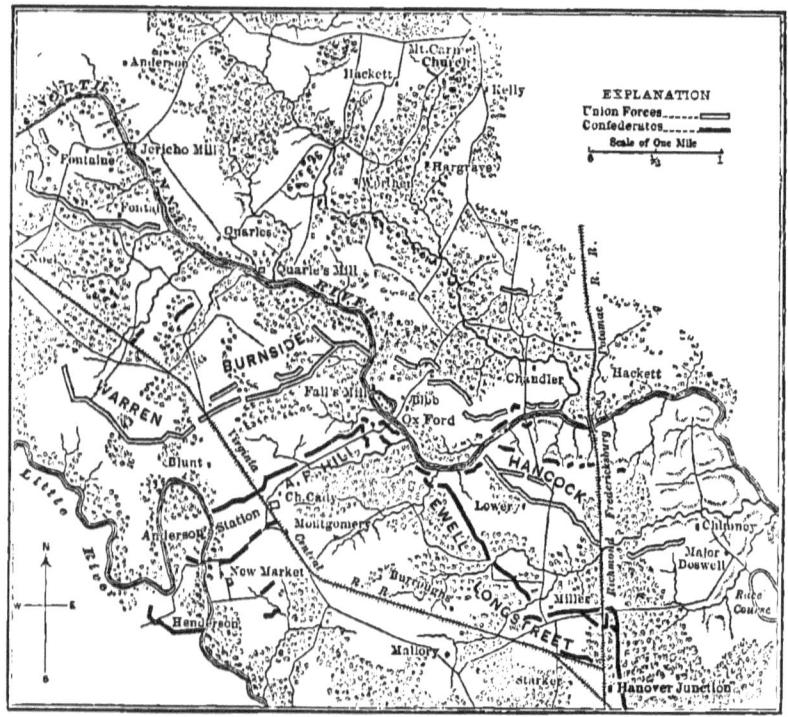

MAP OF THE NORTH ANNA.

ions of cavalry—Gregg's and Torbert's—moved south to Littlepage's Bridge, in the direction of Hanover, followed by Russell's division of the Sixth Corps infantry. A small force of cavalry was left at Littlepage's Bridge to make a feint of crossing at that point, while Sheridan, with the main body, followed by the infantry, pushed on through the night, making a march of nearly twenty miles to Hanover Ferry, crossing the Pamunkey to Hanover Town, encountering a brigade of Confederate cavalry, which was quickly driven, the Union troops capturing forty prisoners. Through the day the main body of the army was moving south-east, crossing the Pamunkey and turning west. General Grant could not learn from his scouts what movement General Lee was making, and directed Sheridan to move towards Mechanicsville. He started with Gregg from Hawes's store, four miles from Hanover Town, which is only seventeen miles from Richmond, but soon found a large force of Confederate cavalry ready to oppose his advance—Hampton's and Fitz-Hugh Lee's divisions, and Butler's brigade of South Carolina cavalry, which had just arrived, armed with rifles of long range. Fitz-Hugh Lee was on the right and Hampton on the left. General Gregg quickly dismounted his men. The Confederates were behind breastworks which they had hastily constructed, and the battle began. Sheridan sent Custer's brigade to Gregg. There were three Union brigades against five Confederate. Through the afternoon the battle went on. The sun went down, but the carbines and rifles were still flashing. The evening twilight was disappearing, when the Union troops made a vigorous assault along the entire line and compelled the Confederates to give way, leaving the killed and a very large portion of the wounded behind them. It was a hard-fought battle, in which there was great loss on both sides; but by winning it the roads were saved for the advance of the Union army towards Totopotomoy River, a little stream with wooded, marshy banks, flowing south-east through Hanover County. Early on the morning of the 28th the army began to cross the Pamunkey on the pontoons, and by noon all except the Ninth Corps were moving west. Burnside was left to guard the trains. From Hawes's store three roads lead towards Richmond. The right-hand one takes us past Polly Huntley's corner towards Atlee's Station, on the Virginia Central Railroad, and crosses the Chickahominy at Meadow Bridge. The middle one leads past Bethesda Church, and is known as the Old Church road, leading to Mechanicsville Bridge. The third runs south and then west through Old and New Cold Harbor. As the troops crossed the Pamunkey, the Sixth Corps moved along the right-hand road, forming the right wing; the Second Corps followed, forming the centre, with the Fifth on the left. General Sheridan was directed to move with the cavalry in the direction of Old Cold Harbor, to protect the road to White House. It was necessary to do this, as it was the highway over which the supplies of food and ammunition would reach the army.

At last General Grant had reached ground with which Meade, Hancock, Warren, and other subordinate commanders were acquainted, although he himself had never seen it. The army was upon ground where it had fought under McClellan, and the map made by the Engineer Corps in 1862 could now be used. The two armies were so near each other that any movement made by either was quickly detected and a corresponding change of position was made by the other. The seizure of the roads at Hawes's store enabled Grant to move in a direct line towards Cold Harbor. But he was looking beyond that point towards James River. He had already sent this despatch to General Hallett: "Send all the pontoon-bridging you can to City Point, to have ready in case it is wanted." Officers of the Engineer Corps were at Fortress Monroe preparing the boats. Steamboats came to that point with material for a bridge twelve hundred feet in length.

The negroes came from all the surrounding plantations—old men with venerable beards, horny hands, crippled with hard work and harder usage; aged women, toothless, almost blind, steadying their steps with sticks; little negro boys, driving a team of skeleton steers, mere bones and tendons covered with hide, or wall-eyed horses, spavined, foundered, and lame, attached to rickety carts and wagons piled with beds, tables, chairs, pots and kettles, hens, turkeys, ducks; women came with infants in their arms, and a sable cloud of children trotting by their side.

"Where are you going?" I said to a short, thick-set, gray-bearded old man, shuffling along the road, his toes bulging from his old boots, and a tattered straw hat on his head, his gray hair protruding from the crown.

"I do'no, boss, where I'se going, but I reckon I'll go where the army goes."

"And leave your old home, your old master, and the place where you have lived all your days?"

"Yes, boss; massa's done gone. He went to Richmond. Reckon he went mighty sudden, boss, when he heard you was coming. Thought I'd like to go 'long with you."

His face streamed with perspiration. He had been sorely afflicted with the rheumatism, and it was with difficulty that he kept up with the column; but it was not a hard matter to read the emotions of his heart. He was marching towards freedom. Suddenly a light had shined upon him. Hope had quickened in his soul. He had a vague idea of what was before him. He had broken loose from all which he had been accustomed to call his own—his cabin, a mud-chinked structure, with the ground for a floor, his garden-patch—to go out, in his old age, wholly unprovided for, yet trusting in God that there would be food and raiment on the other side of Jordan.

It was Sunday—bright, clear, calm, and delightful. There was a crowd of several hundred colored people at a deserted farm-house.

"Will it 'sturb you if we have a little singing? You see, boss, we feel so happy to-day that we would like to praise the Lord."

It was the request of a middle-aged woman.

"Not in the least. I should like to hear you."

In a few moments a crowd had assembled in one of the rooms. A

HEADQUARTERS AT BETHESDA CHURCH.

stout young man, black, bright-eyed, thick-wooled, took the centre of the room. The women and girls, dressed in their finest clothes, which they had put on to make their exodus from bondage in the best possible manner, stood in circles round him. The young man began to dance. He jumped up, clapped his hands, slapped his thighs, whirled round, stamped upon the floor.

"Sisters, less bless the Lord. Sisters, jine in the chorus," he said, and led off with a kind of recitative, improvised as the excitement gave him utterance. From my note-book I select a few lines:

RECITATIVE.

"We are going to the other side of Jordan."

CHORUS.

"So glad! so glad!
Bless the Lord for freedom,
So glad! so glad!
We are going on our way,
So glad! so glad!
To the other side of Jordan.
So glad! so glad!
Sisters, won't you follow?
So glad! so glad!
Brothers, won't you follow?"(*)

And so it went on for a half-hour, without cessation, all dancing, clapping their hands, tossing their heads. It was the ecstasy of action. It was a joy not to be uttered, but demonstrated. The old house partook of their rejoicing. It rang with their jubilant shouts, and shook in all its joints.

I stood an interested spectator. One woman, well dressed, intelligent, refined in her deportment, modest in her manner, using excellent language, said: "It is one way in which we worship, sir. It is our first day of freedom."

The first day of freedom! Behind her were years of suffering, hardship, unrequited toil, heartaches, darkness, no hope of recompense or of light in this life, but a changeless future. Death, aforetime, was their only deliverer. For them there was hope only in the grave. But suddenly hope had advanced from eternity into time. They need not wait for death; in life they could be free. Is it a wonder that they exhibited extravagant joy?

Apart from the dancers was a woman with light hair, hazel eyes, and fair complexion. She sat upon the broad steps of the piazza, and looked out upon the fields, or rather into the air, unmindful of the crowd, the dance, or the shouting. Her features were so nearly of the Anglo-Saxon type that it required a second look to assure one that there was African blood in her veins. She alone of all the crowd was sad in spirit. She evidently had no heart to join in the general jubilee.

"Where did you come from?" I asked.

"From Caroline County."

Almost every one else would have said, "From Old Caroline." There was no trace of the negro dialect, more than one would hear from all classes in the South, for slavery had left its taint upon the language; it spared nothing, but was remorseless in its corrupting influences.

"You do not join in the song and dance," I said.

"No, sir."

Most of them would have said "master" or "boss."

"I should think you would want to dance on your first night of freedom, if ever."

"I don't dance, sir, in that way."

"Was your master kind to you?"

"Yes, sir; but he sold my husband and children down South."

The secret of her sadness was out.

"Where are you going? or where do you expect to go?"

"I don't know, sir, and I don't care where I go."(7)

The conversation ran on for some minutes. She manifested no animation, and did not once raise her eyes, but kept them fixed on vacancy. Husband and children sold, gone forever—there was nothing in life to charm her. Even the prospect of freedom, with its undefined joys and pleasures, its soul-stirring expectations, raising the hopes of those around her, moved her not.

Life was a blank. She had lived in her master's family, and was intelligent. She was the daughter of her master. She was high-toned in her feelings. The dancing and shouting of those around her were distasteful. It was to her more barbaric than Christian. She was alone among them, and felt her degradation. Freedom could not give her a birthright among the free. The daughter of her master! It was gall and wormwood; and he, her father, had sold her husband and his grandchildren!

I had read of such things. But one needed to come in contact with slavery to feel how utterly loathsome and hateful it was. There was the broken-hearted victim, so bruised that not freedom itself, neither the ecstasy of those around her, could awaken an emotion of joy. Hour after hour the festivities went on, but she sat the while upon the step, looking down the desolate years gone by, or into a dreamless, hopeless future.

It was late at night before the dancers ceased, and then they stopped, not from a surfeit of joy, but because the time had come for silence in the camp. It was their first Sabbath of freedom, and like the great king of Israel, upon the recovery of the ark of God, they danced before the Lord with all their might.

We had a hard, dusty ride from the encampment at Mongohick to the Pamunkey. It was glorious, however, in the early morning to sweep along the winding forest-road, with the headquarter's flag in advance. Wherever its silken folds were unfurled, there the two commanders might be found—General Meade, commanding the Army of the Potomac, and General Grant, the commander of all the forces of the Union in the field. We passed the long line of troops, crossed the Pamunkey upon a pontoon-bridge, rode a mile or two across the verdant intervale, and halted beneath the oaks, magnolias, and button-woods of an old Virginia mansion. The edifice was reared a century ago. It was of wood, stately and substantial. How luxurious the surrounding shade; the smooth lawn, the rolled pathways bordered by box, with moss-roses, honeysuckle, and jasmines scenting the air, and the daisies dotting the greensward! The sweep of open land—viewing it from the wide portico; the long reach of cultivated grounds; acres of wheat rolling in the breeze, like waves of the ocean; meadow-lands, smooth and fair; distant groves and woodlands—how magnificent! It was an old estate, inherited by successive generations—by those whose pride it had been to keep the paternal acres in the family name. But the sons had all gone. A daughter was the last heir. She gave her hand and heart and the old homestead—sheep, horses, a great stock of cattle, and a hundred negroes or more—to her husband. The family name became extinct, and the homestead of seven or eight generations passed into the hands of one bearing another name.

When McClellan was on the Peninsula the shadow of the war-cloud swept past the place. Some of the negroes ran away, but at that time they were not tolerated in camp. The campaign of 1862 left the estate unharmed. Sheridan's cavalry, followed by the Sixth Corps, in its march from the North Anna, had suddenly and unexpectedly disturbed the security of the old plantation. There was a rattling fire from carbines, a fierce fight, men wounded and dead, broken fences, trodden fields of wheat and clover; ransacked stables, corn-bins, meat-houses, and a swift disappearing of live-stock of every description.

But to go back a little. The proprietor of this estate ardently espoused Secession. His wife was as earnest as he. They loved the institutions and principles of the South. They sold their surplus negroes in the

Richmond market, parted husbands and wives, tore children from the arms of their mothers, and separated them forever. They lived on unrequited labor, and grew rich through the breeding of human flesh for the market.

When the war began, the owner of this magnificent estate enlisted in the army and was made a colonel of cavalry. He furnished supplies and kept open house for his comrades in arms; but he fell in an engagement on the Rappahannock, in October, 1863, leaving a wife and three young children. The advance of the army, its sudden appearance on the Pamunkey, left the widow no time to remove her personal estate, or to send her negroes to Richmond for safe keeping. Fitz-Hugh Lee disputed Sheridan's advance. The fighting began on this estate. Charges by squadrons and regiments were made through the cornfields. Horses, cattle, hogs, sheep, were seized by the cavalrymen. The garden, filled with young vegetables, was spoiled. In an hour there was complete desolation. The hundred negroes—cook, steward, chamber-maid, house and field hands, old and young—all left their work and followed the army.

Passing by one of the negro cabins on the estate, I saw a middle-aged colored woman packing a bundle.

"Are you going to move?" I asked.

"Yes; I am going to follow the army."

"What for? Where will you go?"

"I want to go to Washington, to find my husband. He ran away a while ago, and is at work in that city."

"Do you think it right, auntie, to leave your mistress, who has taken care of you so long?"

She had been busy with her bundle, but stopped now and stood erect before me, her hands on her hips. Her black eyes flashed.

"Taken care of me! What did she ever do for me? Haven't I been her cook for more than thirty years? Haven't I cooked every meal she ever ate in that house? What has she done for me in return? She has sold my children down South, one after another. She has whipped me when I cried for them. She has treated me like a hog, sir! Yes, sir, like a hog!"

She resumed her work of preparation for leaving. That night she and her remaining children joined the thousands of colored people who had already taken sudden leave of their masters.

Returning to the mansion to see the wounded, I met the owner of the place in the hall. She evidently did not fully realize the great change which had taken place in her affairs, and the change was not complete at

THE FIFTH CORPS AT TOPOTOMOY CREEK.

that moment. The colored steward was there, hat in hand; obsequious, bowing politely, and obeying all commands. A half-hour before I had seen him in the cook's cabin, making arrangements for leaving the premises, and a half-hour later he was on his way towards freedom.

"I wish I had gone to Richmond," said the lady. "This is terrible, terrible! They have taken all my provisions, all my horses and cattle. My servants are going. What shall I do?" She sank upon the sofa, and for a moment gave way to her feelings.

"You are better off here than you would be there, with the city full of wounded, and scant supplies in the market," I remarked.

"You are right, sir. What could I do with my three little children there? Yet how I am to live here I don't know. When will this terrible war come to an end?"(*)

I have introduced this scene because it was real, and because it was but one of many. There were hundreds of Southern homes where the change had been equally great. Secession was not what they who started it thought it would be.

General Grant's headquarters were near a church. The day was warm, and the soldiers brought the settees from the building and placed them under the trees. A messenger arrived from Washington with letters and newspapers. The army, wearied with fighting and marching, was slowly advancing towards Totopotomoy Creek— the Sixth Corps to Hanover Court-house on the right, the Second Corps in the centre, the Fifth Corps on the left on the Shady Grove Church road, the Ninth in reserve at Hawes's store, the cavalry moving south towards Cold Harbor. There was no great battle during the day, only skirmishing.

May 29, 1864.

The morning opened with the Second Corps advancing to the Totopotomoy. The soldiers made their way through the thickets bordering its banks, to find the Confederates strongly intrenched upon the southern bank. The Fifth Corps advanced past Polly Huntley's corner, and was attacked by the Confederates under General Early so vigorously that General Grant ordered the Second Corps to attack in its front. The Union troops drove the Confederates from the line of rifle-pits which they had constructed, while the Fifth Corps repulsed Early and advanced nearly a mile. General Grant saw that General Lee had chosen a very strong position, and resolved to move again by his left flank.

May 30, 1864.

The Government of the United States, from the beginning of the war, maintained its faith with the soldiers. Whenever the term of service of a regiment expired, no matter what the exigency, it was permitted to return home. No individual soldier was forced to serve beyond the time for which he enlisted. Not so with the Confederate Government, which violated its plighted faith, which swept its drag-net over the whole community, and forced men into service from which there was no discharge. The terms of service of several regiments were expiring when the army reached Cold Harbor, and they took their departure, marching to White House, there taking steamers to Fortress Monroe. The losses in battle and the departure of troops was rapidly depleting the army, and as the Army of the James at Bermuda Hundred could do nothing, General Grant ordered General Butler to send him a portion of his troops. So it came about that General Brooks's and General Martindale's divisions of the Eighteenth Corps, and General Devens's and General Ames's divisions of the Tenth Corps, embarked at Bermuda Hundred, descended the James, and ascended York River to White House. They were under the command of Gen. William F. Smith. General Ames's division remained at White House; the others went a long distance out of their way, through the heedlessness of a staff-officer in writing an order. While marching they could hear the booming of cannon far away—Sheridan's guns at Cold Harbor. General Grant had directed General Sheridan to protect the left flank. As the cavalry skirmishers approached a little creek—the Matadequin—they encountered the Confederate cavalry under General Butler, and a fierce battle began. The Confederates had the advantage of being behind breastworks in a strong position. General Sheridan directed the men to dismount, and then, picking their way through a thicket, they attacked as infantry. The fighting was mainly between General Torbert's division of Union cavalry and Butler's brigade of Confederates from South Carolina. The Union troops turned Butler's flank, and compelled him to retreat, with a loss of a large number of men, who were taken prisoners.

Fifteen miles from Hanover southward is the little hamlet of Old Cold Harbor, on the road from Richmond to White House, at the junction of several roads. Before the war, travellers used to water their horses at a well where the roads meet, and while the horses were drinking, the teamsters rested themselves beneath the piazza of the tavern, which still stands there. General Torbert and General Custer, after they had compelled the Confederates to retreat, followed them towards Cold Harbor. The two commanders saw that it was an important point, and so informed General Sheridan, who agreed with them, and Merritt's brigade, followed by Custer's, moved on to occupy it. General Devin's brigade was detached, and moved along a road to the left.(*)

May 31, 1864.

UNION ARTILLERY AT COLD HARBOR.

The cavalry soon found themselves confronted by Fitz-Hugh Lee's division and Clingman's brigade of infantry, which had been brought up from below Richmond. The Confederates were hard at work with axes felling trees, and with shovels throwing up intrenchments. Once more the battle began, and the Confederates were compelled to leave Cold Harbor in the possession of the Union troops. Sheridan was nine miles from any infantry support. A courier galloped up the road and informed General Meade of what had been accomplished, who ordered the Sixth Corps to make a forced march to Cold Harbor. "Hold the place at all hazards," was the order sent to Sheridan. So, through the night the Union cavalry, instead of sleeping after the battle, built breastworks. Boxes of ammunition were distributed, for the pickets could hear the Confederate troops, only a short distance from them, marching into position, to be ready for an assault at daylight.

It was just after daylight when the Confederates of Kershaw's division advanced upon Sheridan, who told his men to wait till they were close up to the intrenchments before firing. The artillery loaded with canister, and the volleys from the repeating-carbines were so destructive that the Confederates fled, leaving many of their number killed or wounded upon the field. Later in the morning they advanced once more, only to be repulsed with great loss. Among the killed was Col. Lawrence M. Keith, who before the war had been a member of Congress, and who was one of the most active in bringing about the secession of South Carolina. ("Drum-beat of the Nation," p. 29.)

June 1, 1864.

General Lee discovered that the Union troops were withdrawing from their intrenchments along the Totopotomoy, that all had gone except the Ninth Corps, and he determined to strike a blow. General Rodes's division of Ewell's corps, now commanded by General Early, came suddenly out of the Confederate intrenchments on the road to Shady Grove Church and captured several of the Union pickets. It was mid-afternoon, and a battle began which became more furious as Gordon's and Heth's divisions, following Rodes's, came on. The Ninth Corps was just moving away, but quickly came into position. The Confederates, under Rodes, pressed on, and captured some of the Union skirmishers. Griffin's division of the Fifth Corps was at Bethesda Church. Cutler's and Crawford's divisions were south of it. General Griffin deployed his line, Ayres's brigade on the left, Bartlett's in the centre, and Sweitzer's on the right. The artillery opened a heavy fire, quickly followed by volleys of musketry. Heth's division fell upon Crittenden's of the Ninth Corps, but Potter's and Wilcox's divisions came to Crittenden's assistance. From mid-afternoon till sunset the battle raged, ending in the repulse of the Confederates, and the death of an able officer, General Dole. While the muskets were flashing and the cannon flaming near Bethesda Church, another tempest was beginning near the Old Tavern, at Cold Harbor. During the morning the Sixth Corps, under General Wright, was coming into position, also the troops from Bermuda Hundred, under General Smith, who had been directed "to hold the road from Cold Harbor to Bethesda Church, and co-operate with the Sixth Corps in an attack."([10]) The troops under General Smith had marched seventeen miles out of their way. They were weary, hungry, covered with dust, when they came into position at six o'clock in the afternoon.

Through the day the Confederate troops, under Longstreet and Hill, had been likewise marching, and were in position, constructing earthworks, felling trees, making abatis, and planting sharpened stakes in the ground. The pickets were hard at work digging rifle-pits and felling trees, in a narrow strip of wood half a mile from the Union troops, who could see the axes and shovels gleaming in the descending sun. A quarter of a mile farther west was the main line of works, a bank of earth, growing wider and higher every moment, with embrasures for cannon, covering every part of the smooth and level field. General Hoke's division was nearest the swamp of the Chickahominy. Then came Kershaw's, Pickett's, and Field's divisions. Going along the line of Union troops, we see Getty's division, commanded by Neill, nearest the Chickahominy, then Russell's, Rickett's, Devens's, Brooks's, and Martindale's divisions—the line extending from the banks of the river to the farm of Mr. Woody.

First came the cannonade—the artillery of both armies, hurling shot and shell across the fields fresh and green with summer verdure. Then the Union skirmishers advanced, followed by the firmly stepping lines. The weak point in a battle-line is where the divisions or brigades unite, where the authority of one subordinate commander ceases and another begins. Rickett's division struck the Confederate line where Kershaw's and Hoke's divisions joined.([11]) The blow fell upon Clingman's brigade of North Carolinians, which gave way, and Rickett's men instantly wedged themselves between Wofford's and Bryan's brigades, capturing over five hundred prisoners. But Hunter's and Gregg's brigades came upon the run, and a new Confederate line was formed. Upton's brigade of Russell's division charged with Rickett's. The Sixth Corps in this attack lost nearly twelve hundred killed or wounded. One regiment—the Second Connecticut—lost in killed, wounded, and missing, three hundred and eighty-six.

General Devens's, Martindale's, and Brooks's divisions of Smith's corps crossed a field under a heavy fire, captured the first line of intrenchments and two hundred and fifty prisoners, advanced almost to the main line of works, but were obliged to fall back, losing in all one thousand men. A soldier in General Burnham's brigade gives this account:

"On the way we file around the burning ruins of a building, said to be Beulah Church, near Mr. Woody's house. We enter thick brush, and move by the right flank into a shoal ravine, halt, and form close columns by divisions. Soon comes the order, given direct by an aide of General Burnham's, 'Load!' While loading our muskets the roll is called, the

ATTACK OF THE EIGHTEENTH CORPS AT COLD HARBOR.

men answering firmly, 'Here! here! here!' in many cases their last roll-call on earth. . . . We have been within range of the enemy's shot and shell for a long time, and hundreds of bullets whistle and whack among the trees, while shells burst over our heads, and the pieces come down among us, or else rip and tear through the trees. One large pine-tree is cut clean off, twenty or thirty feet above the ground, and the great branching top crashes down, and comes near killing General Burnham. . . . The artillery fire increases, the skirmishing rattles louder and louder, the smoke rolls towards us heavier and heavier in volume until the sun is obscured. At six o'clock we are ordered to charge. In a minute we spring out of the pines into the clearer light of open ground, and plunge headlong into the scene of carnage amid the deafening roar of musketry and artillery. Our part of the work is done in less than five minutes. Reliable persons have said in less than three minutes; but in this little time we lose sixty-seven men killed or wounded. We leave our grove of pines at the crest of the bluff, dart on the run three hundred yards across an open field to a little ridge. The enemy withdraws from his rifle-pits."(¹²)

The Confederates, astonished at the suddenness and success of the attack, made their main line of works a sheet of flame. The sun set through dun-colored clouds, illumined by the flashing of cannon and muskets. During the night several attempts were made by the Confederates to regain the captured works, but all such efforts were futile. (¹³)

The loss was severe in killed and wounded; but it was a victory so signal that a congratulatory order was issued by General Meade to the Sixth Corps.

Lying beneath the ever-moaning pines, with the starlit heavens for a tent, I listened to the sounds of the battle—steady, monotonous, like the surf on the beach. An hour's sleep, and still it was rolling in. But all things must have an end. Near midnight it died away, and there was only the chirping of the cricket, the unvarying note of the whippoorwill, and the wind swaying the stately trees around me. Peaceful all around; but ah! beyond those forest belts were the suffering heroes, parched with thirst, fevered with the fight, bleeding for their country. How shall we thank them? How shall we reward them? What estimate shall we place upon their work?

In the advance of Sweitzer's brigade of the Fifth Corps, Sergeant J. H. Abbott, of the Twenty-second Massachusetts, on the skirmish line, came suddenly upon five Confederate soldiers lying behind a log. "Surrender!" he shouted, and to his amazement and their own as well, they dropped their guns, while he sprang behind them and marched them into the lines.(¹⁴)

During the night, General Hancock, with the Second Corps, was moving in rear of the Sixth Corps, and coming into position between the Sixth and the Chickahominy, becoming the left wing of the army. General Grant expected to be ready to attack once more early in the morning, but the night was very dark, and the sun was high in the eastern sky when the troops of the Second Corps reached the position assigned them. They were weary and in no condition to rush into battle, but a battle was going on through the day—a constant pattering of musketry, like steady rain, with the thunder of artillery.

June 2, 1864.

FROM SPOTTSYLVANIA TO COLD HARBOR.

Had we been in the Confederate camp we should have seen men at work with shovels and axes making a massive line of intrenchments, extending all the way from the banks of the Chickahominy to the Shady Grove road. We should have seen the chief of artillery planting cannon to cover the fields with front and enfilading fires. A Confederate writer says: "A portion of the line occupied the edge of a swamp several hundred yards in length and breadth, enclosed by a semicircular ridge covered with beech-wood. On the previous night, the troops assigned to this part of the line, finding the ground wet and miry, withdrew to the encircling ridge, leaving the breastworks to be held by their picket lines."(¹⁶)

SECOND CORPS AT COLD HARBOR.
From a Sketch made at the time.

I rode along the lines from Bethesda Church to the old tavern at Cold Harbor. Russell's division of the Sixth Corps was lying behind the breastworks in front of the house. Shells came singing through the air and crashing through the trees. The Union artillery was replying to the Confederate.

Passing to the right, I saw the men from Bermuda Hundred sheltering themselves behind their breastworks. General Martindale's headquarters were by Mr. Woody's house. The soldiers knew that General Grant was contemplating another assault, and they knew that many lives would be sacrificed, and some of them were writing last letters to loved ones far away.

To judge fairly of military movements, we must put ourselves in the place of commanding generals and see things as they see them at the time. From the Wilderness to Cold Harbor General Grant had endeavored to encounter the Confederate army in an open field, but everywhere he had found it intrenched. What now should he do? Should he order an assault? To do so would result in the killing and wounding of many men; but if he could break the Confederate line he might be able to strike a damaging blow in the falling back of Lee across the Chickahominy. It seemed best to attempt it.

"An assault was ordered," writes General Grant, "to be made mainly by the corps of Hancock, Wright, and Smith; but Warren and Burnside were to support it by threatening Lee's left, and to attack with great earnestness if he should either reinforce more threatened points by withdrawing from that quarter, or if a favorable opportunity should present itself. The corps commanders were to select the points in their respective fronts where they would make the assaults. The movement was to commence at half-past four in the morning." ([16])

The Massachusetts Tenth Battery, commanded by Captain Sleeper, was attached to the Second Corps. When the sun went down, General Gibbon directed the battery to take a position in the works captured from the Confederates, with his first cannon on the right near a tree. Through the night the battery-men were at work with their shovels digging trenches, in which they sank their limber-chests below the level of the ground, and heaping up a great bank of earth. The soldiers cut small pines and oaks and set them outside the embankment, to screen themselves from the Confederate sharp-shooters. Half-past four—the hour had come. The soldiers of the Second, Sixth, and Eighteenth corps were ready and waiting. One of General Gibbon's staff-officers rode to Captain Sleeper with this order, "Fire a single gun as a signal," and the cannon by the tree broke the stillness of the morning. ([17])

June 3, 1864.

Over the breastworks leaped the Union troops. Instantly the Confederate lines burst into flame—a hundred cannon, twenty thousand muskets. Twenty minutes, and the assault known in history as the battle of Cold Harbor was over—lost to General Grant, with from eight to ten thousand men numbered among the killed and wounded. General Grant says of this assault:

"Hancock sent forward Barlow and Gibbon at the appointed hour, with Birney in reserve. Barlow pushed forward with great vigor, under

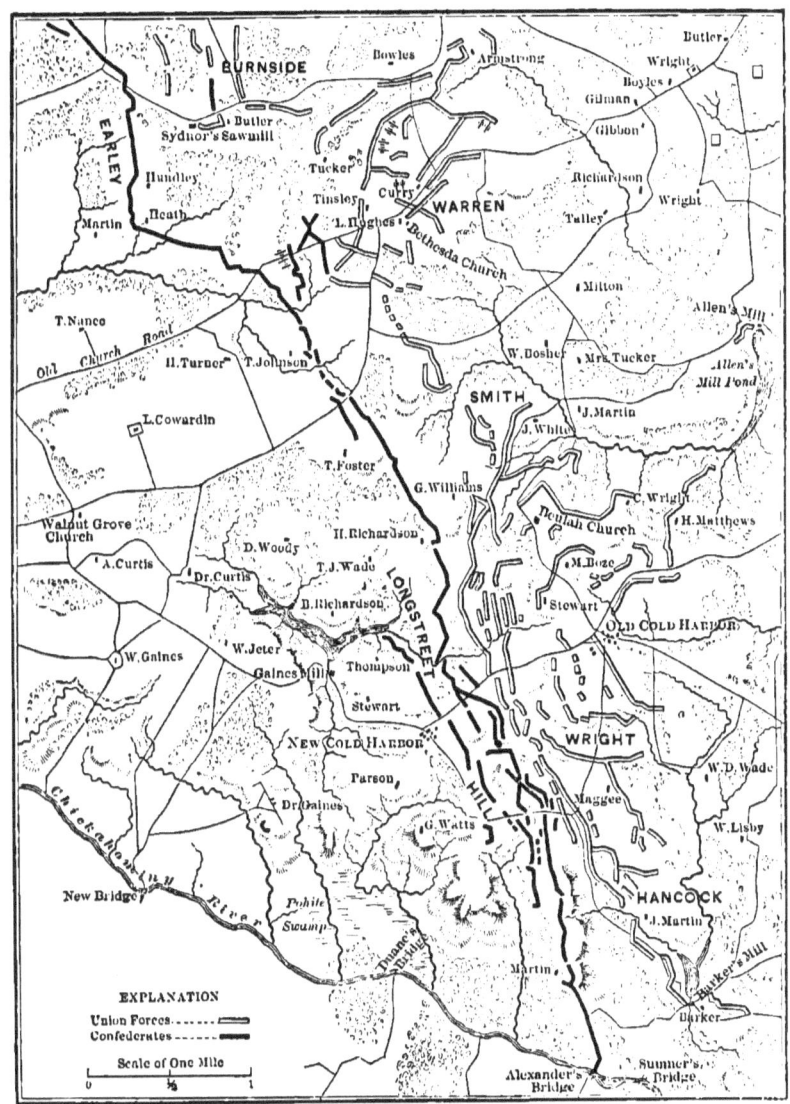

COLD HARBOR.

a heavy fire of both artillery and musketry, through thickets and swamp. Notwithstanding all the resistance of the enemy and the natural obstacles to be overcome, he carried a position occupied by the enemy outside their main line, where the road makes a deep cut through a bank, affording as good a shelter for troops as if it had been made for the purpose. Three pieces of artillery were captured here and several hundred prisoners. The guns were immediately turned against the men who had just been using

THE TAVERN AT COLD HARBOR.

From a photograph taken in 1887 by the author. The Union line of breastworks ran in front of the house. The Confederate lines were from the position of the camera.

them. No assistance coming to him, Barlow intrenched under fire and continued to hold his place. Gibbon was not so fortunate. He found the ground over which he had to pass cut up with deep ravines, and a morass difficult to cross; but his men struggled on until some of them got to the very parapet covering the enemy. Gibbon gained ground much nearer the enemy than that he had left, and intrenched and held fast.

"Wright's corps, moving in two lines, captured the outer rifle-pits, but accomplished nothing more. Smith's corps also gained the outer rifle-pits.

The ground over which the Eighteenth Corps moved was the most exposed of any. An open plain intervened between the contending forces at this point, which was exposed to a direct and cross fire. . . . Warren and Burnside also advanced and gained ground, which brought the whole army on one line."(¹⁸)

Of the assault a Confederate officer says: "I was as well satisfied that it would come at dawn as if I had seen General Meade's order directing it."(¹⁹)

This is the account of one of General Hancock's staff: "At a signal, Barlow advanced and found the enemy strongly posted in a sunken road, from which he drove them after a severe struggle, following them into their works under a heavy fire of musketry and artillery. Two or three hundred prisoners, one color, and three cannon fell into Barlow's hands. The captured guns were turned on the enemy by Col. L. O. Morris, of the Seventh New York Heavy Artillery, and the most strenuous efforts made to hold the position; but the supports were slow in coming up, an enfilading fire of artillery swept down the first line, the works in the rear opened upon them, and large bodies of fresh troops from Breckinridge's division, reinforced by Hill's, advanced with the utmost determination to retake the position. The first line held on with great stubbornness, but was finally forced out, Brooks being severely wounded, Colonel Byrnes and Col. O. H. Morris killed. Though compelled to retire, the men of the leading brigade would not go far. A portion of the line—Colonel Beaver's regiment, the One Hundred and Forty-eighth Pennsylvania—being conspicuous for its soldierly bearing, fell back to a slight crest opposite the enemy's intrenchments and distant only thirty to seventy-five yards therefrom, and proceeded to cover themselves by loosening the earth with their bayonets and scraping it up with their hands or tin plates; and here, at little more than pistol-range, they remained through the day. Miles's brigade also effected a lodgement within the works, Hapgood's Fifth New Hampshire, recently returned from the north, being foremost in the assault; but these troops were also driven out by the enfilading fire of the Confederate artillery, and by the strong lines advanced against them."(²⁰)

A Confederate general has put on record the scene in front of his command:

"I saw what I supposed to be a regiment, with a single flag, and an officer waving his sword and calling upon his men to charge. I asked my men to place their guns on the works and wait for orders. When the advancing line was within seventy yards I ordered my men to fire, when the

THE TENTH MASSACHUSETTS BATTERY FIRING THE SIGNAL FOR THE ASSAULT.
From a Sketch made at the time.

whole line fell to the ground, save one man, who ran behind an oak-tree, but was completely riddled by fifty balls in less time than it takes me to write it. The heroic regiment that made this gallant charge was the Twenty-fifth Massachusetts, which was the only regiment that obeyed the order to advance. The balance of the brigade had refused to go forward, and not since the days of Balaklava has a more heroic act been performed."([21])

In these five minutes two hundred and twenty soldiers and officers, out of three hundred and thirty comprising the regiment, were killed or wounded. Another Confederate general thus describes the scene:

"Our troops were under arms and waiting, when with the light of early morning the scattering fires of our pickets, who now occupied the abandoned works in the angle, announced the beginning of the attack. As the assaulting column swept over the old works a loud cheer was given, and it rushed on into the marshy ground in the angle. Its front covered a little more than the line of my own brigade of less than one thousand men; but line followed line, until the space enclosed by the old salient became a mass of writhing humanity, upon which our artillery and musketry played with cruel effect.... Sending an order for a supply of ammunition to be brought into the lines, I went down to the trenches to regulate the firing. I found the men in fine spirits, laughing and talking as they fired. There, too, I could see more plainly the terrible havoc made in the ranks of the assaulting column. I had seen the dreadful carnage in front of Marye's Hill at Fredericksburg, and on the old railroad-cut which Jackson's men held at the Second Manassas, but I had seen nothing to exceed this. It was not war, it was murder. When the fight ended, more than one thousand men lay in front of our works, either killed or too badly wounded to leave the field.... The loss in my command was fifteen or twenty."([22])

The color-bearer of the Twenty-fifth Massachusetts fell, but one of the color-guards—John E. Lewis, a boy of eighteen—seized the color, and running in advance, shouted, "Come on, boys!" Two men who accompanied him fell. Those in the rear saw the boy reeling; then beheld him take the staff from the socket and attempt to plant it in the ground. His strength was gone, and he fell dead upon the flag. Though the air was thick with bullets, David Casey ran and picked it up, and saved it from capture. Seventy-one per cent. of the men in this regiment fell, a loss exceeding that of any other regiment in a single battle during the war.([23])

Of the twenty officers on duty that morning six were killed, nine wounded, and two taken prisoners.

OFFICERS' QUARTERS AT THE FRONT.

Undaunted through the storm marched one other Union color-bearer, thus described by a Confederate officer:

"We stood three and four deep at the works, which we had strained every nerve and muscle during the night to complete, the men in the rear handing up loaded guns and taking empty ones from their comrades in front. We had never had nor desired a better chance to protect ourselves and damage an enemy. Line after line came out of the opposite woods, only to melt away under our continuous fire, until with the last line, which went the way of all the others, came a tall color-bearer, a sergeant, who bore his charge high in the air, as with steady tread he confidently advanced, looking only to the front and oblivious to his isolation. Amazed at his persistence, our men withheld their fire and called to him to go back; but he did not hear, or if perchance he did, he did not take his orders from our side. However that may be, he gave no sign, and all alone, with not a comrade in sight, he came unfalteringly on. Not even desiring to capture so brave a fellow, our men in gray mounted the works, and waving their hats to attract his attention, fairly shrieked, in their intense admiration and excitement, 'Go back! go back!' 'We don't want to kill you!' 'Go back!' Then this man of iron halted, looked carefully to his right hand as he surveyed the field, and then as carefully to his left—not a man of his regiment in sight! It would have been no disgrace to have dropped or hurried back as fast as he could. Admirable courage! He did neither, nor was there a show of any anxiety. He took

BOMB-PROOF SHELTER.

his flag-staff from its socket, rolled up his color with provoking deliberateness in our faces—the dipping of it we thought an unconscious tribute to our forbearance—and when done, touched his cap to us in grateful appreciation. A right-shoulder shift, an about face, and then began his march back to his own lines with a step as steady as had been his advance. He had quite bewitched us by his nerve, but the spell was broken as he turned, and, tremulous with excitement, we threw up our hats and yelled in admiration until his retiring figure was lost in the deep recesses of the far-away lines."(²⁴)

The soldiers, in charging over the fields of Cold Harbor, swept by Confederate cannon and musketry, knew that many men must necessarily die, but there was no faltering. In no battle was there a more pathetic exhibition of devotion to the flag they loved. Color-sergeant John Mitchell, of the Twenty-seventh Michigan, was carried back mortally wounded.

"I want you," he said to a comrade, "to go to Port Huron, and see my old father and mother, and tell them that I carried the flag until I was shot. I am not afraid to die. It is very little that one can do for so good a cause. Good-bye, boys. Don't forget how John Mitchell died."

Equally touching the pathos of the death of Captain O'Neill, of the Massachusetts Twenty-fifth Regiment, who said: "Doctor, I am willing to die for that dear old flag. I only wish I had two lives to give to my country."(²⁵)

General Grant saw that it was not possible to break through the Confederate lines, for the loss to General Lee probably did not much exceed one thousand. He says: "No advantage whatever was gained to compensate for the heavy losses we sustained. Indeed the advantages, other than those of relative losses, were on the Confederate side."(²⁶)

Many of the Union wounded, who were lying between the opposing armies, could not be relieved. Through the hot, sultry summer day of June 3d they lay in the burning sun. When night came a few Union soldiers crept out on their hands and knees to give the wounded water, but were shot by the Confederates. Through the following day they lay there. On the 5th, General Grant sent a letter by flag of truce to General Lee, proposing that when no battle was raging either party be authorized to send out unarmed men to care for the wounded without being fired upon by either party. General Lee replied on the 6th, that when either party wished to remove the wounded a flag of truce must be sent. General Grant sent a second letter, accepting the conditions, proposing that the wounded be removed between twelve and three o'clock that day, each party bearing a white flag, and that no Union soldier was to go beyond the ground occupied by the Confederate troops. General Lee replied that he could not consent to such an arrangement, but that when either party desired such permission, it should be *asked for* by flag of truce; and that he had directed that any parties coming out as proposed by General Grant be turned back. General Grant thereupon asked for a suspension of hostilities. When the parties went out on the

June 3, 1864.

morning of the 7th to collect the wounded, they found only two alive. Such the indescribable horror of the war brought about by the slave-holders to perpetuate their power.

General Grant regretted that he had ordered the assault, which was so disastrous. As in Burnside's attack at Fredericksburg, Lee's at Gettys-

SHARP-SHOOTERS, EIGHTEENTH CORPS.

burg, the charge upon Cemetery Ridge, and the attempt of the Confederates at Malvern Hill and Knoxville, there was great loss of life, with no compensating advantage.

The soldiers had constructed very strong intrenchments, behind which they were lying. There was a constant firing between the sharp-shooters of the armies ever on the watch. I was at the headquarters of General Grant, who was sitting upon a camp-stool, smoking a cigar. He listened to the firing, and said: "Ever since this army reached the Wilderness, a month ago, there has been scarcely an hour of silence. It has been one prolonged battle. The army is tired and needs rest. It has been fighting or else on the march all the time. I have heard so much firing that I cannot tell the difference between the mus-

June 7, 1864.

ketry and the stamping of the horses out yonder, to rid themselves of the flies."(²⁷)

Before starting from Culpeper General Grant had looked far enough into the possible future to see that he might be obliged to go to the James River. On the first day of June he sent an order to Washington for pontoons to be transported to the James, that he might cross that stream. He had no intention of attempting to advance against Richmond from the region of the Chickahominy. So while the pontoons were on the way from Washington the army rested.

NOTES TO CHAPTER VII.

(¹) Author's Note-book, 1864.
(²) Idem.
(³) Gen. U. S. Grant, "Personal Memoirs," vol. ii., p. 248.
(⁴) Idem, p. 249.
(⁵) Idem, p. 253.
(⁶) Author's Note-book, 1864.
(⁷) Idem.
(⁸) Idem.
(⁹) Gen. Philip H. Sheridan, "Personal Memoirs," vol. i., p. 400.
(¹⁰) Gen. William F. Smith's Report.
(¹¹) Gen. James Longstreet's Official Diary.
(¹²) "History Thirteenth New Hampshire Regiment," p. 344.
(¹³) Gen. U. S. Grant, "Personal Memoirs," vol. ii., p. 268.
(¹⁴) "History Twenty-second Massachusetts Regiment," p. 458.
(¹⁵) Gen. A. L. Long, "Life of Robert E. Lee," p. 347.
(¹⁶) Gen. U. S. Grant, "Personal Memoirs," vol. ii., p. 269.
(¹⁷) "History Tenth Massachusetts Battery," p. 198.
(¹⁸) Gen. U. S. Grant, "Personal Memoirs," vol. ii., p. 269.
(¹⁹) Gen. A. M. Law, *Century Magazine*, June, 1887, p. 298.
(²⁰) Gen. F. A. Walker, " History of the Second Army Corps," p. 511.
(²¹) Gen. T. D. Bowles, *Philadelphia Times*, June 21, 1885.
(²²) Gen. A. M. Law, *Century Magazine*, June, 1885.
(²³) "History Massachusetts Twenty-fifth Regiment of Infantry."
(²⁴) Capt. James H. Franklin, Fourth Alabama—Manuscript transmitted to author, by E. F. Witherby, Shelby, Alabama.
(²⁵) "History Company A, Massachusetts Twenty-fifth Regiment," p. 328.
(²⁶) Gen. U. S. Grant, "Personal Memoirs," vol. ii., p. 276.
(²⁷) Author's Note-book, 1864.

CHAPTER VIII.

FROM CHATTANOOGA TO ALLATOONA.

GENERAL SHERMAN issued his orders as commander of the Military District of the Mississippi at Nashville. It included what had formerly been the Departments of the Ohio, Cumberland, Tennessee, and Arkansas. General Grant wanted one controlling mind west of the Alleghanies. He believed in concentration. We have already seen what his general plan was to be—the movement of the Army of the Potomac against the Confederate army under Lee, in Virginia; the marshalling of the consolidated armies of the west, under Sherman, against the Confederate army at Dalton, thirty miles south of Chattanooga, under Gen. Joseph E. Johnston. Three armies were consolidated into one—the Army of the Ohio, under General Schofield, 14,000; the Army of the Tennessee, under General McPherson, 25,000; the Army of the Cumberland, under General Thomas, 60,000. The entire force, including the cavalry, numbered nearly 100,000, with 254 guns.

March 18, 1864.

A general commanding a great army, and moving into an enemy's country, with a hostile population behind him, has many things to think of, and must take long looks ahead. Chattanooga is one hundred and thirty miles from Nashville, Sherman's base of supplies, reached by a single track of iron rails. From Nashville to Louisville is one hundred and eighty-five miles. The entire distance must be guarded. There must be soldiers ever on the watch, for the Confederates were on the alert to throw a rail from its place, set fire to a bridge, wreck a train, or block the road. To feed one hundred thousand men, and all the mules and horses, would require great energy. The line of advance was to be through a country already exhausted of supplies, and so wasted that the people from Nashville to Chattanooga were on the verge of starvation, and must be supplied with food. General Sherman could not move without accumulating a large amount of food and ammunition at Chattanooga. To the poor people it seemed a cruel order which he issued, limiting the use of the cars to the transportation of food and supplies for the army, and forbidding the issue of provisions to the suffering. He compelled the commanders of posts within thirty miles of Nashville to haul their supplies in wagons. The soldiers going to and returning from the army were obliged to march, and all the cattle purchased for beef were driven instead of being transported in the cars. As there was little for the cattle to eat, they were not much more than skin and bones when they reached the army. By this strict order the capacity of the railroad was nearly doubled; but General Sherman saw that there must be more engines and cars. Necessity knows no law, and military law does just as it pleases. He called the Master of Transportation, Colonel Anderson, the Chief Quartermaster, General Donaldson, and his Chief Commissary, General Beckwith, to Nashville.

"One hundred thousand men and thirty-five thousand animals must be fed, and supplies accumulated," said Sherman.

"You must have one hundred and thirty car-loads a day, and we have not enough cars or engines to do it," is the reply.

"Seize all the cars and engines that arrive in Nashville from the North," was the order, and four hundred cars and forty engines were seized.

"We must have our cars and engines back again, or we cannot bring your supplies from Louisville to Nashville," said Mr. Guthrie, president of the railroad.

"You must stand by me. Seize cars and engines that come to Louisville from Cincinnati," was the reply, and the order was carried out.(¹)

In a short time train was succeeding train in quick succession. General Sherman left the railroads to settle with the Government as best they could. Managers of railroads in the North, wondering what had become of their cars, found them, many months after Sherman was at Atlanta, doing service on this greatest military highway of the country.

Baggage is called impedimenta because it hinders an army in its movements. Stonewall Jackson understood it better than any other commander, Confederate or Union, during the war. Sherman resolved that his army should move in light marching order. Tents were forbidden, except to the sick and wounded. Only one tent was allowed to each headquarters for an office. Sherman himself set an example, neither himself nor his staff having a tent or furniture of any kind. They only had "flies," which they could spread over fence-rails or poles to shelter them from the rain, and which could be carried by soldiers on their shoulders, or strapped to saddles. By this means the wagon-trains were greatly reduced. The campaign was to be through the mountain region, where there were but few roads, and those winding through narrow valleys.(²)

SUFFERINGS OF THE POOR IN EAST TENNESSEE.

The great Appalachian chain of mountains begins to fade out in Central Georgia; but from Chattanooga to Atlanta, a distance of seventy-five miles, the mountains are like the waves of the sea, long, parallel ranges, running north-east and south-west. The little creeks which empty into the Tennessee from the south are not more than twenty or thirty miles long. The railroad which runs from Chattanooga to Atlanta winds along the Chickamauga Creek, through a gap in Taylor's Ridge at Ringgold, then goes on to Rocky Face Ridge, piercing it at Tunnel Hill. The sides of the gorge are steep and rocky. Buzzards wheel and circle high in air above the cliffs, and at night find roost upon the trees. In years gone by, somebody named the place Buzzard's Roost. Four miles farther south we come to Dalton. The rain-drops which fall on the western slope of Rocky Face Ridge flow to the Tennessee, and thence to the Ohio and Mississippi; but the springs which rise on the eastern slope take a much shorter course, to the Gulf of Mexico, through the Coosa. At Dalton a railroad comes down from Cleveland and Knoxville. Ten miles south of Dalton is the town of Resaca, on the north bank of the Oostenaula, one of the branches of the Coosa.

Through the winter of 1863-64 the Confederate army occupied Tunnel Hill and Dalton. No attempt had been made to drive it from its chosen position. The Union army was not ready to move. It was undergoing reorganization and consolidation. We have already seen General Grant made commander of all the armies, with Sherman placed at the head of all the troops west of the mountains.

While Sherman is getting ready to move let us take a near look at the Confederate army at Buzzard's Roost and Dalton.

It was a sad day for General Bragg and the Confederate army, in that last week of October, 1863, when they were swept from Missionary Ridge and compelled to flee southward to Dalton, setting on fire an immense pile of corn in sacks, hundreds of barrels of flour, bacon, bread, pease, sugar, staving in the heads of molasses hogsheads. A river of syrup flowed along the railway at Chickamauga Station. The soldiers filled their canteens and dippers. Those who had no dippers lay down and drank from the flowing stream, getting their uncut beard and hair gummed with the sticky melada. They emptied the corn from the sacks, filled them with bread, flung them across their shoulders, jabbed their bayonets into sides of bacon, filled their pockets with sugar. They had been kept on short rations, but now helped themselves liberally. They cursed General Bragg as the prime cause of all their misfortunes. It was a blunder, they said, to send Longstreet to Knoxville, when every soldier was needed at Chattanooga. Bragg never was liked by his men, neither by his officers.

General Taylor, of the Confederate army, draws this portrait of him: "He was the most laborious of commanders, devoting every moment to the discharge of his duties. As a disciplinarian he far surpassed any of the senior Confederate generals, but his method was harsh, and he could have won the affections of his troops only by leading them to victory. Many years of dyspepsia had made him sour and petulant, and he was intolerant to a degree of neglect of duty, or what he estimated to be such, by his officers."(³)

Some of the retreating soldiers laughed over the misfortune that had come to him who had been so sharp towards them, and were not sorry that he had been defeated. It was a sore blow to Bragg, who asked to be relieved of the command, and was called to Richmond to be Jefferson Davis's military counsellor.

The people of the South demanded that Gen. Joseph E. Johnston should be appointed commander. President Davis did not like him, but the clamor was so great that he was forced to comply, and on December 27th Johnston assumed command. Through the winter he kept a large gang of slaves at work with axes and shovels, constructing fortifications at points along the railroad between Chattanooga and Atlanta, correctly surmising that the Union army would make its next move towards that great workshop of the Confederacy, where founderies were flaming and machinery whirling, turning out arms for the army. A soldier draws this picture of General Johnston: "Fancy, if you please, a man about fifty years old, rather small of stature but firmly built, an open countenance, and a keen, restless eye that seemed to read your inmost thoughts. In his dress he was a perfect dandy. He ever wore the finest clothes that could be obtained, carrying out in dress and the paraphernalia of the soldier the plan adopted by the War Department at Richmond, never omitting anything, even to the trappings of his horse, bridle and saddle. His hat was decorated with a star and feather, his coat with every star and embellishment, and he wore a bright new sash, big gauntlets, and silver spurs. He was the very picture of a general."(⁴)

The army was in a sad plight when he assumed command. The men were losing hope and deserting. They had little to eat. A train came whirling into Dalton, and almost before the cars came to a stand-still the soldiers broke them open and helped themselves to supplies. General Johnston wisely ordered two days' rations to be issued, one of them an extra supply. Bragg had scrimped them, but he gave them all they

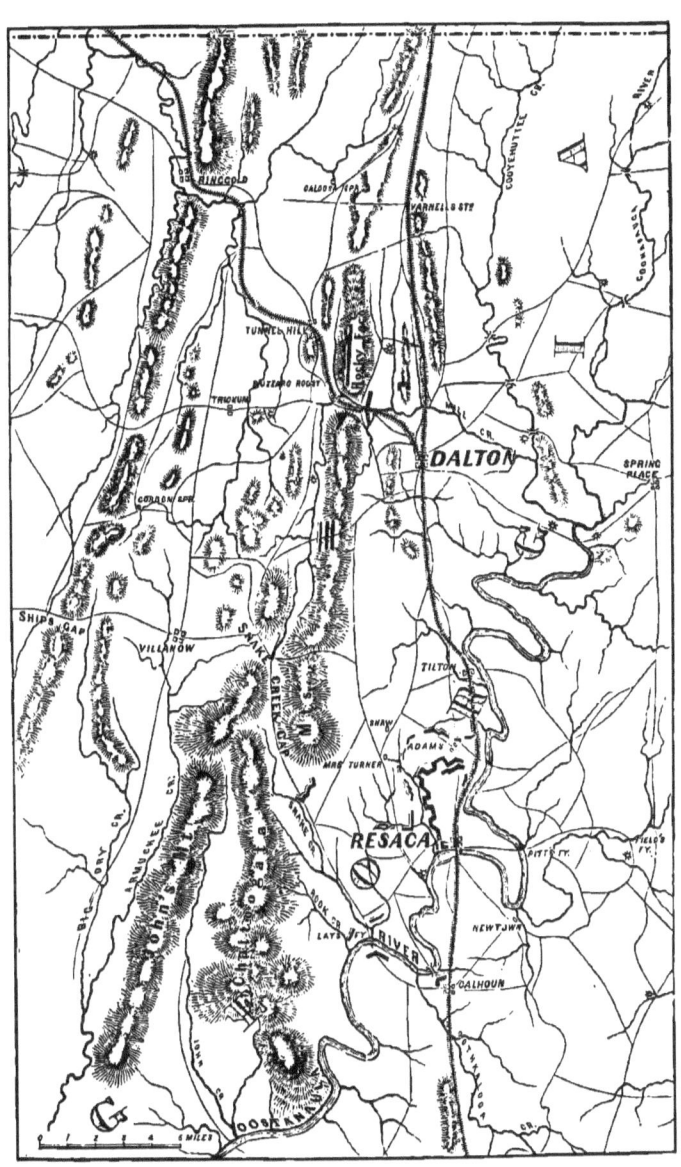

FROM RINGGOLD TO RESACA.

could eat. He ordered tobacco and whiskey to be issued twice a week, and sugar, coffee, and flour instead of meal. He ordered tents, clothes, shoes, and hats, and gave furloughs to one-third of the army at a time, till every soldier had an opportunity to go home; thus imitating General Hooker, who brought up the spirits of the Union army after the defeat of Fredericksburg. Bragg had been strict about small things, ordering roll-call several times a day. We are to remember that volunteering had ceased long before Bragg became commander, and that the largest part of the army had been conscripted, the soldiers compelled to take their places in the ranks. Quite likely Bragg ordered frequent roll-calls as a guard against desertion. Johnston trusted the soldiers, was kind to them, and soon won their confidence. He ordered that they should be paid. True, the money was nearly worthless, but it was something for the Government to keep its faith with them. He ordered that fifty dollars bounty be paid to each man. It cost only the printing. The promises to pay would never be redeemed, but it made the soldiers happy. That was the gain.

General Johnston had brought the Confederate army up to a high state of efficiency. He was severe in discipline. Seventeen men were shot at Tunnel Hill for disobedience, and several more at Rocky Face Ridge. Instead of the whipping-post, he established the pillory. Men who committed petty crimes were incased in barrels. A Confederate soldier gives this picture of an execution: "The snow was on the ground, and the boys were hard at it snowballing. While I was standing looking on, a file of soldiers marched by me with a poor fellow on his way to be shot. He was blindfolded and set upon a stump, and the detail was formed. The command, 'Ready! aim! fire!' was given, the volley discharged, and the prisoner fell off the stump. He had not been killed. It was the sergeant's duty to give the *coup de grâce* should not the prisoner be slain. The sergeant ran up and placed the muzzle of the gun at the head of the poor pleading and entreating wretch, his gun was discharged, and the wretched man only powder-burned, the gun being one that had been loaded with powder only. The whole affair had to be gone over again. The soldiers had to reload and form and fire. The culprit was killed stone-dead this time. He had no sooner been taken up and carried off to be buried than the soldiers were throwing snowballs as hard as ever, as if nothing had happened."(¹)

The army under Johnston, on the last day of April, consisted of Hood's and Hardee's corps, and Wheeler's cavalry, in all 52,992. Reinforcements were on their way. Mercer's brigade of 2800 came three days later. On the 7th, Canty's division of 5500 reached Resaca. General Polk hurried up from Mississippi with his corps of 12,000. Other divisions were forwarded so rapidly that on the second week in May the Confederate army numbered between 70,000 and 80,000 men.

The Union army under Sherman, as we have seen, with headquarters at Chattanooga, on the 1st of May comprised three distinct armies—besides a portion of the Army of the Potomac—the Eleventh and Twelfth corps, which had been sent West after the battle of Chickamauga. Battle, sickness, and the expiration of service had sadly thinned the ranks of the regiments of the veterans from the East. Sherman decided to consolidate them into one corps. The veterans were proud of their achievements. The men of the Eleventh did not want to be merged into the Twelfth, nor did the soldiers of the Twelfth desire to lose their identity in the Eleventh. General Sherman respected the spirit of the men, and created a new corps—the Twentieth—to win new victories, and make a history of its own. General Hooker was appointed commander, and the corps was attached to the Army of the Cumberland. Besides the Twentieth, General Thomas had the Fourth, under General Howard, who had commanded the Eleventh, and the Fourteenth, under General Palmer.

May 1, 1864.

MAJOR-GEN. GEORGE H. THOMAS.

The Army of the Tennessee was composed of the Fifteenth Corps, under General Logan; the Seventeenth, under General Blair; and the Sixteenth, under General Dodge; but only two divisions of the Sixteenth were at Chattanooga. The Army of the Ohio had but one corps, the Twenty-third.

The 5th of May was selected by General Grant for the beginning of the movement, which he desired should be simultaneous with that of the Army of the Potomac in Virginia. On that morning General Thomas was at Ringgold, Schofield east of him, marching down from Cleveland,

FROM CHATTANOOGA TO ALLATOONA. 209

while McPherson was crossing the old battle-field of Chickamauga, to come in upon the right of Thomas.

General Sherman had looked ahead to see about the resources of the country, consulting the census tables of 1860 of every county in Georgia, showing the quantity of corn and the number of cattle, that he might make calculations for the support of the army in case he could not obtain all he needed from the North.

On May 7th General Thomas came upon the Confederates at Tunnel Hill, and drove off the pickets holding it. From the hill Sherman looked down past Buzzard's Roost. He could see the long lines of works, the Confederate cannon reflecting the sunlight, and the dams built across the creek, forming miniature lakes. He had no intention of attacking the formidable position, but he directed McPherson and Hooker to move towards Snake Creek, a little stream which springs from the mountain's side south-west of Dalton. There is a gap in the mountains, with a road winding through it. It seems not to have occurred to Johnston that Sherman would use it to turn his flank and rear. Not till McPherson was through the gap did Johnston see that

May 7, 1864.

MAJOR-GENERAL McPHERSON.

he had left a side-door open, by which Sherman could walk into Resaca. Hooker, with the Twentieth Corps, followed McPherson, who, at two o'clock on the 9th, was within a mile and a half of the railroad at Resaca. He met a brigade of cavalry, which retreated. Had he pressed on he might have seized the railroad; but he acted with caution, and fell back to the gap till morning. The ablest commanders and the best of men err in judgment and make mistakes. McPherson

May 9, 1864.

14

lost a great opportunity. He had twenty-three thousand men, Hooker was behind him, and had he moved on to Resaca there would have been consternation in the Confederate army. Johnston would have been compelled

BUZZARD'S ROOST.

to either divide his army or to retreat eastward, abandoning the line of railroad and his supplies. If the latter, Thomas and Schofield would have been in position to pounce upon him, as hounds upon a startled deer. General

Johnston has been looked upon as one of the ablest of Confederate commanders, but the neglect to guard Snake Creek Gap has been regarded as a glaring defect in his plan of defence. The caution of McPherson was due to the terms of his instructions from Sherman. It was an error of judgment on the safe side, but had he seized the railroad it would probably have been a disastrous day to Johnston. "Had he done so," says Sherman, "I am certain that Johnston would not have ventured to attack him in position, but would have retreated towards Spring Place, and we should have captured half of his army and all his baggage at the beginning of the campaign."(*)

Johnston was thus forced to abandon all the strong works at Dalton. The breastworks, the dam, were of no account. It was not agreeable, but there was no help for it; and so we see the Confederates hastening back

CAVALRY ENGAGEMENT, SNAKE CREEK GAP.

to Resaca, and the soldiers constructing other breastworks, the army no longer facing north, but west. The campaign had opened, and the two mighty armies were in position for the first great battle.

It was startling news to Johnston that the Union troops were moving towards Resaca on the road from Sugar Valley post-office. While he had been watching his front and right, Sherman had been turning his left, and was moving to seize the railroad at Resaca. There were only a few troops at that place to hold McPherson in check.

May 9, 1864.

Just how many were there cannot be ascertained. A citizen of Resaca, who was at home on that afternoon, informed me that there was only a part of a brigade in the village.(') It is quite probable that when the skirmishers of McPherson were seen coming through the woods west of the railroad there were but a handful of Confederates at the station guarding the road and bridge over the Oostenaula. Others under General Canty soon came from the fort, on the hill east of the village. They went upon the run out through the meadow west of the railroad. Some rushed up the hill north-west of the village and opened fire. They strung themselves out in a long line, and made all the racket possible. McPherson's troops, instead of rushing on with a hurrah, as they might have done, came to a halt in the edge of the woods west of Mr. Hill's house. They were only a third of a mile from the railroad and the bridge which spans the Oostenaula. Let them rush on and seize them, and there will be trouble in Johnston's army. All communications with Atlanta will be cut off. No more supplies can be brought up. Let them but rush on, and to-morrow's morn will see Johnston doing one of two things—either bringing a large part of his army from Buzzard's Roost to attack McPherson, or his whole army will be moving eastward along the country roads, attempting to reach Atlanta.

"McPherson," writes General Sherman, "found the Gap undefended, and accomplished a complete surprise to the enemy. At its farther debouche he met a cavalry brigade, which was easily driven and which retreated hastily towards Dalton and doubtless carried to Johnston the first intimation that a heavy force of artillery and infantry was in his rear and within a few miles of the railroad. I got a note from McPherson that day, written at 2 P.M., when he was within one and a half miles of the railroad, above and near Resaca. I renewed orders to Thomas and Schofield to be ready for instant pursuit of what I expected to be a beaten and disordered army, forced to retreat by roads to the east of Resaca, which were known to be very rough and impracticable."(")

A few weeks later McPherson gave up his life, and we shall never know just what considerations turned him back when he was so near the coveted prize. Shall we say that the time had not come? It is General Sherman's view that the country was not ready for the breaking up of the Rebellion. We are to remember that the Confederate Government had taken great offence at the enlistment of negroes as soldiers; that they would not recognize them in exchange of prisoners. In the North were men bitterly hostile to the proclamation of President Lincoln giving freedom to the slaves as a war measure, and were denouncing the war as unrighteous and wicked. If Johnston's army had been annihilated at the outset of the campaign, with such animosity against the colored race, would the measure of freedom be what it is to-day? Would the negroes have become citizens of the republic? Under an all-wise Providence, which sees through from the beginning to the end, which guides the nation to its mighty destiny, McPherson turned back. There must con-

ENGAGEMENT AT DUG GAP.

tinue the outpouring of the precious wine of life, the agony of the battle-field, the hospital, the endurance of the prison, the lengthening trenches of the dead, and ghastly scenes of Andersonville, the sacrifice of thousands of lives, before the government of the people could be established on an enduring basis, with the full measure of liberty to every man, irrespective of race or color, before the United States could take the exalted place of leader and teacher of all the nations in their march towards freedom.

From Dalton a road leads westward up the steep mountain-side to Dug Gap, where there was an engagement just before the battle of Chickamauga ("Marching to Victory," page 396). Again there was a sharp

14*

engagement between the Union troops under General Geary, of Hooker's corps, and General Stevenson's division of Confederates, the Union troops climbing the steep ascent, driving the Confederate skirmishers. General Sherman designed the movement as a feint, a demonstration which had the effect of blinding the Confederates as to his intentions.

Although McPherson had gained the left flank and threatened the rear of the Confederate army, Johnston, finding that he had fallen back, made all haste to hold Resaca till he could withdraw the army from Dalton. Sherman was in no hurry to compel his departure. He was planning a larger movement. He withdrew Schofield, sending Williams's division of Hooker's corps to support McPherson, and waited for Stoneman's division of cavalry, which was coming to join them. He issued orders to Schofield to go through Snake Creek Gap and join McPherson, and so his whole army was in motion towards Resaca.

There was a sudden packing of wagons at Dalton on the afternoon of May 12, 1864. The Confederate artillery went down the road, the horses upon the gallop and the infantry upon the run, towards Resaca. Major-general Polk's corps was in the advance, moving to head off the Union troops under McPherson, which were west of Resaca. The left of the Confederate line rested on the Oostenaula.

RAILROAD DEPOT AT RESACA, GEORGIA.

During the night the soldiers were hard at work with their shovels, throwing up breastworks on the swell of ground by the house of Mr. Hill and on the ridge north-west of the railroad. When morning dawned McPherson beheld a long line of embankments in front of him. A little stream comes down from the north—Camp Creek—and empties into the Oostenaula a half-mile west of the railroad. The ridge of ground along which Johnston was throwing up his line of defence lies between the creek and the railroad. Next to Polk was Hardee with his corps, then Hood. Polk and Hardee faced west, while Hood looked towards the north.

The long lines of wagons belonging to the Union army were parked at the lower end of Snake Creek Gap, guarded by Hovey's division of the Army of the Ohio. General McPherson advanced with Logan's corps on his right, and the cavalry under Kilpatrick going out through the woods and fields towards the south-west, while the other divisions moved along the road and north of it towards Resaca. General Thomas came in from the west towards the house of Mr. Moore, with Hooker opposite the house of Mr. Ruckert, which the Confederates tore down to obtain lumber for their breastworks. General Schofield, with the divisions of Generals Judah and Cox, moved in rear of Thomas, crossed the field near the house of Mr. Wright and the meadows at the head of Camp Creek, turned south, and faced General Hood. General Howard, with the Fourth Corps, was on the march from Dalton, along the railroad, picking up straggling Confederates who had dropped behind in the retreat. General Sherman received word that the Fourth Corps was close at hand, that all the troops were in position, and ordered an advance of the entire line. It was about noon when General Sherman rode up to the point on the line east of Mr. Wright's house, where the Army of the Ohio joined the Army of the Cumberland. General Schofield and General Thomas were both there, and together they watched the movement. There were several little streams to cross, fences which must be torn down, and thick brambles which impeded their way. The artillery found it difficult to get across the miry meadow, and the advance was quite slow. Schofield's two divisions moved south—General Cox on the east side of the Dalton road, General Judah west of it. The artillery begun the battle. A little later a line of skirmishers in blue picked their way along the fences across the meadow, and the musketry opened. The Confederate skirmishers east of the road were driven across the little creek; but those behind the fences and in a thicket by the bridge kept up a sharp fire, and held the ground a while, but were driven at last, and then the whole Army of the Ohio crossed the creek. The battle was fierce east of the road, where Cox's brigades rushed upon the Confederates and drove them from their breastworks. The Confederates fell back to a second line of works. Cox could advance no farther, and the men dropped down behind the breastworks which they had captured.

GEN. LEONIDAS POLK.

holding them until General Howard brought up Wood's and Newton's divisions to support him. The division under General Judah had a harder task to perform, and was less fortunate. The ground over which the troops marched was broken, and there were tangled thickets through which they must charge up a steep hill swept by a cross-fire from the Confederate batteries. Three brigades moved steadily forward. Shells exploded among them, and a pitiless storm beat upon them from the veteran Confederate soldiers under Hood, who had been in a score of battles, and the Union men were repulsed with heavy loss.

General Johnston discovered that General Stanley's division of General Howard's corps, east of the Dalton road, in rear of General Wood's division, had no support, and laid his plans to strike a heavy blow. Hood sent two of his divisions, General Stewart's and General Stevenson's, directing them to come round upon Stanley's left flank and crush it. Very fortunately for the Union army, at the same moment General Sherman, finding that there was not sufficient room to deploy all of Thomas's troops, sent Hooker eastward towards the Dalton road, the troops marching in rear of the Army of the Ohio. Johnston, to conceal his movement and to prevent Sherman from sending supports to Stanley, ordered the Confederate artillery to open all along the line. He did not know that Hooker was on his way towards Stanley's position. The Confederates under Stewart and Stevenson came upon Stanley, making a fierce attack, but soon found themselves confronted by a superior force. Williams's division of Hooker's corps was in advance, and arrived just at the moment when Stanley needed him. The Confederates were repulsed with great loss, and the Union troops held the ground.

Going down now to the Army of the Tennessee, we find General Osterhaus, with a division of Logan's corps, on the road which leads west from Resaca to Sugar Valley post-office. The Confederate troops at this point were west of Camp Creek. There was a bridge across the creek, which they held. There were thick woods along the valley, and the Confederate skirmishers were sheltering themselves behind the trees. The Twelfth Missouri, of Osterhaus's command, was on the skirmish line, and the soldiers gained the rear of the Confederates, who abandoned the west bank and fled across the bridge. General Logan ordered Gen. Giles A. Smith and Gen. C. R. Woods, with their brigades, supported by Veatch's division, to advance. They crossed the creek, drove the Confederates, secured a strong position, and threw up intrenchments. The artillery hastened forward, came into position, and sent shells crashing into the railroad-station and the bridge spanning the Oostenaula.

GENERAL SHERMAN.
From a sketch by T. de Thulstrup, by permission of L. Prang & Co.

General Polk made an attempt to capture the cannon, but his troops were repulsed. From the moment that Logan gained this position General Johnston saw that he must retreat. No railroad trains could bring him supplies across the bridge. He set his engineers to work constructing one bridge near the railroad crossing, and another around the bend a mile east of the railroad bridge, beyond the reach of the Union artillery.

While the cannon were thundering at Resaca, General Sherman was executing another important move. He had no intention of attacking Johnston behind his breastworks, but hoped to gain his rear, intercept his line of communication with Atlanta, and compel him to fight a battle in the open field. The course of the Oostenaula is south-west. The railroad runs nearly south, and he sent Kilpatrick's division of cavalry and Sweeny's division of infantry down the west bank of the river ten miles, to Lay's Ferry, with a pontoon train, with orders to cross the river and secure a position on the east bank. If this could be successfully done, if he could cross the river at that point and seize the railroad near the town of Calhoun, he would compel Johnston either to fight him or retreat across the country towards Kenesaw Mountain. The cavalry reached the river, drove the Confederate pickets across the stream, and pushed out on all the roads. Captain Reese, McPherson's chief engineer, had the pontoons in place in a very short time. One of Sweeny's brigades had crossed, when a messenger came down the road, informing Sweeny that the Confederates were crossing the river above him, to gain his rear and cut off his retreat. The troops were recalled upon the run, and Sweeny marched a mile and a half before he found that it was a false report.

General Johnston learned that General Sherman's troops were crossing at Lay's Ferry, and sent Martin's cavalry and Walker's division of infantry to Calhoun to hold the railroad. Had not Sweeny hastened back, but pushed on to the railroad, he might possibly have seized it; but it is doubtful if he could have held it. Had he done so, it is certain that there would have been a sudden commotion in Johnston's centre at Resaca. On the evening of the 15th of May we see Sweeny once more crossing the Oostenaula, and moving towards Calhoun; but he was not strong enough to take possession of the railroad.

At sunrise the following morning the skirmishers were firing all along the line. General Sherman was intending to make a vigorous demonstration. During the night the Fourteenth Corps had moved to the ground occupied by Schofield, who in turn had moved east, thus lengthening the line. Johnston saw what was

May 15, 1864.

going on, and withdrew a portion of Hardee's and Polk's troops to reinforce Hood.

It is past noon before the demonstration begins. Butterfield's division of Hooker's corps, and Stevenson's of Hood's, are the first to clash. Instead of a demonstration it soon becomes a furious battle. Stevenson brings forward a battery to a knoll, from which he will hurl a storm of shell upon the Union army, but the sharp-shooters in blue pick off the gunners, who abandon their cannon. Through the afternoon the uproar

DRAGGING OUT THE CANNON.

goes on, the Union men gaining inch by inch, driving Stevenson, who is not able to withdraw the cannon. The Union soldiers crouch under the breastworks, holding the ground gained. Night closes over the scene, and then, under cover of the darkness, illumined by the flashing of guns, they dig away the earth and drag the captured cannon from the trenches. Through the night the intrenchments are strengthened.

General Sherman intends to make them so strong that a few troops will be able to hold them, while he withdraws the remainder of the army for the movement by Lay's Ferry to gain Johnston's rear.

Commanders of armies are often obliged to do things that are exceedingly distasteful. General Johnston had been compelled to give up his strong position at Dalton because he left a door open at Snake Creek Gap, by which Sherman outflanked him. There were no mountain passes around him at Resaca; but the Oostenaula was at his back, too deep to be forded. The Union army was moving to get in his rear, and there was but one course to pursue. He must retreat before Sherman can transfer his troops across the Oostenaula at Lay's Ferry. He must be quick about it. He must abandon all the lines of breastworks which have been thrown up, and find another position. He issues his orders accordingly. Before the sun goes down the wagon-trains are ready to move. As soon as it is dark the troops begin to withdraw, Polk's corps crossing the railroad bridge, Hardee's corps the bridge immediately above it, Hood's corps the bridge beyond the bend. Morning dawns, but no Confederate troops are at Resaca; all have gone, and the bridges are on fire.

The newspapers of the South said that Johnston was falling back to get Sherman away from his supplies, that he might utterly crush him in a great battle which would soon be fought; that Sherman would have fewer troops the farther he advanced, because he would be obliged to detach a large force to guard the railroad. Johnston, on the other hand, would be getting nearer his base of supplies, while his army would be growing stronger day by day. Governor Brown, of Georgia,

May 17, 1864.

BURNING BRIDGE AT RESACA.
From a Sketch made on the morning of May 16, 1864.

called out the militia, which would guard the railroad, while the regular troops could all be employed against Sherman. A Confederate soldier gives this picture of affairs:

"We had stacked our arms and gone into camp, and started to build fires to cook supper. I saw our cavalry falling back, I thought, rather hurriedly. I ran to the road and asked them what was the matter. They answered, 'Matter enough; yonder are the Yankees. Are you infantry fellows going to make a stand here?' I told Colonel Field what had been told to me and he hooted at the idea; but balls that had shucks tied to their tails were passing over, and our regiment was in the rear of the whole army. I could hardly draw any one's attention to the fact that the cavalry had passed us, and that we were on the outpost of the whole army, when an order came for our regiment to go forward as rapidly as possible, and occupy an octagon house in our immediate front. The Yankees were about a hundred yards from the house on one side, and we were about a hundred yards on the other. The race commenced as to which side would get to the house first. We reached it, and had barely gotten in when they were bursting down the paling of the yard on the opposite side. The house was a fine brick, octagon in shape, and as perfect a fort as could be desired. We ran to the windows, up-stairs and down-stairs, and in the cellar. The Yankees cheered and charged, and our boys got happy. Colonel Field told us he had orders to hold it until every man was killed, and never to surrender the house. It was a forlorn-hope.

"We felt we were 'gone fawn-skins' sure enough. At every discharge of our guns we would hear a Yankee squall. The boys raised a tune—

"'I'se gwine to jine the rebel band,
A-fighting for my home'—

as they loaded and shot their guns. Then the tune of—

"'Cheer, boys, cheer, we are marching on to battle!
Cheer, boys, cheer, for our sweethearts and our wives!
Cheer, boys, cheer, we'll nobly do our duty,
And give to the South our hearts, our arms, our lives.'

"Our cartridges were almost gone, and Lieut. Joe Carney, Joe Sewell, and Billy Carr volunteered to go and bring a box of a thousand cartridges. They got out of the back window, and through that hail of iron and lead made their way back with the box of cartridges. Our ammunition being renewed, the fight raged on. Capt. Joe P. Lee touched me on the shoulder and said, 'Sam, please let me have your gun for one shot.' He raised it to his shoulder and pulled down on a fine-dressed cavalry officer, and I saw that Yankee tumble. He handed it back to me to reload. About twelve o'clock, midnight, the One Hundred and Fifty-fourth Tennessee, commanded by Colonel McGevney, came to our relief.

"The firing had ceased, and we abandoned the octagon house. Our dead and wounded were there—thirty of them—in strange contrast with

THE BATTLE OF RESACA.

the furniture of the house, fine chairs, sofas, settees, pianos, and Brussels carpeting being made the death-bed of brave and noble boys, all saturated with blood; fine lace and damask curtains all blackened by the smoke of battle; fine bureaus and looking-glasses and furniture being riddled by the rude missiles of war; beautiful pictures in gilt frames, and a library of valuable books, all shot and torn by musket and cannon balls. Such is war."(*)

It is twenty-five miles due south from Resaca to Kingston, where the railroad turns east towards the little village of Cassville, the place selected by Johnston where he would fight a great battle. His engineers reported to him that that was a very strong position. He issued an order to his army, informing his soldiers that he should retreat no farther, and that they would have an opportunity to fight a decisive battle. The Union scouts obtained a copy of the order, which they brought to Sherman. General Thomas had been advancing, a portion of the Confederate troops contesting his way, but they fell back, and he finally discovered them drawn up in line of battle. It was on Sunday afternoon, May 19th, when he sent the information back to Sherman, who was delighted at the intelligence. "Come up on Thomas's right," was the order from Sherman to McPherson. Hooker and Schofield were on the left of Thomas, and advanced with him towards Cassville. Sherman rode forward to the front line, and beheld upon a swell of land a line of newly constructed earthworks. It would seem that General Sherman took pleasure in letting Johnston know that he was close at hand and ready to accept battle. It was almost night when he ordered two batteries into position to begin the cannonade. The battery was quite a distance from the Confederate lines, but the gunners elevated their pieces and the shot enfiladed the trenches. We shall presently see what came of this cannonade. Through the night the Union troops were closing in and taking position. "Attack at daylight," was the order. The soldiers, as they sat by their bivouac fires, said that there would be a battle unless the Confederates retreated. Johnston had retreated so many times that they feared he would not make a stand.

May 19, 1864.

The morning dawns, but not a Confederate soldier is to be seen at Cassville. Why has Johnston, with between sixty and seventy thousand men, so suddenly abandoned a strong position? Why has he exposed himself to be the laughing-stock of the army? At sunset on the evening of the 19th Hood was on the right, Polk in the centre, and Hardee on the left—the troops all in position, the artillery behind the breastworks—everything in readiness for the battle. No Union troops were in his rear. Sherman was making no movement to out-flank

May 20, 1864.

15

him. He had issued his order for a battle, and yet in the morning he was making haste towards Kenesaw Mountain. What was the meaning of it?

After the Confederate troops were all in position, Johnston, Hood, and Polk sat down to supper together in a house at Cassville. Johnston had nothing to eat, and was dining with Hood. "My troops are not in good position; the enemy's cannon enfilade my line," said Hood. "They also enfilade my line, and I fear I shall not be able to hold my ground," said Polk.([10])

General Johnston was astonished and irritated, for he saw that it was a criticism upon his plan. General Hood was brave and energetic, but a restless officer. He had found fault with Johnston for abandoning Resaca, and maintained that he should have fought a battle at that place. There was a long discussion. Johnston learned that Hood had a plan of his own that he wanted to carry out. Johnston believed in making a defensive fight—to stand behind his intrenchments and let Sherman make the attack. Hood, instead, wanted to take the offensive. He believed in giving blows instead of receiving them. He wanted to march with his own and part of Polk's corps and fall upon Schofield, who was five miles away from Thomas. He thought that he could defeat Schofield, drive him pell-mell to the rear, and then hasten back and get into position once more before Thomas could begin a battle. It is quite possible that Hood thought that he could repeat the tactics of Stonewall Jackson at Chancellorsville. He had ever been regarded by his fellow-officers as brave, but lacking in judgment. Johnston did not believe that any such strategy could succeed. He was irritated and angry. The newspapers of the South had been finding fault with him—had asked why he did not fight a battle. He knew that a portion of his officers had been criticising him also; and now that he was ready to fight, instead of hearty, unquestioning co-operation, Hood and Polk were opposing his plans. He accused them of having conferred together, of having lost heart, of being beaten before a battle had begun. At last he said: "I am not willing to engage in a critical battle with an army much larger than my own, with two of my corps commanders dissatisfied with my plan, and unwilling to fight upon the ground which I have chosen, or in the position which I have assigned them."([11]) He rose from the table in anger, and issued orders for the army to retreat at once. Behind him a few miles was Etowah River, beyond which was the strong position of Allatoona. Beyond Allatoona was Kenesaw, equally strong. In both places he could stand on the defensive. Couriers went with the order, and the Confederate soldiers took up the line of march towards the Etowah. It is a stream easily forded, and in the morning they were passing through the Allatoona Hills, coming once more into position on the east bank of Pumpkin-vine Creek. Morning dawned, the Union army was ready to attack, but not a Confederate soldier was to be found at Cassville.

NOTES TO CHAPTER VIII.

(1) "Memoirs of Gen. W. T. Sherman," vol. ii., p. 11.
(2) Idem., p. 22.
(3) Gen. Richard Taylor, "Destruction and Reconstruction," p. 100.
(4) S. R. Watkins, "First Tennessee Regiment," p. 111.
(5) "Memoirs of Gen. W. T. Sherman," vol. ii., p. 34.
(6) S. R. Watkins, "First Tennessee Regiment," p. 116.
(7) Dr. Johnston to Author.
(8) "Memoirs of Gen. Wm. T. Sherman," vol. ii , p. 34.
(9) S. R. Watkins, "First Tennessee Regiment," p. 129.
(10) "Memoirs of Gen. W. T. Sherman," vol. ii., p. 40.
(11) Idem.

CHAPTER IX.

NEW HOPE AND KENESAW.

THE army commanded by General Sherman had little baggage. It could pack all its camp equipage in a few moments. The commander was quick in all his movements, and had the faculty of infusing his own energy into his subordinate officers. He detailed a body of men to build bridges and repair the railroad. The Confederates, when they retreated from Resaca, burned the bridge across the Oostenaula; but in three days Colonel Wright, who had charge of the repairs of the railroad, had it rebuilt, and the cars running to Kingston, south of Resaca. Day and night the trains rolled into Kingston, and on the banks of the Etowah, on May 22d, rations for twenty days were issued, and the army once more took up its line of march. General Sherman had not been able to obtain any reliable maps of the country, and he organized an engineer corps, which soon had every road and stream platted and photographed and distributed to the officers. As fast as the army moved, additions were made and new maps issued.

May 17, 1864.

The Confederate army had retreated across the Etowah River, which rises in north-eastern Georgia, runs south, finds its way through the mountains and hills north of Allatoona, and flows on westward to Rome, where it is joined by the Oostenaula. Together they form the Coosa. It was a very strong position at Cassville from which Johnston had retreated, but he had selected another much stronger at Allatoona.

The railroad, after crossing the Etowah, runs south-east. At Allatoona there is a deep cut through a range of hills. Pumpkin-vine Creek rises amid the hills around the town of Dallas, twenty miles or more south-west of Allatoona, runs north, then north-west to the Etowah.

When General Sherman was a young man, in 1844, he rode over the country between Atlanta and Chattanooga. He was quick to see things. Through all the years he remembered the topography of the region.(¹) He thought that Johnston would be likely to select Allatoona for a defensive position, and he had no intention of advancing against it. If he

BATTLE OF NEW HOPE—ATTACK OF HOOKER'S CORPS ON THE RIGHT.

could turn Johnston's flank, Allatoona would be of no value to the Confederates.

Were we to stand on the hill near Allatoona and look south, we should see Pine Mountain, rising so beautifully and conspicuously that it is a landmark for a wide reach of country. Beyond it in the south-west is Lost Mountain standing by itself. Another beautiful mountain, Kenesaw, rises higher than either of these, from the top of which we can look many miles in all directions. It is eighteen miles from Allatoona. The town of Marietta, with its public square and shaded streets, is only three miles south of Kenesaw. This section of country was to be the second great battle-ground of the campaign. Going now south-west from Allatoona to Dallas, we find that Pumpkin-vine Creek winds through a narrow valley with steep banks. North-east of Dallas four miles is New Hope Church, where a branch of the Pumpkin-vine comes in from the south. Three miles farther on towards the north-east, upon a small stream emptying into Pumpkin-vine, is Mr. Pickett's mill. Keeping these points in mind, we shall see how Sherman laid his plans, and how Johnston met his advance. A general invading the country of an enemy must take long looks ahead. General Sherman, on the banks of the Etowah, spread out his map and studied through the night the roads along which the troops were to move. After issuing his orders, he leaned against a tree and dropped off to sleep, undisturbed by the tramping of the columns of soldiers moving past, until a soldier seeing him, said, "A pretty way we are commanded." The commander of the army heard it, and said, "My man, while you were asleep I was making my plans, and now I am taking a little nap."(²)

Sherman is on the Etowah River, about eighteen miles north of Dallas. The troops crossed the river and marched south, the Army of the Tennessee, under McPherson, away out on the right, moving towards the town of Van Wert, north-west of Dallas. The Army of the Cumberland, under Thomas, with the Twentieth Corps, under Hooker, in advance, took the road leading to Burnt Hickory. Schofield, with the Army of the Ohio, was still farther east.

Johnston quickly discovered Sherman's movement. Between Van Wert and Dallas the cavalry under General McCook captured a Confederate cavalryman who was carrying a despatch from Johnston to General Jackson, commanding the Confederate cavalry around Dallas, informing him that Sherman was marching in that direction. McCook sent the despatch to Sherman, who had ordered Hooker and Thomas to go slow, that McPherson, who had much farther to march,

May 25, 1864.

might reach Dallas before he came in collision with the enemy. McCook pushed on to see if the Confederates were advancing to head off the movement. It was three in the afternoon of May 25th when McCook reached Pumpkin-vine Creek, near Owen's mill. Confederate cavalry held the bridge, which was in flames, but McCook put out the fire. Geary's division of Hooker's corps followed the retreating Confederates towards New Hope Church. The Seventh Ohio was deployed as skirmishers, and came suddenly upon the Thirty-second and Fifty-eighth Alabama and a battalion of sharp-shooters, the whole under Colonel Jones, of Hood's corps.

"Make all the noise and resistance possible," was Hood's order to Jones.([3]) The Confederate army was on the march from Allatoona towards New Hope, but was not yet in position. Geary deployed Candy's brigade, and drove Jones back upon the other Confederate troops of General Stewart's division.

General Sherman heard the firing, hastened down to see what was going on, and directed Hooker to bring up his other divisions. It was five o'clock when Williams's division came into the fight on Geary's right, and still later when Butterfield arrived. Hood's troops were on a ridge covered with thick woods. A storm was rising at the moment in the west, the lightning flashing and thunder rolling. Up the slope rushed the men of the Twentieth Corps, to be cut down by the hot fire of Hood's men behind their breastworks. It was a gallant but fruitless attack, Hooker losing many men, Hood very few. Night settled over the scene.

General Howard, commanding the Fourth Corps, under Sherman, says: "Again and again Hooker's brave men went forward through the forest only to run upon log barricades, which were so thoroughly manned by the enemy, and so well protected by well-posted artillery, that to take them under a galling fire was impossible. This meant for Hooker a succession of bloody repulses."([4])

This General Johnston's description: "A little before six o'clock in the afternoon, Stewart's division, in front of New Hope Church, was fiercely attacked by Hooker's corps, and the action continued two hours without lull or pause, when the assailants fell back. The canister-shot of the sixteen Confederate pieces and five thousand infantry at short range must have inflicted heavy loss upon Hooker's corps."([5])

General Sherman knew, on the evening of the day of the first battle at New Hope, that the whole of Johnston's army, except a small force left at Allatoona, was marching rapidly towards that point.([6]) We can see after a battle has been fought how the movements might have been made in other directions, and possibly with better re-

May 26, 1864.

BATTLE OF NEW HOPE—ATTACK OF HOOKER'S CORPS ON THE LEFT.

NEW HOPE AND KENESAW. 235

sults. General Sherman's main object was to crush Johnston's army, and he had made the movement to New Hope to compel Johnston to give up the fortified position at Allatoona. He could not venture very far from the railroad, by which he must receive his supplies. He had cut loose from it in order to turn Johnston's flank, but must soon return to it. If Sherman, on the evening of the 25th, had issued an order for the army to turn north-east and make a rapid march through the night, while Johnston was marching south-west, the morning of the 26th would have seen Schofield and Thomas on the right flank of Johnston. Getting between him and the railroad, in the direction of Ackworth, McPherson would have been close at hand. The movement would have compelled Johnston either to attack Sherman on ground of Sherman's choosing, or hasten to secure the lines in front of Kenesaw. At sunset Schofield was only six miles

ACKWORTH STATION.
From a Sketch made May, 1864.

distant, Thomas nine miles, and McPherson's advance only twelve miles from the nearest point on the railroad, three miles south of Allatoona. At the same time Hood and Polk were twelve miles and Hardee ten miles south-west of Ackworth, the nearest point.

Instead of such a movement, the Union troops moved on towards Pumpkin-vine, the Fourth Corps under Howard coming in upon Hooker's left, while Davis's and Palmer's divisions of the Fourteenth came upon

Hooker's right. McPherson marched through Dallas, the Sixteenth Corps under Dodge continuing the line to the left of Davis, and the Fifteenth under Logan reaching still farther to the south, with the cavalry under Garrard covering the flank. Schofield, with the Army of the Ohio, was marching towards Owen's mill, to come in on the left of Howard. Stoneman's division of cavalry was covering the left flank of the army.

At daybreak Sherman was sitting on the log beside which he had slept, drawing a map. The army, after a night's march in the rain, was in position, the troops at work building intrenchments.(¹) The artillery on both sides opened fire, and the pickets began a fusillade, which was to go on almost without cessation for several days. McPherson was confronted by Hardee, and the lines were so close that not an officer or soldier could show his head without a rattling fire along the line. A skilful general never will attack a strong position in front if he can get round it. Sherman had made his intrenchments so strong that he could hold them with a portion of his troops, while he made the attempt to gain Johnston's right flank with the remainder. He withdrew Wood's division of Howard's corps, Johnson's of Palmer's, and McLean's brigade of Schofield's, and moved them north-east towards Pickett's mill, which is on a branch of Pumpkin-vine Creek.

May 27, 1864.

The movement was through thick woods. General Howard thought that he had gone far enough to gain the flank of the Confederates, and turned south. What he supposed to be the right flank of the Confederate line was an angle instead. It was a costly mistake. Hazen's and Scribner's brigades led the attack, to find cannon flaming in their faces and musketry cutting them down.

The Confederates had seen the movement. "Howard's corps is on my right. I have extended my own lines as far as I can, and need reinforcements," was the message sent by Hood to Johnston. Cleburne's division was placed under Hood to act as he should order. Cleburne was directed to form his troops in a column of brigades in the rear of Hindman's division. The Union cavalry scouts had seen what they thought was the extreme right of the Confederate line, but they had not seen the column of brigades standing behind Hindman. It was this that had deceived Howard, who suddenly found himself confronted by Cleburné on ground which the cavalry had reported as all clear. When Howard faced south and marched to strike Hindman, Cleburne quickly changed front, and stood a solid wall of men, with batteries in an advantageous position.

It was five o'clock in the afternoon when the battle began. General Hazen led Howard's advance, driving the Confederate skirmishers into

THE BATTLE OF PICKETT'S MILL.
From a Sketch made at the time.

their intrenchments. Johnson's division was on the left of Hazen, and swept round by Pickett's mill. Scribner's brigade had the advance in Johnson's division. It was on the east bank of the little stream, when a volley was poured down upon the brigade. Scribner halted, changed front, crossed the stream, and returned the fire. General Wood was still farther on the left, and also received a terrific volley with a storm of shell. Through a mistake, McLean's brigade did not come up on Wood's flank to protect it, and Wood was obliged to fall back.

From five o'clock till after dark the battle went on. The artillery all along the lines on both sides sent their missiles into the intrenchments. Newton and Stanley, of Howard's corps, made a feint of advancing. Out on the left, Cox's and Hascall's divisions of Schofield's corps swung south against the Confederate cavalry under Wheeler, which fought as infantry. The Confederate commander, General Johnston, says of the attack: "The enemy came on in deep order and assailed the Texans with great vigor, receiving their close and accurate fire with great fortitude, such as is always exhibited by General Sherman's troops in the actions of this campaign. The contest with Granberry was a very fierce one. The enemy left hundreds of corpses within twenty paces of the Confederate lines."(ª)

Till past ten o'clock the battle went on, Howard falling back under a charge of the Confederates a short distance, but holding a position much in advance of the ground of the morning. There had been a loss of fully fifteen hundred men. The attack was not well planned. The troops were massed in brigades, one behind another, in thick woods, which was a mistake, as Howard, Sherman, and every other officer soon discovered. The rear lines, under such a formation in the woods, could take no part in the fight without firing upon those in the front line.

The engagement is known as the battle of Pickett's Mill. Lieutenant-general Johnston has given this record of the bravery of the Union troops which fought Granberry's brigade of Texans: "When the United States troops paused in their advance within fifteen paces of the Texan front rank, one of their color-bearers planted his colors eight or ten feet in front of his regiment and was instantly shot dead; a soldier sprang forward to his place, and fell also as he grasped the color-staff; a second and third followed successively, and each received his death as speedily as his predecessors; a fourth, however, seized and bore back the object of soldierly devotion."(')

General Bate held the left of the Confederate army, and was directed to ascertain by a forced reconnoissance whether or not the Union troops were still behind their intrenchments. The Confederates advanced upon Logan's corps. Harrow's division held the right, Morgan L. Smith's the centre, and Osterhaus's the left. Smith was on the road leading from Dallas to Marietta. Three of the cannon of the First Iowa Battery were on the skirmish line in an advantageous position. The Union skirmishers saw Bate's division of Confederates appear on the crest of the ridge, and then descend the slope, advancing rapidly. The three guns opened upon them; the rattle of the skirmishers' muskets began. Men dropped in the Confederate ranks, but the lines moved on. No Union infantry had been sent forward to support the three guns. In a twinkling, almost, the Confederates were laying hold of the cannon, but could not use them, for the artillerymen carried off the rammers in their retreat.

The Confederates gave a cheer and charged upon Walcott's brigade of Harrow's division. Instantly a line of light streamed from the Union intrenchments, and the Confederate line melted like lead in a crucible. On came the other divisions of Hardee's corps, attacking with great spirit. General Logan rode along the lines, waving his hat and encouraging the men, who responded with a cheer. For a time the battle raged fiercely, but the Confederates were repulsed with heavy loss. It has been called the battle of Dallas.

The cannon on both sides were thundering, and the muskets of the pickets flashing, but no attempt was made on either side to flank or charge the other. The lines were so near that no soldier could lift his head above the breastwork without being fired upon. When night came, and darkness settled over the scene, the men rose from the ground and cooked their supper. Suddenly all the Confederate batteries opened, and the landscape was illumined by the cannon-flashes. Sherman's cannon replied, and for two hours the thunder of the cannonade rolled over hill and dale, forest and field, sending its reverberation far away to Lost Mountain and Kenesaw. The fire was so terrific, and such a storm of shot and shell was hurled from the Union and Confederate guns, that the soldiers changed the name of New Hope to Hell Hole.

May 29, 1864.

On the afternoon of May 30th General Sherman, General Logan, General McPherson, General Barry, and Colonel Taylor were standing together, when a minie-bullet passed through the sleeve of Logan's coat, and struck Colonel Taylor in the breast, who fell, not killed, but disabled from further service.

May 30, 1864.

General Sherman's supplies were running short. The time had come for a new movement which should bring the army nearer to the railroad. The cavalry under General Stoneman had already seized Allatoona, and

GENERAL LOGAN CHEERING HIS MEN.

NEW HOPE AND KENESAW. 243

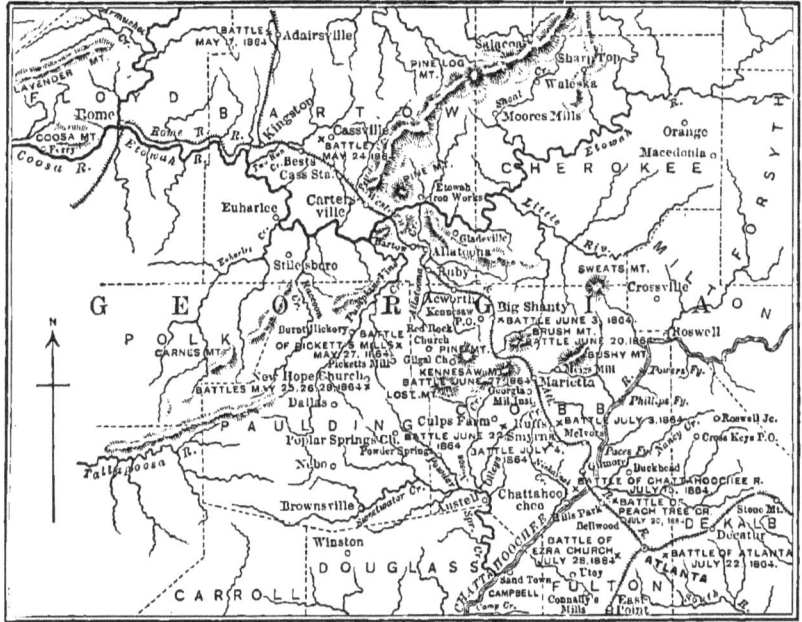

FROM RESACA TO KENESAW.

Sherman could reach the railroad at Ackworth. Johnston saw that he would be powerless to stop such a movement and that he must fall back to a new position. During the night of June 3d the Confederates filed out from their strong intrenchments and took up their line of march towards the works already thrown up by gangs of slaves at Lost Mountain and northward of Kenesaw. With great bravery they had held the lines at New Hope, which was no longer a new hope to them; for thousands in the Confederate ranks were beginning to see that theirs was a hopeless cause, and were asking why such a sacrifice of life, for what were they fighting? Some of them with clearing vision saw that in reality they were not fighting for any great principle of right, but for the perpetuation of slavery, and they cursed those who began the war. Every day there were desertions from the Confederate ranks, those on picket throwing down their guns and entering the Union lines.

June 7, 1864.

The month of May had been delightful, but rain began to fall. The soldiers of General Sherman and the Confederate army alike suffered. The roads were almost impassable. Reinforcements came to the Union army — two divisions of the Seventeenth Corps, under General Blair.

Their arrival made good the losses, so that the army still numbered nearly one hundred thousand. A portion of the Union troops were at Big Shanty. Looking south, they could see the Confederate signal-flags waving on the summits of Lost, Pine, and Kenesaw mountains, and long lines of intrenchments. The officers, with their glasses, could see cannon in position. The intrenchments thrown up by the slave gangs were ten miles in length, extending east to the railroad, and west to the carriage road leading from Marietta to New Hope.

June 1, 1864.

General Sherman was advancing, with McPherson on the railroad. Thomas west of it, and Schofield beyond Thomas, moving towards Lost Mountain. Colonel Wright was so energetic in building bridges and repairing the railroad that he soon had a train of cars rumbling into Big Shanty, and the engineer, uncoupling the engine, ran down the road to a water-tank near the skirmish line. The Confederate artillery on Kenesaw opened fire with their long-range rifled guns, and the shot and shell came crashing through the trees and around the locomotive; but the engineer kept on filling the tank, then tooted his whistle, and went back to Big Shanty, the soldiers waving their hats and cheering him.

General Sherman was standing with General Howard in front of Pine Mountain, reconnoitring the Confederate lines to see where he could best attack them. He noticed a battery on the crest of the mountain, and a line of intrenchments, and a group of officers around the guns, looking through their glasses.

June 14, 1864.

"Open fire upon them with one of your batteries, and make them keep under cover," he said to General Howard.

"General Thomas wishes me to be sparing of my artillery ammunition," was the reply.

"That, as a general rule, is all right, but I wish to keep up a vigorous offensive. By using your artillery you will make the enemy timid. Let one of your batteries give three volleys."([10])

General Sherman knew that six cannon sending that number of shells at once into the group, and twice repeated, would be far more effective than if the cannon were fired separately. The gunners of Simonson's Indiana Battery loaded their cannon. The Confederate officers were General Johnston, General Hardee, and General Polk, with their staffs. General Bate's division of Hardee's corps held the intrenchments, and the soldiers gathered around their generals with the freedom characteristic of the Southern soldiers. It was a large group, and to Simonson's gunners seemed like the clustering of bees upon the side of a hive on a midsummer day. They calculated the distance, and elevated the muzzles of the

BATTLE OF DALLAS—ATTACK ON HARROW'S DIVISION.

guns to send the shells into the group. General Johnston was looking through his glass, and could see the gunners preparing to open fire.

"Go to your positions. They are getting ready to fire!" he exclaimed, and himself hastened behind the intrenchments.

General Polk was very dignified. He came from a family which prided itself on its dignity. His brother was President of the United States from 1845 to 1849. When the war began he was a bishop in the Episcopal Church and wore his robes with much dignity. He was stout in person and walked slowly, and never had been known to hurry. General Bragg found fault with him at Chickamauga because he was slow in getting into action. He was brave, and had been in many battles where the bullets were singing around him. He walked slowly towards the breastworks. Possibly he wished to let the soldiers see that he was in no hurry. Simonson's six guns all flashed at the same instant. The shells screamed through the air and tore across the Confederate earthworks.

WHERE GENERAL POLK FELL.
From a Sketch made in 1864.

General Polk did not hasten; he partially turned, as if to see where they came from. Again the cannon flashed, and a shell struck him in the breast. A moment before he was in the vigor of life; now the soldiers beheld a mangled body, his life-blood crimsoning the yellow earth. He had been educated at West Point Military Academy by the United States, but at the outset of the Rebellion had laid aside the robes of his high calling, left the service of the Church, accepted a commission from Jefferson Davis as major-general, had been a believer in the doctrine that the rights of a State are superior to those of the nation, yet he invaded Kentucky and seized Columbus, thus violating the theory of State rights. He did it without orders from the President of the Confederacy, who afterwards sent this telegram: "The necessity justifies the action." He had done what he could for the establishment of a government based on slavery, but his work was ended. A Union signal-officer on the roof of a shed sheltering a cotton-gin, and watching the waving of the Confederate signal-flags, who had studied them till he had discovered the key, read the despatch waved to Marietta, "Send an ambulance for the body of General Polk." A Confederate soldier wrote this about him: "He was looking through his field-glass when a shot struck him in his left breast, passing through his body and his heart. I saw him while the infirmary corps were bringing him from the field. He was as white as a piece of marble. Every private soldier loved him. Second to Stonewall Jackson, his loss was the greatest the South ever sustained."(")

On the morning of the 15th General Sherman was ready to attack Pine Mountain, but when daylight came the Confederates had disappeared. Johnston saw that his lines were too long, that they could be easily flanked. Sherman's troops pushed on and captured many prisoners —those who had been asleep and did not know that the army had gone. Johnston also concluded to give up Lost Mountain and make Kenesaw his line. Sherman pushed on. He organized a brigade of shovellers, employing the negroes who flocked into his camp, setting them to building intrenchments, thus relieving the soldiers. The negroes were paid ten dollars a month and their rations.

We are to keep in mind the fact that the war was a conflict between two systems of labor. We have the spectacle of General Johnston employing gangs of slaves, impressed into service from their owners to build his intrenchments. He was careful to keep them beyond the range of the Union guns, because they were property, and valuable to their owners; and the other spectacle of negroes, who a few weeks before had been slaves, earning wages under the Stars and Stripes.

The springs which ooze from the ground at the northern end of Kenesaw form Noonday Creek, which runs north to the Etowah River, while those which bubble up at the southern end of the mountain form Noses Creek, which flows south to the Chattahoochee. The banks of Noonday Creek are covered with thick woods. The Confederate cavalry under General Wheeler held the east bank, while General Garrard, with a division of Union cavalry, occupied the west bank. Garrard kept a sharp lookout, expecting that Wheeler would march north-east, and come round upon Cassville and destroy the railroad. Sherman had a force at Resaca which

DESERTERS ENTERING THE UNION LINES.

he brought down to that point, and also a brigade under Gen. John E. Smith from Huntsville, Alabama.

If Johnston thought of making such a movement it was not attempted. The Confederate line extended from Noonday Creek across the railroad, over the top of Kenesaw, over the rugged hill south of Kenesaw, then along the east bank of Noses Creek to the road which leads from Marietta

UNION SIGNAL-STATION ON PINE MOUNTAIN LOOKING TOWARDS KENESAW.

to Powder Springs. It was twelve miles long. Next to Dalton, it was the strongest position of the campaign. Along the entire line there were breastworks which had been thrown up by the slaves. At the foot of Kenesaw there was a line of rifle-pits; half-way up, a strong line of intrenchments, with a third line on top. The artillery would sweep every part of the ground. General Loring was appointed to the command of

Polk's corps, which held Kenesaw, from the top of which the Confederate soldiers could overlook all the surrounding country and detect Sherman's movements. General Johnston could spread out his map on the top of the mountain, and, by noticing the smoke rising here and there, locate the exact positions of the divisions of the Union army.

French's division of Loring's corps held the south-western side of the mountain; Walthal's the summit and north-eastern slope down to the railroad: Hood was east of the railroad, on the hill overlooking Noonday Creek; Hardee held the line west of Marietta, along Noses Creek; Walker's division joined French's; then came Bate's, Cleburne's, and Cheatham's. In the last retreat Johnston swung his left flank back eight miles, while Hood had fallen back only two. The line was thus in the form of a semicircle.

From the 1st to the 19th of June it had rained every day. Noonday and Noses creeks were torrents, overflowing their banks and covering the lowlands. The roads, cut up by the wheels of Johnston's wagons, were impassable. Sherman was obliged to make new ones. McPherson moved along the railroad with the Seventeenth Corps, under Blair, on the extreme left, next to Garrard's cavalry; then came the Fourteenth Corps, under Logan; then the Sixteenth Corps, under Dodge. The Army of the Cumberland fronted Kenesaw, the Fourteenth Corps, under Palmer, holding the left against the south-western slope; then the Fourth Corps, under Howard, whose centre was on the road leading from Gilgal Church to Marietta. When Schofield reached Noses Creek his skirmishers found the meadow overflowed. The Confederates had taken the planks from the bridge, and the water was sweeping over the stringers. On the hill east of the stream was a battery, while along the bushes lay the Confederate sharp-shooters.

June 19, 1864.

General Schofield placed a battery on a knoll, and opened fire. General Cameron's brigade of Schofield's corps advanced, and the One Hundred and Third Ohio dashed through the water, crossed the creek on the stringers, and rushed up the bank, driving the Confederate skirmishers. The Confederate battery limbered up and retreated to the higher ground in the rear. A few minutes later Cameron's brigade and Cox's whole division were across the creek. From the top of Kenesaw Johnston could see that Schofield and the Twentieth Corps, under Hooker, were threatening to turn his left flank towards Marietta. He resolved to make a bold movement. Hood was east of Kenesaw; he would transfer him from the extreme right to the extreme left, and strike Schofield a sudden blow. Night came. Hood left his intrenchments, marched south-west through the town of Marietta, going out past the Georgia Military Institute and Zion Church. General Loring strung out his men along the earthworks which Hood had evacuated. General Wheeler was instructed to make as much noise as he could in front of McPherson. At daylight Hood was at Zion Church, north-east of Mr. Culp's farm. Hindman's and Stevenson's divisions were in the front line, with Stewart's in support. The men were weary with the night's march, and it was mid-afternoon before Johnston was ready to strike the blow which he fondly hoped would crush Schofield and Hooker.

While Hood was making his march Schofield had been changing his position, Hascall's division coming into position on Hooker's right on Culp's farm, with Cox's division at the forks of the road near Mr. Cheney's house, two miles farther south. Going north from Schofield, we see Williams's division of Hooker's corps joining Hascall; then Geary's, with Butterfield's in support. Hooker's pickets captured a prisoner.

"Whose corps do you belong to?"

"Hood's."

This was important news, for at sunset Hood was east of Kenesaw.

"Hood is getting ready to attack you," said the prisoner.

"Deploy your divisions, and throw up intrenchments," was the order of Hooker.

The men threw down their muskets and went to work with shovels and axes, cutting down trees and piling logs. It was a little after three o'clock when a line of gleaming bayonets was seen in the fields and pastures on both sides of the road west of Zion Church.

The Confederates advanced rapidly, striking Geary and Williams. Instantly the Thirteenth New York Battery, Captain Winegar, and Captain Woodbury's battery of 12-pounders, opened fire. The shells made sad havoc in their ranks, but the Confederates pushed bravely on. A little nearer, and the line of partly finished breastworks was a sheet of flame. Hood's left came against Hascall, who had sent out the Fourteenth Kentucky as skirmishers. Their fire was so deadly that the next morning sixty Confederate dead were found lying where they delivered their volleys. Colonel Galloup, the commander of the regiment, held the ground stubbornly, but fell back under orders to the intrenchments that the artillery might begin firing. The Nineteenth Ohio and Sixth Michigan batteries used canister, and the slaughter of the Confederates was terrible. It was a bravely executed but ill-judged attack. No one will ever know how many were killed and wounded. General Johnston admitted that more than one thousand fell in the few minutes of the struggle. The Union loss was less than three hundred. Instead of crushing Hooker and Schofield, Hood fell back towards Zion Church with his lines in disorder. To cover the attack Johnston ordered the artillery to open all along the line, and so for the entire distance of twelve miles the cannon of both armies were thundering.

We come to June 26th. The two armies were behind strong intrenchments. What should General Sherman do? The mud was so deep that he could not make any flanking movement, nor had he sufficient supplies to do so. The troops farthest from the railroad had scant rations. He came to the conclusion that if a bold attack were to be made along the entire line, a weak place might be found where he could break through. He resolved to make the attempt.

June 26, 1864.

During the night, the troops were placed in position, but as soon as day dawns, June 27th, the Confederates on Kenesaw could see what changes had been made in the Union lines. There was no long waiting. The Union artillery began the battle by sending a storm of missiles into the Confederate lines; Johnston's guns responded, and such a racket never before was heard along the hills of Kenesaw. As daylight streamed up the east, Cox's division, south-west of Marietta, advanced. Reilly's and Cameron's brigades made a vigorous attack, drove the Confederates, and secured an advantageous position on the ridge east of Olley's Creek, which runs south-west of, and parallel with, Nickajack Creek. It was a great gain. From that position the artillery could send shells across Nickajack Creek almost into Marietta.

June 27, 1864.

While Cox's division was advancing, the battle opened all along the line. McPherson's artillery was directing its fire against Kenesaw. Howard's and Palmer's corps of the Army of the Cumberland moved together. A terribly destructive fire burst upon them. The soldiers reached the abatis in front of the Confederate lines. They were amid fallen trees; they came upon a line of sharpened stakes. They could go no farther, but lay down, many of them never to rise again. The advantage was all on the side of the Confederates. But through the day the Union troops remained there, keeping up a steady fire. When night came they went to work with shovels, and threw up intrenchments, holding the ground gained by such a fearful sacrifice of life. Smith's division crossed Noses Creek, and advanced against the rocky sides of the hill, which the soldiers called Little Kenesaw. The Fifteenth Corps, under Logan, attacked Featherstone's division of Loring's corps. The Confederate sharp-shooters killed and wounded in Logan's corps seven officers commanding regiments. One of them (Colonel Bunhill, of the Fortieth Illinois) was within a few feet of the intrenchments when he fell.

KENESAW FROM LITTLE KENESAW.

General Palmer's corps almost pierced the Confederate line, but General Cheatham, seeing the danger, hurried up a brigade in reserve, and forced back the Union troops. General Sherman had selected three points where he thought it possible to break through. The Confederates could see just where he was massing his troops, and could hurry their soldiers from one point to another to resist him. No advantage was gained by the attempt other than on the right by Olley's Creek. Night beheld the two armies behind strong breastworks. But it was a sickening scene where the ambulance corps were gathering up the wounded, their torches and lanterns casting a lurid light upon the trees, green with midsummer foliage, and the bleeding forms beneath. It is the scene after a battle that dispels

MARIETTA, 1864.
From a Sketch made at the time.

the illusion of the pomp and glory of war. After such a sacrifice of life the soldiers asked the question, "What is all this for?" They knew that it was not for glory; not that they wanted to fight; not that they had any hatred towards their opponents; but that this government of the people should not be destroyed, and a government based on slavery set up on its ruins.

It would have been far better if General Sherman had not ordered the assault. The Confederate army was in a very strong position, and was larger than at the beginning of the campaign. The returns for June 10th show that there were 71,000 Confederate officers and men present for

17

duty, and that there were 187 cannon.([12]) At the battle of New Hope the Confederate army numbered 75,000; the Union army, 93,600.([13]) By flanking movements General Sherman had compelled General Johnston to give up Dalton, Resaca, and the line of Pumpkin-vine Creek; a movement southward of Kenesaw would have compelled Johnston to retire from the strong position from which he could not be dislodged by direct assault.

Gangs of slaves, and ten thousand old men and boys who had been ordered into service by Governor Brown of Georgia, were hard at work throwing up intrenchments at Smyrna, six miles south of Marietta.([14]) Another party was building fortifications along the Chattahoochee River, while down by Atlanta a third gang was building forts and a line of fortifications around that city, where there were rolling-mills, machine-shops, and a great supply of military stores. General Johnston knew that although the direct assault of Sherman had failed, the position which General Schofield had secured south-west of Marietta would enable the Union army to reach the railroad south of that place, and that sooner or later he must give up Kenesaw.

Schofield's pickets during the night could hear trains rumbling southward, and came to the conclusion that Johnston was getting ready to abandon his strong position. General Sherman, however, could not move without supplies. Nearly every day rain had fallen; wagons could hardly move. Day and night trains came to Big Shanty bringing supplies; but before they were received and distributed, the Confederate troops, under cover of the night, filed down from Kenesaw, and abandoned Marietta.

June 28, 1864.

The Union pickets, as day dawned, looking towards the line of Confederate works, saw that they were deserted. Swiftly the word ran along the lines. General Sherman ordered General Garrard, commanding a division of cavalry, to make swift pursuit, and many stragglers from Johnston's army were picked up. With bands playing, drums beating, and colors waving in the morning breeze, the army entered Marietta, marching through the public square. It was one of the most beautiful towns in Georgia, pleasantly situated, with many elegant residences. Before the war, on market-days, a great crowd of teams loaded with cotton were to be seen in the spacious streets. When the thunder of the cannonade at New Hope and Dallas reverberated over hill and vale, the people, by riding to the top of Kenesaw and looking westward, could see the battle-clouds rising above the dark-green woodlands, and some of them, fearing what might happen — that the Union army might reach Marietta — packed up what goods they could, and hastened to Atlanta.

July 3, 1864.

When the terrible conflict raged around Kenesaw, when shot and shell from the Union cannon aimed at the Confederate batteries on the top of the mountain began to fall in the streets, there was a hurrying of men, women, and children away to the country. Little had the people of the South imagined, in 1861, when they advocated the secession of the State, when they welcomed the formation of the Confederacy, that the sound of Union cannon would ever echo from Kenesaw, as on the morning of July 4th—anniversary of the Independence of the United States; that a victorious army would be marching through Marietta. To the people of that town, flying from their homes, it was a sad and mournful day.

NOTES TO CHAPTER IX.

(1) "Memoirs of Gen. W. T. Sherman," vol. ii., p. 42.
(2) Gen. O. O. Howard, *Century Magazine*, July, 1887.
(3) Gen. J. B. Hood's Report.
(4) Gen. O. O. Howard, *Century Magazine*, July, 1887.
(5) Gen. J. E. Johnston, *Century Magazine*, August, 1887.
(6) "Memoirs of Gen. W. T. Sherman," vol. ii., p. 44.
(7) Idem.
(8) Gen. J. E. Johnston, "Narrative of Military Events," p. 330.
(9) Idem.
(10) "Memoirs of Gen. W. T. Sherman," vol. ii., p. 53.
(11) S. R. Watkins, "First Tennessee Regiment," p. 138.
(12) E. C. Dawes, *Century Magazine*, December, 1887.
(13) Idem.
(14) Gen. J. E. Johnston, "Narrative of Military Events," pp. 345–347.

CHAPTER X.

THE VALLEY OF THE SHENANDOAH.

VERY beautiful is the valley of the Shenandoah, with its green fields, rich pastures, and verdant woodlands, bounded by the Blue Ridge on the east and a succession of mountain ranges on the west. The fertile farms yield luxuriant harvests of wheat and corn. Millwheels plash in the silver streams gurgling down from the mountains. In no section of the South was there before the war more comfort and prosperity than in this peaceful valley.

From its topographical features it became, in a military point of view, a region of great importance alike to Union and Confederate commanders. From Winchester, the most important town, General Johnston had marched across the Blue Ridge, in 1861, to join Beauregard upon the field of Bull Run, and win the first great battle of the war.

In 1862 Stonewall Jackson had compelled General Banks to make a hasty retreat to Harper's Ferry. After Antietam, General Lee retreated to the Rapidan, behind its sheltering mountain walls. In advancing to Gettysburg his troops marched over its macadamized roads, screened from the observation of Union scouts by the Blue Ridge, with its passes held by the Confederate cavalry. His retreat was over the same highways. Union and Confederate armies in succession, like the ebbing and flowing of the tides of the ocean in an estuary, had swept through the valley, each helping themselves to wheat and corn from the granaries of the people. When General Grant assumed command of all the armies he found General Sigel in command of the Department of West Virginia, whose headquarters were near Winchester. A portion of the troops in the department were in the valley of the Kanawha, commanded by General Crook. General Grant, while advancing with the Army of the Potomac against General Lee, with Butler menacing Richmond from the south, directed Sigel to advance up the Shenandoah and threaten the Virginia Central Railroad at Staunton, while Crook was to destroy the East Tennessee Railroad, also the salt-works at the town of Saltville, where great kettles had been placed, and which were bubbling and steaming night and day to furnish salt for the curing of meat for the Confederate armies.

General Averill, with two thousand cavalry, started from Charleston, West Virginia. His line of march was to be over mountain ranges, and through narrow valleys, along winding roads. He had no cannon and very few wagons. After five days' marching he learned that there was a Confederate force with several cannon at Saltville, and he decided not to attempt its capture, but to march to Wytheville, where there were lead-works. When he reached that town he found that the Confederates, learning of his movement, had been whirled over

May 1, 1864.

DESTROYING THE EAST TENNESSEE RAILROAD BRIDGE.

the railroad from Saltville, and outnumbered him. Instead of attacking, he himself was assailed and obliged to retreat. He stole away in the night, made a swift march eastward to Christiansburg, where he tore up a portion of the railroad, burned the repair-shops, and then made all haste to join General Crook, who was marching eastward up the Kanawha valley. General Crook had three brigades—one commanded by Col. Rutherford B. Hayes, of Ohio, since then President of the United States; the second by Colonel White, the third by Colonel Sickel. He had four hundred cavalry—in all, six thousand men, with twelve cannon. Starting from the town of Fayette and marching south, he reached Cloyd's Mountain, where he was confronted by a large force of Confederates, under Generals Jones and Jenkins, behind breastworks, with cannon planted to sweep the fields in front of them. To attack them in front, the Union soldiers must cross a brook where the water was knee-

May 8, 1864.

deep, climb a steep hill, with Confederate sharp-shooters behind rifle-pits ready to pick off the men. General Crook could see the lines of intrenchments, the bank of yellow earth, the Confederate soldiers and cannon. He looked a long while. "It is a strong position. He may whip us, but I guess not," he said.(¹)

His troops were in thick woods and screened by the fresh green foliage. White's brigade, with two of Sickel's, stole round upon the Confederate right, and opened a vigorous fire. When the rolls of musketry began to break upon the morning air, the troops remaining in the woods waded the brook, rushed up the bank, charged across the fields, leaped over the intrenchments, capturing between two and three hundred prisoners and two cannon. While the escaping Confederates were streaming along the fields a train of cars came down the railroad from the west, bringing reinforcements from Saltville. Those fleeing rallied, but were again put to flight. The Union troops moved on to New River, where they found the Confederates, holding the bridge across that stream; but once more they were obliged to flee. The Union troops set the bridge on fire. General Crook, having accomplished what he set out to do, returned to the town of Union.

General Sigel, with a small force, partly composed of German troops— in all, about four thousand men—was at Winchester, guarding the lower end of the valley. General Grant directed him to advance up the valley for the purpose of attracting the attention of the Confederates while General Crook executed his movement. General Sigel was moving towards New Market, his troops scattered, when he suddenly found himself confronted by a Confederate force.

New Market is on the valley turnpike. The north fork of the Shenandoah winds northward west of the town, and Smith's Creek runs in the same direction east of it. A road leads due east from New Market, crosses Smith's Creek, ascends the slope of Massanutten Mountain, and goes on to Luray, where, since the war, wonderful caves have been discovered.

May 15, 1864.

General Breckinridge had advanced from Staunton with the brigades of Generals Echols and Wharton, old soldiers who had fought many battles. He had also two hundred and fifty cadets from the Virginia Military Institute at Lexington, which was established in 1839, and which had been well cared for by the State before the war. Many men who distinguished themselves in the Confederate army graduated from this institution. Stonewall Jackson was one of its professors at the outbreak of the struggle. It was a noble battalion which marched northward to join

Breckinridge. Some of the veteran soldiers, wearing clothes colored with butternut bark, laughed at the boys in their cadet uniforms, and derisively sang, "Rock-a-bye baby," and asked them if they wanted rosewood coffins, lined with satin.([2])

Rain fell, swelling the streams and saturating the ground. The newly ploughed fields around New Market were sticky with mud, and the soldiers of both armies sank ankle-deep in attempting to march.

May 15, 1864. Colonel Moor, with the One Hundred and Twenty-third Ohio, Eighteenth Connecticut, and Twenty-fourth Massachusetts, was in the advance. At nightfall he came upon small parties of Confederates, and cavalrymen riding in informed him that a large force was not far away. At daybreak on the morning of the 15th Sigel's force was widely scattered, the main part being two miles distant from Colonel Moor. The Confederates had advanced from New Market, starting at midnight. No bugle had sounded, no drum had been beaten; the order to advance as noiselessly as was possible had been obeyed.

"I do not wish to put the cadets in if I can avoid it, but if occasion calls I shall use them freely," said General Breckinridge to Colonel Skip, commanding the striplings from the Institute.([3])

General Breckinridge formed his lines with Wharton's brigade in front, and Echols's and the cadets two hundred and fifty paces in the rear. Imboden, commanding the cavalry, was to go down Smith Creek, and gain Sigel's left flank and rear. It was Sunday morning, but there was no gathering of worshippers in the little church of New Market, no bell sending its resounding tones over the valley; but

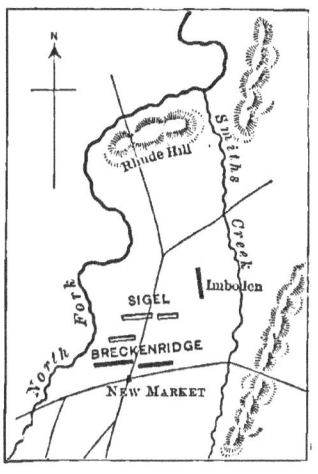

BATTLE OF NEW MARKET.

cannon, instead, opened their brazen lips amid the white head-stones of the cemetery. Through the morning the skirmishers of both armies were engaged, but it was past noon when the battle began by the advance of Breckinridge's troops. A Confederate officer gives this account:

"Wharton's line advanced; Echols's followed at two hundred and fifty paces in the rear. As Wharton's ascended a knoll it came in full view of the enemy's batteries, which opened a heavy fire, but not having gotten the range, did but little damage. By the time the second line reached the same ground they had gotten the exact range, and the fire began to tell upon our lines with fearful accuracy. It was here that Captain Hill and others fell. Great gaps were made through the ranks, but the cadet, true to his discipline, would close in to the centre to fill the interval, and push steadily forward. The alignment of the battalion under this terrible fire, which strewed the ground with killed and wounded for more than a mile on open ground, would have been creditable even on a field-day."(⁴)

A Confederate cadet portrays the scene: "Away off to the right is Luray Gap, of the Massanutten range. Our signal-corps was telegraphing the position and numbers of the enemy. Our cavalry was moving at a gallop to the cover of the creek, to attempt to flank the town. Echols's brigade was moving from the pike at the double-quick by the right flank, and went into line of battle across the meadows, the left resting on the pike. Out of the orchards and meadows arose puff after puff of blue smoke as our sharp-shooters advanced, the 'pop,' 'pop' of the rifles ringing forth exultingly. Thundering down the pike came McLaughlin with his artillery, and, whirling out into the meadows, let fly with all his guns. . . . Down the green slope we went, answering the wild cry of our comrades as their musketry rattled its opening volleys. In another moment we should expect a pelting rain of lead from the blue line crouching behind a stone wall at the base. Then came a sound more stunning than thunder, that burst directly in my face; lightnings leaped, fire flashed, earth rocked, the sky whirled round, and I stumbled. My gun pitched forward, and I fell upon my knees. Sergeant Cabell looked back at me sternly, pityingly, and called out, 'Close up, men!' as he passed on. I knew no more. When consciousness returned, it was raining in torrents. I was lying on the ground, which was torn and ploughed with shell, which were still screeching in the air and bounding on the earth. Poor little Captain Hill was lying near, bathed in blood, with a fearful gash over the temple. Reed, Merritt, and another, also badly shot, were near at hand. The battalion was three hundred yards away, clouded in smoke and hotly engaged, and the Federal battery in the graveyard had fallen back to higher ground."(⁵)

Colonel Moor, with the front line of the Union troops, had fallen back to join Colonel Thoburn's brigade. They had vigorously withstood the Confederate onset, but had been overlapped on both flanks. Upon an eminence north of the town stood the Union troops. From the outset the Confederates had the advantage in numbers, they also knew from the Signal Corps, who were waving their flags on the summit of Massanutten, the exact position and number of Sigel, who was ignorant of the movement of Imboden, stealing down through the woods along the east bank of Smith Creek to gain his rear. Imboden crossed the creek at the Luray bridge, moved west, and came upon Sigel's flank. At the same moment Wharton and Echols and the cadets—the entire Confederate force—moved forward. Imboden had two cannon, which opened upon the Union cavalry covering Sigel's flank. Though thus attacked the Union troops fought bravely. From three o'clock till past six the battle went on, when the Union troops fell back, in such order that though Sigel had lost five cannon, he was able to save all his wagons and supplies.

A Confederate officer in his official report says: "Sigel's entire line retired slowly. His artillery was especially damaging, and Breckinridge determined to silence the most mischievous battery directly in front of the centre of his line, and Colonel Smith, of the Sixty-second Virginia, and Colonel Wise with his cadets, were ordered to charge and take it. The battery was taken, but with fearful loss on both sides. . . . The Sixty-second lost 241 killed and wounded, including seven of ten captains. The cadets lost 69 out of 250."([4])

A Union officer gives this account: "Our front fire was heavy, and the artillery had an enfilading fire under which their first line went down. The Confederates staggered, went back, and their whole advance halted. Their fire ceased to be effective. A cheer ran along our line, and the first success was over. I gave the order to cease firing. Just then Colonel Thoburn, brigade commander, rode along the lines, telling the men to prepare to charge. He rode by me shouting some order I could not catch, and went to the regiment on my left, which immediately charged. I supposed this to be his order to me, and commanded the men to fix bayonets and charge. The men sprang forward. As we neared the crest of the hill the regiment on my left turned and went back. I shouted to my men to halt, but could not make a single man hear or heed me, and it was not till they had climbed the intervening fence, and were rushing ahead on the other side, that I was able to run along the lines, and seizing the color-bearer by the shoulder, held him fast as the only way of stopping the regiment. The alignment rectified, we faced about, and marched back to our position in common time. On reaching it the regiment halted, faced about, and resumed its fire. The path of the regiment was sadly strewn with our fallen. I saw to my surprise that the artillery had limbered up, and was moving off the field, and that the infantry was gone, saw our regiment, which was gallantly holding the ground, far to the left. The Confederates had advanced until I could see above the smoke their battle-flags where the artillery had been posted. I ordered a retreat; but the men either could not hear or would not heed the order. I was finally obliged to take hold of the color-bearer, face him about, and tell him to follow me to get the regiment from the field. They fell back slowly, firing in retreat, and encouraging each other not to run."(')

The Union troops fell back to a strong position on a hill and spent the night, retreating the next day to Cedar Creek. Breckinridge made no attempt to follow. The Union loss was 482 killed and wounded, and 250 who were taken prisoners. Affairs in the Shenandoah had been so badly managed by Sigel that General Hunter was appointed to command the Department. Reinforcements were sent him increasing his force to 8500 men, with twenty-one guns.

General Hunter received orders from General Grant to push on if possible to Charlottesville and Lynchburg, and destroy the railroads and canals. General Hunter, wishing to move rapidly, determined to take no large supply-train, but to depend upon the country for food. He allowed very little baggage. He forbade pillaging, but all food was to be collected by authorized officers, and all citizens who were loyal to the United States were to be paid for the articles taken. A supply-train moving down the turnpike from Martinsburg was captured by Confederate guerillas and destroyed. Had Hunter issued his orders for living upon the country he could not have advanced.

May 26, 1864.

Immediately after the battle of New Market, General Lee, finding that General Grant was moving to the North Anna, ordered General Breckinridge to hasten to his assistance. Quite likely General Lee thought that as General Sigel had been defeated there would be no immediate movement of Union troops in the Shenandoah, but General Hunter moved on to New Market, Harrisburg, and Piedmont.

At daybreak the Union troops were on the march, the cavalry in advance. Not far from Piedmont they came upon a body of Confederates. Gen. William E. Jones, with about five thousand men, had selected a strong position, thrown up intrenchments, and was ready for a battle. It was seven o'clock in the morning when the Union skirmishers advanced, but they found that the Confederates were also advancing. The Union soldiers could hear a Confederate band playing the Marseillaise Hymn. Grandly its strains floated out upon the morning air, mingling with the reverberating echoes of the cannonade.

June 5, 1864.

General Jones concentrated the most of his troops against the right of the Union line; and General Hunter, discovering it, sent Thoburn's brigade to its support. The Thirty-fourth Massachusetts was sent through fields and woods, and fell upon the flank of the Confederates. The Union troops pressed on with great vigor, and in five minutes nearly sixty of that regiment were killed or wounded. A half-hour and the battle was over, the Confederates defeated, losing more than one thousand in killed, wounded, and prisoners—the Confederate commander being numbered among the killed.

By this victory the troops of Crook and Averill were enabled to join Hunter at Staunton, giving him an army of eighteen thousand, and thirty guns. At Staunton were factories which supplied the Confederate army with saddles, harnesses, clothing, and shoes, all of which were destroyed, together with six miles of the railroad-track.

General Hunter waited several days at Staunton for supplies of clothing and shoes for Crook's troops. It would have been far better if he had hastened on at once to Lynchburg, as we shall see.

Through a wide and beautiful valley the troops of Hunter went on to Lexington. Some of the cadets fired upon the Union soldiers from the buildings of the Military Institute, whereupon the buildings were burned, together with several iron-mills which had been manufacturing iron for the Confederate Government. John Letcher, who was Governor of Virginia in 1861, and who did what he could to bring about the secession of the State, published a proclamation calling upon the people to become guerillas, and then ignominiously fled, whereupon General Hunter issued an order to burn his house. Several canal-boats loaded with supplies, and six cannon, were captured. The Union cavalry under Duffie, after the battle of Piedmont, followed the fleeing Confederates to Waynesboro, but finding them intrenched, turned south, crossed the Blue Ridge by Tye River Gap, reached Amherst, moved on to Arrington Station, on the railroad leading from Charlottesville to Lynchburg, and tore up the track.

June 10, 1864.

The Confederate cavalry under Imboden came upon him, and there was a sharp engagement, resulting in the repulse of the Confederates, who lost one hundred men, four hundred horses, and a portion of their wagons. Turning back, Duffie recrossed the Blue Ridge at White's Gap, rejoining General Hunter at Lexington June 13th.

It was startling news that reached General Lee at Cold Harbor—the defeat of Jones at Piedmont. Breckinridge's troops were sent back with all possible speed to Lynchburg, a vital point to General Lee. It is on the James River, in a rich and fertile section. It had numerous manufactories and flouring-mills. If General Hunter were to take it, the Confederate army and the people of Richmond would be cut off from a large portion of their supplies. The emergency was so critical that he directed General

Early, commanding Stonewall Jackson's old troops, to make all haste westward. The fortifications at Cold Harbor had been made so strong that he could hold them with Longstreet's and Hill's corps and the troops that had come from the south. So it came about that Early's troops were quietly withdrawn and started westward. As the railroad to Gordonsville had been destroyed, they were obliged to march; but they had learned under Stonewall Jackson how to make long marches, and thought nothing of making twenty miles a day. While Hunter was waiting at Lexington for Duffie's return and for a wagon-train of shoes and clothing and ammunition, a rich opportunity for him was passing away.

But the Union troops were not all idle. General Averill, commanding a division of cavalry, reached Buchanan. The Confederate cavalry under McCausland was there, but was driven. McCausland, thinking to prevent the Union cavalry from following him, set the bridge crossing the James on fire, against the wishes of the citizens. Eleven buildings were burned. The Union troops did what they could to save the other buildings. General Hunter's scouts informed him that Breckinridge had returned with his two brigades, and was holding Rock Fish Gap and the road to Charlottesville. The prisoners taken by Duffie said that a large body of Confederates was coming from Lee's army to hold Lynchburg. They also said that Sheridan had been defeated by the Confederate cavalry at Louisa Court-house. What should General Hunter do? If he were to advance directly towards Charlottesville he would encounter Breckinridge, with six or eight thousand, in Rock Fish Gap; but there were no Confederates to oppose his direct march to Lynchburg. He decided to make a rapid march to Buchanan, twenty-four miles from Lexington, and thence cross the Blue Ridge and reach Lynchburg if possible before the arrival of Early.

June 13, 1864.

While the army was marching from Lexington to Buchanan two hundred Union cavalrymen on good horses were moving from Buchanan across the ridge to Amherst. If they had torn up a mile or two of track they would have rendered great service; but without doing much damage to the railroad, they turned south-east, reached James River, crossed it below Lynchburg, came to the Southside Railroad, tore up a portion of the track, burned two trains of cars at Concordia Station, turned west, and rejoined Hunter at Liberty, thus riding round Lynchburg.

The Union army, the while, was crossing the Blue Ridge. At four o'clock in the morning the *reveille* was sounded, and the troops began to wind up the mountain. Those in the rear could see the column far above them, and hear the rumbling of the artil-

June 15, 1864.

lery; those above could look down upon the long line stretching far away. The road was narrow, its windings frequent. Some of the wagons were lost by rolling down the almost perpendicular cliffs. Guerillas fired on the troops from behind rocks. Slow and tedious the ascent, but at night the troops encamped upon the summit.

The Union army was marching through Liberty eastward. The cavalry under Crook was tearing up the rails on the road leading to East Tennessee from Liberty to Big Otter Creek, burning the ties and bending the rails. Two hundred wagons were leaving Liberty for Lewiston, on the Great Kanawha, guarded by soldiers from Ohio,

June 16, 1864.

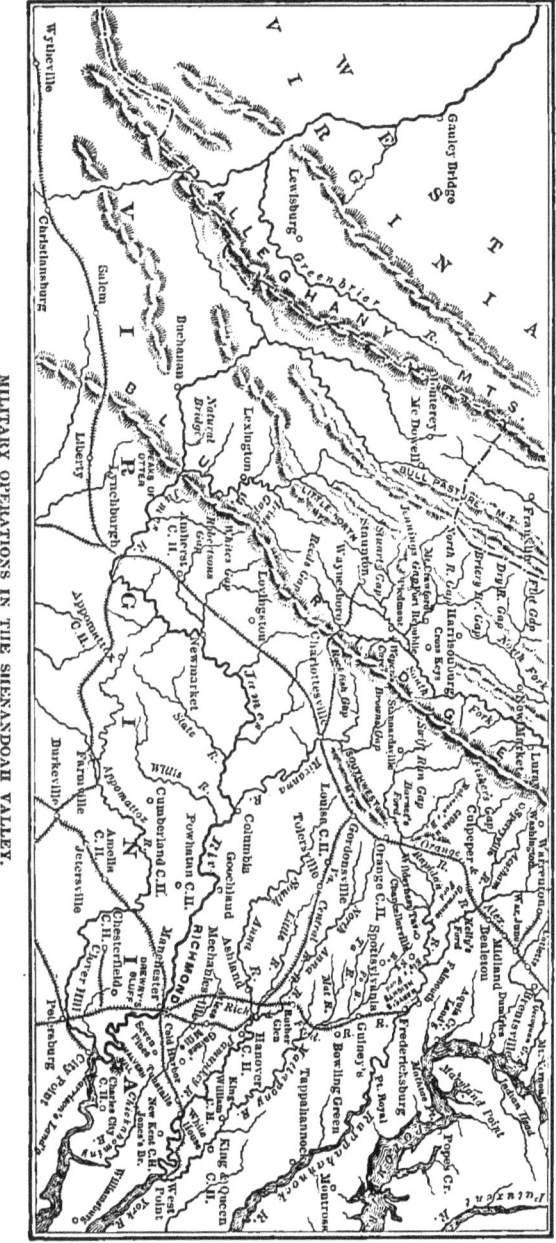

MILITARY OPERATIONS IN THE SHENANDOAH VALLEY.

returning home, their term of service ended. In the afternoon the Union cavalry found the forces of Imboden and McCausland disputing their advance.

Hunter was within four miles of Lynchburg. Averill's cannon opened fire upon the Confederates. Crook came to Averill's assistance, charged, and captured two cannon. Through the afternoon the Union soldiers could hear railroad-trains, and when night came, with its stillness, they could hear the people cheering Early's troops, who were being whirled into the city from Charlottesville.

June 17, 1864.

During the night the Confederates were constructing intrenchments. The first glimmer of dawn was lighting the eastern horizon when the Union troops were aroused from sleep. A little later the artillery began. Crook and Averill were upon the right, Duffie upon the left. The pickets began a fusillade, and then came a sharp contest, the Confederates charging but meeting a repulse, some of the Union troops following them to their breastworks, losing two hundred men.

June 18, 1864.

General Hunter saw that the opportunity for capturing Lynchburg had passed. His provisions were nearly gone; the last piece of hard-bread had been eaten. He had only six ounces of flour per day for the men.

"No fires to-night," was the order. The sun went down behind the peaks of Otter, and darkness settled over the valley. Silently the Union troops departed, the pickets remaining till near midnight. General Hunter saw that he could not well retreat down the valley of the Shenandoah; for if he took that direction, the Confederates, by using the railroad, would be able to reach the valley before him and block his way. He decided to retreat down the valley of the Great Kanawha. While on the march, the Confederate cavalry under McCausland came suddenly upon the artillery-train. No infantry were at hand, and the Confederates cut out three pieces before being repulsed. So many horses had been lost that five other cannon had to be abandoned.

Supplies were gone. There was little food in the mountain region. Men dropped by the road-side, weary and faint from marching. "Hundreds of my men are starving," said General Crook.

A Union officer wrote thus in his diary: "Started at three this morning and halted about noon, when meat and a little coffee were issued. The boys look so gaunt and are so hungry, it makes our hearts ache to see them. At the halt I saw two dollars refused for one small griddle-cake."(¹)

June 27, 1864.

The soldiers were without food on one occasion for two days. During

GENERAL CUSTER.

the last week of the march they had one ounce of flour only per day, and a little meat. In this movement against Lynchburg the soldiers marched nearly six hundred miles, and suffered bitter hardships, besides fighting three battles. A soldier wrote this to his mother: "Seven days after leaving Salem we were in the mountains and woods, not a house within ten miles. We had no bread, no meat, no nothing. The men grew poor and thin. When I looked into a glass for the first time I was startled at the change. I hardly knew myself. My face was black and thin, my eyes large, and of such expression they looked as if they would eat me up."(*)

We have seen that General Hunter was directed to move upon Charlottesville and Lynchburg. General Grant, with this in mind, directed General Sheridan to move in that direction, destroy the Virginia Central Railroad, meet Hunter at Charlottesville, and retire with him to the Army of the Potomac. General Sheridan started with two divisions, marching north, crossing the North Anna at Carpenter's Ford, on the road to Trevilian's Depot.

June 7, 1864.

General Lee learned of Sheridan's departure, and sent Hampton and Fitz-Hugh Lee with the Confederate cavalry, to see what he was intending to do.

When evening came, on the night of June 10th, Sheridan was northeast of Trevilian's. Hampton, with his division, was in Green Spring Valley, three miles north-west of the depot, and Fitz-Hugh Lee at Louisa Court-house, six miles south-east of it. About half-way between the railroad and Carpenter's Ford was a little store, owned by Mr. Clayton, from which a road ran to Louisa Court-house. Hampton decided to move from Spring Valley to the depot, and thence to Clayton's. Fitz-Hugh Lee was to join him there, and together they would attack the Union cavalry.

June 10, 1864.

General Sheridan's men were early in the saddle, moving west. Hampton was also on the move at three o'clock. Just as day was breaking, Torbert's division came against Hampton's. The meeting was in thick woods, Butler's and Young's Confederate brigades being on the main road, and Rosser's on a parallel road farther north. The Confederates had dismounted, and were making a breastwork of fence-rails.

June 11, 1864.

General Sheridan quickly decided to send General Custer to gain Hampton's rear. He directed Gregg to fall upon Fitz-Hugh Lee, while Torbert was to confront Hampton. Custer made his way through the woods and attacked with vigor, capturing Rosser's supply-train, and seizing fifteen hundred of the horses of the men who had dismounted to meet

Torbert. Custer turned them over to the Fifth Michigan Regiment to take back to Sheridan; but Hampton intercepted the escort, recaptured most of the horses, and seized Custer's own headquarters wagon. Most of the escort reached Sheridan, and reported what had happened. Custer found himself surrounded. He had only four small regiments and four cannon, but fought his way out. The Confederates charged upon Pennington's battery and seized one cannon. "I have lost one of my guns," said Captain Pennington. "We will see," said Custer. "Charge!" he shouted, and sixty cavalrymen, led by himself, went tearing across the field, cutting down the Confederates around the cannon. "Here is your gun, take it," said Custer.

Through the day the strife went on, Gregg pushing Fitz-Hugh Lee, while Sheridan, dismounting Torbert's men, assailed Hampton's troops behind their breastworks, carrying them, and driving the Confederates back upon Custer, capturing nearly five hundred prisoners. The loss on both sides was very heavy. Hampton and Fitz-Hugh Lee fell back towards Gordonsville.

General Sheridan learned from the prisoners that Breckinridge was at Gordonsville. They said that Early was on his way to Lynchburg to head off Hunter. Sheridan's horses were jaded; there was little forage to be had, and the supplies of the country were so exhausted that he could not support his troops. As he could learn nothing directly concerning Hunter he decided to rejoin General Grant.

June 12, 1864.

We have seen that the victory of General Hunter at Piedmont was won on June 5th, that the escaping Confederates fled towards Waynesboro. It is only a good day's march from that town to Charlottesville. We can now see that if General Hunter, instead of moving to Staunton after the battle of Piedmont, had vigorously followed the fleeing Confederates he would have reached Waynesboro on the next day before the arrival of Breckinridge. Then tearing up the railroad between Charlottesville and Lynchburg, he would have been free to move on; but by turning towards Staunton, waiting for the arrival of a wagon-train, and the tarry at Lexington, enabled Lee to send Early, and thus foil him at Lynchburg and compel him to retreat down the Great Kanawha. Thus an army of fifteen thousand men was rendered useless for service for several weeks at a moment when, if he had taken the route to Charlottesville the day after the victory at Piedmont, he would have been of inestimable service to General Grant.

The time had come for a bold movement on the part of the Confederates. When General Lee sent Early to head off Hunter he contemplated

BEGINNING OF THE BATTLE IN THE WOODS.

a larger movement, the menacing of Washington. Hunter was retreating down the valley of the Kanawha, towards Ohio; there were no Union troops in the Shenandoah. Early had seventeen thousand troops, veterans who had been in many battles, and who were inured to hardships, four divisions—Ramseur's, Echols's, Rodes's, and Gordon's—between forty and fifty cannon, and a large force of cavalry, with few Union troops to oppose him. General Early saw that he could choose his own course and made quick preparation. He issued orders to take very little baggage, compelling the officers to carry whatever clothing they might need. He knew that he would find cattle, flour, corn, and supplies in abundance, and so was not hampered by long trains of wagons. On the 27th he started from Staunton. The roads were in excellent order. Imboden, with his division of cavalry, swept on in advance, crossing North Mountain, moving to tear up the track of the Baltimore and Ohio Railroad west of Martinsburg, burning bridges so that Hunter, when he reached the Ohio, could not be whirled through Wheeling eastward to gain his rear.

June 27, 1864.

General Sigel was at Martinsburg, with a few troops, guarding the large amount of Government supplies stored in that town. When the Union scouts informed him that Early was on the march, he telegraphed to Baltimore for cars and removed the supplies. When the Confederate cavalry dashed into town they found empty warehouses, no engines or cars to be destroyed, and the Union troops retreating towards Shepherdstown. Gen. Bradley T. Johnson, of Baltimore, commanded a division of Confederate cavalry, and dashed towards Leetown in pursuit of Sigel, but was confronted by Colonel Mulligan, who held him in check till Sigel, with his trains, was on the north bank of the Potomac, holding Maryland Heights. General Weber held Harper's Ferry, and also retreated across the Potomac. To prevent the Confederates from using the railroad bridge, one span was destroyed. When Early's troops attempted to take possession of the village of Harper's Ferry they were driven back by the fire of the Union cannon on Maryland Heights. Sigel had about six thousand men, two veteran regiments, four regiments of militia from Ohio, twenty-five hundred dismounted cavalry, and between forty and fifty cannon. In addition, there was a brigade of cavalry, under General Stahl, in Pleasant Valley. The Confederate cavalry crossed the Potomac at Shepherdstown, moved over the battle-field of Antietam, and dashed into Hagerstown, made a requisition for twenty thousand dollars, burned a great deal of hay and grain, creating a panic among the people, who collected their cattle and horses and started them in droves northward into Pennsylvania. Many of the farmers packed their household

July 2, 1864.

goods into wagons, and hastened away from their houses. General Early intended to advance towards Washington directly from Harper's Ferry, but could not do it because the Union troops held Maryland Heights. He found every approach swept by the artillery, and was compelled to move north to Sharpsburg and Boonsborough, and then eastward over South Mountain to Frederick.

The military authorities in Washington thought that it was only a small raiding party of Confederates.

General Grant supposed that after the retreat of Hunter General Lee would recall Early to the defence of Richmond; when he learned the state of affairs, he offered to send an army corps; but General Halleck thought that if Grant would send up the cavalrymen who had lost their horses, they would be all the troops needed. General Grant thought otherwise, and sent not only the dismounted cavalry but Ricketts's division of the Sixth Corps. The dismounted cavalry were of little account, most of them being sick or convalescents from the hospitals.

July 5, 1864.

The troops of the Sixth Corps embarked on a steamer at City Point, went down the James and up the Chesapeake to Baltimore; for General Halleck was in doubt whether Early was intending to attack Washington or the former city.

While the steamboats were on their way up the Chesapeake, Gen. Lew Wallace, in command at Baltimore, sent what few troops he had westward to Monocacy River, near Frederick, as they would be in position along that stream to confront Early in his movements towards either city. The Eighth Illinois Cavalry, under Colonel Clendennis, made a reconnoissance to Frederick, and thence along the turnpike towards Middleton. They encountered the division of General Johnson. There was a sharp skirmish, ending in the falling back of the Union troops to Frederick, the Confederates to Middleton.

July 7, 1864.

General Wallace had only a handful of troops who had been hastily collected from the forts around Baltimore and along the railroads—twenty-five hundred—many of them soldiers who had enlisted for one hundred days, and who never had been in battle. They were commanded by General Tyler. Soon after sunrise a train of freight cars came from Baltimore bringing a portion of General Ricketts's division of the Sixth Corps from Petersburg. The cars came to a standstill outside the city; the soldiers, weary with their all-night ride, kindled fires and cooked their coffee, and then marched across fields, threw up breastworks, then were marched to another field. General Wallace kept

July 8, 1864.

THE VALLEY OF THE SHENANDOAH. 279

them moving, with the design of deceiving Early as to his numbers, hoping to delay the advance of the Confederates till the arrival of the whole of Ricketts's division.([10])

General Early was cautiously advancing towards Frederick. There was skirmishing between the cavalry, the Union troops retreating towards the Monocacy, and the Confederates entering the city, helping themselves to boots, shoes, clothing, bacon, and flour. General Early demanded two hundred thousand dollars in money, which was paid him. During the

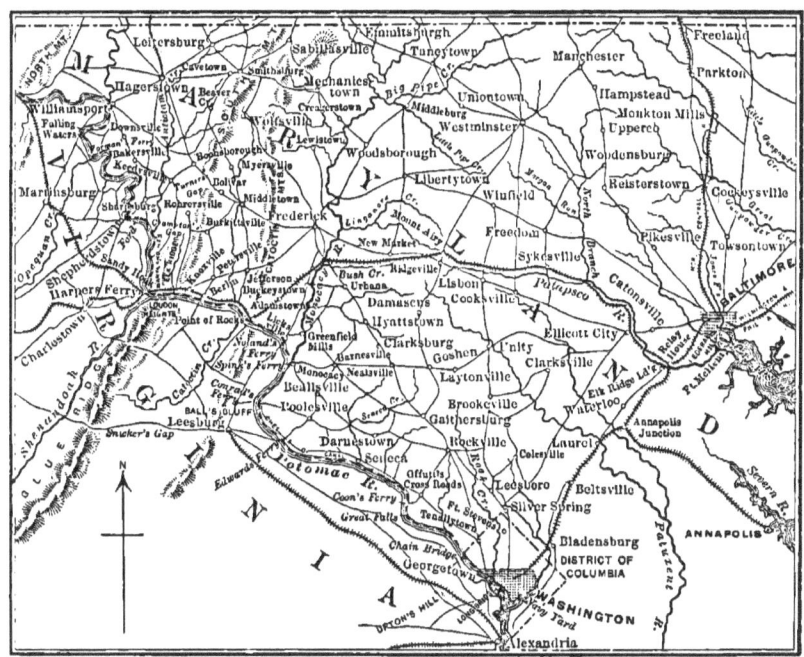

EARLY'S MOVEMENT TO WASHINGTON.

day the entire force of Ricketts's division arrived, giving General Wallace six thousand men and six cannon, against twenty thousand Confederates and forty cannon.

The morning dawned, with the little force under General Wallace posted along the banks of the winding Monocacy. The troops under General Tyler held the right of the Union line. Upon no
July 9, 1864. other field during the war was there such a collection of odds and ends of regiments marshalled to fight a battle, which might

result in consequences of vital moment to the parties; for if Early should sweep this little line of men from their position by such an onset as those same Confederate regiments had made at Chancellorsville under Jackson, there would be no other Union force to oppose his entrance to the capital of the United States. The troops of Tyler were—the Third Regiment of Potomac Home Guards, Eleventh Maryland Regiment, seven companies of the One Hundred and Forty-ninth, three companies of the One Hundred and Fifty-ninth Ohio Militia, two hundred and fifty Eighth Illinois Cavalry, Captain Lieb's battalion of one hundred mounted infantry, Captain Brown's company of one hundred Maryland Home Guards, Captain Alexander with three cannon—these, numbering, in all, twenty-five hundred, extended from the stone bridge across the Monocacy on the Baltimore turnpike southward, a distance of more than two miles. Only the men of the Eighth Cavalry had ever been in battle. General Ricketts's line covered another mile, from the railroad bridge south. General Early moved out from Frederick with Rodes's division marching down the turnpike leading to Baltimore; Ramseur's division took the road leading to Washington, while Gordon marched through the fields nearer the Potomac River, to cross the Monocacy, turn Ricketts's flank, and win the battle. General Wallace placed a body of skirmishers on the west bank of the river to harass the Confederate advance. When closely pressed, they were to retreat across the wooden bridge, which was to be set on fire so that the Confederates should not use it.

The Union troops, from their position on the east bank, could see the long lines of Confederates, three times their own number, deploying in the green meadows and trampling down the fields of wheat ripe for the reaper. It was a beautiful spectacle, as the veterans' ranks filed from the turnpike, their battle-flags waving in the summer breeze, the sunlight glinting from their bayonets. So many of them were dressed in blue uniforms captured from the Union army that some of the Home Guards in the Union ranks could hardly be persuaded to fire upon them, confidently believing that they were' Union soldiers, and not till they saw them fire could they believe that they were Confederates.([11])

It was a great surprise to Mr. C. K. Thomas that Saturday morning to find that a battle was to be fought on his farm—to see the men of the Tenth Vermont and Fifty-first New York regiments standing in line of battle around his buildings and beneath his peach-trees. It was a large brick house, and instead of fleeing, Mrs. Thomas and the family remained to cook bread and do what they could for the soldiers, and find shelter in the cellar when the battle began.

The Confederate cannon sent their shells into the ranks of the Union troops. It was a feeble fire which the six Union guns made to the six batteries opposing them. It was half-past ten when the Confederates advanced, and it was a surprise to them when a steady volley was poured into their ranks by the veterans of the Sixth Corps. Their officers had informed them that they would meet only the Home Guards. The volleys were given by the Tenth Vermont and One Hundredth New York, and were so destructive that the Confederates fell back with disordered ranks.

Again the Confederates advanced. A Union officer says of the second attempt:

"The second charge and repulse was a grand scene, such as made the blood tingle in our veins. It was in marked contrast to Petersburg riflepit style of fighting. Here our men had the advantage of position, acting on the defensive, with fair protection, an open field, and a full view. . . . About 10.30 the long wooden bridge at my left over the river was burned by order of General Wallace, to guard against a flank attack upon General Ricketts." (¹²)

A portion of General Ricketts's troops—nearly three regiments—were several miles in the rear. They were sent for, but did not make an appearance upon the field. General Wallace says: "I could probably have retired without much trouble, as the rebels were badly punished. The main object of the battle was unaccomplished—their strength not yet developed."

From eleven o'clock till past two in the afternoon the contest went on sharply between the skirmishers. Gordon's division was making its turning movement, fording the Monocacy and marching to gain Wallace's left flank. The Union troops changed position to present a front line to Gordon, who turned north-east after crossing the stream. It was past three when the white-heat of battle came on between Ricketts and Gordon. Ricketts was obliged to pivot the right flank of his division on the Monocacy, to prevent Ramseur from crossing. The Confederate artillery on the west bank sent a storm of shells into Ricketts's ranks, partly enfilading the line. General Tyler, the while, was resolutely confronting Rodes, who made no great effort to cross the stream, knowing that Gordon's movement would soon put to flight the Union troops, so few in number, comparatively, to Early's. Wallace, seeing the line could not be held, ordered Ricketts to retire. Rodes made a rush upon the Union troops holding the bridge, several hundred of whom were captured, their retreat being cut off by Gordon. Had they been withdrawn ten minutes earlier they would have escaped. Wallace fell back along the turnpike

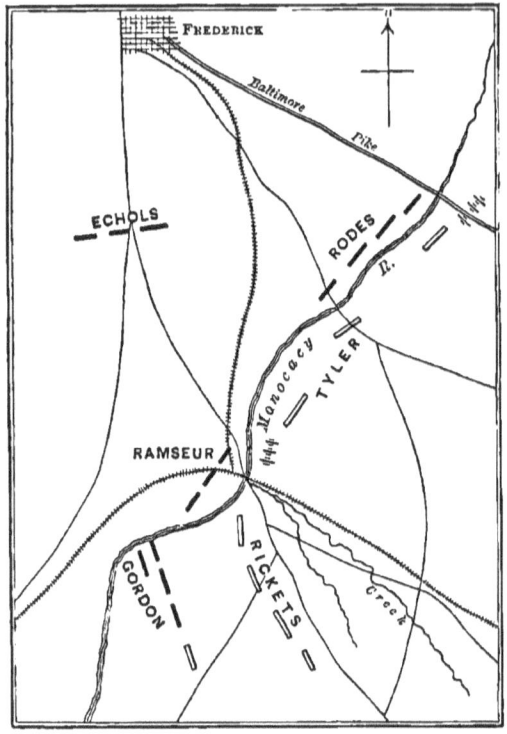

BATTLE OF MONOCACY.

to New Market, the Confederates making no pursuit in that direction, but preparing to advance upon Washington. The battle was stubbornly fought on the part of the Union troops, who lost nearly two thousand in killed, wounded, and missing. Nearly seven hundred were captured by Early. It is supposed that the Confederates lost nearly one thousand in killed and wounded. The stand thus resolutely made by Wallace when he knew that he was vastly outnumbered, and the advantages gained by delaying Early in advancing upon Washington, were incalculable. There was no panic in the ranks of the Sixth Corps as they retreated from the field. Wallace brought off his six cannon. Early had gained a victory, but at great comparative loss.

With the break of day, while the birds were singing their morning songs, the Confederate troops were astir, the long column moving down the Georgetown turnpike towards the nation's capital.

July 10, 1864.

In Baltimore the church bells were clanging, calling the citizens, not to worship, but to the fortifications erected for the defence of the city. Wallace had fallen back to Ellicott's Mills, leaving the road open for Early to march to Washington. The Confederate cavalry under Johnson, who came from Maryland, and who knew all the roads, were sweeping northward to Westminster and eastward to the railroad leading from Baltimore to Harrisburg, tearing up the track, capturing mules and horses, and sending them south to the fords of the Potomac at Edwards Ferry, and hastening droves of cattle into Virginia. The Confederates rode north-east of Baltimore, came to the long bridge at Gunpowder River, captured two trains of passenger cars, backed the trains upon the bridge, and set bridge and cars on fire. They burned Governor Bradford's house. This was done by men who before the war were citizens of Maryland—a State which had not seceded from the Union—who could not plead, as could the people of the Southern States, that they were defending the rights of their respective States. The troops which destroyed the bridge and cars were led by Harry Gilmor, a citizen of Maryland.

At the beginning of the campaign, General Grant, foreseeing that he would need reinforcements in his great contest with General Lee, had ordered the corps commanded by General Emory, which had been a year in Louisiana, to embark at New Orleans for Fortress Monroe. Was it chance alone that brought the troops of that command to Fortress Monroe at the moment when they were most needed? The steamships transporting these veterans reached Fortress Monroe, and were sent up the Potomac to Washington. The telegraph, a few hours after the battle of Monocacy, flashed the news to General Grant, who instantly ordered the remaining division of the Sixth Corps to hasten to Washington. I was at City Point when they arrived, after a march of fourteen miles from the trenches. Steam was hissing from the escape-pipes of the steamers lying at the wharves. Without breaking step, the bronzed veterans filed across the gang-planks, the cable was cast off, and the wheels turned and the vessels disappeared down the James.

In Washington, on that Sunday, men were hurrying here and there, orderlies and lieutenants riding in hot haste. Gen. C. C. Augur was in command. He issued orders to gather up the convalescents from the hospitals, the soldiers on detached service, the marines and sailors from the Navy Yard, the militia, the clerks in the quartermaster's department. These, together with the veteran reserves and the heavy artillerymen, numbered nearly twenty thousand; but they were widely scattered and could not readily be concentrated. The chances were that Early, by a determined assault, would somewhere break through the line of intrenchment and make his way into the city.

Down the James and up the Potomac steamed the vessels bearing the men of the Sixth Corps, reaching the wharves in Washington at the foot of Sixth Street at two o'clock in the afternoon. As the steamers came to the dock the soldiers saw a tall man standing there to welcome them—Abraham Lincoln—and they rent the air with their cheers. The great ocean steamer from New Orleans, with eight hundred men on board, came in at the same moment. Rested and refreshed, the soldiers marched down the gang-plank and up Seventh Street, amid

July 11, 1864.

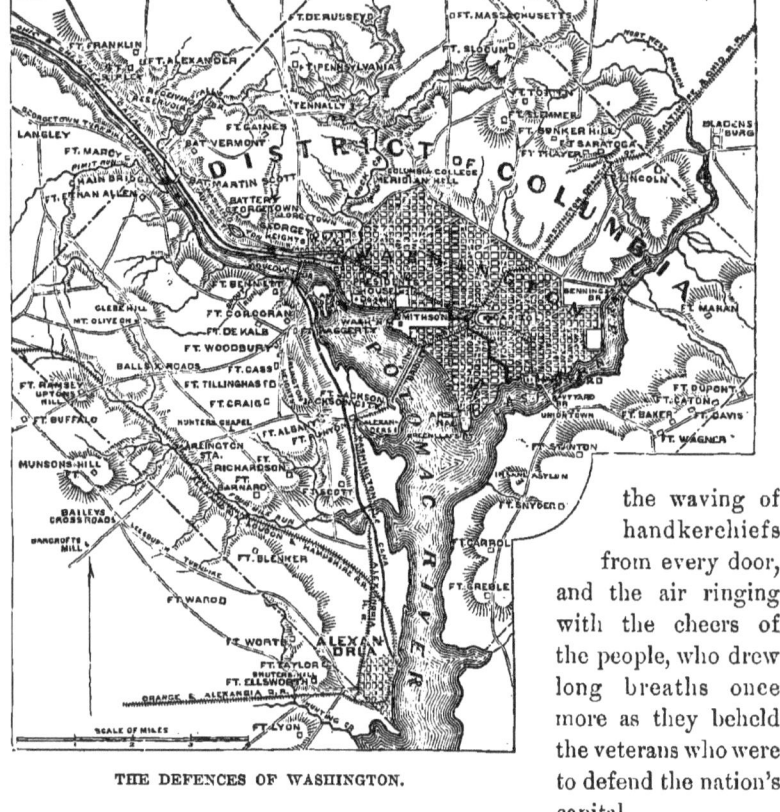

THE DEFENCES OF WASHINGTON.

the waving of handkerchiefs from every door, and the air ringing with the cheers of the people, who drew long breaths once more as they beheld the veterans who were to defend the nation's capital.

On Sunday morning, after burying the dead at Monocacy and sending the wounded to Frederick, the Confederates started for Washington, marching twenty miles and halting for the night near Rockville, the Confederate cavalry under McCausland having a sharp skirmish with the Sixteenth Pennsylvania and a portion of the Eighth Illinois, the Union troops driving the Confederates. Early had detailed Ramseur's division to guard his rear, and now Sigel's cavalry from Harper's Ferry was picking up stragglers from his ranks. Early saw that he must advance rapidly if he would seize the capital, and soon after daybreak on Monday his troops were moving on. At nine o'clock the Confederate cavalry were at Tenallytown, north of Georgetown; and the infantry, a little later, looking across the fields, could see the white and unfinished dome of the Capitol gleaming in the mid-day sun. The day was hot, and Early's men began to droop. During a period of thirty days they had marched from Cold Harbor to Lynchburg, from Lynchburg to Harper's Ferry, from there to Boonsborough, from Boonsborough to Monocacy, had fought a battle, and now were at Washington. They had suffered great hardship, and could not longer march under the blazing sun.

The Union cavalry fell back, and formed a picket line in front of the fortifications. The men of the Sixth Corps, while marching down the gang-plank, heard the booming of the 32-pounder cannon in Fort Stevens, out on Seventh Street, announcing the advance of the Confederates. Under the vigorous fire of the great guns the Confederate skirmishers came to a halt.

Fort Stevens and Fort De Russey stood west of Seventh Street, and Fort Slocum east of it. There was a deep, wooded ravine between Forts Stevens and De Russey, with Rock Creek winding through it. The forts were so situated that if the Confederates were to carry either of them it could be swept by the fire of the others. It was two o'clock when the Sixth Corps and the troops of the Nineteenth landed. Two hours later General Wright was in Fort Stevens surveying the ground, and his troops were filing into the fields. General Early's opportunity had gone by. Never was a Confederate army to march triumphantly through the streets, or to fling out the flag of the Confederacy as an emblem of sovereignty and power above the dome of the nation's capitol.

General Early says: "The day was so exceedingly hot, even at a very early hour in the morning, and the dust was so dense, that many of the men fell by the way, and it became necessary to slacken our pace. When we reached the fortifications the men were completely exhausted, and not in condition to make the attack. . . . I determined to make the assault, but before it could be made it became evident that the enemy had been strongly reinforced. . . . After consultation with my division commander I became satisfied that the assault, even if successful, would be attended with great sacrifice, or would insure the destruction of my whole force before the victory could be made available, and if unsuccessful would necessarily have resulted in the loss of the whole force." ([12])

There was a dripping fire from the skirmishers in front of Fort Stevens; but General Early showed no signs of bringing on a battle. General Wright, commanding the Sixth Corps, determined to attack. The heavy cannon in the forts sent their shells upon the Confederates in the fields and orchards on the farm of Mr. Rives. General Wright and Abraham Lincoln stood on the parapet of Fort Stevens, together with several ladies who had come from Washington in car-

July 12, 1864.

riages to see a battle. It was two o'clock in the afternoon when Getty's division, commanded by General Wheaton, moved out from Fort Stevens, Bidwell's brigade driving the Confederate skirmishers. The rattling fire deepened into volleys of musketry; the battle going on till sunset, the Confederates falling back, and during the night retreating to Rockville, signalling their departure by burning the house of Mr. Blair, one of the members of President Lincoln's Cabinet.

The Union force at Washington was not strong enough to march out and bring on a pitched battle, nor was General Early disposed to engage in such a contest. He had come to seize the capital, but had been foiled in his efforts. Had he hastened on after crossing the Potomac, instead of lingering at Boonsborough and Frederick, there would have been no battle at Monocacy, and the chances were that he would have been able

CONFEDERATES RETREATING ACROSS THE POTOMAC WITH THEIR PLUNDER.

to seize the intrenchments. Had he entered the city he doubtless would have committed great havoc, but quite likely, in the end, would have lost his army through the closing around him of Union troops from every quarter.

The Confederates were making their way to the fords of the Potomac with a drove of horses and cattle which they had taken from the people of Maryland. It was time for Early to be gone, for had he remained a day or two longer, Sigel and Hunter would have been closing in upon him from the west. Hunter, upon reaching the Ohio River after his retreat down the Kanawha, embarked his troops on steamboats, ascended the river to Wheeling, and they were on their way eastward over the Baltimore and Ohio Railroad. The force closing around Early from the west and from Washington was much larger than his own. Had he lingered, it is probable that his army would soon have been scat-

July 13, 1864.

THE VALLEY OF THE SHENANDOAH. 287

tered to the winds. He had lost heavily at Monocacy and in the engagement at Fort Stevens. His troops were weary. He had gathered large herds of cattle and horses, much corn and flour; but he had not brought about what the Confederate Government hoped would be the result of the movement—the withdrawal of Grant from Petersburg or the capture of Washington.

NOTES TO CHAPTER X.

([1]) E. Pond, "Shenandoah Valley," p. 12.
([2]) J. S. Wise, *Century Magazine*, January, 1889.
([3]) Lieutenant-colonel Ship, "Report of the Battle of New Market," p. 7.
([4]) General Breckinridge's Report.
([5]) J. S. Wise, *Century Magazine*, January, 1889.
([6]) General Imboden's Report.
([7]) Colonel Wells's Letter to Governor Andrew, Massachusetts Archives.
([8]) "History of Thirty-fourth Massachusetts Regiment," p. 230.
([9]) Sergeant-major Black, "History of Thirty-fourth Massachusetts Regiment," p. 324.
([10]) Capt. George Davis's Paper read before Stannard Post No. 2, Grand Army of the Republic, Burlington, Vt.
([11]) Idem.
([12]) Idem.
([13]) Gen. J. A. Early, "Memoir of the Last Year of the War," p. 58.

CHAPTER XI.

THE "ALABAMA" AND "KEARSARGE."

IT was on a Sunday morning in August, 1862, that the Confederate flag was hoisted above the decks of the *Alabama*. In "Marching to Victory" (chaps. ii., iii.), the story of the building of that vessel in England and her departure has been told. Her career as a destroyer of vessels belonging to the merchants of New York and New England began on that Sunday morning, three miles from one of the islands of the Azores. Up to that hour the *Alabama* had been the British ship *Enrica*.

August 24, 1862.

Captain Semmes stepped upon a gun-carriage, read the commission which he had received from Jefferson Davis appointing him a captain in the Confederate navy, and then the Confederate flag rose to the peak. "This vessel henceforth is to be called the *Alabama*," he said. The officers and crew uncovered their heads. The flag of England came down, and the flag of the Confederacy floated in the sunshine.(¹)

Up to that moment the *Alabama* had no crew. The men on board had been shipped for a trip to the West Indies, a reckless set, who cared little what might become of them. Captain Semmes made a speech. Those who might desire to go back to England could do so; but if they would ship with him on the *Alabama*, there would be plenty of excitement and adventure; they would destroy a great many vessels; there would be no end of plunder; they would have prize-money paid them in gold, voted them by the Confederate Congress. The temptation of prize-money glittered in their imaginations, and eighty out of ninety enlisted. This is what Semmes said: "The democratic part of the proceedings closed as soon as the articles were signed. It was the last public meeting ever held on board the *Alabama*, and no other stump speech was ever made to the crew. When I wanted a man to do anything after this, I did not talk to him of nationalities, liberties, or double wages, but gave him a rather sharp order, and if it was not obeyed on the double-quick, the delinquent found himself in limbo. Democracies may do for land, but monarchies, and pretty absolute monarchies, are the only successful governments at sea." (²)

Thus, off the Azores, the *Alabama* began her career, spreading her sails and starting her engines, to destroy the unarmed ships of the Northern merchants, in order to build a government and establish a nation which should be an aristocracy, with slavery as its foundation. The officers were nearly all from the South, but the men were mostly English, Welsh, or Irish.

What was the status of this vessel thus flying the Confederate flag, and how shall she be classified? Semmes had a commission as captain in the Confederate navy. The *Alabama* was an English-built vessel; she never

THE "ALABAMA."

had been in a Confederate port; her crew were English; her guns were made in English founderies; her engines in an English machine-shop; all her supplies were from England; the powder in her magazine, the shot in her locker, were of English manufacture. She was English built, equipped, and manned.

The next day the man upon the lookout aloft sang out: "Sail, ho!" It was the whaling ship *Ocmulgee*, which had captured a whale, and the crew were cutting out the blubber. Little did the men at work think that the neat, new, and trim steamer approaching them with the Stars and Stripes, which had been run up by Semmes, instead of the flag of the Confederacy, was a privateer. When the *Alabama* was close upon the whaler

19

the Stars and Stripes came down, and the other went up. No need for such strategy, for the *Ocmulgee* could not have escaped. But it was Captain Semmes's way. In a few minutes all the valuable articles to be found on the ship, together with the crew, numbering thirty-seven, were transferred to the *Alabama*, and then the torch was applied, and the ship was quickly a mass of flame.

The *Alabama* ran near one of the small islands, landed the captured crew, paroling them as if they had been captured from a ship-of-war. While the prisoners were being sent on shore, the man aloft shouted once more "Sail, ho!" The schooner *Starlight*, which had just left the port of Fayal for Boston, was passing the island with several ladies on board. The *Alabama*, like a fox stealing upon a lamb, hoisted the English flag, and ran out to capture the ship. The *Starlight*, unsuspicious of danger, kept on her course till a gun suddenly flamed. It was a blank shot. The captain of the *Starlight*, instead of rounding to, thought that he could get within three miles of land, where he would be safe from capture, under international law, and kept on till a shot came across the deck of the schooner. The captain saw that he could not escape. The schooner's head came into the wind, and the sails flapped against the masts. A few minutes later the captain and crew, numbering seven, were in irons on the *Alabama*.

When the Confederate steamer *Sumter* was at Gibraltar the paymaster of that vessel went over to Tangier, in Africa, where, at the instigation of the American consul, he was arrested and delivered to the consul, under a treaty with Morocco, who sent him to the United States on the ship *Harvest Home*, the captain of which put him in irons. The arrest and the action of the captain of the ship were unwarranted. Semmes was determined to be revenged. He would make those unoffending sailors feel his power; and not only these, but the crews of several other vessels were to be treated as if they were felons, thieves, and murderers. Other vessels, mostly whalers, were captured and burned. Whales at certain seasons of the year frequent the seas around the Azores, where they feed upon the food brought by the Gulf Stream and other ocean currents. Semmes knew that he would find vessels there, and nearly every day a great black column of smoke rose from a burning ship.

Having destroyed nearly all the whaling vessels, the *Alabama* steered north-west, to burn the ships which were carrying grain from New York to Liverpool. In six weeks she destroyed seventeen. He sent the crews to the Azores, and the ships to the bottom of the sea. One of the ships was the *Tonawanda*, with a large number of passengers, several of whom were women. Semmes did not know what to do. He wanted to burn the vessel, but could not bring so many women on board the *Alabama*, for he had no room for them. He kept the ship until he captured another, and then sent the women and the captured crews to Boston.

He says: "There being no claim by any neutral for the cargo, both ship and cargo were a good prize of war; but unfortunately we could not burn the ship without encumbering ourselves with the passengers, and thirty of the sixty were women and children. I kept her cruising with me a day or two, hoping that I might fall in with some other ship of the enemy that might be less valuable, or might have a neutral cargo on board, to which I could transfer the passengers, and thus be enabled to burn her."(*)

Captain Semmes experienced great pleasure in seeing the flames leap up the rigging of the noble ships which fell into his hands. The motives which animated him to carry on his work of destruction will be seen in the following quotation from his book:

"We captured the whaling schooner *Courser*, of Provincetown, Mass. Her master was a gallant young fellow and a fine specimen of a seaman, and if I could have separated him in any way from the universal Yankee nation, I should have been pleased to spare his pretty little craft from the flames, but the thing was impossible. There were too many white-cravated, long-haired fellows bawling from the New England pulpits, and too many house-burners and pilferers inundating our Southern land, to permit me to be generous; and so I steeled my heart, as I had done on a former occasion, and executed the laws of war."(*)

He captured the *Brilliant*, in regard to which he says: "I was much moved by the entreaties of the master to spare his ship. He was a hard-working seaman, who owned one-third of the vessel. He had built her, was attached to her, and she represented all his worldly goods. But I was forced to steel my heart. He was like other masters who had remonstrated with me—in the same boat with the political rascals who had egged on the war, and I told him he must look to those rascals for redress. The ship made a brilliant bonfire, lighting up the Gulf Stream for many miles around. Having been set on fire at night, and the wind falling to a calm, we remained in sight of the burning wreck nearly all night."(*)

It was charged upon Semmes that he decoyed ships into his power by thus setting those captured on fire at night, so that other ships, seeing the light, would hasten to the rescue of those whom the sailors supposed were in distress. He denies this in his volume, and says that he never lay by a ship longer than to see her well on fire.

We are not to forget that the South was fighting for the establishment of a government based on slavery. Captain Semmes carried out the idea practically. One of the captives on the *Tonawanda* was a negro boy, seventeen years old, owned by a gentleman from Delaware, who was on his way to England, and who had taken the boy along as his servant.

RAPHAEL SEMMES.

Under the laws of that State, the boy would be free when he was twenty-one. He would also be free the moment he reached England. Captain Semmes knew this, but he took the boy for a waiter. This is his reason: "The little State of Delaware, all of whose sympathies were with us, had been ridden over rough-shod by the vandals north of her, as Maryland afterwards was, and was arrayed on the side of the enemy. I was obliged, therefore, to treat her as such. The slave was on his way to Europe with his master. He came necessarily under the laws of war, and I brought him on board the *Alabama*, where we were in want of good servants."(')

Captain Semmes had the power, and acted accordingly. Delaware, instead of giving her sympathies to the South, was loyal to the old flag from the beginning. He wanted a servant and took him. It was the spirit of slavery.

Having captured a large number of vessels loaded with grain, and knowing that several United States war-ships would soon be after him, Semmes, who did not want to fight, but only to destroy instead, sailed south towards the West Indies, capturing, among other ships, the *Wales*, from India, on which were several ladies. That, however, did not deter him from setting the vessel on fire. He removed the ladies to the *Alabama*, making his conduct meritorious from the fact that he permitted them to bring on board their wardrobes. One of the ladies was the daughter of a general in the British army, married to an American gentleman, and had three children. What Captain Semmes would have done had he fallen in with the *Kearsarge* with these captives on board, we do not know; but he had no desire just then to encounter a war vessel.

Off St. Domingo the *Alabama* captured the *Parker Cooke*, of Boston. The following, from Captain Semmes's book, shows once more the spirit of the commander of the *Alabama:* "It was sunset, the twilight hour, when the breeze was dying away, that we applied the torch. As we filled away and made sail I could but moralize on the spectacle. Sixty years before, the negro had cut the throat of the white man, ravished his wife and daughters, and burned his dwelling in the island of St. Domingo, now in sight. The white man of another country was now inciting the negro to the perpetration of the same crimes against another white man, whom he called his brother. The white man thus inciting the negro was the Puritan of New England, whose burning ship was lighting up the shores of St. Domingo.

"That Puritan, only a generation before, had entered into a solemn league and covenant to restore to the Southern man his fugitive slave, if he should escape into his territory. This was the way he was keeping his plighted faith. Does any one wonder that the *Alabama* burned New England ships?"(')

Bitterness and hate grow by what they feed on. When Captain Semmes began the work of destruction, in command of the *Sumter*, there were some qualms of conscience—an unwillingness and reluctance to take a crew from a ship, strip them of all except the clothes on their backs, and consign a noble vessel to flames. There was so much of the highwayman about the transaction that his better nature revolted; but as vessel after vessel fell into his hands, the reluctance gave place to an unquenchable desire to burn and destroy.

His book was written in 1869, four years after the war. Were he living, it is charitable to believe that he would wish it had never been written; but it presents a true picture of the motives, feelings, and actions of the men who attempted to build a nation with slavery for its corner-stone.

In December, Captain Semmes made his way from the West Indies westward into the Gulf of Mexico. He had two objects in view—one to waylay one of the California steamers, with the expectation of getting possession of a million dollars or more in gold; the other, to intercept the expedition under General Banks, on its way to the Mississippi. Captain Semmes put himself in the path of the California steamers, and waited for his prey. He soon had the satisfaction of seeing a large steamer approaching, but it was steering south instead of north; it was the *Ariel*, bound to Panama, with a great number of passengers, many of whom were women and children. Captain Semmes says: "I was very anxious to destroy this ship, as she belonged to Mr. Vanderbilt, an old steamboat captain, who had amassed a large fortune in trade, and was a bitter enemy of the South."(*) He kept the *Ariel* several days, hoping that another ship would come along to take her passengers, so that he could burn her; but none came, and he was obliged to let the vessel go on her way.

The engines of the *Alabama* were repaired, and her course was taken across the Gulf to Galveston.

The story of the engagement with the *Hatteras*, one of the blockading fleet, has already been told ("Marching to Victory," p. 39). After the easy victory over a ship that was no match for the Confederate vessel, Semmes entered the harbor of Kingston, Jamaica, landed his prisoners, and repaired his ship. Three English war-ships were there, the officers of which received Captain Semmes with great cordiality. The *Alabama* had been built in England, and they had a pride in her. The sympathies of the English officers were all on the side of the South. They had not forgotten that the pride of Great Britain had been humbled when the *Constitution*, in 1812, sent the *Guerriere* to the bottom of the sea, and all the other victories of that war, which compelled her to resign her title of "Mistress of the Seas."

Commerce has its highway on the ocean as well as on the land. Such a path lies along the coast of Brazil, where the ships sailing to that country, together with those that go round Cape Horn, those that come from the East Indies, and the Cape of Good Hope, find favoring winds and currents. Captain Semmes had destroyed the whalers in the region of the Azores, the grain ships off Newfoundland, and now he would carry destruction to the fleets on this great South Atlantic highway. It would not do for him to remain long at Kingston, for in a few days the North would know it, and it might be difficult to get away. He sailed eastward.

One day's sail brought him into the great highway, where he picked up the ship *Golden Rule*, which was soon in flames. This his exultant account: "The islands of Santo Domingo and Jamaica were sufficiently near for their inhabitants to witness the splendid bonfire which lighted up the heavens soon after dark. A looker-on would have seen a beautiful picture; for besides the burning ship there were the islands, sleeping in the dreamy moonlight, on the calm bosom of a tropical sea, and the rakish-looking 'British Pirate' steaming in for land, with every spar and line of cordage brought out in bold relief by the bright flame, with the very 'pirates' themselves visible, handling the bales and boxes of merchandise which they had 'robbed' from this innocent Yankee, whose countrymen at home were engaged in the Christian occupation of burning our houses and desolating our fields."(²)

The next day the *Chastelaine* was captured, on the 3d of February was captured the *Palmetto*, and two days later the *Olive Jane* and the *Golden Eagle*. Semmes saw a great many other vessels, but they were of other nations. The man at the mast-head saw not less than seven ships at a time on this great highway of the ocean. There was scarcely a day that an American vessel did not fall into the clutches of the *Alabama*, followed by the lighting up of the sea.

Day after day the work of destruction went on as Semmes made his way slowly towards Brazil, running into the Island Fernando de Noronha, which lies just off the coast. A remarkable peak rises from the sea, and, once seen, is always remembered by sailors. All vessels on the great highway take their bearings from it. Here Captain Semmes violated the neutrality laws of nations by taking two of his captured vessels into port. While there, two American vessels came sailing towards the harbor, and disregarding all the laws of nations, he steamed out to capture them and set them on fire. For two months the *Alabama* hovered along the coast, taking ten vessels. But it was time for Semmes to be gone, for he knew that a powerful and swift steamer was after him—the *Vanderbilt*.

The course of the *Alabama* had been well predicted by the Navy Department at Washington, and the *Vanderbilt* was chosen to follow her, commanded by Captain Baldwin, who was ordered to hasten to the West Indies, and then go down the coast of Brazil and on to the Cape of Good Hope. He was at Martinique on the 28th of February. Rear-admiral Wilkes was in command of the United States fleet in the West Indies, and the *Vanderbilt* was so much nicer than his own ship that he took possession of her, holding her as his flag-ship. There cannot be much doubt that this interference with the plan of the Government enabled the *Alabama* to go on with her work of destruction. When the Secretary of the Navy learned that Wilkes had interfered with the plan, he was summarily ordered home, and had no other important service during the war.

Having stayed as long as prudence dictated at Brazil, Semmes steered for the Cape of Good Hope. No need that we should follow the *Alabama* in her cruise in the Indian Ocean during the next six months. The *Vanderbilt* followed to the Cape of Good Hope, but was a month behind, in consequence of the detention of that steamer by Wilkes. The *Wyoming* was in the East Indies, but Semmes carefully avoided her. There were but few ships for him to capture in those distant seas, and he turned back, stopped once more at the Cape, where he was treated with great consideration by the English officers, then made his way north, passing the Azores, capturing several vessels and setting them on fire. He steamed into the harbor of Cherbourg, on the northern coast of France. He did not quite dare to venture into an English home port, for possibly he would

June 11, 1864. not be allowed to leave. The *Alabama* had been built in England; she had a captain and officers who held commissions in the Confederate navy; but the civilized world regarded England as, in fact, responsible for her. Some of the thinking men of Great Britain, now that the armies of the North were winning victories, were beginning to see that a day of reckoning was coming in the future for England. Semmes intended to have the *Alabama* thoroughly repaired. The news of her arrival was quickly flashed to Paris, London, and all over Europe, for the story of her exploits had been published far and wide.

Opening our maps to Holland, we see the river Scheldt pouring its flood into the ocean through several mouths. A vessel flying the Stars and Stripes — the *Kearsarge* — was lying in one of the outlets opposite the village of Flushing. Some of the officers were on shore when, looking towards the ship, they saw a signal-flag flutter out at her masthead, ordering them to return at once. They also saw the flash, and heard the roar of one of her guns, fired as a signal. Arriving on board, they were informed that Mr. Dayton, the American Minister at Paris, had sent a telegram that the *Alabama* was at Cherbourg. A few minutes

CHART OF THE CRUISE OF THE "ALABAMA."

later the propeller began to whirl, and the *Kearsarge* steamed west, with the lowlands of Holland on the port bow, and the white, chalky cliffs of Dover, in England, on the starboard. She steamed into the harbor of Cherbourg, but did not come to anchor, for were she to do so, and the *Alabama* go out, the *Kearsarge* would be compelled to remain twenty-four hours. Her captain was careful not to be hampered in any way. The *Kearsarge* was named for a mountain in New Hampshire, beneath the shadow of which Daniel Webster, the great defender of the Constitution was born. Her commander, John A. Winslow, was born in North Carolina, but, though his State had seceded, he remained true to the old flag. The crew of the *Kearsarge* were seamen

June 14, 1864.

THE "KEARSARGE."

who, when the war began, were on merchant vessels, but who had enlisted to defend their country.

Backward and forward, now east, now west, the ship moved, with a man up in the foretop looking with his glass into the harbor, patiently waiting for the appearance of the ship which had done so much destruction upon the seas, and brought poverty to so many homes. Captain Winslow determined that the *Alabama* should not escape from Cherbourg as she did from Jamaica.

But Captain Semmes did not intend to steal away. He could not afford to attempt it. He was in command of a ship built after a model prepared originally for an English gunboat. She had stolen away from an English port at the outset; away from the *San Jacinto* at Kingston,

Jamaica, another English port. She was armed with English guns; the great majority of her crew were English. Captain Semmes had been banqueted by officers of the English navy in the West Indies, at the Cape of Good Hope, Gibraltar, Singapore, Liverpool, and London. He was regarded as a hero. Clergymen of the Church of England had made him their welcome guest. Merchants had invited him to grand dinners. He was their benefactor, for through his destruction of the property of American merchants they had been able to purchase a great fleet of swift-sailing ships for a song. Through the destruction of so many vessels they had become the world's carriers. The burning wrecks illuming midnight skies on lonely seas, reducing opulent families to beggary, had lighted their paths to fortune.

There are times when men must show what stuff they are made of. Such a time had come to Semmes. Were he to steal away now, men who had fraternized with him might in the future pass him by without notice; for outside Cherbourg harbor was an antagonist, a ship almost the counterpart of the *Alabama* in size, armament, and crew. Were he to run away, people might think he was lacking courage. More than this, a good many people in Europe were beginning to see that the course pursued by the *Alabama* was not a manly method of warfare.

In social circles, in the club-houses of London and Paris, men whose sympathies sided with the North were likening the conduct of Semmes in waylaying peaceful, defenceless vessels to the bandit who steals upon his victim, or the prowler who robs a house and fires it at night. A ship was a seaman's home; he had no other. On shipboard only could he obtain bread for himself and family. In burning a ship Semmes might injure the American merchants, but at the same time he was doing grievous injury to a great many sailors who were not Americans, who were earning bread for themselves and families by shipping on American vessels. Even if Semmes had acted strictly in accordance with the laws of nations, which he had not, his setting men on shore in out-of-the-way places, without food for more than a day or two, without clothing, without means of any kind to save themselves from starvation—men who were not fighting against the South, who were not American citizens—was abhorrent to the advancing humanity of the age. It was not sufficient for Semmes to say in excuse that the armies of the North were burning Southern homes. A ship was not like a house on shore. If the house were destroyed the land was still there, and harvests might still be grown and reaped, and there were kind neighbors to supply the homeless and destitute.

For the sailor whose ship had made "a beautiful bonfire" there was no sheltering home, no helping hand, no food, no sympathy from the men who had fired their vessels. It is possible that Semmes, on his passing the Azores, over the waters where the *Alabama* began her work of destruction, experienced a momentary depression of spirits. There is an undertone of melancholy in the pages of his book, as if the memories of the past were not altogether satisfactory. He knew that the prospects of the South were waning. Grant had taken Vicksburg; Gettysburg had been fought. All England knew that the resources of the South were rapidly diminishing; that the North was redoubling its energies. Men who had been enthusiastic for the South were beginning to see that it was only a question of time when the Confederacy would disappear, and that possibly there might come a time when John Bull would have to make some apology or reparation to the United States for what the *Alabama* had been doing; or that possibly the time might come when privateers of other nations would be lighting up the ocean with bonfires of British ships.

Semmes knew that it would be difficult for him to get away from the *Kearsarge*, eying with sleepless vigilance the narrow entrance to the harbor. There is no evidence that he desired to steal away. He knew that he must fight or suffer loss of prestige and character. He did not send a challenge direct to Captain Winslow, but wrote a letter to a gentleman in Cherbourg, saying that after he had made repairs he intended to go out and engage the *Kearsarge*. The telegraph flashed the information to Paris and London, and those who desired to see the battle hastened to Cherbourg. Four days passed, in which Semmes was getting ready for battle, sending all valuable articles on shore — chronometers, watches, and gold captured from the vessels burned. The coal-bunkers were filled, to protect the engines. All Cherbourg was buzzing with the news that there was to be a battle which everybody would be able to see. The news was flashed again to Paris and London. Men talked about it in the cafés, and rushed to the cars, which whirled them to Cherbourg.

Saturday morning came. The officers of the French navy at Cherbourg invited Semmes to a dinner-party, together with some of his officers. The talk was of the battle which Semmes informed them he intended to fight. He was confident of winning the victory. He would either sink the *Kearsarge* or add another vessel to the Confederate navy. It is not quite easy to see what grounds Semmes had for his confident expectations. He had never been in a battle save in the attack upon the *Hatteras*, which was no match for the *Alabama*. He did not know from experience the quality of his crew in battle. He only knew they were a reckless, rollicking set, whom he had controlled by his iron will.

Quite likely the capture of so many merchant ships without resistance led Semmes to overrate his own strength and to underrate that of the *Kearsarge*. Possibly, also, the contempt which he had for the men of the North, in common with the people of the South, at the beginning of the war, that one Southerner was equal to five Yankees, had its effect. The officers drank their wine, and assured the French officers that they would celebrate the victory on Sunday night at a grand dinner.

On the *Kearsarge*, this Saturday night, the officers were talking of the battle which they expected might be fought, though they did not know what Semmes's intentions might be. They expected it to be a hard-fought contest. There was no boasting; they were not confident of winning the victory, but they had one resolution—to go to the bottom of the sea before they would surrender the ship to a craft that had done so much damage, and which had the character of a corsair rather than that of a ship-of-war.(¹⁰) The *Kearsarge* was ready, and had been throughout the week, with her pivot-guns pointed starboard, shot and shell, grape and canister all piled beside the guns.

When Admiral Farragut ran past the forts below New Orleans, he hung his chain-cables in loops along the sides of his ships to protect them. Captain Winslow, more than a year before, hung his spare chains up and down the sides of the *Kearsarge*, and covered them with light planking, painted like the rest of his ship. His coal-bunkers were not full, and the chains might be some protection to the machinery.

Let us look at the two vessels on this Saturday night—one thoroughly English, though officered by Confederates; the other thoroughly American. They are almost exactly of the same size—the *Alabama* of 1016 tons, the *Kearsarge* 1031 tons. This was their respective armament: *Alabama*, six long 32-pounders, one rifled 100-pounder, one 8-inch shell gun—eight guns. *Kearsarge*, four short 32-pounders, two 11-inch smoothbore pivots, one 30-pounder rifle—seven guns.

Though the Confederate vessel has one more gun than the Union ship, the seven solid shot of the latter, if they could be thrown at the same moment, would be sixty pounds heavier than the eight solid shot of the *Alabama*; but in the coming contest the *Kearsarge* would be able to use only five guns, so that the weight of the shot would be nearly equal. Discipline, coolness, precision, were to be factors in a contest where everything else was so evenly matched. Patriotism would also come in. The crew of the one were Britishers, who had enlisted for adventure, prize-money, and

CAPT. JOHN A. WINSLOW.

loot: they cared very little for the Confederacy or its flag; while the men on the other looked up to the flag above them as the brightest banner in the world. They had not enlisted for pay; they could make more money catching codfish. They had not enlisted with the expectation of obtaining plunder, but to serve their country.

Sunday morning. The sunshine falls upon a glassy sea. There is little wind to ruffle the water. The *Kearsarge* is off the northern entrance to the breakwater, three miles from land. Her decks have been holy-stoned and washed, the brass-work around the wheel and binnacle rubbed and polished. The crew are in their Sunday muster suits. They have been inspected. It is ten o'clock, the hour for

June 19, 1864.

religious service. The bell is tolling. Captain Winslow is ready to begin the reading of prayers.

"The *Alabama* is coming!" The man up in the foretop-gallant shouts it. The officer of the deck repeats it. The drummer beats to arms. Captain Winslow lays aside the prayer-book and grasps his speaking-trumpet. A moment ago the men were standing reverently in worship; now they are beside their guns, with jackets thrown aside, ready for action.

The *Kearsarge* turns her bows seaward, but she is not going to run away. Captain Winslow intends that the contest shall be so far from land that the French Government shall not have cause for complaint or interference, and also that the *Alabama* shall not have a chance to run back to the harbor in case she is crippled. As for the *Kearsarge*, she is to go to the bottom, or win the victory.([11])

Cherbourg harbor is alive with boats. Every fisherman has hoisted the sails of his little craft. The French ship-of-war *Couronne* is steaming alongside the *Alabama* to see that she goes beyond the three-mile limit. When it is reached, the *Couronne* turns about and courteously retires, not staying to be a witness of the contest. The English yacht *Deerhound* follows the *Alabama*. Her owner and his family are on board: his sympathies are with the South. His children want to see the battle, and he wishes to gratify them.([12]) What a scene along the shore!—thirty thousand men, women, and children clustering on the beach or on the housetops, gazing seaward. The sweet-toned bells up in the cathedral tower are tolling for service, but the priests chant the mass alone.

It is almost eleven o'clock when the *Kearsarge*, seven miles from land, turns in a circle, and, bringing her bow towards the shore, steers for the *Alabama*. There are moments when men hold their breath, when their hearts beat like sledge-hammers, when every faculty is at the utmost tension. Such a moment has come to the sailors on the deck of the *Kearsarge*. The vessels are three-fourths of a mile apart, when the *Alabama* opens fire. Had we been on board the *Alabama* we should have seen officers wearing their uniforms, and the crew neatly dressed. Every needful preparation had been made for the contest; the decks cleared. "The ship is ready for action, sir," said the executive officer, Mr. Kell, saluting Captain Semmes. "Send all hands aft," said the captain, who, standing on a gun-carriage, made a speech to the crew, who responded with cheers. Captain Winslow thought that the *Alabama* intended to fight the battle at long range. "More steam," was his order, and the *Kearsarge* surged through the water, rapidly narrowing the distance between the vessels. Again the cannon of the *Alabama* flamed. Still no answer from the

"KEARSARGE" AND "ALABAMA".—HAULING DOWN THE FLAG.
From a sketch by T. de Thulstrup, by permission of L. Prang & Co.

Kearsarge, whose guns had been loaded with shells the fuses of which were cut to explode in five seconds. Nine hundred yards—half a mile— and the 11-inch starboard guns break the silence. Broadside to broadside are the two vessels steaming in circles, each using her starboard guns. The tide drifts westward. A shot carries away a rope on the *Alabama*, and the flag comes down upon the run. The sailors on the *Kearsarge* regard it as a good omen, and give a cheer. ([13])

But the battle had only just begun, and the flag again fluttered in the breeze at the mizzen of the *Alabama*, whose guns were fired rapidly; but the gunners, in their excitement, did not take good aim. Not so the firing of the *Kearsarge*. "Take direct aim. Aim the heavy guns below the water-line. Sweep the *Alabama's* decks with the lighter guns," the instructions to the gunners. ([14])

The men of the *Kearsarge* watched their shells as they sped through the air.

"That's a good one! Hurrah! Give her another like the last! Now we have her! Hurrah!" they shouted, and rammed down the cartridges.

Eleven o'clock and fifteen minutes. A 68-pounder shell crashes through the starboard bulwark of the *Kearsarge*, explodes with terrible concussion, wounding three of the men working the aft pivot-gun. The men are carried below to the surgeon so quietly that those in the forecastle do not know that any one has been injured. Two shots enter the ports, but do no injury. Another shell explodes on board. "The ship is on fire!" is the cry; but it is quickly extinguished.

On board the *Alabama* Captain Semmes is by the mizzen-mast with his spy-glass, watching the effect of the shot upon the *Kearsarge*. He sees a shell strike and fall into the water. He does not discover the chain cables which Captain Winslow has hung against the side of the ship. "Use solid shot, Mr. Kell; the shells fall into the water," ([15]) he says to the executive officer; and solid shot and shell alternately spin across the water from the guns of the *Alabama*. The 11-inch shells of the *Kearsarge* are making fearful havoc the while. Three successively explode, killing and wounding several of the men. The great guns of the *Kearsarge*, aimed below the water-line of the *Alabama*, have pierced her sides and the water is pouring in through the shot-holes, and the vessel begins to settle. Captain Semmes sees that the battle is going against him. "Be ready to make all sail possible," his order to Mr. Kell. The decks are strewn with killed and wounded, and slippery with blood. So many are killed that Mr. Kell directs the crew to throw the mangled bodies into the sea. Sails are hoisted and the bowsprit turned towards the shore.

"The fires are out, the engine will not work," said the chief engineer, coming on deck.

"Go below, Mr. Kell, and see how long the ship can float," said Captain Semmes. Mr. Kell goes down the gangway into the wardroom, where stands the assistant-surgeon, Mr. Llewellyn, an Englishman. A wounded sailor is lying on the table, and the surgeon is dressing the wounds, when an 11-inch shell crashes through the side of the ship, and table and sailor are hurled across the room.

Mr. Kell sees that the water is pouring in, and runs upon the deck. "We cannot keep afloat ten minutes," he shouts.

"Cease firing. Shorten sail. Haul down the colors! It will not do for us to go down with our decks covered with wounded," are the words of Semmes.(¹⁶)

The colors of the *Alabama* came down, and the *Kearsarge* ceased firing. Captain Winslow, to prevent the *Alabama* from reaching the shore, steamed ahead, and was in position to pour in a raking fire. According to the report of Captain Winslow, the *Alabama* again fired. "He is playing us a trick; give him another broadside," he said, and again the cannon of the *Kearsarge* sent their shells into the sinking ship.(¹⁷)

"Show a white flag," was the order from Semmes, and the quarter-master ran up a white flag on the stern. "Send a boat and an officer to the *Kearsarge*, and tell them that we are sinking," was the order of Semmes to Mr. Kell, and the quartermaster's mate jumped into the small-boat, the only one not injured, and hastened to the *Kearsarge*, while another boat, not badly injured, was lowered, and the wounded placed in it.

Lower in the water settles the *Alabama*. Captain Semmes is at the stern. "Every man for himself," is his last order. The stern is almost to the water's edge. With a life-preserver on, and throwing his sword into the sea, he drops overboard and swims towards the *Deerhound*, which has been watching the contest and which is steaming up. With a lurch, at 12.24 o'clock, the *Alabama* goes down beneath the waves.

"For God's sake do what you can to save them!" shouted Captain Winslow to Mr. Lancaster, owner of the *Deerhound*, and the boats of the yacht were quickly lowered, picking up Captain Semmes, Mr. Kell, twelve other officers, and twenty-six men. The boats of the *Kearsarge* were quickly lowered, and rescued all that could be found—about seventy. The owner of the *Deerhound* had been requested by Captain Winslow, in the interest of humanity, to save the struggling men, but having picked up Captain Semmes, and nearly all the officers, instead of coming alongside the *Kearsarge*, he began to move away.

"She is steaming away. Why not send a shot after her?" said an officer.

"Oh no; she is only coming round. No Englishman flying the flag of the Royal Yacht Squadron would go away without communicating with me," said Captain Winslow.(¹ˢ)

But his confidence was misplaced; the *Deerhound* kept her course, her owner, senseless to the dishonorable act, carried the Confederate officers to England, when by every principle of honor he was bound to remain alongside the *Kearsarge*. It was a British vessel, manned largely by Englishmen, which had been sunk, and his sympathy for the Confederacy and chagrin over the discomfiture of a British-built ship outweighed his better judgment and sense of honor.

Very little damage had been done to the *Kearsarge*. One 100-pound shell lodged in the stern part which, if it had exploded, quite likely would have left the ship unmanageable, and might have resulted in her going to the bottom of the sea instead of the *Alabama*. One of the Confederate officers, Lieutenant Armstrong, refused to go on board the *Deerhound*, when picked up by a French pilot-boat, but came and personally delivered up his sword to Captain Winslow.

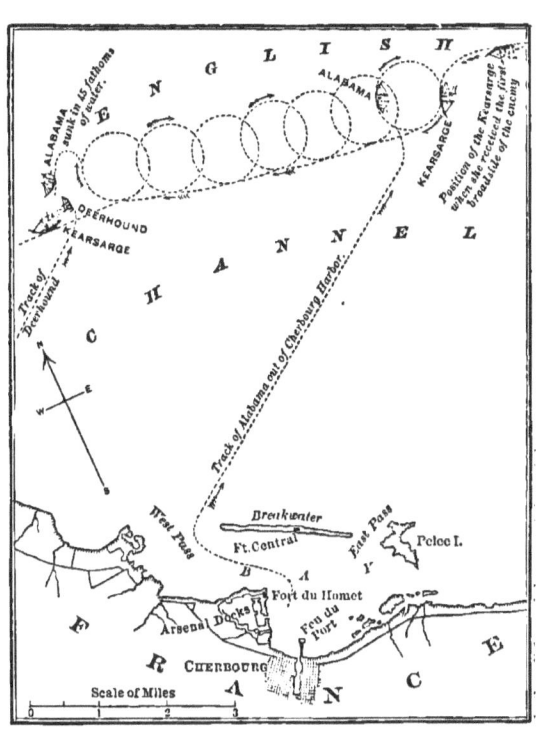

MOVEMENTS OF THE "ALABAMA" AND "KEARSARGE."

In strong contrast to this noble action was the conduct of Mr. Fullam, who, after reporting to Captain Winslow that the *Alabama* was sinking, asked permission to help save the men, and who promised to return to the *Kearsarge*, but who, instead, went on board the *Deerhound*. Captain Semmes had hauled down his flag, and raised the white flag in token of surrender. "Where shall I land you?" said the owner of the *Deerhound* to Captain Semmes. "I am now under English colors, and the sooner you put me with my officers and men on English soil the better," he replied.([19]) The *Deerhound* could not have picked him up except at the request of Captain Winslow; he could not honorably avail himself of the opportunity to escape; and his course, together with that of the owner of the yacht, will ever stand in dishonorable contrast to that of Lieutenant Armstrong.

One of the crew of the aft pivot-gun of the *Kearsarge* was William Gowin, who was wounded. He fell upon the deck, but dragged himself towards the hatch, and was lowered to the surgeon's table.

"Doctor, I can fight no more, and so come to you; but it is all right. I am satisfied, for we are whipping the *Alabama*. I will willingly lose my leg."

There was exultation throughout the United States when the news came that the *Alabama* was lying at the bottom of the sea; but in England there was chagrin and mortification among those who sympathized with the South, and who had rejoiced to know that the *Alabama* was lighting the sea with burning American vessels, thus bringing more commerce to the ships of Great Britain. When Captain Semmes reached London he was invited to a banquet, received as a hero, and presented with a sword.

During the months that the *Alabama* roamed the seas, Captain Semmes burned fifty ships, released ten on bond, changed one — the *Conrad*—into a tender to the *Alabama*, and renamed it the *Tuscaloosa;* one vessel was sold; making in all sixty-two vessels. It was not merely the burning of the vessels which entailed loss upon the citizens of the United States, but it compelled the merchants to transfer their ships to parties in England, thus driving the American flag from the seas, and giving the commerce of the world into the hands of Great Britain. Nearly a third of a century has gone by, and the United States, during the period, has not been able to recover what it thus lost through the destruction of ships by this vessel, which the British Government criminally allowed to sail from Liverpool, against the oft-repeated protestations of the Government of the United States. Great Britain has acknowledged her culpability by the payment of fifteen million dollars, awarded by the Conference of Arbitrators at Geneva in 1871, which settled all matters in dispute; but no court of claims can wipe out the sense of wrong and the indignation engendered in the United States against the Government of Great Britain during the career of the *Alabama*. Not till the Stars and Stripes are seen once more in just proportion in the carrying trade of the world, will the sense of wrong be wholly obliterated from the minds of the American people.

NOTES TO CHAPTER XI.

([1]) Raphael Semmes, "Memoirs of Service Afloat," pp. 566, 409, 464, 459, 465, 524, 535, 566.
([2]) Idem.
([3]) Idem.
([4]) Idem.
([5]) Idem.
([6]) Idem.
([7]) Idem.
([8]) Idem.
([9]) J. M. Browne, *Century Magazine*, April, 1886.
([10]) Idem.
([11]) J. McIntosh Kell, *Century Magazine*, April, 1886.
([12]) J. M. Browne, *Century Magazine*, April, 1886.
([13]) Idem.
([14]) J. McIntosh Kell, *Century Magazine*, April, 1886.
([15]) Idem.
([16]) J. M. Browne, *Century Magazine*, April, 1886.
([17]) Idem.
([18]) J. McIntosh Kell, *Century Magazine*, 1886.
([19]) Idem.

CHAPTER XII.

FROM COLD HARBOR TO PETERSBURG.

WE left the Army of the Potomac resting at Cold Harbor after its repulse and great loss of men in the attempt of General Grant to carry the Confederate intrenchments. While the army was thus at rest, while the cavalry under Sheridan was having an engagement with the Confederate cavalry, near Louisa Court-house and Trevilian's Depot, General Gillmore and General Kautz were moving quietly from Bermuda Hundred with the intention of seizing Petersburg.

General Butler had laid a pontoon-bridge between Bermuda Hundred and City Point, across the Appomattox; but he had not taken the precaution to cover the planks with grass or earth. The night was calm and still, and when the cavalry horses and the wheels of the cannon came upon the planks, the trampling and rumbling were heard in Petersburg, and General Wise, who was in command of the Confederates there, at once comprehended the meaning of it; that it was a movement for the capture of that town. If seized, it would be a serious blow to Lee, for Wilmington, in North Carolina, was the only seaport which blockade-runners bringing supplies from England could enter, except now and then a vessel, perchance, might slip into Charlestown. If Petersburg were lost, all supplies must come from Danville, and the south-west. General Beauregard, in front of Bermuda Hundred, had seen the danger. He had only a small force, most of his troops having been sent to Lee after the battle of Drewry's Bluff. Just before the pickets in front of Petersburg heard the trampling of the horses' hoofs on the bridge, Beauregard, at ten o'clock in the evening, sent this to General Bragg, at Richmond: "Pickets on the lower part of James River report one steamer towing up canal-boats and pontoons; also schooners going up heavily loaded, whereas those going down are light. This may indicate future operations of Grant." (¹)

June 9, 1864.

Before the army moved from Culpeper—before the battle of the Wilderness—Grant had looked forward to the time when he might possibly be at Petersburg. In his tent at Culpeper he had informed his private secretary of the possible outcome of his movements. When he was on the North Anna he said to those about him, "I feel that our final success over Lee's army is already insured." He was not aiming to take Richmond, but to defeat the Confederate army. Up to that time there had been a feeling in the Army of the Potomac that there was no commander under the Stars and Stripes quite able to inaugurate and carry out an aggressive and successful campaign against General Lee, but that feeling was gone; and though there had been fearful loss of life at Cold Harbor, the soldiers had faith in their general. He had reached the Chickahominy. Orders had already been issued for the sending of pontoons up the James, and Beauregard's pickets had discovered the steamboats ascending the river with a long train of boats at their sterns.

The James, below the Appomattox, is a wide, majestic stream, flowing south-easterly to the Chesapeake. Twelve miles below City Point is Wilcox's Landing, three miles from Charles City Court-house. The river is two thousand one hundred feet wide, and eighty feet deep. This is the point which General Grant had selected, on the report of the engineers, as the place where the bridge of boats was to be placed. It is thirty-five miles from Cold Harbor, and twenty from Petersburg. It was a great problem which confronted Grant. How should he transfer the army, with all its artillery, wagons, and supplies, to the south side of the James without exposing it to attack from Lee, who had a very much shorter line, with a railroad by which he could quickly transport his troops? Would not Lee, as soon as he discovered what was going on, transfer enough brigades to Bermuda Hundred to overwhelm the small force under Butler? McClellan was much praised for making a change of base from the Chickahominy to Harrison's Landing, a distance of ten miles. While doing it Lee pushed down the Charles City road, and attacked him. Would he not do the same now, with the army drawn out upon a thin line? Would it be possible to withdraw the troops without their being attacked? If Petersburg could be captured in advance it would greatly simplify the problem. It was to that end that the cavalry under Kautz, and the infantry under Gillmore, were marching across the pontoon-bridge at Point of Rocks, on the Appomattox, at midnight. Kautz had one thousand five hundred horsemen, and Gillmore three thousand infantry.

Had we been in Petersburg that morning of June 9th, we should have seen a great commotion. General Wise was there with his brigade of two thousand. He called upon the citizens to take their places in the ranks, and old men and boys were hastening to obey the orders, arming themselves with muskets. The convalescent Confederate soldiers in the hospitals were called out to stand guard in the breastworks. In the jail and guard-houses was a motley collection of criminals. The doors were unlocked, and they were hustled out, supplied with arms, and hurried to the intrenchments east of the city. General Wise called those from the hospitals his corps of "Patients"; those from the jails, "Penitents."(²)

General Beauregard, in front of Bermuda Hundred, learned what was going on, and sent a brigade of cavalry, under General Dearing, which came later in the day upon a gallop across the Appomattox, rode through the city, and pushed south-east to meet Kautz. Wise had a battery of artillery under Graham. The Union force, all told, was not far from four thousand five hundred; the Confederate, two thousand six hundred, with the advantage of position greatly on the side of the Confederates. At seven o'clock in the morning Gillmore, with the infantry, was in front of the Confederate intrenchments. Kautz had gone south-west, and was five miles away. Gillmore examined the intrenchments, saw the sunlight glinting on the Confederate cannon. The Confederate "patients" and "penitents" were marching and countermarching along the breastworks, and he came to the conclusion that they were too strong to be assaulted. It was nine o'clock before Kautz was in position. After a short struggle he turned the Confederate flank, pushed on almost into the town, when Dearing, with the Confederate cavalry, confronted him. At that moment Gillmore, having heard nothing from the Union cavalry, began his return to City Point, the movement a failure, with nothing attempted, no assault, no manifestation of energy, and the result a complication which made the movement of the army much more difficult than it otherwise would have been, and enabled Beauregard to hold the city, the loss of which would soon have compelled Lee to evacuate Richmond.

General Grant had not only the James, but the Chickahominy, to cross. Eight miles from Cold Harbor was Bottom's Bridge. Long Bridge was fifteen miles, Jones's twenty miles, and Windsor twenty-four miles distant, all of which had been destroyed. Two miles below Bottom's Bridge the creek which winds through White Oak Swamp empties into the Chickahominy. How to get the army across the two streams, how to get troops to Butler sufficient to hold Bermuda Hundred, how to cover the movement, were the three features of the problem. The Eighteenth Corps, under Smith, which had come to Cold Harbor from Butler by York River, was the first to move, going by the same route, marching in the night, having the right of way over everything else. The soldiers reached White House, went down York River, and up the James, before Lee learned of their departure. A brigade of cavalry, under Wilson, crossed the Chickahominy, and moved up the roads towards Richmond. Pontoons were laid, and the Fifth Corps, under Warren, the Second, under Hancock, crossed at Long Bridge, Warren following the cavalry. The Sixth Corps marched towards Jones's Bridge, while the long lines of wagons went farther down, to Windsor, crossed the stream, and then made their way towards Windmill Point, all moving like clock-work.

It was one o'clock on the morning of June 13th when the pontoons were laid at Long Bridge. A few moments later the cavalry were moving up the road to Riddel's shop, near which three roads diverge, all leading towards Richmond. They came upon the Confederate cavalry at the shop, and just at daylight there was the rattle of carbines; but Warren, with two divisions of the Fifth Corps, was close at hand, which made their way a short distance up the Charles City and Central roads, driving the Confederates. While this was going on, the Second Corps crossed the Chickahominy, and marched straight on towards the James, paying no attention to the rattle of musketry up by Riddel's. The soldiers took the long swinging step which carried them rapidly on, and at five in the afternoon were at Wilcox's Landing. At the same hour the Fifth was at St. Mary's Church, covering the movement of the Sixth and Ninth corps from Jones's Bridge. At five o'clock on the next afternoon the entire army, with the trains, were on the bank of the James. It was four o'clock that afternoon when the engineers, under Major Duane, began to put the pontoons in place. Vessels were anchored above with strong cables trailing from their sterns, to which the boats were fastened. The river was so wide that one hundred and one boats were needed. So well had everything been planned by the engineers that at midnight the last plank was in place, and the bridge ready for the crossing. Before it was completed, the Second Corps, under General Hancock, began to cross on ferry-boats, and at four o'clock in the morning of the 15th the whole of that corps and four batteries were on the southern bank.

June 13, 1864.

June 14, 1864.

When the sun rose on the morning of the 13th the Confederate pickets at Cold Harbor found no men in blue before them. A little later General Lee learned that Grant was advancing upon Richmond south of the Chickahominy. He had no suspicion of the real movement, and sent Anderson's corps down the Charles City road, while A. P. Hill's corps crossed the Chickahominy and moved down to Riddel's shop, but when Hill arrived there he found that the Fifth Corps was no longer there.

Little things, quite as often as great things, overturn the best laid plans. The wagons of the Second Corps had not arrived. General Grant had seen that they could not reach Wilcox's Landing until some hours after the troops. He had issued orders to General Butler to have sixty thousand rations there for General Hancock. Upon receiving them, Hancock was to march as rapidly as possible towards Petersburg, to a point where the Norfolk Railroad crosses Harrison's Creek. Hancock had twenty thousand men, and the rations would last him three days. But the supplies were not there. General Meade, at 7.30 on the morning of the 15th, ordered Hancock to move without waiting for his rations. The signal-officer who received the despatch did not immediately deliver it, and it was not till 10.30 that the troops began the seventeen-mile march which would take them to their assigned position. This was a serious delay, as we shall presently discover.

June 15, 1864.

We have seen the Eighteenth Corps steaming down the York and up the James. It reached its old camp at Bermuda Hundred just as the sun was setting on the 14th. The troops had rested on the steamer, and were fresh and vigorous. General Smith was ordered to move at daylight on the 15th from Point of Rocks, on the Appomattox, following General Kautz, who was directed to start at once, but who did not move till morning. Smith was to seize the intrenchments at Petersburg. He had, with the cavalry, seventeen thousand men. General Hancock had not been informed that Smith was to move, which was a serious error. Hancock was moving towards what he supposed to be Harrison's Creek; but the map was wrong, and he took a road several miles longer than the one he otherwise would have taken.

Smith had only six miles to march. We see him moving south, the colored troops, under General Hinks, marching from City Point. Two miles, and Kautz came upon the Confederates, who fired upon the advancing skirmishers. Two miles farther, and a battery of artillery opened fire from behind a breastwork. It was nearly noon before the troops of General Hinks were in position to attack the battery. It was to be the first battle of the colored soldiers, who, a few months before, were in slavery. It had been no light task to enlist and discipline them. Men who hated them because they were negroes predicted that they would run like sheep the moment they heard the whistling of bullets or the thunder of cannon. They are in the edge of a piece of woods facing west; before them is a cleared field. On the farther side they see a bank of earth, with four cannon and soldiers behind it. The shells come crashing through the trees around them. They do not flinch, but move out of the woods in a compact line. With a yell they rush across the field.

THE SECOND CORPS, GENERAL HANCOCK, CROSSING THE JAMES.
From a sketch made at the time.

There is a quick limbering up of cannon by the Confederates, the drivers lashing their horses to a run. The troops rush upon the hindmost, shooting the horses and capturing the piece. The air resounds with their triumphant shouts. They pat the muzzle of the captured gun, mount the carriage, swing their caps, and make the air ring with cheers. (³)

They had proved their manhood. Northern opposers of the war, who had denounced the enlistment of negroes, were silenced by the exhibition of their manhood at Wagner, Fort Pillow, and Petersburg. By their bravery and discipline they won the respect of the army, silenced their opponents, and accomplished great things for their race.

Let us go now into the Confederate lines and take a survey of affairs. At eight o'clock in the morning General Beauregard sent a telegram to Lee, informing him that a deserter had come into his lines with the information that Butler had been reinforced by the arrival of Smith. Beauregard was at Swift Creek, three miles north of Petersburg. He had only Wise's brigade and two regiments of cavalry, the citizens of Petersburg, and the men from the jail—in all, about twenty-seven hundred men, with twenty-two pieces of light artillery and heavy cannon. The entire force under Beauregard south of Richmond was about six thousand.(⁴) Slaves, during preceding months, had constructed a line of earthworks, beginning at the Appomattox, north-east of the city, and extending south, then west, round to the river—a line seven miles in length. Wise placed his troops behind the breastworks east and south of the town, leaving those on the south-west for a distance of four miles wholly undefended.

June 14, 1864.

Hoke's division, which was at Drewry's Bluff, had been ordered to hasten to Petersburg. It started at six in the morning; the distance was eighteen miles. It reached Petersburg after sunset. General Lee, with his whole army, the while, was on the north bank of the James, his lines extending from Malvern Hill, where he had been defeated in 1862, north to White Oak Swamp. General Beauregard was sending telegrams and messages to him, informing him that Grant was moving in force upon Petersburg. Lee did not credit the reports.

It was noon when the Union cavalry skirmishers approached Petersburg. They discovered a line of works two miles east of the city, with a formidable array of cannon. General Smith arrived and reconnoitred. He saw a broad valley, with the Appomattox on the north. East of the city, where he was about to attack, were ravines, ditches, breastworks, and fallen trees. The ground in front was swept by a cross-fire of the artillery. General Smith could see few Confederate troops, but more than twenty cannon behind the breastworks opened fire, and he thought that with so many guns in position there must be a large body of troops at hand. It took a long time to look over the ground, and to decide where it was best to attack. He sent Martindale's division towards the Appomattox to form the right, placed Brooks's division in the centre and Hinks's on the left, with the cavalry, dismounted, still farther on the left. The Confederate artillery had such a sweep, he decided to mass his own artillery in the centre, and after silencing the Confederate cannon, to send forward a strong skirmish line to capture the works. Heavy artillery-firing was going on against Kautz. Time was flying, the day fast waning. It was five o'clock before he had made up his mind what to do, and when the order was given for the artillery to wheel into position and open fire, it was found that the horses had been sent to the rear to be watered, and it was past six o'clock before they returned. Precious every moment to the Confederates! Through the day Wise had kept up as best he could an appearance of strength. Hoke's division, which started from Drewry's Bluff at six in the morning, had not arrived.([)

Going down now to Prince George Court-house, four miles from Smith's position, we see General Hancock receiving a message from Grant, who was at City Point, informing him that he must march as rapidly as possible to reinforce Smith. Hancock had been hunting for the railroad crossing at Harrison's Creek, to which he was ordered, but had not been able to find it, because his map was wrong. This was the first intimation he had received that Smith was about to make an attack. He turned towards Petersburg. Birney's division was in advance, and reached Smith just before he was ready to attack.

The sun was going down at the moment. The skirmishers met a sharp fire, but worked their way on, rushing at last upon the intrenchments. The brunt of the fire came upon the colored troops. They did not quail, though more than five hundred were killed and wounded. As in the forenoon, they went resolutely into the fight, and astonished the army by their steadiness under a galling and destructive fire. Five redans were captured, with sixteen pieces of artillery. The colored troops were the first inside the works. They seized four of the cannon and wheeled them upon the retreating Confederates. Three hundred prisoners were captured.

At the hour of 8 P.M. no reinforcements had reached the south side of the Appomattox to aid the Confederates in holding the city. Smith had only to press on, make one more determined assault with his whole line, reinforced now by two divisions of the Second Corps, and the Con-

GENERAL GRANT AT CITY POINT.

federates would be swept out of Petersburg. Why did not General Smith see that he had come to the supreme moment of his life? His troops had not suffered greatly. They had marched only six miles; had lain upon the ground while the Confederate shells had been hurled at them; had suffered a tension of nerve, which had made them all the more ready to finish the victory by sweeping the Confederates into the Appomattox. He asked Hancock to relieve his troops while he retired. And so we have the spectacle of thirty thousand Union troops lying down to rest with less than two thousand five hundred Confederates before them, who had been driven from their outer works, and who were ready to flee once more before a determined advance of the overwhelming force in their front! The great opportunity went by never to return.

Of the failure General Hancock said in his report, written the following week: "It should have been captured by the Eighteenth Corps, which was directed to assault the town with, I believe, fifteen thousand men; and certainly with the assistance of the two divisions of the Second Corps, which I offered to General Smith just after dark on the 15th, these two divisions being massed at Bryant's house, on the left and rear of General Hinks's division, about one mile from General Smith's line. Had I arrived before dark, and been able to have seen the general myself, I should have taken decisive action."(*)

Great events hang on little things. Whoever studies the history of the war will see it very often. The Second and Eighteenth corps were in front of the Confederate works at Petersburg, the colored troops holding those which they had captured. General Hancock was now in command. He had his own corps and the Eighteenth Corps, fully thirty-five thousand men. The Ninth Corps would be up by noon, and the Fifth before night. What Smith failed to accomplish was now within Hancock's grasp, as we shall presently see. It was a little thing that turned the scale and lost the second great opportunity to take Petersburg. It was the breaking-out afresh of the wound which Hancock received at Gettysburg. For six weeks the commander of the Second Corps had been in the saddle, directing the movements of his troops in the march or on the field of battle. The constant action, the loss of vital force from lack of sleep, the physical and mental strain, had told upon his system, and during the movement from Cold Harbor he had been compelled to ride in an ambulance, suffering intense pain. Pieces of bone were, on the morning of this 16th day of June, protruding through the flesh, rendering him incapable of directing the movements of the troops in person to the extent of seeing to the details, as was his custom.

June 16, 1864.

At midnight he issued his orders to his division commanders to seize all important points at daylight. Instead of moving at that hour, it was past eight o'clock, the sun three hours high, before there was any advance. General Birney was near the house of Mr. Avery, and might have occupied an advantageous position at daylight which at eight o'clock was held by the Confederates. General Egan's brigade moved to the assault of a redoubt behind which at daylight there was not a Confederate soldier. After a sharp struggle it was carried, but the division could make no further advance. It was sent towards the left to reconnoitre. General Meade arrived at noon and assumed command, General Hancock having been obliged to hand over the corps to General Birney. The Ninth Corps arrived, and the troops at hand numbered nearly fifty thousand. The afternoon wore away before General Meade was ready to attack. It was six o'clock when the three divisions of the Second Corps—Birney's, Barlow's, and Gibbon's—advanced, supported by two brigades of the Eighteenth and two of the Ninth. They captured three redoubts after a severe struggle, which could have been taken at daylight with but little opposition.

No censure can be cast upon Hancock, for he was unable to be in the saddle in the morning; but it is plain that his division commanders were dilatory in the execution of their orders. Had Grant demanded of Smith the utmost energy; had Hancock set forth the same in his orders to his subordinates, or had Meade ordered a general advance of all the troops at one o'clock, far different, in all probability, would have been the issue of events.

General Beauregard, seeing that Grant's movement was wholly against Petersburg, ordered Johnson's division, which was holding the intrenchments in front of Bermuda Hundred, to hasten south of the Appomattox.(¹) Lieutenant-colonel Greeley, of the Tenth Connecticut, was in command of the Union pickets at Bermuda Hundred. It was a bright, moonlight night. His ears were open to every sound, his eye quick to see all that was going on. He could hear a trampling of feet behind the breastworks. Creeping on his hands and knees, he came close up to the Confederate pickets, and could see that the troops were moving away. He crept back as noiselessly as he had advanced, and reported to General Terry. A little later Lieutenant-colonel Greeley was sweeping down upon the Confederate pickets, capturing nearly all of them, then rushing upon the thin line left to hold the breastworks, capturing them, which General Terry at once occupied.(")

General Beauregard had concentrated his troops with great vigor on the night of the 15th, had thrown up a line of new intrenchments in the rear of those captured by the colored troops, and had not far from fourteen thousand men by nine o'clock on the morning of the 16th. Through the day the Confederates were hard at work with shovels and axes strengthening the lines which ran from the Appomattox south three miles to the railroad leading to Norfolk, then west four miles to the Weldon Railroad, then north two miles to the Appomattox River.

Two and one-half miles east of Petersburg stood the house of Mr. Shand; General Potter's division of the Ninth Corps was directly east of it, half a mile distant. It was a large house, with a chimney at both ends. There was a peach orchard around it, with the young fruit forming on its branches. Fifty paces eastward was a ravine fifteen or twenty feet deep, with a little rivulet winding through it. Directly west of the house, about the same distance, was another ravine with a rivulet, both streams running north, and uniting twenty rods distant from the house. A Confederate brigade held this tongue of land, protected by breastworks. They had four cannon by the house. The Union artillery were sending their shells towards it. One of the Confederate officers was playing the piano which stood in the parlor, but suddenly found himself sitting on the floor, the piano-stool having been swept from beneath him by a shot. He was uninjured, but his playing was unceremoniously interrupted.

June 17, 1864.

It is a mile or more from the house of Mr. Shand to that of Mr. Dunn, north, towards the Appomattox, and the Confederate line ran from house to house. The works had been thrown up in 1862, and the tall pine-trees in front had been felled. During the summer of 1863 the fire had run through the fallen timber, burning the dried foliage and blackening the trunks. We are to think of the Union troops as being drawn up in the edge of the woods a third of a mile east of the breastworks, waiting orders to advance. Solid shot and shell come crashing amid the trees. One of the regiments standing there was the Fifty-seventh Massachusetts, with a boy only seventeen years old in the ranks—Edward Schneider, who was born far away on the head-waters of the Euphrates, where the patriarch Abraham once tended his flocks. His father was a missionary, but had sent his son to the United States to obtain an education at Phillips Academy, in Andover, Mass. A few weeks after the battle of Gettysburg the students of that institution invited me to tell them the story of that great struggle. When I finished my address the boy from the far East came and talked about it. He was so greatly interested that he thought about it through the night, and his lesson was not learned in the morning. Day after day he failed in his recitations. He said to his teacher, when re-

21*

proved: "I cannot study; I must go to the war. My country calls me," and enlisted as a soldier. He was deeply religious, and had the moral courage the first night in camp to kneel before his comrades and silently offer his evening prayer. His messmates respected him all the more, and the next night asked him to pray aloud, and so under his sweet and persuasive influence they too became religious. His first battle was at North Anna, where he was wounded, and sent to the hospital. His soul was on fire, and, without asking leave of the surgeon, he returned to his regiment. Here he stood, looking across the blackened trunks of the fallen trees towards the Confederate lines, knowing that his regiment was to cross the intervening space and charge the works. The chaplain of the regiment was walking along the lines. "We are going to capture the works, and I mean to be the first one inside," he said. The line moved on. Shells exploded in the ranks. Muskets flashed. There was no faltering. When near the works the boy leaped from the line, mounted the embankment in advance of all others. "Come on!" he shouted, and fell with a mortal wound. He was taken to the hospital. The chaplain went to see him. "Write to my father, and tell him that I have tried to do my duty." He divided his money—$10 to the Christian Commission, $10 to the American Board of Missions. "Write to my school-mates and tell them that I die content. Write to my brother in the navy, and tell him to stand up for the old flag, and cling to the cross of Christ." The surgeon bent over him. "Doctor, I am going home. I am not afraid to die. I don't know how the valley will look when I get into it, but it is all bright now." He broke into singing:

> "Soon with angels I'll be marching,
> With bright laurels on my brow;
> I have for my country fallen,
> Who will care for mother now?"

It was a song often sung by the soldiers. Death stole on. Sunday morning dawned, and just as the sun was rising he passed into the light of eternal day. Had he lived a century, he could not have completed life more fully.(⁹)

Several attempts were made by a brigade of the Second Corps to carry the position on the evening of the 16th, without success, and night came on with the Union troops in the ravine. They were relieved by Potter's division of the Ninth Corps. The men packed their tin plates and cups in their haversacks, that there might not be any rattling. No one spoke. There were two brigades—Griffin's and Curtin's—twelve regiments. They made their way into the ravine, and were only fifty-seven paces from the

Confederate breastworks. They were to rush up the steep bank, cross the narrow terrace, leap over the breastworks, and gather in the line of men in gray. Cannon would flame in their faces. There would be a blast of leaden rain. It required nerve and hardihood to move at midnight silently down the ravine, the rising moon throwing its light along the moving column, to take their places, speaking no word above a whisper, to lie upon the ground till the first gleam of daylight appeared on the eastern sky. Fifteen minutes past three was the time fixed. The officers had regulated their watches. The hands stole on to the appointed moment. Up to the hour of midnight the cannonade rolled along the line. After that hour both armies had been resting. The men in the ravine rose and dressed their ranks, elbow touching elbow, and grasped their muskets with nervous energy. There was no clicking of locks, but each soldier brought his musket to the "charge." With watches in one hand and swords in the other, the commanders of regiments waited. Their swords waved. It was the signal. The moon was high in the heavens, shining from a cloudless sky. The soldiers caught the gleam of the flashing blades, and moved up the bank. Cannon flashed, men went down, but the lines rolled on, up to the breastwork, over it. "Surrender!" Six hundred and fifty Confederates threw down their muskets. The six cannon were seized, one thousand five hundred muskets and four stands of colors were captured. It was the work of three minutes.(¹⁰)

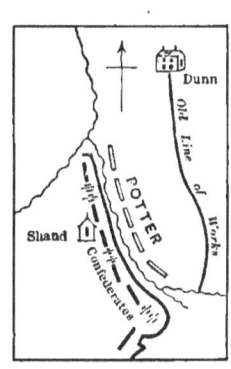

ASSAULT OF POTTER'S DIVISION, NINTH CORPS.

During the day Wilcox's division of the Ninth Corps, supported by Barlow's of the Second, attacked near the Norfolk railroad, and drove the Confederates. Just before night Ledlie's division of the Ninth, commanded by Colonel Gould, captured a portion of the intrenchments and one hundred prisoners; but having used up all their ammunition, and no troops being sent to their assistance, they were driven out, losing heavily. Nearly all of the Second Corps and Crawford's division of the Fifth were engaged. There was little concerted action on the part of the Union troops. The divisions attacked separately, and at a disadvantage. General Beauregard, on the contrary, handled his troops most effectively. He had not far from twenty thousand, but had great advantage of position, behind breastworks, with the trees cut down in front, their branches interlaced, with here and there a thick growth of brambles.

General Beauregard saw that he must reduce his line—make it shorter. He sent his engineer, Colonel Harris, to lay out a new line on the west bank of Harrison's Creek, which rises south of the house of Mr. Shand, and runs north to the Appomattox. The engineer drove a line of white stakes. Shovels were distributed. Silently, at midnight, the main line fell back, leaving only skirmishers in front. The men seized the shovels, and in a very short time a new breastwork was thrown up, and the artillery placed in position.(11)

General Meade was preparing for a grand assault. It was to be made at four o'clock on the morning of the 18th. The whole of Grant's army had arrived. The Eighteenth Corps, with the exception of Martindale's division, was recrossing the Appomattox to join General Butler. Neill's division of the Sixth Corps had taken its place. At the appointed hour, the Second, Fifth, and Ninth corps moved forward, but no musketry flamed from the intrenchments which yesterday were manned by the Confederates, who were now behind the new intrenchments, a third of a mile nearer Petersburg. General Meade was compelled to make new dispositions. Time went by, and with the swiftly flying hours went all chance for taking Petersburg by assault. At seven o'clock the troops of Kershaw's division, and a little later Field's division, of Lee's army, came across the Appomattox in the cars, and took positions behind the newly made works.

June 18, 1864.

Just after dark on the evening of the 12th of June, General Warren, commanding the Fifth Corps, started from Cold Harbor for the movement towards James River. He was followed by the Second and Ninth. We have seen how Warren crossed the Chickahominy and moved up the Charles City road towards Riddel's shop. General Grant intended to accomplish two things by the movement of this corps—make Lee think he was about to move upon Richmond from that direction, and at the same time screen the real movement of the army, in both of which he was successful. We have seen the Second Corps making a rapid march to the James, followed by the Ninth, taking the shortest route to Petersburg, with the Sixth taking the longer route, and the trains making a still longer journey. We have seen the Second crossing the James, followed by the Ninth, the Second arriving in front of Petersburg just before sunset on the 15th. Let us see what Lee was doing upon the afternoon of the 17th, at the hour when the whole of Grant's army was near Petersburg.

General Beauregard forecast the probable movement. On the afternoon of the 7th he telegraphed this to Bragg at Richmond: "Should Grant have left Lee's front, he doubtless intends operating against Rich-

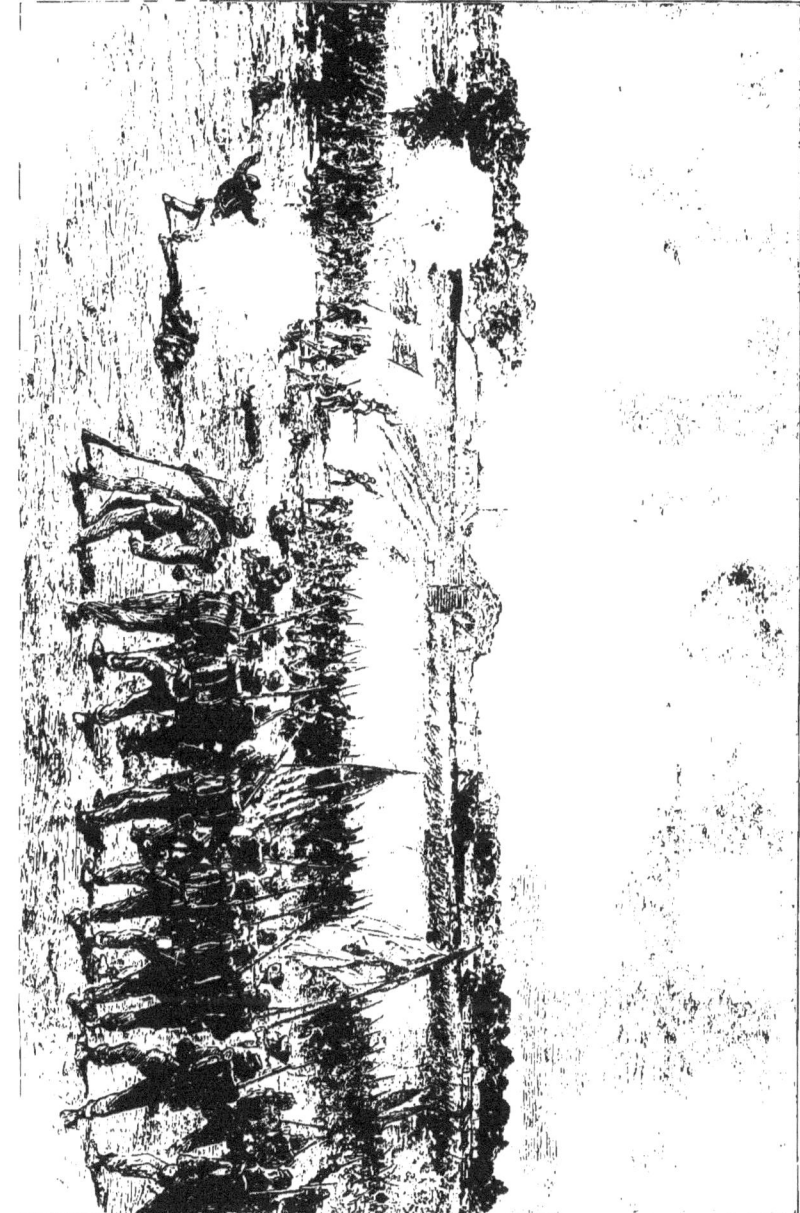

ATTACKING THE CONFEDERATE INTRENCHMENTS AT PETERSBURG.
From a war-time sketch.

mond along James River, probably on the south side. Petersburg, being nearly defenceless, would be captured before it could be reinforced." The next day Beauregard sent a long letter to Bragg, giving his reasons for believing that Grant was swinging round to the James, and that he would probably attack between Bermuda Hundred and Richmond, and at the same time seize Petersburg. Neither Bragg nor Lee paid any attention to Beauregard. On the 13th, Warren was south of the Chickahominy, and Lee was hastening from Cold Harbor, through Richmond, and down the Charles City road, to meet Grant's whole army, which he supposed was to advance from that direction. At three o'clock on the afternoon of the 13th Grant was at Bermuda Hundred, giving directions to Butler. On the 15th Lee had his army extending from Malvern Hill north to White Oak Swamp, supposing that Grant's whole army was before him, when there was only the Fifth Corps, which was getting ready to move to the crossing at Windmill Point. On the morning of the 16th Lee was still there, but the Fifth Corps was well on its way to Petersburg, where were the Second, Ninth, and Eighteenth, already engaged with Beauregard.

At 10.30 on the morning of the 16th Lee sent this to Beauregard: "I do not know the position of Grant's army. Cannot strip north bank of James River." On the afternoon of the 17th, at 3.30, he sent this to W. H. F. Lee, who was at Malvern Hill: "Push after the enemy, and endeavor to ascertain what has become of Grant's army." Gen. A. P. Hill was at Riddel's shop, just south of White Oak Swamp, where he had been three days, confronted part of the time by Warren and the rest by the Union cavalry. But Warren was now at Petersburg, and the cavalry, by their bold front, had successfully deceived the Confederate commander.

At 4.30 on the 17th Lee sent this to Beauregard: "Have no information of Grant's crossing the James River, but upon your report have ordered troops to Chaffin's Bluff." At ten o'clock that evening he informed Beauregard that he had ordered Kershaw's division of Anderson's corps to report to him. Kershaw marched to the cars, which whirled him to Petersburg, where he arrived at seven o'clock on the morning of the 18th, while the Union army was moving to assault the new line taken up by the Confederates. Had not Beauregard taken his new line, it is probable that he would have been swept out of the position held the day before, and that at the hour of seven Kershaw would have seen him retreating across the Appomattox. Not till the close of the 17th did Lee comprehend Grant's movement. That it came upon him with great force at last is seen in the haste with which he made his way to Petersburg, where he arrived at 11.30 on the forenoon of the 17th.

There has been a disposition on the part of the admirers of Lee to belittle the part performed by Beauregard, and give undue credit to the Confederate commander-in-chief, but the truth of history will give the honor of holding Petersburg to Beauregard; and the truth of history will also give to Grant the credit of planning a movement which Lee did not comprehend, and which, had General Smith

June 18, 1864.

AVERY HOUSE, HEADQUARTERS OF GENERAL WARREN, IN FRONT OF PETERSBURG.

From a war-time Sketch.

acted with energy, would have given him Petersburg on the 15th of June, and changed the whole aspect of the war.

When it was discovered, on the morning of the 18th, that the Confederates had fallen back to a new position, General Meade ordered the army to press forward. The Second Corps very soon became engaged near the house of Mr. Hare. It had only a short distance to advance, while the Ninth Corps had a mile, and the Fifth a still greater distance. The forenoon passed before the Fifth and Ninth were in position. All the while the Confederate cannon were sending shells upon the Union troops. General Burnside, with the Ninth, advanced to the railroad leading from Petersburg to Norfolk, but could not drive the Confederates from an excavation in which they were sheltered. Not till the sun was going down were the different divisions in position. We are to think of a great uproar of artillery, more than one hundred and fifty cannon on both sides sending solid shot and shell into the opposing ranks. Down in the ravine, through which winds Harrison's Creek, were the men in blue, struggling amid fallen trees to make their way up to the Confederate lines. By the railroad, cannon were flaming in the faces of the men of the Ninth Corps, who worked their way to within one hundred yards of the Confederate intrenchments. Very gallant was the charge of Griffin's division close by the house of Mr. Avery, near which General Warren established his headquarters.

I climbed to the roof of the building, through which Confederate shells had crashed. "Do not let them see you use your glass," was the injunction of General Warren, who was sitting on the step of the portico.

GENERALS HUNT AND DUANE.

At my feet were the Union soldiers reclining on the ground; eastward, screened from the Confederates by woods, were the wagons of the Fifth Corps; westward, across the storm-swept plain, were the Confederate intrenchments, bristling with cannon and battle-flags waving above them; beyond were the spires of the city and the winding Appomattox.

The Union troops did not retreat, but held the ground already won, went to work with shovels, and when once more the daylight appeared in the east, they were behind a line of works which they would hold from that hour to the close of the mighty struggle, ten months later, when the Confederacy would disappear like a bubble in a swirling stream.

June 19, 1864.

During the three days' struggle for the possession of Petersburg, nearly eleven thousand Union soldiers had been killed, wounded, or taken prisoner. It will never be known how many went down upon the Confederate side; but as Beauregard's troops were sheltered behind intrenchments, the loss could not have been as great. General Grant knew when the sun went down that Lee's army had arrived; that the intrenchments could not be carried by assault, and that there were long months of weary struggle before him. He accepted the inevitable, and began his plans for the future. Both armies were worn and weary. The immediate object which Grant had in view, the taking of Petersburg, had not been accomplished; but there was no despondency visible in his face. It was nine miles to City Point, his base of supplies. A few days, and the soldiers heard the scream of the locomotive, and a train of cars came into their very encampments, bringing fresh supplies. So the siege of Petersburg began. General Duane, of the Engineer Corps, marked out the lines for the fortifications, and General Hunt, commanding the artillery, selected the positions for the heavy guns.

NOTES TO CHAPTER XII.

(¹) Alfred Roman, "Military Operations of Gen. P. T. Beauregard," vol. ii., p. 566.
(²) General Wise, Report quoted by Alfred Roman, in "Military Operations of Gen. P. T. Beauregard," vol. ii., p. 224.
(³) Author's Note-book, June, 1864.
(⁴) Alfred Roman, "Military Operations of Gen. P. T. Beauregard," vol. ii., p. 230.
(⁵) Idem.
(⁶) Major-general Hancock's Report.
(⁷) Alfred Roman, "Military Operations of Gen. P. T. Beauregard," vol. ii., p. 281.
(⁸) "Military History of Connecticut," p. 611.
(⁹) Author's Note-book, June, 1864.
(¹⁰) Idem.
(¹¹) Alfred Roman, "Military Operations of Gen. P. T. Beauregard," vol. ii., p. 233.

CHAPTER XIII.

APPROACHING ATLANTA.

MILITARY law in the Confederacy was very powerful. It not only swept all able-bodied citizens of the military age into the army, but it impressed the slaves of the planters into the service to build fortifications. When General Johnston found that General Sherman would soon compel him to fall back from the strong fortifications which he had erected on Kenesaw, he sent Colonel Prestman, of the engineers, to lay out a new line of fortifications, ten miles south of Marietta, and called upon the slaveholders to send their slaves to construct them, also a strong line of forts, redoubts, and breastworks around Atlanta. So through the last days of June three large gangs of slaves were toiling with picks and shovels, one south of Marietta, a second party along the Chattahoochee River, and the third around Atlanta.([1])

With Sherman's troops closing around Marietta, and threatening Johnston's communications, the Confederate commander could tarry no longer at Kenesaw, and retreated once more to the new line of intrenchments. For twenty-six days the two armies had stood face to face around Kenesaw, but this retreat took the Confederate army away from the hills and mountains, and made a flanking movement all the easier for General Sherman.

July 3, 1864.

While the cars were bringing supplies to Sherman he was studying his next move. He had no intention of attacking the Confederates behind their breastworks. He would gain Johnston's rear. The Chattahoochee River was swollen by the rains. The only bridge, the one at Roswell, twenty miles up-stream, above the railroad to Atlanta, had been burned. The river was too deep to be forded, and he must lay pontoons. He sent Garrard's cavalry north-east eight miles from Marietta, to the village of Stop-and-Swap. The troopers pressed on to Roswell, burning a cotton-factory, which was making clothing for the Confederacy; also a paper-mill.

The French flag was flying over the building, and the men who were running the mill said that the property belonged to citizens of France; Garrard did not stop for that, but set the building on fire. General Davis on his march to join Sherman destroyed an iron-foundery at Rome. So, day by day the Confederate Government saw that not only were the armies being pressed back, but that the resources of the country were rapidly diminishing.

July 5, 1864.

General Schofield rode along the banks of the Chattahoochee up to Soap Creek, above Roswell, looking at all the crossings. Garrard's scouts said that there was only one company of Confederate cavalry with a single

THE FISH-TRAP ON THE CHATTAHOOCHEE WHERE GENERAL SCHOFIELD CROSSED.

cannon guarding the crossing just above the creek. Schofield saw that a farmer who lived near by had made a fish-trap at that point, and that the water was rippling over the rocks. He also saw that the boats for the pontoon-bridge could be put into the creek where the Confederate cavalry could not see them, and that in a few moments a strong force could be put across the river. The place was selected for the crossing.

Cox's division and the Army of the Ohio reached the creek. The men marched in silence. No camp-fires were kindled. The wagons with the boats came up, and five hundred men launched them in the little stream. Byrd's brigade was to make the crossing, and the Twelfth Kentucky was to take the lead. While the boats were getting ready Cameron's brigade

TURNER'S MILL, NICKAJACK CREEK.

was making its way to the fish-trap, half a mile above the creek. The scouts, who crept along the bank of the river, peeping through the bushes, saw a Confederate cannon on the other bank. In the camp near at hand some of the soldiers were playing cards; one was writing a letter to his

MAJOR-GENERAL SCHOFIELD.

wife. He had just written that she need not be alarmed about him, for no Yankees were to be seen anywhere; they were all down in front of Johnston, and he was just as safe there as he would be at home.(²) While he was writing it the hand on General Cameron's watch moved on to 3.30. Upon the instant Colonel Casement, with the One Hundred and Third

Ohio, the men who ran across the stringers of the bridge at Culp's farm, dashed down the bank by the fish-trap, made their way across the river, and rushed up the other bank. At the same instant the boats, filled with Kentuckians, shot out from the mouth of Soap Creek into the river. Strong-armed rowers pulled the oars. There was a commotion in the Confederate camp; the soldiers seized their guns; the unfinished letter dropped upon the ground; the cannon flashed, but the next moment the air was humming with bullets fired by the advancing Union men. The Confederates fled, carrying the news to Johnston that the Union army was crossing the river. Before night the bridge was completed and Cox's division across the stream.

Once more Johnston was compelled to retreat. Through the night his troops were on the march across the river.(³) Sherman followed to close in upon Atlanta, marching east to approach the city on its northern and eastern sides. Such a movement would enable him to protect the railroad over which he received his own supplies, and at the same time cut the road leading east from Atlanta. General Thomas took position nearest the Chattahoochee, along the north bank of Peach-tree Creek. McPherson and Schofield moved farther east, turned south to destroy the railroad leading east, with the intention of cutting off Johnston from direct communication with Lee at Richmond.

July 9, 1864.

The intrenchments which the slave gangs had erected for the defence of Atlanta began at the railroad two miles south of the Chattahoochee, ran east six miles to Pea-vine Creek, then turned south and extended to the railroad leading from Atlanta eastward. General Johnston saw that McPherson was separated from Thomas, and was thinking of giving battle to Sherman.

Just at this moment General Bragg arrived at General Johnston's headquarters. After his defeat at Missionary Ridge he had been called to Richmond, and had been appointed chief of staff as military adviser to Jefferson Davis. He said that he was on his way to see two other Confederate commanders—Generals S. D. Lee, in the south-west, and E. Kirby Smith, who was west of the Mississippi(⁴)—to ascertain what reinforcements they could send to General Johnston. He said that Governor Brown, of Georgia, had called for ten thousand militia of that State to aid in holding Atlanta, and that they would be hurried into the city at once, which was welcome news to General Johnston. General Bragg did not stay long, for he said that his visit to the army was not official. Jefferson Davis, as has before been stated, did not like General Johnston. Before the Southern States seceded from the Union

July 14, 1864.

there had been a disagreement between them which the President of the Confederacy had not forgotten, though after the defeat of Bragg at Missionary Ridge he had been compelled to comply with the public demand, and appoint him to command the Army of the West. While the Confederate army was at Dalton an intrigue was started in Richmond against Johnston. A Confederate writer says: "An intrigue was commenced at the time he first moved from Dalton, at the very commencement of the campaign, and Mr. Davis only waited a convenient opportunity and an available pretext to put his sinister design into execution."(*)

GENERAL HOWARD'S CORPS CROSSING THE CHATTAHOOCHEE.

From a sketch made at the time.

General Bragg remained but a short time in Atlanta, and instead of going on to Mobile to confer with Gen. S. D. Lee, returned to Richmond. Had we been in the large room in the President's mansion in which the Confederate Cabinet held its sessions, we should have seen the President and his Cabinet discussing the question of removing General Johnston summarily from command. We are not to think that the members of the Cabinet had personal animosity towards General Johnston, and it is hardly probable that Jefferson Davis allowed his personal difference with him to unduly affect his judgment as President; but the people of the South, the members of the Confederate Congress, were disheartened over the falling back of the Confederate army from Dalton to Resaca, from there to Cassville, and successively to Dallas, Kenesaw, Smyrna, and across the Chattahoochee, until at last General Sherman was closing around Atlanta. The newspapers were publishing accounts of Confederate victories, and had informed the people that General Johnston was only falling back to lead Sherman farther from his base of supplies; but now that the Union army was across the Chattahoochee,

July 17, 1864.

there was a tone of discontent and disappointment, and a demand for an aggressive movement on the part of the Confederates. The Cabinet, it is said, favored the removal of Johnston and the appointment of General Hood. It is also said that the President of the Confederacy walked up and down the room with his hands behind him in deep anxiety, saying that he doubted the propriety of it.(⁸)

Going back to Atlanta, we see General Johnston in his tent talking with Colonel Prestman about the intrenchments around Atlanta. It is ten o'clock at night(⁷) when the telegraph operator hands him this despatch from Adjutant-general Cooper at Richmond: "Lieutenant-general J. B. Hood has been commissioned to the temporary rank of general under the late law of Congress. I am directed by the Secretary of War to inform you that, as you have failed to arrest the advance of the enemy to the vicinity of Atlanta, far in the interior of Georgia, and express no confidence that you can defeat or repel him, you are hereby relieved from the command of the Army and Department of Tennessee, which you will immediately turn over to General Hood."(⁸)

General Johnston read it, and with a smile handed it to General Lovell, saying, "What do you think of that?"(⁹) Possibly it was not unexpected, for he knew that there was an intrigue going on against him. General Lovell had confidence in General Johnston, and felt that his removal would be a great mistake. He saw Generals Hardee, Stewart, and Hood, and induced them to send a petition to Jefferson Davis to continue Johnston in command. A Confederate historian says: "They protested against the change, deputizing General Hood, as a matter of courtesy, to send the protest. General Hood sent the despatch, but it was worded in such a way as to carry no force and no effect. Mr. Davis declined to withdraw the order."(¹⁰)

General Johnston turned over the army to General Hood and sent this despatch to Richmond: "As to the alleged cause of my removal, I assert that Sherman's army is much stronger, compared with that of Tennessee, than Grant's compared with that of Northern Virginia; yet the enemy has been compelled to advance much more slowly to the vicinity of Atlanta than to Richmond and Petersburg, and penetrated much deeper into Virginia than into Georgia."(¹¹)

July 18, 1864.

General Hood was a brave, bold, energetic commander. He had led his troops in many battles; he could strike heavy blows. Whether General Hood was, or was not, a party to the intrigue against General Johnston may never be certainly known. He had objected to the policy of falling back, and abandoning intrenchment after intrenchment, but had opposed the plan of Johnston to give battle to Sherman at Cassville. He accepted the command.

One of General Sherman's spies came from Atlanta, bringing a newspaper which gave information of the appointment of Hood. General Schofield and General Hood were classmates at West Point. "What sort of a man is Hood?" was Sherman's question.

"He is bold even to rashness, and courageous in the extreme."

"His appointment means fight," said Sherman, who sent notice of the change to all parts of the army, and who told the division commanders that they must be always prepared for battle, and that he would like nothing better than to have Hood come out and attack in the open ground.([12])

General Hood had three corps—Hardee's, Cheatham's, and Stewart's, formerly commanded by General Polk. Stewart was on the left in front of Thomas, Hardee in the centre, and Cheatham on the right. Beyond Cheatham, in the intrenchments east of the city, were the State troops of Georgia, under Gen. G. W. Smith.

The Army of the Tennessee, with Garrard's cavalry, early in the afternoon reached the railroad leading east from Atlanta. The soldiers tore up the rails, heaped up the ties, laid the rails on top, and set the ties on fire. When the rails were red-hot they bent them double around the trees, so that they could never be used again. While McPherson was destroying the railroad, Thomas was getting across Peachtree Creek, four miles north of Atlanta, which winds through a deep ravine with steep banks. Shoal Creek is a little stream which rises amid the hills near Atlanta, runs north, turns the wheel of Mr. Collier's mill, and just beyond the mill joins Peachtree. Mr. Collier's house is about a quarter of a mile east of the mill, and Mount Zion Church about the same distance west of it, on the road leading south, through Mr. Embury's farm, to Atlanta.

July 19, 1864.

General Palmer's division of the Army of the Cumberland was on the right, then came Williams's and Geary's divisions of Hooker's corps, on Mr. Embury's farm, between the church and Peachtree Creek. If we walk now from the left of Geary's line to the mill across Shoal Creek and go up the eastern bank, we come to a piece of woods, in which we find Ward's division of Hooker's corps in reserve. Going a short distance south and east, we find Wood's and Newton's divisions of Howard's corps. Beyond Newton's we come to another little stream—Clear Creek—beyond which, more than a mile from Newton, is Stanley's division of Howard's corps. Off in the south-east, six miles away, are Schofield and McPherson. General Sherman in this movement has divided his army, and Hood believes that with such gaps between Thomas and McPherson and Schofield, and with Stanley so far away from Newton, he can fall upon Newton, roll him back on Wood's division, drive both in confusion down into the muddy ravine of Peachtree Creek, and then sweep Williams, Geary, and Palmer in turn across the creek. Having done this, he will then turn about and fall upon Stanley, thus defeating Thomas before Schofield and McPherson can arrive to assist him.

General Hood was a firm believer in what he called the Stonewall Jackson school—to march with a portion of his army and strike a blow in one direction, then turn and give another in an opposite direction. He wanted Johnston to pursue such tactics at Resaca, New Hope, and Kenesaw. He detailed Smith and Cheatham to hold the breastworks in front of McPherson. It was one o'clock in the afternoon when Hardee, with Bate's division on the right, Walker in the centre, Maney on the left, and Cleburne in reserve, moved to attack Thomas, directing the main assault on Newton's division. Stewart at the same time moved towards Zion Church, to strike Williams and Geary. It was nearly four o'clock when Bate's division, marching through a thicket of pines and oaks along the west bank of Clear Creek, came upon Newton's left flank. At the same moment, south of Zion Church, Stewart was riding along his lines, telling his troops that they were to drive Geary and Williams back across Peachtree Creek. It was very well for him to arouse the enthusiasm of his troops, and tell them how they could put Williams and Geary to rout, but the regiments in blue, stretched across the road and fields, had been in a score of battles. They climbed Lookout Mountain and fought the battle among the clouds. At Gettysburg, at the second Bull Run, Chancellorsville, and on the Peninsula, they showed what stuff they were made of. They were not in the habit of running from a battle.

This was Hood's plan : The troops were to advance in echelon by division; that is, first Bate's division on the extreme right was to get between Newton's left flank and Clear Creek; then Walker's division, three hundred yards in rear, was to march against Newton's centre ; Maney's division was to be three hundred yards in the left rear of Walker's; Stewart's divisions were to move in the same order. Hood expected that Bate would have little difficulty in getting behind Newton's left flank. The troops were ordered to charge with the bayonet, give a triumphant yell, and sweep all before them. It was well planned, but General Hood had not correctly calculated the staying qualities of Thomas's men. Instead of getting behind Newton, Bate found that officer quickly changing his line of battle, swinging his left flank back towards the creek, conforming it to

Bate's line, and holding his ground. Walker and Maney, as they advanced, were met by a terrific storm of shell and musketry. Newton and Wood resisted the onset. Wood came into position, ready to take part in the contest. West of Shoal Creek, Stewart's men were rushing upon Geary by the mill, and upon Williams near the church. They were met by a remorseless fire. General Thomas was on the north side of the creek, opposite the ravine through which Shoal Creek trickles to Peachtree.

He massed several of his batteries, which poured a destructive fire upon the Confederates by the mill. It was a terrible slaughter; the ground was quickly covered by the killed and wounded. Not one of the Union divisions yielded their ground.

General Hood was in trouble, for a courier brought word that Schofield and McPherson were attacking Cheatham, and that he must have reinforcements. Hood was just ready to put Cleburne into the fight against Newton, but was obliged to send him, instead, upon the run to hold the intrenchments east of the city. Night came, and the thunder of battle died away. Hood's troops were returning to their intrenchments. They had accomplished nothing, and had lost more than four thousand brave men.

Cleburne hastened out to a hill south of the railroad, two miles east of Atlanta, across which the slave-gang had thrown up a line of intrenchments. It was an important position, overlooking not only the city, but the ground over which McPherson was advancing. Cleburne's artillery, from that position, could send their shells into the lines of the Fifteenth Corps.

McPherson determined to drive Cheatham from the hill, and directed General Logan to do it, who selected General Leggett's division of the Fifteenth Corps, instructing Leggett to be ready at daylight to make the assault. Leggett formed his division during the night, with Force's brigade on his right, facing the hill, Scott's brigade on the left of Force, and Malloy's in rear of Scott's, to protect the left flank. In Force's command were the Twentieth, Thirtieth, Thirty-first, and Forty-fifth Illinois, and the Twelfth and Thirteenth Wisconsin. The Twelfth Wisconsin had just joined the division with full ranks. Some of the men were new recruits. They knew that Cleburne's division was regarded as one of the best in Hood's army. When Leggett moved to the attack, the division under Giles A. Smith, on his left, was also to advance, to prevent the sending of reinforcements to Cleburne.

July 20, 1864.

The sun was rising when the signal was given. Colonel Munson, in command of the skirmishers, advanced rapidly from a belt of timber. The Confederates on the hill looked over their breastworks, and saw the line of skirmishers closely followed by two well-formed lines.

"Don't fire a gun until you are inside of the works," was the order of General Force.

From the line of breastworks on the hill the storm burst forth. Men dropped from the advancing ranks, which did not for a moment falter, but which moved on up the slope. Then came quick flashes, followed by the bayonet-thrust and pistol-shot. A moment of *mêlée* and the veterans of Cleburne's division, who had stood like a wall of adamant in a score of battles, were fleeing down the western slope of the hill, across the little rivulet trickling through the ravine at its base, and up the hill-side beyond to the inner line of intrenchments. It was a bitter mortification to Cleburne, for from the summit of the hill, which Force had won, the Union cannon would send shot and shell into the streets of Atlanta.

The attack upon Thomas at Peachtree Creek had resulted in disaster to Hood, and now Cleburne had been driven from Bald Hill, east of Atlanta. He had lost five thousand men. The Union artillery—Elliott's Eighth Michigan Battery, and the Third Ohio, Williams's battery of 20-pounder Parrot-guns—were sending shells into Atlanta, which was a mortification to Hood. General Wheeler, commanding the Confederate cavalry south-east of the city, during the day brought word that the rear of McPherson was open to attack; that there was a large Union wagon-train at Decatur, seven miles east of Atlanta.

The roads were in excellent condition, and there was nothing to prevent Hood from making a movement in that direction. He decided to leave Stewart and the Georgia militia to hold the lines of intrenchment,

VIEW OF ATLANTA, FROM THE UNION SIGNAL-STATION EAST OF THE CITY.

From a sketch made at the time.

and to use Hardee's and his own corps, under Cheatham, to crush McPherson. Hardee's corps was the largest in the Confederate army. Hood ordered the troops to be ready to move at sunset. Hardee's men marched through Atlanta, down the road along the Intrenchment Creek, crossing it at Mr. Cobb's mill, and turned north-east. Bate's division was in advance, then Walker's, followed by Cleburne and Maney. Hardee was to gain the rear of McPherson, turn west, and attack Bald Hill. Cheatham, at the same time, was to attack from the west. His design was to grind to powder the Fifteenth Corps, which held the hill, and the Seventeenth Corps, immediately north of it.

General McPherson had not grown careless by the success that followed Sherman's movements, but, on the contrary, had become active and vigilant; during the night he issued an order for the Sixteenth Corps to move south of the railroad, and strengthen the left of the Seventeenth. At daybreak the Sixteenth was on its march. Going now up to Bald Hill, we find that the soldiers of Leggett's division had changed the breastworks captured the day before, so that now they faced west, towards Atlanta. When daylight came they discovered that the Confederates had abandoned a part of the second line in front of them, and Malloy's brigade went out and took possession. General Leggett's division faced west, while Gen. Giles A. Smith's division, on his left, faced south. The angle was on the southern slope of the hill. Most of Smith's line was in thick woods. The Fifteenth Corps was north of Bald Hill, Morgan L. Smith's division joining Leggett, then came Harrow's and Wood's divisions, the last being on the railroad. Going now from the left of Giles A. Smith's division, three-fourths of a mile east of Bald Hill, we come to Morrell's brigade of General Fuller's division of the Sixteenth Corps, which had come down from north of the railroad to be in position to support the Seventeenth Corps. Sprague's brigade of Fuller's division had been sent east to Decatur to protect the wagon-train from Wheeler's cavalry. Sweeny's division of the Sixteenth Corps was north of Fuller's, near the railroad. The fields around were thickly covered with wagons.

July 22, 1864.

Yester-night, before the sun went down, the troops on Bald Hill could see a column of Confederates marching out of Atlanta towards the south. Now that the sun was rising, they could still see them, infantry and artillery, moving in the same direction. Was Hood evacuating Atlanta? Was the repulse at Peachtree and the driving of Cleburne from Bald Hill so damaging that it was useless for him to attempt to hold the place, now that McPherson's shells were exploding in the streets? Those who knew Hood best could not quite accept the conclusion that he was abandoning the city. Through the night the pickets of Leggett, down south of Bald Hill, had heard the rumbling of artillery wheels and the tramping of men. General Sherman was at McPherson's headquarters,([19]) near the house of Mr. Howard, north of the railroad. He found that the Confederates in front of Thomas, as well as those in front of McPherson, had fallen back, but that they were hard at work building intrenchments, which did not look much like evacuation. Thomas's artillery was sending shells into the new Confederate line. The air was still, and the boom of the guns came to Sherman's and McPherson's ears as they sat on the piazza of the house. They could hear the pickets firing in front of the

Fifteenth Corps. They walked down the road a little distance and sat beneath the grateful shade of the trees. General Sherman spread out his map and pointed to the positions. They were in rear of Schofield, whose cannon were also hurling shot and shell towards the Confederate line. The Confederate cannon replied, and a shot came hurtling through the trees near them. They heard a rapid firing of musketry towards the south-east. Sherman took out his pocket-compass to note the direction.

"What is the meaning of it?" he asked. McPherson could not tell, but gathered up his papers and rode away with General Hickenlooper, Chief of Artillery, Adjutant-general Clark, Inspector-general Strong, Captain Steele, Captain Gile, and Orderly Thompson towards the firing.(")

It was near noon, and the pickets out towards Decatur had caught a glimpse of Confederate cavalry advancing from the south-east towards the trains and hospitals. The first dropping fire of musketry came from the pickets. As the noise increased, the Sixty-third Ohio, commanded by Colonel Welles, of Leggett's division, was ordered in that direction to protect them. On its way the regiment suddenly came upon a line of Confederate skirmishers, the advance of Bate's division. Colonel Welles deployed his men, and the battle began.

General Dodge, commanding the Sixteenth Corps, and General Fuller, were eating dinner. They dropped their knives and went out to see what was going on.

"The Rebel cavalry must be raiding our rear. Post your regiments to protect our train," said Dodge, as he leaped into his saddle.

The firing was becoming every moment louder in the rear, where they did not expect to be attacked. Fuller's soldiers were quickly in line, forming on the western edge of a field, and facing east. The Second division of the Sixteenth Corps, under Sweeny, was forming at the same moment north of Fuller. A little rivulet rising in the woods runs along the western edge of the field, then turns eastward. Fuller's line was along this stream; the Thirty-ninth Ohio on the west, the Twenty-seventh next in line. The Sixty-fourth Illinois was on the west bank of the stream, and the Eighteenth Missouri in reserve in rear of the Thirty-ninth Ohio; the Fourteenth Ohio Battery, Captain Laird, was on a knoll farther north; the Eighty-first Ohio was near the battery. The fields in the immediate vicinity were filled with wagons. There was a sudden harnessing of horses, and the trains began to move north towards the railroad. The pickets were streaming from the woods, followed by the Confederates of Bate's and Walker's divisions of Hardee's corps. The six guns of Laird's battery opened fire. The Confederates evidently did not see Fuller's regiments, which were partly concealed in the woods.

But suddenly a line of fire burst forth in front of them. They halted, fell back, rearranged their lines, and once more advanced. They were a quarter of the way across the field. "Charge the battery!" was the word which ran down the Confederate lines. They rushed towards the guns, when suddenly the Eighty-first Ohio, rising like an apparition from the ground, stood before them. With a cheer the men from Ohio rushed to meet the Confederates half-way across the field. Enthusiasm is contagious. In a time of excitement, what others do spontaneously we ourselves are pretty certain to do.

The cheer and the action stirred the blood of the Thirty-ninth Ohio. The soldiers of that regiment fired a volley, sprang to their feet, and rushed upon the Confederates of the Sixty-sixth Georgia. The enthusiasm reached the Twenty-seventh Ohio, and that regiment also dashed across the field. There were no regiments on Fuller's right to oppose the Confederates in that direction, and there was the remarkable scene of the Ohio regiments rushing east, while just south of them the Confederates were pushing past them towards the west.

The Sixty-fourth Illinois was armed with Henry repeating-rifles, with which they could fire fourteen rounds without stopping to reload. It was like the firing of a brigade. The Confederates were commanded by a brave officer, General Walker, who saw his line wavering, and brought forward other regiments from the woods. He rode in front of them bareheaded, waving his hat and encouraging his men. The Eighteenth Missouri came down at the moment and joined the Sixty-fourth Illinois, pouring in its volleys. The brave Confederate officer fell from his horse, mortally wounded. Hood had lost one of his ablest division commanders.

The Confederate troops fell back into the woods, but reformed and advanced once more to strike Fuller's flank. That commander saw that he must change front. There are times when actions are better than commands. Some of his men did not comprehend his order, whereupon he seized the colors of the Twenty-seventh Ohio, planted them where he wished to form his new line, and the regiment came into position upon the double-quick. General Fuller was once the colonel of the Twenty-seventh, and the men gave a cheer and, together with the Thirty-ninth, drove the Confederates once more into the woods.

The Sixteenth Corps was holding its ground against Hardee, but there was a wide gap between Fuller and the left of Giles A. Smith's division of the Seventeenth Corps. While Bate's and Walker's divisions were attacking the Sixteenth Corps, Cleburne and Maney were falling upon Smith. Cleburne's men were smarting under the loss of Bald Hill the day before. It is a noble faculty of the soul that stirs us to regain what we have lost, and bring victory out of defeat. Cleburne's blood was on fire to turn the disaster of yesterday into a victory to-day. Never had his troops gone into battle with such determination to win a victory as now. They paid no heed to the line of Union skirmishers in front of them, but brushed them away as you brush aside a spider's thread floating in the air.

McPherson had ordered General Blair, commanding the Fifteenth Corps, to send Wangelin's brigade, which was in reserve, to fill the gap between the Sixteenth and Seventeenth corps. It was on the march, but had not arrived. Cleburne was just ready to strike the left of Giles A. Smith's division. It was at that moment that McPherson gathered up his papers, put them into his pocket, and rode south across the railroad with his staff to find out the meaning of the uproar. He came to the wagon-train, and saw the teamsters lashing their horses to a run.

"Please stop those teams; they will get up a stampede," he said, and his staff rode away to control the panic-stricken teamsters. One of General Leggett's staff, with his horse upon the run, rode up and saluted McPherson:

"General Leggett wishes me to inform you that the enemy are attacking him, and he desires orders."

"Tell him to straighten his line parallel with this road."

The road ran south into the woods, towards the position of Giles A. Smith. Captain Raymond rode in advance, followed by McPherson and Orderly Thompson. In all probability McPherson supposed that Wangelin was in the position to which he had been ordered, but he was not. He was on the march, but had not reached the ground. They entered the woods, were in a bend of the road, when suddenly there was a volley of musketry and Captain Raymond's horse went down. "Halt! halt! Surrender!" was the cry of a hundred Confederates. General McPherson wheeled his horse, lifted his hat as if to salute, but the next moment fell headlong to the ground. Orderly Thompson, swept from his saddle, also fell to the ground. A moment later and McPherson's horse was running wild across the field in front of the Ohio troops. The faithful orderly sprang to his feet and ran to his beloved commander. "Are you hurt, general?" "Oh, orderly, I am!" They were his last words.(") A moment of convulsion, and his heart ceased its beating. The country had lost one of its ablest commanders. The Confederates swarmed around the lifeless body and searched General McPherson's pockets, taking his pocket-book and papers. Captain Raymond and Orderly Thompson were marched away as prisoners, and Cleburne's line moved on over the body of the dead commander. It was between twelve and one o'clock. General Sherman was walking up and down the porch of the Howard House when one of McPherson's staff rode up with the startling news that McPherson was killed or a prisoner.

"Ride to Logan, and inform him that he is the senior officer in the Army of the Tennessee. Direct him to refuse his left flank, drive back the enemy, and hold the hill. Tell him that I will send him all needful reinforcements."

The officer reached Logan and informed him that he was commander. Cleburne at that moment was sweeping past Giles A. Smith, whose left regiments had crumbled in part, some of the men fleeing, but others sullenly falling back towards Leggett's division. Cleburne intended to annihilate Smith and then toss Leggett over against Cheatham.

The death of General Walker had deprived Cleburne of an important ally. More than this, the battery of Captain Laird was sending shells into his flank. The Sixty-fourth Illinois, with their Henry rifles, were doing him great damage. The soldiers of that regiment made a dash and captured forty Confederates of the regiment which fired the volley upon McPherson. In the pockets of one of the prisoners they found McPherson's papers, and among them an important letter from General Sherman forecasting the Union commander's plans, and about which Sherman had been uneasy; but it was quite certain that no Confederate officer had seen it, and Sherman breathed easier.("") The Sixty-fourth pushed on and recovered the body of their beloved commander, which was borne back to the Howard House. The Confederates rallied, and the Sixty-fourth Illinois and Twenty-seventh and Thirty-ninth regiments in turn were forced back into a thicket; but their resolute attack had retarded Walker's and Cleburne's divisions. So stubborn the resistance that every third man in the Twenty-seventh and every fourth man in the Thirty-ninth was either killed or wounded; but they held their ground till ordered to a new position.

In obedience to the last order issued by McPherson, Giles A. Smith endeavored to form his new line parallel with the road, but was forced back by Cleburne until he stood back to back with Leggett.

Going up now to the top of the hill, to the intrenchment which Leggett had constructed, let us take a look from that position. Looking south along the line of breastworks, we see a part of Scott's brigade, the Seventy-eighth Ohio, nearest the fortification; then the Twentieth Ohio, which turns a sharp angle, the right of the regiment facing west and the left south-east.

WHERE McPHERSON FELL.

The line is along the western edge of woods, with a field sloping westward towards a ravine, beyond which is the Confederate line of intrenchments, where Hood's old corps is in waiting to come out and do its part of the grinding up of the Fifteenth and Seventeenth corps. Hood himself is there to see it done. The right flank of Giles A. Smith's division of the Seventeenth Corps joins the Twentieth Ohio regiment. General Force's brigade of Leggett's division is in the fortification on the top of the hill and along the breastworks.

As we have already seen, the first blow of Cleburne was on the left side of Smith; but as Cleburne advances, the attack runs down the line to the Twentieth Ohio, as the white foam of an ocean billow rolls against a long reach of sea-beach, striking at last a jutting headland. They who stand at the angle hear at first a ripple and then a roar of musketry. Onward sweeps the tide, the Confederate soldiers sending out their loudest yells, their bayonets flashing in the sun, the earth resounding the tread of the advancing host. The veteran Union soldiers know that there must be a desperate struggle. In an instant they leap over the breastworks, turn about, and face to the south-east, bring their muskets to a level, and fire a volley.

The great body of the Confederate column under Cleburne sweeps on towards the hill, while Maney's division swings west of the angle, then turns east to rush upon the Twentieth and Seventy-eighth regiments. In an instant the Ohio troops leap back to the other side of the breastworks, turn about, and deliver their volleys upon Maney, strewing the ground with killed and wounded. Leggett's chief of artillery, Captain Williams, has placed Elliott's battery of Rodman guns between Force's and Scott's brigades, the 24-pound howitzers of Captain Hooper's battery on the top of the hill, and the Third Ohio Battery of 20-pound Parrot-guns on the right of the division. Cleburne's troops rush up the eastern slope of the hill. Then comes a terrible hand-to-hand struggle, men firing into each other's faces across the breastworks, stabbing each other with their bayonets, beating out each other's brains with the butts of their muskets. Such a *mêlée* cannot continue long. Cleburne's men are out of breath with their running up the hill. Their aggressive force has spent itself; many have been killed or wounded, and the shattered lines fall back into the woods.

General Hood was on the breastworks east of the city. He had intended that Cheatham, with his own old corps, should rush up the western slope of the hill the same moment that Cleburne attacked, but it was not possible for him to arrange for exact concert of action. Cheatham started when he heard the uproar, but before he could reach the hill Cleburne had been repulsed. The Confederates under Cheatham rushed up the western slope, but the Union troops leaped back again over the intrenchments and were ready to receive them. The howitzers, the Rodman and Parrot-guns poured in a terrific fire. Cheatham could make no headway and was easily repulsed. Cleburne was not ready to give up the struggle, and reformed his lines in the woods and again advanced. Once more the Union men leaped over the breastworks and faced the east. General Walcott, commanding a brigade in Morgan L. Smith's division of the Fifteenth

Corps, swung his troops out from the main line and delivered a destructive enfilading fire. The hill once more was aflame. Fuller, of the Sixteenth Corps, was opening on Cleburne's rear, whose troops again fled to the shelter of the woods.

Over towards Atlanta Cheatham meanwhile had rallied his troops and advanced from the west. The men of Leggett's and Giles A. Smith's divisions once more jumped over their breastworks and fired upon the advancing lines. The soldiers called it practising "Hardee's Tactics." There was humor in the remark, for before the war General Hardee published a volume with that title. This advance of Cheatham was mainly against the Fifteenth Corps. Walcott's brigade, the first north of Leggett, had its right flank in a thicket, its left flank on a knoll. The other brigades of Morgan L. Smith's division were farther east. Smith ordered Walcott to fall back, but General Leggett asked him to remain.

"I am ordered," said Leggett, "by Sherman to hold this hill at all hazards, and if you fall back my flank will be exposed." Walcott saw that it would be better to remain where he was.(") We come to the critical moment of the battle. It was four o'clock—possibly later, for men take little note of time in battle—when Hardee's artillery opened fire from the south-east, followed once more by an attack on Giles A. Smith.

In the morning we saw the Sixty-eighth Ohio, under Colonel Welles, taking part in the repulse of the attack upon the Sixteenth Corps. The regiment had returned, was coming down from the north, and was in position to deliver its fire squarely into the faces of the Confederates. Leggett moved Malloy's brigade to face the south, and the 24-pound howitzers were turned in the same direction. While Hardee was getting ready to attack, Leggett's men seized their shovels, and in a few moments had a line of breastworks running eastward at a right angle with that on the hill. Hardee had captured two of Giles A. Smith's cannon, had wheeled them, and was firing upon the hill. General Blair, commanding the Seventeenth Corps, had his line admirably arranged, and was ready to receive the last grand assault. The men who had held the hill through the day had no intention of yielding it now, although Hardee was to attack from the south and Cheatham from the north and west.

Cheatham's sharp-shooters sheltered themselves behind a house, fired from its windows, picked off the gunners of De Gress's battery, and shot the horses. Manigault's brigade of Confederates was massing behind some buildings. Suddenly they swarmed out, rushed upon the battery, seized the guns, and turned them upon Smith's troops. De Gress went back to Sherman with tears dropping from his eyes. His cannon were first heard at Shiloh, had thundered in nearly all the great battles, and he was heartbroken over his loss. The Confederate assault was so vigorous that Smith's and Wood's troops by the railroad were driven from their intrenchments. General Wood hastened to Sherman for orders.

"My left is driven in, and my connection with Leggett broken," he said to his commander-in-chief.

"Wheel your brigades to the left, advance in echelon, and strike the enemy in flank," was the order.

Sherman sent a messenger to Schofield with this order: "Mass your artillery on yonder hill and open fire." Schofield put twenty pieces into position a short distance west of the Howard House, and opened a destructive fire upon the Confederates. Wood's brigades wheeled round from the north-east, coming upon the flank of the Confederates under Manigault. Down by the railroad Logan, with hat in hand, was riding along the line shouting, "Remember McPherson! Avenge his death! Don't let the Fifteenth Corps be disgraced!"

Going north now, along the line of the Fifteenth Corps, we find Morgan L. Smith's division extending to the railroad. Two cannon of De Gress's battery (A, First Illinois) were near a house by the railroad, supported by the One Hundred and Eleventh Illinois Regiment. When the battle began in the morning the other regiments of Martin's brigade went upon the double-quick to the assistance of the Sixteenth Corps. They were the Fifty-fifth and One Hundred and Seventh Illinois, Fifty-seventh Ohio, and Sixth Missouri. The withdrawal of these regiments left a weak line at this point near the railroad, north of which was C. R. Wood's division, reaching to Schofield. Sherman's headquarters were in the rear of Wood's at the Howard House.

It was late in the afternoon when Cheatham again advanced, rushing upon the battery, overwhelming the regiment in support.

The Union lines which a few moments before were disorganized took form once more. Soldiers who for a moment had been fainthearted were themselves again under the magnetism of their commander. Martin's brigade came into position, and resolved that the cannon whose thunder had been music to their ears in many battles should be recaptured. Captain De Gress was running along the lines pleading with the soldiers to get them back.(") Sweeny's brigade of the Sixteenth Corps was there to help the Twelfth and Sixty-sixth Illinois and Eighty-first Ohio. The advance of the lines of both brigades was like the rush of a whirlwind that sweeps everything before it. They recaptured the guns, and drove the Confederates in complete rout towards Atlanta.

While Cheatham was thus being rolled back from his position the rest of the Union troops were giving the final repulse to Cleburne, driving him back into the woods. The sun went down with the guns still flashing. A portion of Maney's division of Confederates crept along the intrenchments south of the fort, still hoping that by some sudden movement they might get possession of the hill; but Sherman's lines were stronger than when the battle began, while Hood's were terribly shattered. The Union loss in killed, wounded, and prisoners was about thirty-five hundred, while the Confederate loss is supposed to have been nearly ten thousand. To the Confederates it was one of the most disastrous conflicts of the war. Walker's division never again appeared as a separate organization, but the brigades were broken up and distributed to other commands. The battles of Peachtree Creek and Atlanta, brought on by General Hood, had both resulted in irretrievable disaster to the Confederate cause.

NOTES TO CHAPTER XIII.

(1) Gen. J. E. Johnston, "Narrative of Military Events," p. 345.
(2) Copy of Letter in possession of the Author.
(3) Gen. J. E. Johnston, " Narrative of Military Events," p. 347.
(4) Idem, p. 348.
(5) E. A. Pollard, "Lost Cause," p. 377.
(6) J. W. Avery, " History of Georgia," p. 279.
(7) Geu. J. E. Johnston, "Narrative of Military Events," p. 348.
(8) Idem, p. 349.
(9) J. W. Avery, "History of Georgia," p. 279.
(10) Idem.
(11) Gen. J. E. Johnston, "Narrative of Military Events," p. 349.
(12) "Memoirs of Gen. W. T. Sherman," vol. ii., p. 72.
(13) Idem, p. 76.
(14) Idem.
(15) Account of Orderly A. G. Thompson, in possession of the Author.
(16) "Memoirs of Gen. W. T. Sherman," vol. ii., p. 78.
(17) General Leggett's Account.
(18) "Memoirs of Gen. W. T. Sherman," vol. ii., p. 81.

CHAPTER XIV.

THE SIEGE OF PETERSBURG.

THE siege intrenchments which were begun by General Grant east of Petersburg consisted of redoubts, connected by lines of parapets with ditches and fallen trees, sharpened stakes, and *chevaux-de-frise*. When those were constructed, it was intended that they should be held by a portion of the army, while another portion should make a movement towards the south-west, to gain possession of the railroads, and attack General Lee whenever any advantage could be gained.

The Second Corps crossed the Norfolk railroad and the Jerusalem plank road, which runs south-east from Petersburg, and took position on the left of the Fifth Corps. General Meade ordered the movement with the intention of reaching the Weldon Railroad, which also runs south from Petersburg. Barlow's division was on the extreme left, and within two miles of the railroad. During the night the Sixth Corps came up on the left of the Second, to be ready to move with it. General Lee discovered the change in position, and directed Gen. A. P. Hill to march out from the intrenchments and meet the movement.

June 21, 1864.

In years gone by the region had been a tobacco-field, but by long cultivation the fertility of the soil had been exhausted, and where once the slave-gang tilled the ground stood an impenetrable thicket of scrubby pines. It was so difficult for the two corps to move connectedly that the Sixth Corps took a road which led past the house of Mr. Williams, separating it from the Second Corps, which was making its way towards the Globe Tavern, which stood near the railroad. It was three o'clock in the afternoon, and the troops of Gibbon's and Mott's divisions of the Second Corps were building breastworks, and Barlow's division was on the march towards the tavern, when Mahone's and Johnson's divisions of Confederate troops came through the woods and fell upon Barlow's flank and rear. The attack was so sudden that Barlow's troops had no time to form. Some were taken prisoner, and the whole command scattered. Mott's division, next in line, retreated before the Confederates,

June 22, 1864.

RETURN OF THE CAVALRY.

who rushed upon Gibbon, capturing a large number of prisoners and four cannon. There was little fighting. It was a very successful movement on the part of A. P. Hill, who fell back to his intrenchments with the four cannon and seventeen hundred prisoners. The disaster was keenly felt by the Second Corps, which, through all the war, up to that moment, had not lost a gun.

Recovering from the disaster, the Second Corps moved forward in compact order, accompanied by the Sixth, both corps building breastworks about a mile and a half from the railroad, with the picket line well advanced towards it.

June 22, 1864.

It was two o'clock on the morning of the 22d that Generals Wilson and Kautz, with five thousand cavalry, started south-west, and reached the Weldon Railroad at Ream's Station, where they tore up the track. Turn-

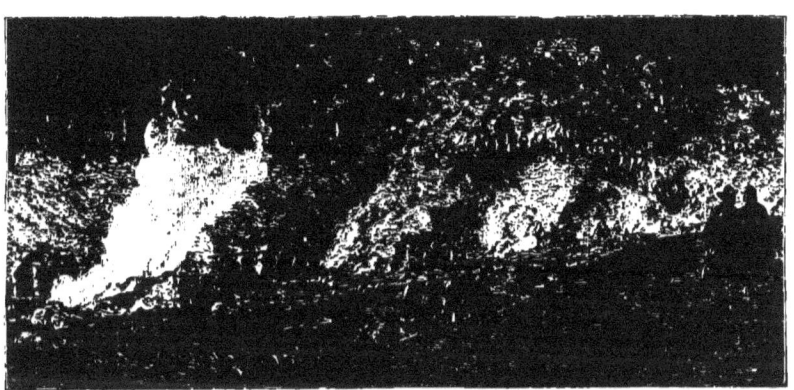

TEARING UP THE RAILS.

ing north-west, the cavalry pushed on to the South Side Railroad, leading west from Petersburg, striking it fourteen miles west of the city, tearing up the rails for thirty miles to Staunton River. General Kautz found the bridge across that stream protected by a strong military force, with cannon, and he could not burn it.

The Confederate cavalry under W. H. F. Lee attacked the rear of Wilson's troops nearly one hundred miles west of Petersburg. Finding that his provisions were nearly gone, and having committed great havoc along the railroad, General Wilson turned south-east, came to the Weldon road at Stony Creek Station, ten miles below Ream's Station, where he was confronted by a division of cavalry under Hampton. A battle began which

23—*

lasted till ten o'clock at night. General Kautz at midnight started north up the Halifax road, towards Ream's Station. It was daylight before Wilson could withdraw from his position. Hampton's troops followed him two miles, but the Confederate commander, seeing the direction which Wilson was taking, hastened along another road to cut him off. Kautz reached Ream's Station, and found himself confronted by Fitz-Hugh Lee.

Captain Whittaker, with a message to Meade, dashed through the Confederate lines. It was eleven o'clock in the morning when he reached General Meade's headquarters on the Jerusalem plank road, eight miles from Ream's Station. General Lee was informed of the situation, and sent Mahone's division to help capture the Union cavalry. Finding themselves cut off from the Union army, Wilson and Kautz destroyed their wagons and caissons, issued all their ammunition, and at noon turned south, along the Halifax road, towards Nottoway River, intending after crossing that stream to move eastward twenty miles, and then turn north. Before they could get away, Mahone and the Confederate cavalry advanced, separated Kautz's division from Wilson's, throwing the rear of both into confusion. Kautz, finding that he could not reunite with Wilson, made a movement which the Confederates did not mistrust he would attempt—crossed the railroad between Ream's Station and Rowanty Creek. In passing through a swamp his cannon sunk so deep in the mire that he spiked and abandoned them, but just at dark reached the army.

June 28, 1864.

General Wilson the while was pushing south towards Stony Creek, accompanied by more than one thousand negroes who had left their masters to find freedom, as they hoped, under the Stars and Stripes; but they could not keep pace with the cavalry and were left behind. The Union troops reached Jarrett's Station on the Weldon road, rested a little while, and then moved on, and came to Nottoway River at Peter's Bridge. They found it partly destroyed, but in a short time trees were felled, stringers put in place, and the bridge made passable. When the last man was over, it was again destroyed, thus foiling Hampton and Fitz-Hugh Lee, who were close behind. On the afternoon of July 2d, Wilson reached the Army of the Potomac, having been gone ten days, during which time he had marched over three hundred miles, and destroyed sixty miles of railroad. Twelve cannon had been abandoned, and fifteen hundred men were missing; most of them had fallen out of the ranks through the breaking down of their horses, and had been captured by the Confederates. So arduous and fatiguing this march that many of the soldiers fell asleep while sitting in their saddles, and some of them dropped off to sleep in

FIRST CONNECTICUT ARTILLERY SIEGE GUNS.

battle. A large number of horses broke down and were abandoned. The men were covered with dust, were worn and weary. They had lived on scant rations. The longest halt made at any time did not exceed six hours.

Although so long a line of railroad-track had been destroyed, the Confederate Government soon had a large force of negroes and white men at work repairing it, and in a few weeks the cars were once more in motion.

SOLDIERS' WELLS.

The sun shone during these summer days from a cloudless sky. For a period of forty-seven days no rain fell. The springs dried. The dust was ankle-deep, but the surface soil was porous, and a few feet below it in the clay subsoil there was water in abundance. The soldiers dug wells behind the intrenchments, erected sweeps, attached buckets, and so had delicious cool water to drink.

Through the days the sharp-shooters of both armies were on the lookout. If a soldier raised his hat above the breastwork it was sure to be pierced by a bullet. Here and there along the lines, day and night the cannon were thundering and mortars sending their shells in parabolic curves through the air. Colonel Abbott, of the First Connecticut Artillery, was in command of the siege-train. He had forty rifled 30-pounder Parrot-guns, sixty mortars of various sizes, and six 100-pound Parrot-guns.

In the Ninth Corps was a regiment from Pennsylvania, the members of which, before the war, were engaged in mining coal. It was the Forty-eighth Regiment, commanded by Colonel Pleasants, who knew all about mining. The regiment was in a ravine behind breastworks only a few hundred feet from the Confederate works. Colonel Pleasants, after surveying the ground, thought that he could dig a passage-way into the bank of the ravine, carry it under a Confederate redoubt where there were several cannon, and lay a mine, which, when exploded, would make such a break in the Confederate works, and create so much havoc and confusion, that with troops massed, ready to rush in when the mine was touched off, the whole line of Confederate earthworks in that vicinity might be seized. The engineer officers of the army doubted if a mine could be excavated, but General Burnside thought that it could be done. General Meade gave his consent. The men went to work digging the gallery, bringing out the earth in bags at night, and distributing it so that the Confederates should not detect any change. Although carried on with great secrecy, the Confederates discovered that something was going on. A countermine was attempted and given up for want of tools;(¹) but a second line of works was erected in the rear, and cannon placed to pour a cross-fire upon the spot which General Beauregard expected would be blown up. He also gave minute instructions to the officers in the menaced quarters, so that when the explosion came there would be no panic or confusion, but a quick concentration of troops. The gallery was five hundred and eleven feet in length, with two branches, one thirty-seven and the other thirty-eight feet long.(²) There were eight magazines, each charged with one thousand pounds of powder. While the mine was being excavated through the month of July, a sharp fire was kept up between the Ninth Corps and the Confederates. Every day from thirty to fifty men were killed or wounded by the sharp-shooters or by shells from the mortars. The casualties were equally great on the Confederate side.

It was thought that if a movement were made towards Richmond north of the James, the Confederate line near Chapin's Bluff might be success-

BEHIND THE BREASTWORKS.

fully assaulted, and that such a movement would compel Lee to send troops from Petersburg to meet it, which would give greater chance for success with the mines.(')

While the miners were carrying in the powder and doing the last work, the Second Corps, under Hancock, who had returned to it, marched to Point of Rocks, on the Appomattox, crossed that river, and kept on north, in rear of General Butler's troops, towards Deep Bottom, on the James, accompanied by the cavalry under Sheridan. Going up to Deep Bottom, we see a little stream named Bailey's Creek coming down from the north and emptying into the James. Were we to go up the creek we should come to the New Market road, which leads to Richmond. Beyond it is the mill of Mr. Fressell, on the Derbytown road, also leading to Richmond. General Foster, commanding the Tenth Corps, had two bridges across the James, one above the mouth of Bailey's Creek, the other below it.

July 27, 1864.

General Grant intended that the Second Corps should cross the upper bridge and move towards Chapin's Bluff, while the cavalry should cross the lower bridge and move rapidly towards Richmond up the roads leading to the city. When General Hancock reached the upper bridge he found that the Confederates had a strong line of works beyond it. He did not think it best to attempt to attack at that point, and so turned east, crossed the lower bridge, and marched up the east bank of Bailey's Creek, but very soon found his march disputed by Kershaw's division behind breastworks with several cannon. The Union skirmishers deployed in the fields, the Ninety-ninth and One Hundred and Seventh Pennsylvania and Seventy-third New York, the One Hundred and Eighty-third Pennsylvania, Twenty-eighth Massachusetts, and Forty-sixth Michigan, under Gen. Nelson A. Miles, who looked over the ground and led the troops through a ravine, and rushed upon the breastworks, capturing four 20-pound Parrot-guns and some prisoners. Great the rejoicing in the Second Corps over the success thus attained. The troops tossed their caps in the air, and gave a grand hurrah! They felt that they had made good the loss of McKnight's battery in the movement towards the Weldon Railroad. The Second Corps moved on to Bailey's Creek, but found that the Confederates had a strong line of works along the western bank, and that the trees had been cut down in front, making a barrier which could not be carried. General Grant arrived, and looked over the ground and saw that nothing could be accomplished, for Lee had hurried a large number of troops across the Appomattox to resist the movement; not only Kershaw's but Wilcox's and Heth's divisions. Sheridan found himself confronted by

Confederate infantry and W. H. F. Lee's division of cavalry. In a sharp contest Sheridan captured two hundred prisoners.

General Grant, knowing that more than half of Lee's army was north of the Appomattox, detached Mott's division from the Second Corps, and directed it to hasten back to Petersburg, to be ready for an active part if the explosion of the mine was as successful as was anticipated, leaving Sheridan and Hancock with two divisions of his corps to make a strong demonstration at Bailey's Creek; but when night came they also took up their line of march for Petersburg.

All preparations had been made for the explosion. In 1864 science and invention had not discovered that an electric battery might be used for firing mines, and Colonel Pleasants was obliged to use several sections of fuse. To insure the firing, a train of powder was also laid on the night of the 29th.

July 30, 1864.

General Meade at the outset doubted if the mine could be excavated, but it had been completed. He objected to the selection of the colored troops to lead the assault, although General Ferrero had drilled them with that object in view. He thought that if they were to fail, it would be said that they were putting the colored people in to get killed; but no such criticism would be heard if white troops were to lead. General Burnside had great confidence in the efficiency of the colored troops. He thought that the other troops had been so long accustomed to shelter themselves under the intrenchments that General Ferrero's troops would be more efficient as soldiers. His objections were overruled by General Meade, and it was then decided that lots should be drawn in the selection of troops to lead the assault. The lot fell to General Ledlie's division.(¹) Butler's troops were placed in position to open fire upon the Confederate batteries, and the troops of the Second, Eighteenth, and Fifth corps were to be ready.

The mine was under the Confederate redoubt held by Elliott's brigade, south of which was Wise's and then Colquitt's; north of Elliott's were Rawson's and Gracie's. These brigades constituted Johnson's division. Hoke's division continued the line to the Appomattox; Mahone's was on the right of Johnson's, extending towards the Weldon Railroad.

On this midsummer morning, at half-past three, just as day is breaking, the fuse is lighted. The troops of the Ninth Corps are waiting. The artillerymen are by their guns, ready to open fire. An hour passes, but there is no sign of explosion. Lieut. Jacob Douty and Sergt. Henry Rees, of the Forty-eighth Pennsylvania, who have excavated the mine, creep into the gallery and find that the fire has gone out; that the powder laid in the

CAPTURE OF GUNS BY MILES'S BRIGADE.

trough has become damp by the thirty hours' exposure. They strike a match, relight the fuse, and flee from the gallery. Five minutes pass and then there is a trembling of the ground, a rumbling like that of an earthquake, and a great mass of earth rises in the air, together with timbers, cannon, and men. The explosion has made a crater nearly two hundred feet in length, sixty in width, and nearly thirty deep. The Confederate troops are appalled at the spectacle. A moment later the Union cannon open fire. Ten or fifteen minutes pass before General Ledlie's troops reach the crater. They do not rush through it, but halt within it, when they should be pushing across the space beyond, to seize the several lines of intrenchments. Fatal delay! Confederate batteries soon open upon them, and the troops, which for nearly two months have been sheltering themselves from the fire of the enemy behind breastworks, are loath to advance. Wilcox's and Potter's divisions reach the crater, but are not led by their division commanders, and in a short time there is a mass of men huddled into the excavation and under the breastworks. The Confederates, seeing the Union troops halting in the crater, quickly opened a destructive fire. General Beauregard, awakened by the explosion, sent Colonel Paul to General Lee for troops, and then hastened towards the scene, and directed the movements of the troops.([4]) A Confederate officer says: "In less than five minutes' time our men recovered from their panic, and we fired rapidly and with great execution. About the same time the battery on the left of the ravine, a short distance in rear of Rawson's brigade, did great execution, and fired about six hundred shots in a short time. The others, in rear and on the right, also did good execution."([5])

The Confederate batteries poured their shells and canister with great precision into the crater, doing such execution in the halting troops that many of the soldiers began to run. It was half-past seven when the colored troops, under General Ferrero, were ordered forward. None of the divisions of the Ninth Corps advanced so bravely. A Confederate writer gives this testimony: "They moved across the open space between the Federal and Confederate lines into, out of, and beyond the crater; but at this point they broke, under the fierce artillery fire there concentrated upon them, and after having been partially reorganized, broke again, now fleeing in wild disorder into and out of the crater back to General Burnside's lines."([7])

We are not to think that the Union troops are doing nothing; on the contrary, a fierce fight is going on as they attempt to force their way along the trenches. "Numbers of them got into the ditch of the gorge line," writes a Confederate historian, "where a hand-to-hand fight ensued;

while others, creeping along the glacis of the exterior line, got over the parapet of the main trench. The troops on the right and left fought them from behind the traverses, and from the barricades thrown up at the angles of the trenches; while the adjacent brigades, from their main parapets, the covered ways and ravines running to the rear, from bombproofs, concentrated a deadly fire on such of the Federal forces as were marching across from the river."(⁵)

There is much discrepancy in the reports and accounts of the Union officers in regard to the battle, but for want of prompt and energetic action the opportunity to win a victory went by. General Grant came at nine o'clock, surveyed the scene, saw that every chance of success was lost. "These troops must be immediately withdrawn. It is slaughter to leave them there," he said.(⁹) General Meade directed the withdrawal of the men, but not till nearly eleven were they back once more in their intrenchments—not all of them, for more than thirty-five hundred had been killed, wounded, or taken prisoner, while the Confederate loss was about fifteen hundred.(¹⁰)

So what promised to be a cheering victory ended in disheartening disaster to the Army of the Potomac, but with exultation to the Confederates.

Though the attempt to break the Confederate lines had ended in failure, there was no letting up of effort and vigilance on the part of General Grant. The Engineer Corps established its posts of observation in tall trees, whence, with their glasses, they could overlook the Confederate lines; the batteries and earthworks were made stronger, so that they could be held by fewer troops. Had we been inside the Confederate lines we should have seen General Lee doing the same, that he might have a movable body to be used wherever most needed.

NOTES TO CHAPTER XIV.

(¹) Alfred Roman, 'Military Operations of General Beauregard," vol. ii., p. 260.
(²) Colonel Pleasants' account, "Attack on Petersburg," p. 4.
(³) Gen. U. S. Grant, "Personal Memoirs," vol. ii., p. 310.
(⁴) Gen. A. E. Burnside's account, "Attack on Petersburg," p. 17.
(⁵) Alfred Roman, "Military Operations of General Beauregard," vol. ii., p. 263.
(⁶) Colonel McMaster's Report, quoted, 'Military Operations of General Beauregard," vol. ii., p. 263.
(⁷) Idem, p. 264.
(⁸) Idem.
(⁹) Gen. A. Badeau, "Military History of General Grant," vol. ii., p. 482.
(¹⁰) Gen. B. R. Johnson's and Colonel McMaster's statements, in "Military Operations of General Beauregard," Appendix to chap. xxxix.

ENGINEER'S LOOKOUT.

CHAPTER XV.

MOBILE BAY.

THE rain-drops falling on the mountains of northern Alabama, and the springs which gurgle from their sides, give rise to two great rivers—the Alabama and Tombigbee—which pour their floods into Mobile Bay, an estuary of the Gulf of Mexico, whose entrance was guarded before the war by Fort Morgan and Fort Gaines. When Alabama seceded from the Union in January, 1861, Governor Moore, of that State, ordered the forts to be seized and garrisoned by the militia. For three years the flag of the Confederacy had floated above their ramparts. Fort Morgan was situated on the main-land and guarded the eastern entrance. It was built of brick, and the walls were nearly five feet thick and mounted eighty-six cannon. Outside the fort, in batteries, were twenty-nine additional guns behind banks of sand. Within the fort was a citadel or stronghold, whose brick walls were four feet thick, with loop-holes for musket-firing. The fort was garrisoned by six hundred and forty men.

Three miles westward of Fort Morgan is Dauphin Island, upon which stood Fort Gaines, also built of brick, in the form of a star, mounting thirty heavy cannon, and garrisoned by eight hundred men. To guard against the entrance of small vessels to the bay at flood tide, lines of piles had been driven by the Confederates across the reaches of shoal water between the forts and the channel, narrowing the passage-way to three hundred yards, so close to Fort Morgan that a vessel would be subjected to the fire of all the guns of the fort and the batteries. Six miles west of Fort Gaines was another channel, through which vessels of light draught might enter the bay. It was called Grant's Pass, to guard which the Confederates constructed Fort Powell, upon which several heavy guns were mounted.

While the Union and Confederate governments during the winter of 1863–64 were preparing for the great struggles in Virginia and northern Georgia, wood-choppers were felling trees in Alabama, and floating them down the river ten miles to Selma, hewing them into timbers for the construction of an iron-clad vessel to aid in preventing a Union fleet from entering the bay, and for breaking the blockade. When the hull was completed it was floated down the Alabama River to the city of Mobile. The craft was two hundred and nine feet long, forty-eight broad, with sloping sides two feet thick, covered with six inches of iron plating manufactured in the rolling-mills at Atlanta. A sharp-pointed iron spur projected from the bow below the water—a beak to be thrust into the side of the wooden ships of the Union fleet, should they attempt to enter the bay. The vessel was named the *Tennessee*, and carried six heavy rifled Brooke cannon, two of which were pivot-guns that could be fired in any direction, and threw solid projectiles that weighed one hundred and ten pounds; the other four cannon threw solid shot that weighed ninety-five pounds. The *Tennessee* was far more formidable than the *Merrimac*, which created such havoc off Fortress Monroe in March, 1862 ("Drum-beat of the Nation," chap. viii.). The steering apparatus was not well planned, and the engines, taken from a river steamboat, were weak; but aside from these defects, the vessel was more than a match for all the wooden ships of the United States navy. The Confederates had no machine-shops for the construction of powerful marine engines, and the *Tennessee*, with her cannon and coal on board, could make only six knots an hour. The vessel drew so much water that not till the cannon were taken out and great flat-boats, called "camels," were fastened to her sides and filled nearly full of water, and the water pumped out, thereby lifting the *Tennessee*, could the vessel be taken across the bar below Mobile. It was a task requiring so much labor that not till May did she steam slowly down the bay, and drop anchor on the east side of the channel near Fort Morgan, accompanied by three wooden gunboats—the *Morgan*, carrying six guns; the *Gaines*, six; and the *Selma*, four.

May, 1864.

Further, to prevent the Union fleet from entering the bay, two lines of torpedoes were anchored between Fort Morgan and Fort Gaines.

Not much was known by the Government at Washington about the *Tennessee*. The newspapers of the South gave no information. Deserters from the army of General Johnston, at Dalton, told great stories about the vessel which some calm night would send to the bottom of the sea the Union fleet blockading the entrance.

From the beginning of the war the Confederate sentinels, facing the ramparts of Fort Morgan, looking seaward, could always see the Stars and Stripes flying above the decks of several war-ships. On calm nights they could hear, perchance, the dipping of oars in the water as the adventurous sailors paddled their boats close up to the channel, ever on the watch for any swift steamer built in England, arriving from Nassau. laden with goods, or departing with a cargo of cotton.

Admiral Farragut, after his great service on the Mississippi, was given command of the fleet off Mobile Bay, and after recruiting his health by a visit to New York, hoisted his flag once more above the deck of the *Hartford*, and began preparations to attack the Confederate fortifications. In the light-draught gunboat *Octorora*, accompanied by the *Itasca*, on a clear bright day, he steamed up to Sand Island, and took a look at the fortifications and the Confederate gunboats.

Jan. 20, 1864.

OFF MOBILE BAY AT NIGHT.

"I am satisfied," he said, "that if I had one iron-clad at this time I could destroy their whole force in the bay, and reduce the forts at my leisure, by co-operation with our land force—say five thousand men. We must have about two thousand five hundred men in the rear of each fort, to make regular approaches by land, and to prevent the garrison from receiving supplies and reinforcements; the fleet to run the batteries and fight the flotilla."(¹) But he had no iron-clad vessels. Men were hard at work in the ship-yards at Brooklyn constructing a fleet of monitors.

A few days later Admiral Farragut steamed up Grant's Pass with the small gunboats, and bombarded Fort Powell. The Confederates replied with their rifled guns, striking a mortar schooner four times, but only wounding one man. Admiral Farragut wrote this in his journal: "We silenced them in an hour and a quarter, causing them to remain in their dodging-holes until we stopped at sunset. We were four thousand yards off, lying fast aground, and could get no closer."(²)

Feb. 24, 1864.

Admiral Farragut could not carry out his plan for capturing the forts, for want of co-operation on the part of the army. General Canby, in command at New Orleans, had no troops to spare for such an expedition till midsummer.

What Admiral Farragut had waited for came at last—four monitors and a division of troops under Gen. Gordon Granger. There were not enough troops to invest both forts, and they were landed on Dauphin Island to begin the investment of Fort Gaines. How loyal and noble was the man commanding the fleet of war-vessels off the bar of Mobile Bay is seen from the letter which he wrote to his wife on the evening before he was to fight a great battle.

Aug. 4, 1864.

"I am going into Mobile Bay in the morning, if God is my leader, as I hope he is, and in him I place my trust. If he thinks it is the proper place for me to die, I am ready to submit to his will in that as in all other things. My great mortification is that my vessels, the iron-clads, were not ready to have gone in yesterday. The army landed last night, and are in full view of us this morning, and the *Tecumseh* has not yet arrived from Pensacola. God bless and prepare you, my darling, and my dear boy, if anything should happen to me."(³)

The *Tecumseh* arrived, making the fleet complete. Admiral Farragut paid attention to things which might seem to most people to be of little moment. He studied the ebb and flow of the tide, the direction of the winds during the summer day. He noticed that at a certain hour the water was ruffled by a gentle breeze from the west, which would carry the smoke of his guns towards Fort Morgan and envelop it in such a cloud that the Confederate gunners would not be able to take good aim. The sailors had gone up the channel in the night, and secured a torpedo, which he examined; and he saw that if he went in on the flood tide, the apparatus by which the torpedo was to be exploded would be tilted towards the harbor by the swirling current, and would be less likely to explode than if tilted seaward by an ebb-tide. Besides, if the engine of a vessel should become disabled, flood tide would be likely to sweep it into the harbor. As the channel was within two hundred yards of Fort Morgan, and two miles distant from Fort Gaines, he would pay no attention

ADMIRAL FARRAGUT.

MOBILE BAY.

to the latter, but pour his broadside upon Fort Morgan. He ordered the heavy guns of the port side to be shifted to starboard. The boats of the ship were lowered into the water upon the port side, to be ready for use should they be needed. Bags were filled with sand and piled against the bulwarks, making a wall of sand four feet in thickness.

Admiral Farragut had fourteen wooden ships which he intended to use in passing the forts and fighting the Confederate fleet, leaving six gunboats outside to maintain the blockade. The vessels were to be

SECURING A TORPEDO.

coupled, lashed side by side, so that if one, perchance, were disabled, the other would carry both safely past the forts, with the tide setting into the bay. It was to be a procession of ships. This the order:

1. *Brooklyn*, twenty-four guns, Captain Alden; *Octorora*, six guns, Lieutenant Greene. 2. *Hartford*, twenty-one guns, Admiral Farragut and Captain Drayton; *Metacomet*, six guns, Lieutenant Jouett. 3. *Richmond*, twenty guns, Captain Jenkins; *Port Royal*, six guns, Lieutenant Gherardi. 4. *Lackawanna*, eight guns, Captain Marchand; *Seminole*, eight guns, Commander Donaldson. 5. *Monongahela*, eight guns, Commander Strong; *Kennebec*, five guns, Lieutenant McCann. 6. *Ossipee*, eleven guns, Commander Le Roy; *Itasca*, five guns, Lieutenant Brown.

7. *Oneida*, nine guns, Commander Mullany; *Galena*, ten guns, Lieutenant Wells.

The *Octorora*, *Metacomet*, and *Port Royal* had side wheels, and sharp sterns as well as bows, so that by reversing the engines they could go backward and forward alike. They were built to navigate rivers, and were called "double-enders." The others were screw steamships.

The four monitors were to form a procession by themselves, the *Tecumseh*, carrying two guns, leading, followed by the *Manhattan* with two guns, the *Winnebago* and *Chickasaw* four guns each. They were to pour their fire upon Fort Morgan till the wooden ships were past it. Admiral Farragut intended to lead in the *Hartford*, but as the *Brooklyn* had an apparatus projecting from her bow for picking up torpedoes, that ship was permitted to lead the column. The vessels were to steer east of a red buoy, which was supposed to mark the beginning of the torpedoes. The Confederates had placed the buoy in position for the benefit of vessels running the blockade.

Admiral Buchanan, who commanded the *Merrimac* in the battle with the *Monitor* ("Drum-beat of the Nation," chap. viii.), commanded the *Tennessee*. He knew by the arrival of Admiral Farragut's ships from Pensacola on the afternoon of August 4th, and by what was going on in the fleet, that the ships would soon make the attempt to pass the forts. He believed that the *Tennessee*, with two feet of solid timber on her sloping sides, plated with seven inches of iron, was invulnerable. He had good reason for believing that she would prove more than a match for all the fourteen wooden ships; but possibly remembering what took place in Hampton Roads, he stood in some fear of the four monitors, which he could see at anchor under the lee of Sand Island down the harbor.

As the fleet, after entering the bay, was to co-operate with the army for the capture of Fort Gaines, signal-officers from the army were placed on the several vessels of the fleet—very fortunately, as we shall see. That he might survey Fort Morgan and the *Tennessee* once more before going into battle, Admiral Farragut stepped on board the little steamer *Cowslip*, which made its way well up towards the fort. He was accompanied by Captain Percival Drayton of the *Hartford*. Farragut had just passed his sixty-third year. He was still hale, hearty, vigorous, energetic. He had a kind heart and resolute will. Everybody loved him. He looked at the fort with his glass, and saw that it had been greatly strengthened by the Confederates, who had piled bags filled with sand against the walls. He saw the *Tennessee*, lying like a huge black turtle in the calm waters beyond the fort, with the three Confederate wooden vessels near at hand.

We are not to think that every man born in the Confederate States fought against the Stars and Stripes. On the contrary, there were notable examples of loyalty. Captain Winslow, who sent the *Alabama* to the bottom of the sea, was from North Carolina. Captain Percival Drayton, who stands by the side of Admiral Farragut, was born in South Carolina, and showed his loyalty and devotion to the Union in the bombardment of the forts at Port Royal, although his brother commanded the Confederates in the forts ("Drum-beat of the Nation," p. 123). Here he is scanning eagerly the forts, the Confederate fleet, the reach of water where with the rising sun of to-morrow he will again render great and honorable service to his country.

At sunset the last orders are issued. Every commander knows what he is expected to do. In the fading hours of the summer day a gentle breeze born of the sea is wafted inland with the tide. It enters the open ports of the ship, cools the heated air of the wardroom, where the officers are writing letters to loved ones far away. Possibly their hands never again will hold the pen; that with to-morrow's sunset their voices will be silent evermore. But there is no blanching of faces. Not one of them but would think it a hardship were he to be ordered otherwheres and not take part in the battle. Not that they delight in carnage; not that they thirst for glory, but that they are to sustain the honor and dignity of the flag that was first dishonored at Sumter. Duty nerves them; and so with firm step they walk the deck, look up to the eternal stars in the heavens above them—ready to die, if need be, that the nation may live.

"Admiral," said one of the officers to Admiral Farragut, "won't you give the sailors a glass of grog in the morning—not enough to make them drunk, but just enough to make them fight well?"

"Well," replied the admiral, "I have been to sea a good deal in my life, and have seen a battle or two, but I never found that I needed rum to enable me to do my duty. I will order two cups of good coffee to each man at two o'clock, and at eight o'clock I will pipe all hands to breakfast in Mobile Bay."(⁴)

Three o'clock. Day is breaking, and on every ship the boatswains' whistles are piping. "How is the wind?" Admiral Farragut asks from his berth. "South-west, sir," is the reply from the steward of the *Hartford*. "Then we will go in this morning."(⁵) It is spoken cheerily, as if the day had been selected for a picnic or a pleasant excursion up the bay. After midnight there had been fog, but it was drifting landward and the rising sun would burn it away.

Aug. 5, 1864.

25

The gunboats selected to accompany the larger vessels ran alongside their consorts, and were lashed together by heavy cables. All the topmasts and spars had been left at Pensacola. The sun appeared before the signal to move on fluttered from the main-mast of the *Hartford*, and then the grand procession, like a brigade of troops at review, moved slowly up the channel, the *Brooklyn* and her consort leading, and the monitors keeping pace in a procession by themselves a short distance to the left.

Six o'clock. The Confederate vessels move from their anchorage into the channel, the *Selma* on the right in advance, the *Tennessee* near the red buoy. Two guns break the stillness of the morning, fired by the *Tecumseh*, and then comes an interval of silence. The fleet is yet too far away for effective work. Ships and fort alike wait.

Six minutes past seven. From the barbette and casemates of Fort Morgan, from the batteries on the sand-hills, flames leap forth, and the air is filled with strange screechings as the solid shot and shell stream upon the *Brooklyn*. And now forts, batteries, monitors, and ships, from stem to stern, are clouds of flame and smoke. In the turret of the *Tecumseh* stands Captain Craven and John Collins, his pilot, looking through the narrow peep-holes in the dome of iron towards the red buoy, which from this position seems to be very near the beach. "It is impossible that the admiral means us to go inside that buoy; I cannot turn my ship," said Craven to the pilot. "Starboard the helm!" he shouts.(°) It was a sad mistake. The *Tecumseh* turns her prow westward towards the *Tennessee*, which has moved in that direction. Her cannon are loaded with sixty pounds of powder and jointed steel shot; but suddenly, as if a giant were attempting to lift the monitor, the *Tecumseh* rolls on one side, and her propeller whirls in the air. A torpedo has exploded beneath her. Pilot and captain instantaneously attempt to get through the narrow passage leading from the dome. "After you, pilot," are the courtly words of the great-hearted Craven. John Collins and a few of the sailors leap from the turret into the sea, but before the others can reach the deck the vessel disappears beneath the waves. Of one hundred and fourteen men on board, only twenty-one are saved.

The smoke was so thick that Admiral Farragut climbed to the main rigging to see what was going on. Captain Drayton, fearing that a sudden jar might jostle him, sent Quartermaster Knowles to tie him to the shrouds with a rope.(') The pilot, Martin Freeman, was farther up in the main-top, giving directions to the men at the wheel how to steer. The admiral saw the *Brooklyn* stop and begin to back. "What's the matter with the *Brooklyn?* She must have plenty of water there." "Plenty

OPENING OF THE BATTLE OF MOBILE BAY.

and to spare," is the pilot's answer.(⁸) Down in the hold of the *Hartford*, where the surgeon is ready to care for the wounded, is army Signal-officer John C. Kinney, with his signal-flag. Admiral Farragut has ordered him to remain there during the battle.

"Send up a signal-officer; the *Brooklyn* is signalling!" is shouted down the hatchway. Lieutenant Kinney runs up with his flag, waves it in response, and receives the message, "Monitors right ahead."

"Order the monitors ahead, and go on," the reply.(⁹) This the account of Lieutenant Kinney. More dramatic the scene as recorded by Admiral Farragut's son:

"What is the trouble?"

"Torpedoes."

"—— the torpedoes! Go ahead, Captain Drayton! Four bells. Full speed, Jouett!"(¹⁰)

The bells in the engine-rooms of the *Hartford* and *Metacomet* tinkled, and the two ships shot ahead of the *Brooklyn*, taking the lead of the column, passing harmlessly across the line of torpedoes planted beneath, which failed to explode. So the *Hartford* took her position with the *Metacomet* at the head of the line. To have halted under the full fire of the fort, with the *Selma* raking the decks, with the fleet pressing on, would have resulted in disaster.

The *Hartford* is receiving the fire of nearly all the Confederate cannon. The men in the fort see the admiral's flag flying above her deck. It will be something to boast of, if they can send her to the bottom of the sea. A shot strikes the foremast; then one weighing one hundred and twenty pounds splinters the main-mast. Timbers are crashing, shells exploding, men are torn to pieces; but all the while her guns are thundering, sending such a torrent of shrapnel upon the batteries that the Confederate gunners are compelled to lie down under their breastworks. In the water, struggling for life, are the men who leaped from the *Tecumseh*. Admiral Farragut sees them. "Send a boat for them, Mr. Jouett; pick up the poor fellows," he shouts to the captain of the *Metacomet*. But Captain Jouett has already sent Ensign Nields with a boat. Nields is but a boy, but he bravely steers the boat, unmindful of the shells bursting around him, or the solid shot screeching through the air, to within a few hundred yards of the Confederate cannon, unfurling a flag, placing it in the socket, so gallantly that the Confederates looking out from the embrasures of the fort will not fire upon so brave a boy, saving the lives of drowning men.(¹¹) He picks up Ensign Zetlich and eight men, takes them to the *Oneida*, and stands ready to take part in the battle.

25*

The *Brooklyn*, by her backing, is lying across the channel, with her bows pointed towards the fort, and the whole fleet is brought to a standstill, with the cannon of the fort and the *Tennessee*, *Selma*, and *Gaines* doing terrible execution on the ships, one shot cutting off both legs of one sailor, and, as he throws up his arms, another shot cuts off both hands. In this moment of confusion Admiral Farragut does not lose his head, but with clear comprehension as to what ought to be done, what must be done, issues his orders to go ahead, and the *Hartford*, with the *Metacomet* by her side, obeys her helm, passes the *Brooklyn*, and with full steam sweeps on. A few moments and she is a mile distant from the rest of the fleet, beyond the reach of the guns in the fort, but alone with the *Tennessee* and the other Confederate vessels.

It was this decision of the moment that brought order out of confusion, and the *Brooklyn*, followed by the other vessels, moved on — each vessel pouring grape and shrapnel into the Confederate batteries—all passing safely except the *Oneida*, last of the line. A rifled shot exploded in one of her boilers, another in her cabin, cutting the wheel-ropes, a third set the ship on fire. The escaping steam scalded the fireman and coal-heavers, but the engine had still one boiler left and the vessel went on. The sailors put out the fire, new ropes were attached to the wheel, and all the while her guns were flaming. Assisted by the *Galena*, the *Oneida* went on as if nothing had happened.

Brave deeds were being done in these moments. On the *Hartford* six men were tugging at a pulley, lifting shells from the hold, when a shell from the fort exploded among them, killing or wounding all six. John Lamson was wounded in the leg and hurled against the bulwarks, but he would not go below. A few moments later he was once more tugging at the rope.

The cannon in charge of Coxswain Thomas Fitzpatrick was disabled by having its gearing cut away. Seven of his men were killed, and several others wounded, himself among them; but he had the wounded cared for, repaired the tackling, got a new crew, and once more had his gun in action. On the *Brooklyn* the rod of the sponge broke in one of the guns, but Coxswain Edwin Price poured powder into the vent and touched it off, thus blowing out the broken part, and went on with the firing.

> "Right abreast of the fort
> In an awful shroud they lay,
> Broadsides thundering away,
> And lightning from every port—
> Scene of glory and dread!

"A storm-cloud all aglow
With flashes fiery red—
The thunder raging below ;
And the forest of flags overhead."

Up the narrow channel moved the *Hartford* and *Metacomet*. The *Selma* had chosen a position from which her guns raked the *Hartford* from stem to stern, doing great damage. On her starboard bow were the *Gaines* and *Morgan*, but the broadsides of the *Hartford* were turned upon them, and they moved away, the *Gaines* in a sinking condition. The *Tennessee* was in motion towards the *Hartford*, which attempted to strike the iron-clad but failed. Both vessels fired as they passed, the shells of the *Tennessee* missing their aim, the solid shot of the *Hartford* making no more impression upon the iron-clad than gravel thrown against a house.

Buchanan determined to send the *Hartford* to the bottom of the sea by thrusting the iron prow of the *Tennessee* through her side, but Farragut avoided her thrusts. The Confederate commander then started for the *Brooklyn*, sending two shots which went clear through the latter vessel, then passed on to the *Richmond*, which hurled her shot against the iron-clad, as did the *Lackawanna*. Captain Strong, of the *Monongahela*, determined to give the *Tennessee* a blow, but it only turned the iron-clad partly round. The Confederate vessel then sent a raking fire upon the *Oneida*, wounding Commander Mullany. The three monitors, up to this moment, had remained in front of Fort Morgan pouring in their fire.

"Gunboats, chase enemy's gunboats," was the signal from the *Hartford*.(¹²)

"Ay, ay, sir. Cut the ropes there!" the response of Captain Jouett.

The *Metacomet* swung away from the *Hartford*, followed by the *Itasca*, *Port Royal*, and *Kennebec*. The fleet was past the forts, and no longer was there need of being coupled ; they were inside the bay, and had only to deal now with the Confederate fleet. The *Morgan* stranded upon a shoal, but backed off, and ran to find shelter under the guns of the fort. The *Metacomet*, flying like the wind, was soon pouring her fire upon the *Selma*, one shot killing the executive officer and several of the men, whereupon the flag was hauled down in token of surrender. A shell made a great rent in the side of the *Gaines*, disabling the vessel, which was burned.

At nine o'clock, three miles above the fort the vessels of Admiral Farragut's fleet came to anchor. The sailors cleared the wreck from the decks and sat down to eat their breakfast.

The *Tennessee*, the while, was lying near the fort, and the officers and men were looking to see what damage, if any, had been done. They saw only a few holes in the smoke-stack, and dents where the Union shot had struck. Admiral Buchanan, believing that the vessel was impregnable, resolved to attack the fleet, first sinking the wooden ships and then engaging the three monitors. Admiral Farragut the while was laying his plans to wait till night and then attack the *Tennessee* under the walls of the fort with the three monitors.(¹³) "She's coming!" was the cry from every Union ship. "Attack her, bows on, full speed!" the order from Farragut. The boatswain's whistle rang sharp and clear, piping all hands again to quarters. The *Monongahela* was the first to strike the *Tennessee*, receiving two shots, while the shots of the *Monongahela* only struck and rolled into the water, doing no harm. Not so the bolts from the *Chickasaw*.

THE "SELMA" SURRENDERING TO THE "METACOMET."
From a Sketch made at the time.

This the story, as told by an officer of the *Tennessee*: "The *Monongahela* was hardly clear of us when a hideous monster came creeping up on our port side, whose slowly revolving turret revealed the cavernous depths of a mammoth gun. 'Stand clear of the port side!' I shouted. A moment after a thundering report shook us all, while a blast of dense sulphurous smoke covered our port-holes, and four hundred and forty pounds of iron, impelled by sixty pounds of powder, admitted daylight through our side, where, before it struck us, there had been over two feet of solid oak, covered with four inches of solid iron. It did not come through; the inside netting caught the splinters. I was glad to find myself alive."(")

Down upon the *Tennessee* came the *Lackawanna* and the *Hartford*, striking a fearful blow, each firing every gun of her broadside—the shot

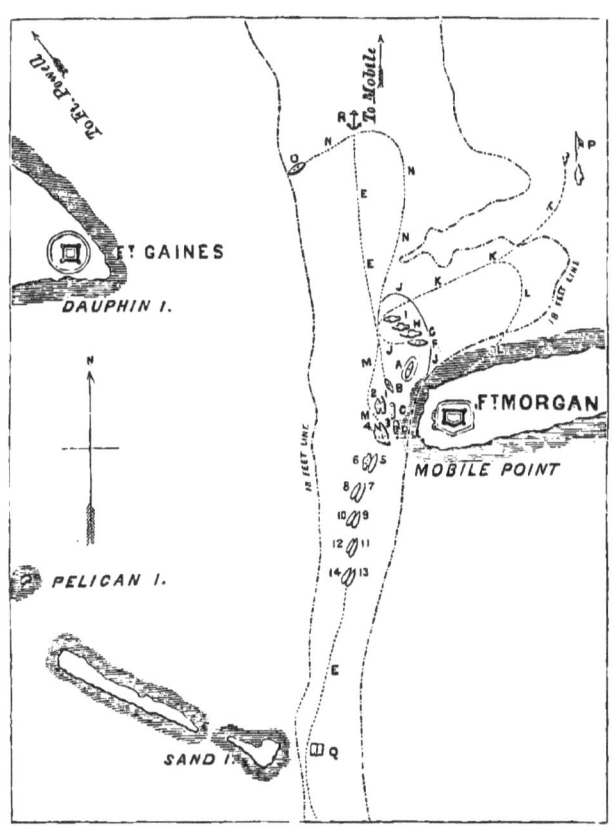

THE BATTLE OF MOBILE BAY.

1. Brooklyn................
2. Octorora................
3. Hartford................
4. Metacomet...............
5. Richmond................
6. Port Royal..............
7. Lackawanna.............. } Wooden Vessels.
8. Seminole................
9. Monongahela.............
10. Kennebec................
11. Ossipee.................
12. Itasca..................
13. Oneida..................
14. Galena..................
A. Tecumseh, sunk by torpedo.... } Iron-clads.
B. Manhattan..................

C. Winnebago............... } Iron-clads.
D. Chickasaw...............
E. Course of Union Fleet.
F. Ram Tennessee...............
G. Morgan..................... } Rebel Vessels.
H. Gaines.....................
I. Selma......................
J. Course of Ram.
K. Retreat of Rebel Wooden Vessels.
L. Morgan and Gaines's course towards Fort Morgan.
M. Hartford turning out for Brooklyn to back.
N. Course taken by Ram during second attack.
O. Ram surrendered.
P. Selma surrendered to Metacomet.
Q. Formed line; read prayers.
R. Union Fleet anchored.

only denting the iron plating. The *Lackawanna*, in attempting to strike the Confederate craft, came in collision with the *Hartford*, almost sinking both vessels. All were pouring in their shot, but it was the *Chickasaw* which followed the *Tennessee* as the kingbird follows the hawk, sending at fifteen rods solid shot, cutting the rudder-chain of that vessel. The *Ossipee* was just ready to strike her. Admiral Buchanan was wounded. "Well, Johnston, they have got me. You'll have to look out for her now!" his words to Captain Johnston.

"I'll do the best I know how,"(¹⁶) the reply.

The shot of the Union cannon had jammed the covers of the fore-and-aft port-holes so that they could not be opened. The smoke-stack of the iron-clad tumbled to the deck, and the furnaces would no longer draw, nor would she obey her helm. None of the guns could be trained upon the Union vessels. Like the blows of a giant's sledge-hammer were the solid shot from the *Chickasaw* pounding at the stern.

"I cannot bring a gun to bear upon them," the words of Captain Johnston.

"Well, if you cannot do that any more you had better surrender," was the reply of Admiral Buchanan.(¹⁶)

The flag-staff had been shot away, but a white flag, hung upon a boat-hook, was raised above the *Tennessee*. The *Ossipee* was bearing down at the moment to give another blow. Captain Stevens, in command, saw Johnston standing upon the deck, with the white flag above him. Before the war they were friends; during the conflict they had been enemies. This the hail from the commander of the *Ossipee*:

"Hullo, Johnston, old fellow! how are you? This is the United States steamer *Ossipee*. I'll send a boat alongside for you. Don't you know me?"

Captain Stevens meets him at the gangway with cheery words. "I'm glad to see you. Here's some ice-water; I know you are dry. I've something better down in the cabin for you." In the cabin they drink a glass of wine. "Steward, attend to Captain Johnston's wishes."(¹⁷) Such the kindness and courtesy to an old friend in the hour of his humiliation.

On the *Hartford* the brave old admiral was standing beside the row of dead, twenty-five in number, with the tears rolling down his cheeks as he beheld their mangled forms awaiting befitting burial. Three hundred and thirty-five had been killed, drowned, or wounded on the Union ships; ten killed and sixteen wounded on the Confederate.

THE CONTEST WITH THE "TENNESSEE."
From a Sketch made at the time.

"Up went the white! Ah, then
The hurrahs that, once and again,
Rang from three thousand men,
All flushed and savage with fight!

"Our dead lay cold and stark,
But our dying, down in the dark,
Answered as best they might,
Lifting their poor lost arms,
And cheering for God and right.

"Ended the mighty noise—
Thunder of forts and ships;
Down we went to the hold.
Oh, our dear, dying boys!
How we pressed their poor, brave lips,
(Ah, so pallid and cold!)
And held their hands to the last!
(Those that had hands to hold.)

"Still thee, O woman heart!
(So strong an hour ago.)
If the idle tears must start,
'Tis not in vain they flow.

"They died, our children dear,
On the drear berth-deck they died;
Do not think of them here;
Even now their footsteps near
The immortal, tender sphere—
(Land of love and cheer,
Home of the Crucified!)

"And the glorious deed survives;
Our threescore, quiet and cold,
Lie thus; for a myriad lives,
And treasure, millions untold.
(Labor of poor men's lives,
Hunger of weans and wives—
Such is war-wasted gold.)

"Our ship and her fame to-day
Shall float on the storied stream
When mast and shroud have crumbled away,
And her long white deck is a dream."

While this contest was going on near Fort Morgan a fleet of five gunboats was bombarding Fort Powell, guarding the western entrance to Mobile Bay at Grant's Pass, and at the same time the troops upon Dauphin Island, under General Granger, after a long and wearying march through the sand, were closing around Fort Gaines, which was adding to the uproar of the morning by opening fire with its heavy guns. Very little damage was done to Fort Powell by the gunboats, which did not approach very near; but at two o'clock in the afternoon, the *Chickasaw*, having made her way across the bay, steaming up close to the fort, opened fire with its 11 and 15 inch guns upon its eastern face, with such effect that Lieutenant-colonel Williams, in command of the Confederate garrison, telegraphed this message to Colonel Anderson, in Fort Gaines: "Unless I can evacuate, I will be compelled to surrender within forty-eight hours."

"Save your garrison," (") the reply.

The tide was out; the Union fleet had not yet moved up to prevent the Confederates from making their way in boats to the main-land. Night settled down. It was past ten o'clock, when there came a bright flash, a deep, heavy roar, and timbers, gun-carriages, cannon, shell, and a great cloud of earth rose in the air, to rain down again upon the calm waters. The Confederates had evacuated the fort, lighted a fire connecting with the magazine, and made their escape.

The troops on Dauphin Island had mounted fourteen rifled guns, and were ready to begin the bombardment of Fort Gaines from the west, while the fleet was preparing to assist on the north.

Aug. 6, 1864.

Anxious to save men from being killed, Admiral Farragut sent a flag of truce to the fort, inviting Colonel Anderson to visit the *Hartford* for a conference. The invitation was accepted by that officer, who was accompanied by Major Brown. General Granger and Captain Drayton, and other Union officers of the army and navy, were present when the two Confederate officers entered the cabin. "Surrounded on three sides by my vessels, and on the fourth by the army, you cannot hold the fort. Submit like a man to the hard necessity, and prevent further loss of life," were the words of the admiral.

Colonel Anderson could not deny that the fort was surrounded, and he appreciated the humanity that dictated the demand. Not so Major Brown. "Let us fight it out," he said. "Gentlemen, if hard fighting would save the fort, I would advise you to fight to the death, but by all the laws of war you have no chance to save it," Farragut replied.

Major Brown saw that with the Confederate fleet destroyed, with no means of reaching the land, there was no chance for escape, and it was agreed that the fort and garrison should be surrendered the next morning. So Fort Gaines came once more under the control of the United States.

A summons was sent to General Page, commanding Fort Morgan, who declined to surrender.

Aug. 9, 1864. The troops were transported from Dauphin Island and landed in Navy Cove, four miles east of Fort Morgan, thus cutting off the retreat of the garrison. From that point they advanced westward, closing round the fort, throwing up breastworks, mounting twenty-five heavy guns, and placing sixteen mortars in position within five hundred yards of the fort.

Aug. 22, 1864. Ten days passed, the sharp-shooters the while keeping up such a fire that no Confederate would show his head above the intrenchments. At daylight the monitors, and all the vessels of the fleet, steamed down towards the fort, and all the cannon on shipboard, together with the mortars and artillery on land, opened fire, continuing it through the day, sending a continuous stream of shot and shell upon the

CAPTURE OF FORT MORGAN.
From a Sketch made at the time.

fortification. The sun went down, but a portion of the guns continued to thunder, a shell setting the barracks in the citadel on fire. When the flames burst forth, once more the cannon of the fleet redoubled their firing. Within the fort the Confederate soldiers were throwing kegs of powder into the cisterns, fighting the flames, and spiking the cannon.

Aug. 23, 1864. With the dawn of the morning a white flag was flung out above the fort, whose walls had been honey-combed, whose guns had nearly all been disabled, together with sixty of the four hundred men of the garrison. With its surrender, vessels running the blockade could no longer enter Mobile. Once more the Stars and Stripes waved over the fortification from which it had been removed when Alabama seceded from the Union.

The taking of the fort closed another port to the blockade-runners, leaving only Wilmington, Charleston, and Galveston—the last so far away that vessels entering there with supplies from Europe could contribute nothing to maintain the waning fortunes of the Confederacy.

NOTES TO CHAPTER XV.

(1) "Life and Letters of Admiral Farragut," p. 302.
(2) Idem, p. 392.
(3) Idem, p. 405.
(4) W. H. Seward, "Diplomatic History of the War for the Union," vol. v., p. 492.
(5) A. T. Mahan, "Gulf and Inland Waters," p. 230.
(6) Idem, p. 231.
(7) J. C. Watson, "Battles and Leaders of the Civil War," vol. iv., p. 406.
(8) "Life and Letters of Admiral Farragut," p. 410.
(9) J. C. Kinney, "Battles and Leaders of the Civil War," vol. iv., p. 387.
(10) "Life and Letters of Admiral Farragut," p. 416.
(11) Gen. R. L. Page, "Battles and Leaders of the Civil War," vol. iv., p. 408.
(12) "Life and Letters of Admiral Farragut," p. 419.
(13) A. T. Mahan, "Gulf and Inland Waters," p. 240.
(14) Lieutenant Wharton, quoted by Commodore Foxhall A. Parker, "Battle of Mobile Bay," p. 35.
(15) Capt. J. D. Johnston, "Battles and Leaders of the Civil War," vol. iv., p. 404.
(16) Idem.
(17) Idem.
(18) Commodore Foxhall A. Parker, "Battle of Mobile Bay," p. 38.

CHAPTER XVI.

FALL OF ATLANTA.

THE siege of Atlanta began. General Sherman had no intention of assaulting the Confederate works, made strong by the gangs of slaves at the outset, and made still stronger by the Confederate troops. General Hood, on the other hand, after the disastrous battles of Peachtree Creek and Atlanta, had no inclination to again march out from his intrenchments, and assail the Union troops in the open field. The Union cavalry under General Garrard had destroyed thirty miles of the railroad leading east from Atlanta. There was still another road which must be destroyed before Sherman could cut off Hood's supplies—that leading south from Atlanta to East Point, six miles. From that station one line runs south-west to Newnan, thirty-nine miles, and then on to Montgomery; the other line runs south eighteen miles to Jonesborough, and from thence to Macon. If these could be effectually destroyed, Hood would soon be compelled to abandon Atlanta. General Rousseau, with a division of cavalry, had torn up a railroad in the south-west, at Opelika, and if the lines of communication could be broken in all directions, the Confederate army would be greatly hampered in its operations.

July 23, 1864.

Day and night men were at work constructing a bridge across the Chattahoochee, which was completed in six days, and trains of cars arrived from Nashville bringing supplies.

General Sherman called his officers together, not to ask them what they thought he ought next to do, but to tell them what he intended to do. They were seated on camp-stools in front of a small house. " I intend to place this army south-west of Atlanta," he said. He had approached the city from the north and east in order to destroy the railroad leading directly eastward, the shortest line of connection with Richmond. He had received a despatch from General Grant, informing him that the Confederate Government had become aroused at the critical state of affairs around Atlanta, and that possibly reinforcements would be sent from the east to Hood.(¹) By moving the army south-west, Sherman would be nearer the

26

railroad which brought him his own supplies than if he were to march from the position he had already gained.

General Stoneman, commanding the cavalry, presented a proposition that one body of cavalry, under General McCook, should start from the left flank of the army, tear up the track of the railroad leading south-west to Alabama, and then move on to Lovejoy's Station, on the Macon road, and tear up that track. Another body of troops, commanded by Stoneman himself, was to start from the east side of Atlanta, and make a forced march to Andersonville, one hundred and ten miles in a straight line, and liberate more than thirty thousand Union prisoners at that place, who were suffering the horrors of starvation, and dying by the thousand through want of proper food, and from diseases generated by crowding so many men into a small prison-pen.

It was a plan which awakened the sympathy of General Sherman and all the officers. If it could be carried out, it would soon return a large number of soldiers to the army; but beyond that, it would release them from a prison where they were suffering indescribable horrors. The cavalry of Garrard's division had just returned from destroying the railroad leading eastward, and the division under General Rousseau had arrived from a raid westward. The horses and men of those divisions were so worn that they were not included in the forces selected for these movements. The troops commanded by Stoneman were about five thousand, those under McCook numbered four thousand. It was a mistake, as we shall see, to divide the troops into two parties. United, and moving together on parallel roads sufficiently near for quick concentration, they would have been strong enough to have met any force that could have been brought against them. We can now see that the plan was faulty in one other respect; it aimed to accomplish two things: cripple Hood by destroying the railroads, and to release the prisoners. To release the prisoners, the expedition ought to make a forced march and sweep down upon Andersonville as an eagle upon its prey, before there could be any great concentration of Georgia militia or Confederate troops to defend the prison. The Confederates would have the advantage of whirling troops by rail to that point, not only from Atlanta but from Charleston and Savannah. It was therefore quite doubtful if even nine thousand Union cavalry would be able to overcome the force that would be likely to confront them from behind fortifications. By stopping to destroy long sections of railroad-track valuable time would be lost. Starting from two points, with a watchful foe before them, and a Confederate cavalry force as large as the two Union divisions combined, was a serious mistake. It would have been

"I INTEND TO PLACE THIS ARMY SOUTH OF ATLANTA."

far better if the expedition had moved as one body, with a single object in view, and that the thorough destruction of long sections of each railroad. With that accomplished, the cavalry might have returned, and after two or three days' rest, before Hood could have relaid the tracks, the entire force with Garrard — a body of twelve thousand — could have made a forced march to Andersonville, with a fair prospect of reaching the prisoners before any large body of Confederate troops could have been concentrated there. We have seen how nearly Kilpatrick came to reaching Richmond;

the chances for success in the movement to Andersonville would have been much better if the cavalry under Stoneman and McCook had been united, and reinforced by Garrard.

McCook was west of the Chattahoochee, and marched down its west bank to Campbellton, crossed on pontoons, made a quick movement east to the railroad leading to Montgomery, striking it at Lovejoy's Station, thirty miles from Atlanta, and tore up a section of the track, burned several trains of cars, destroyed the locomotives and five hundred wagons, and captured four hundred prisoners; but the Confederate cavalry were soon upon him, and cars loaded with troops came rolling down from Atlanta. McCook could hear nothing of Stoneman, and made the mistake of attempting to return over the same route by which he had advanced. He was attacked at Newnan, and lost his prisoners and nearly six hundred of his men, but rejoined the army. The burning of the locomotives, cars, and wagons, however, was a serious loss to Hood.

General Stoneman was at Flat Rock, south-east of Atlanta, and moved east to Covington, crossed the Ocmulgee River, turned south, struck the railroad leading eastward from Macon, and tore up a portion of the track, destroyed seventeen engines and one hundred cars, sent a portion of his troops eastward, and burned a bridge over the Oconee River, and then advanced to Macon. General Hood had discovered the movement, and saw what Stoneman intended to do. The Confederate cavalry were following him. The telegraph summoned troops from every quarter. Stoneman was east of the Ocmulgee, which he must cross before he could enter Macon. He planted his artillery, had a skirmish, fired shells across the river, and then fell back northward towards Clinton. He was more than forty miles from Andersonville, and saw that he could not reach it. He thought himself surrounded, and prepared to surrender, but authorized his brigade commanders to cut their way out, while he, with seven hundred of his men, held the others in check. We now know that he greatly over-estimated the number of Confederates confronting him. Had he acted with resolution and vigor, it is probable that he would have cut his way through and saved his command. The result, instead, was that General Stoneman and seven hundred surrendered, and that several hundred others were gathered up by the Confederates before the main body reached the army. General Stoneman had been directed by General Sherman first to destroy the railroad leading to Macon, and then move on to Andersonville. He had not done so, but had ridden directly away from the railroad. The damage to the railroads was soon repaired, and General Hood's army did not materially suffer from what had been done.

In the Confederate army Lieut.-gen. S. D. Lee was appointed to take command of Hood's old corps in place of Cheatham, who went back to his division. In the Union army General Howard was appointed to command the Army of the Tennessee in place of McPherson, and General Stanley to command the Fourth Corps. General Hooker thought that his experience as commander of the Army of the Potomac and in command of the Eleventh and Twelfth Corps at Lookout Mountain and Chattanooga, and of the Twentieth Corps during the campaign, entitled his promotion to command the Army of the Tennessee. Feeling himself aggrieved by the selection of General Howard, he asked to be relieved from the further command of the Twentieth Corps. His request was granted. His troops loved him, and showed their affection for him when he bade them farewell by gathering around him as school-children around a beloved teacher. His departure from the army marked the closing of his military service.

General Sherman began his new movement. The Sixteenth Corps, which had been camping where it fought on the 22d, marched in rear of the Army of the Ohio, also in rear of the Army of the Cumberland, and came to a road which leads west from the city to a village bearing the strange name of Lickskillet. General Blair, with the Seventeenth Corps, followed the Sixteenth, passed it, and came into position at Ezra Church.

July 27, 1864.

General Hood had anticipated such a movement, and the slave-gangs had been hard at work west and south-west of the city throwing up intrenchments. He determined to fall upon the Seventeenth Corps at the church and crush it. He withdrew Loring's and Walthall's divisions of Stewart's corps from the intrenchments north of the city, and his own old corps under Lee, and brought them out over the Lickskillet road. Lee was to begin the attack at the church, while Stewart and Loring were to strike the Seventeenth Corps from the south, turning its flank.

General Sherman saw what the probable movement of Hood would be, and ordered General Davis, with the Fourteenth Corps, to march in rear of the Sixteenth and Seventeenth towards the village of Lickskillet to head off any possible movement which Hood might make. General Sherman and General Howard were with Logan, of the Fifteenth Corps, at Ezra Church when the Confederates advanced. Logan's troops had thrown up intrenchments. The attack was upon Morgan L. Smith's and Harrow's divisions. General Howard massed the artillery, which opened with a terribly destructive fire. The Confederates advanced bravely, but were cut down by the shot, shells, and musketry.

July 29, 1864.

They wavered, but were rallied by their officers, and advanced once more only to be hurled back, with Generals Stewart, Loring, Brown, and Johnson numbered among the wounded. The Union position was so well chosen, and the Fourteenth and Sixteenth corps so near at hand, that there could be but one result—failure to Hood. The loss in Logan's corps was less than six hundred. It will never be known how many Confederates fell, but six hundred and forty-two bodies were gathered after the battle, which, with the usual number of wounded, would make the Confederate loss not far from five thousand. The Confederates had fought bravely at Peachtree, and again east of the city, and now west of it, but had lost heavily and gained nothing. They were discouraged, and in the last assault many of them refused to advance.

"How many of you are there left?" shouted a Union picket to a Confederate.

"About enough for another killing," was the answer.

The soldiers of the Twentieth Corps out on the picket line at a signal rushed upon the Confederate line so suddenly that they captured eight officers and more than one hundred men, and held the ground which they thus gained, erecting new breastworks.

July 30, 1864.

General Sherman began to extend his line south-west of the city, but the Confederates had large working gangs building breastworks reaching towards Jonesborough. He sent to Nashville for Parrot siege-guns, placed them in battery with all his field artillery, and began a bombardment of the city, sending a continuous stream of shot and shell, which riddled the houses, and made it very uncomfortable for the people, who were obliged to live in cellars or in holes in the ground.

General Kilpatrick came from the Army of the Potomac to command the cavalry. He tore up several miles of the railroad leading to Macon, but the Confederates soon repaired it, and two days later the cars were running into Atlanta. While Kilpatrick was thus engaged the Confederate cavalry under Wheeler moved north-east from Atlanta, crossed the Chattahoochee River, struck the railroad near Resaca, and captured one thousand of Sherman's beef-cattle. Wheeler demanded a surrender of Dallas, but Colonel Raum, who was there with a small force, held him at bay till Gen. J. E. Smith came with a brigade, compelling Wheeler to retreat. He burned the bridge across the Etowah River and tore up the track, but the railroad men soon had the trains running again. Wheeler continued north, intending to burn the bridge across the Tennessee River and destroy the railroad, so that Sherman would not be able to obtain supplies. Jefferson Davis recommended the movement. Wheeler could do

BATTLE OF EZRA CHURCH.
From a war-time Sketch.

FALL OF ATLANTA.   409

but little harm, for the bridges were well guarded. A few days later, when too late to recall Wheeler, Hood found that he sorely needed him.

Sherman determined to compel Hood to give up Atlanta, which was a railroad centre, where there were iron-founderies and machine-shops, not by throwing his troops against the intrenchments, but by leaving a portion

EZRA CHURCH.

of his army at the railroad bridge across the Chattahoochee. "It was evident," says General Sherman, "that we must decoy the enemy out to fight us on something like equal terms, or else with the whole army raise the siege and attack his communications."(²)

To carry out the plan, the Twentieth Corps was sent back to the Chattahoochee River to protect the bridge, the trains, hospitals, supplies, and ammunition accumulated at that point.

Aug. 13, 1864.

General Sherman was much pleased with the spirit manifested by General Kilpatrick, who had torn up the railroad, and decided to suspend the movement of the army a few days, in order that Kilpatrick might make another movement to strike the railroad near Jonesborough, hoping that it would force Hood to give up the city, and that when the Confederates evacuated the place he could strike him a damaging blow.(³)

Two of Garrard's brigades of cavalry were sent from the east side of the city round to Kilpatrick, who was west of it, and placed under command of that officer. It was after dark when Kilpatrick reached the railroad. He cut the telegraph wires, burned the station, tore up three miles of the track, but was then attacked by a body of Confederates. He did not return the way he advanced, but turned north, rode round Atlanta, and rejoined General Sherman. He had captured a battery and destroyed three of the cannon, and brought in one as a trophy. He thought it would take the Confederates ten days to repair the road, but two days later the Union troops on picket could see the cars rolling into Atlanta, and General Sherman came to the conclusion that cavalry alone could not do much damage to a railroad before they would be compelled to retreat. All of the attempts to permanently destroy communications, whether by Union or Confederate cavalry, whether in Virginia or the west, had ended in failure, while the hard riding necessary to reach the distant points had resulted in the breaking down of horses and men. General Sherman has this to say of the cavalry movements on both sides:

Aug. 18, 1864.

"We saw trains coming into Atlanta from the south, and I became more than ever convinced that the cavalry could not or would not work hard enough to disable a railroad properly, and therefore resolved at once to proceed with the execution of my original plan. Meantime the damage to our own railroad and telegraph by Wheeler about Resaca and Dalton had been repaired, and Wheeler himself was too far away to be of any service to his own army, and where he could not do us much harm."(⁴)

Aug. 23, 1864.

General Sherman sent this despatch to General Halleck in Washington: "Heavy fires in Atlanta all day, caused by our artillery. I will be all ready, and will commence the movement around Atlanta by the south to-morrow night, and for some time you will hear little of us. I will keep open a courier line back to the Chattahoochee bridge, by way of Sandtown. The Twentieth Corps will hold the railroad bridge, and I will move with the balance of the army, provisioned for twenty days."

Aug. 24, 1864.

General Sherman was confident that the Confederate cavalry under Wheeler could not seriously interfere with the running of railroad trains. It was soon seen by the Confederate troops that Hood had made a mistake in sending Wheeler northward into the State of Tennessee. A Confederate writer says that "it was an irreparable blunder."(⁵) A Confederate has pictured the scene in Atlanta: "There are excavations in the

GEN. JUDSON KILPATRICK.

ground, roofed with heavy logs, over which is heaped a mountain of earth. The garden to almost every house which does not boast of a cellar has one of these artificial bomb-proofs. They are perfectly secure against the shells, and many of them are quite comfortably furnished with beds, chairs, and other furniture. Women and children are huddled together in them for hours at a time, and when the city is furiously shelled at night, the whole community may be said to be underground."(⁶)

The Twentieth Corps was marching north-west, to be the guard at the Chattahoochee. The Fourth Corps, under General Stanley, was marching south towards Utoy Creek. Garrard's cavalry picketed their horses in the woods where the Confederates could not see them, and took the place of the departing troops in the trenches. As soon as it was dark on the night of the 26th, the Army of the Tennessee, under the command of Howard, left its trenches and moved south, unseen by the Confederates.

Aug. 26, 1864.

When day dawned there was silence in the Union trenches—no bugle-call or rallying drum-beat, no smoke ascending from bivouac fires. The Confederates did not know what to make of it. The Confederate artillery opened fire, to see if the exploding shells would not awaken the Union troops. A Confederate writer has penned this description: "We sprang to our feet and grabbed our muskets, and ran out and asked some one the meaning of it. We were informed that they were 'feeling' for the Yankees. The comment that was made by a private soldier was simply two words—'Oh shucks!' The Yankees had gone, no one knew whither, and our batteries were shelling the woods, feeling for them. 'Oh shucks!'"(⁷)

Aug. 27, 1864.

Hood's scouts discovered the movement of the Twentieth Corps north-west, away from Atlanta. They reported that Sherman was retreating. Hood was delighted. He concluded that Wheeler was doing great things in Tennessee. He did not comprehend Sherman's tenacity of purpose, or the meaning of his movement, and telegraphed to Richmond that Sherman was retreating.(⁸)

It is reported that a party of ladies and gentlemen came from Macon to rejoice with their friends over the falling back of Sherman's troops.

The Army of the Cumberland took its noonday rest in a beautiful grove of oaks around Shoal Creek Church. General Sherman was there, talking with General Thomas in regard to the movement. "It is somewhat hazardous for seventy thousand men to cut loose from their base of supplies and be dependent upon what we can pick up here and there," said General Thomas, as they stood by a fire

Aug. 30, 1864.

where a soldier was down on his knees roasting an ear of corn. General Thomas was very kind to his troops, who loved and respected him as dutiful children a kind father. He talked with them, gave them counsel and advice, but required strict obedience to orders. "What are you doing?" said General Thomas, addressing the soldier.

"Why, general, I am laying in a supply of provisions," said the soldier, with a smile overspreading his face.

"That is right, my man, but do not waste your provision."

The two commanders walked on, but they heard the soldier say, "Good old man; economizing as usual."(⁹)

There was humor in the remark, for there were hundreds of acres of corn near at hand, the ears ripe for roasting. While talking with the soldiers, they could hear the booming of the cannon of the Army of the Tennessee near Jonesborough.

When General Hood learned from his scouts what General Sherman was doing, he sent off a large amount of supplies, and had trains of freight cars, with engines fired up, ready for a rapid transfer of troops to any point. General Hardee was near the village of Rough and Ready, with Lee's corps on his right at East Point. General Hood, with Stewart's corps and the Georgia militia, were in Atlanta, when the cannon were heard at Jonesborough.

Logan's corps of the Army of the Tennessee had crossed Flint River and was only a mile from the railroad, and had fallen upon Lewis's brigade. "Move at once to Jonesborough," was the order from Hood to Hardee. Lee was directed to follow. "Attack with all force in the morning, and drive the enemy, at all hazards, into the river."(¹⁰)

If the attack was successful, General Hood intended to bring back Lee's corps the next night to Rough and Ready, to join them with Stewart's corps and drive Sherman down Flint River, while Hardee was to advance from Jonesborough.(¹¹)

General Ransom, who had succeeded General Dodge in command of the Sixteenth Corps, was on Logan's right, covering his flank. During the night, the Seventeenth Corps, under Blair, arrived and covered Logan's left. The soldiers could hear the rumbling of the trains, and knew that the Confederates were arriving from Atlanta. Howard ordered the soldiers to build intrenchments, and waited for the Army of the Cumberland.

It was three o'clock in the afternoon when the Confederates of Lee's corps advanced to attack Logan and Ransom, making a spirited assault on Hazen's division, which was easily repulsed, with severe loss to the Con-

FALL OF ATLANTA. 415

federates. Just after noon, Schofield, with the Army of the Ohio, reached the railroad north of Jonesborough, at Rough and Ready. The troops came near capturing a train, but the engineer made his way back to Atlanta with the startling news. Hood, thinking that Sherman was marching north to close in upon the city, and not knowing that Hardee had attacked Howard and had been repulsed, sent a courier ordering Hardee to march back to Atlanta. Lee thereupon moved northeast to avoid Schofield at Rough and Ready, and was half-way back to Atlanta before Hood discovered that Sherman, instead of marching to Atlanta, was closing upon Hardee. There was but one thing to be done now; he must give up Atlanta and reassemble his scattered troops farther south. He sent word to Lee to stop where he was till he could join him.

Aug. 31, 1864.

While Hood was preparing to evacuate the place, the Fourteenth Corps, under Davis, was moving down the railroad towards Jonesborough to strike Hardee's right flank. The Confederates had thrown up a long line of intrenchments, beginning east of the railroad, running west, crossing it, then turning south on the west side of the village, and again crossing the railroad below the Baptist church, thus enclosing three sides of a quadrangle. General Logan was west of the village, General Ransom south-west, while General Davis, with the Fourteenth Corps, was northwest, and General Stanley, with the Fourth Corps, was on his way down the railroad.

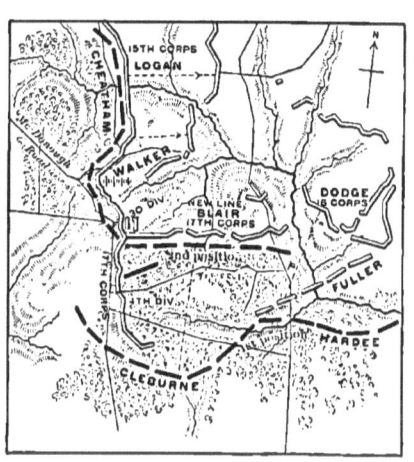

POSITIONS OF THE UNION AND CONFEDERATE ARMIES AT JONESBOROUGH.

General Thomas sent an order to Stanley to take position on Davis's left flank. The afternoon was waning, and Sherman getting impatient. He desired Stanley to come round in Hardee's rear, but Stanley was so far away that Davis advanced to the attack without waiting for him. The Thirteenth, Sixteenth, Eighteenth, and Nineteenth United States Infantry, commanded by Lieutenant-colonel Edie, constituted a brigade in Carlin's division. Their position was in front of Govan's brigade in the

Confederate works. Moore's brigade was to support Edie on the left. Estes's brigade of Baird's division was on their right flank, and Morgan's division was beyond Estes's brigade.

Going over now into the Confederate lines, we find Govan's brigade of Cleburne's division holding the angle, with Lewis's brigade extending east across the railroad, and Granberry's extending from the angle southward. It was a very strong position, for the angle was on a knoll, with open ground in front. Hardee's men had used their shovels and axes to good advantage. Govan had two batteries near the angle, which sent their shells down into the Union lines. General Thomas's batteries replied. Captain Prescott's battery sent an enfilading fire along the Confederate trenches.

The Union troops came into position while the artillery duel went on. General Baird and General Carlin rode along the line, giving their orders and encouraging the men. It was about one hundred rods from Edie's position to the breastworks, across open ground swept by Confederate cannon. It was five o'clock in the evening of a beautiful summer day, when Edie and Estes moved up the slope towards the breastworks, together with Morgan's division on the west and Moore's on the north. They crossed the open ground, and rushed upon the intrenchments, leaped over the breastworks, and captured a large number of prisoners, driving the Confederates, who rallied and who were joined by a brigade in reserve, and the Union men in turn were driven. But they also rallied, regained the works and held them. The struggle was short and vigorous. Morgan's division closed in upon the right, and Moore's brigade on the left. It was like the springing of a net by a pigeon-catcher—a brief but desperate contest, in which Govan's brigade was annihilated. The number of killed and wounded in Hardee's corps was about twelve hundred, with between eight and nine hundred taken prisoners.

The movement of General Sherman had placed the whole of his army, with the exception of the Twentieth Corps, near Jonesborough. It was a compact body, while Hood's was widely scattered, with Stewart's corps and the Georgia militia in Atlanta, thirty miles distant from Hardee's corps; while Lee's corps was about half-way between the two, on its way back to Atlanta. A Confederate soldier has pictured the situation:

"We could see the Yankee battle-flags waving on the top of red earthworks not more than four hundred yards off. Every private soldier knew that General Hood's army was scattered all the way from Jonesborough to Atlanta, without any order, discipline, or spirit to do anything. We could hear General Stewart in Atlanta blowing up arsenals, smashing

FALL OF ATLANTA. 417

things generally; while Stephen D. Lee was somewhere between Lovejoy Station and Macon, scattering. And here was a demoralized remnant of Cheatham's corps facing the whole Yankee army. . . . We had everything against us. The soldiers distrusted everything. They were broken down with their long day's hard marching, were almost dead with fatigue and hunger. Every one was taking his own course, and wishing and praying

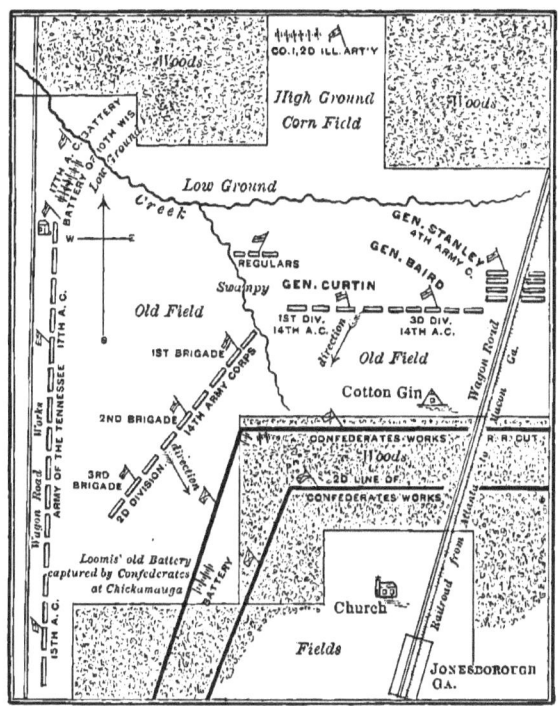

BATTLE OF JONESBOROUGH.

to be captured. Hard and senseless marching, with little sleep, half rations, had made their lives a misery. Each one prayed that all this foolishness might end, one way or the other."(¹²)

The pickets of the Twentieth Corps near Atlanta through the night could hear a commotion in the city. They saw the light of burning buildings; then came explosions of shells. General Slocum heard it, and ordered his troops under arms. He was confident that Hood was evacuating the city, and soon after sunrise the men

Sept. 1, 1864.

27

of the Twentieth Corps, with their banners waving above them, keeping step to the drum-beat, marched through the streets.

General Sherman, twenty miles away, heard the explosion. He did not know what to think of the volleys, and walked to the house of a farmer and roused him from sleep.

"Have you lived here long?" asked the general.

"Yes."

"Have you heard the cannonade and musketry of the battles around Atlanta?"

"Yes, sir; and these sounds are just like those of a battle."

General Sherman thought it possible that Slocum had been attacked. The sounds died away, but at four o'clock in the morning the explosions began again. Daylight dawned, and the Union troops around Jonesborough were ready to renew the battle, but not a Confederate was to be seen.

CAPTURE OF CONFEDERATE WORKS AT JONESBOROUGH.
From a war-time Sketch.

All had gone. A courier came with a letter from Slocum written in the city. He had entered it unopposed. General Sherman sent the letter to General Thomas, who whistled, snapped his fingers, and was almost beside himself with joy, while the soldiers swung their caps, hurrahed and danced, and made the woods ring with their yells. A courier rode up to the Chattahoochee, and this message flashed from Sherman to President Lincoln: "Atlanta is ours, and fairly won." President Lincoln sent it to General Grant, in front of Petersburg, who ordered all the cannon to be loaded with shot and shell, and then at a signal all were fired at once, while the Union soldiers in the trenches yelled and screamed themselves hoarse over the news so joyful to them, so disheartening to the Confederates.

CONFEDERATE PRISONERS TAKEN AT JONESBOROUGH.
From a Sketch made at the time.

Had General Sherman known at midnight the true state of affairs within the Confederate lines, it is quite probable that Hood would have found it difficult to reunite his army; or if General Davis had moved his corps, as he might have done, on the evening of August 30th, Hardee would have been completely isolated from the other Confederate corps.

The troops entering Atlanta found the smoking ruins of the founderies, machine-shops, and railroad cars, together with six disabled locomotives, a company of woe-begone men and women, and altogether an indescribable scene of desolation. Through the night Hood had been making a forced march towards the south-east, reassembling the shattered corps of his army at Lovejoy's Station, leaving behind a large number of wounded. Sherman advanced a portion of his troops to that point, but Hood retreated still farther, whereupon Sherman, needing supplies, decided to give his troops a little rest, and the army exultingly marched back to Atlanta. Hood had left twenty cannon, eight locomotives, and eighty-one cars which he had not time to remove, loaded with ammunition and supplies.

"Atlanta is not taken, nor is it likely to be," were the exultant words of one of the newspapers in Richmond on the 25th of August. (¹³)

"So much for the removal of General Johnston.... The result is disaster at Atlanta in the very nick of time when such a victory alone could save the party of Lincoln from irretrievable ruin," were its words on the morning of September 5th. (¹⁴)

The loss of Atlanta—a railroad centre, with its machine-shops and founderies—the retreat of the army under Johnston from Chattanooga, the successive defeats under Hood, with the great losses, cast a deep gloom over the Confederate States, while throughout the Northern States there was great rejoicing.

A large number of speculators who wanted to obtain cotton, and traders who wanted to open stores, had gathered at Nashville, expecting to reap a rich harvest at Atlanta, but General Sherman would not permit them to enter it. More than this, he determined to compel the few people who were there to leave, giving them the privilege of going South or North as they might choose. These were his reasons:

"I was resolved to make Atlanta a free military garrison or depot, with no civil population to influence military measures. I had seen Memphis, Vicksburg, Natchez, and New Orleans all captured from the enemy, and each at once garrisoned by a full division of troops, if not more; so that success was actually crippling our armies in the field by detachments to guard and protect the interests of a hostile population.... I knew, of course, that such a measure would be strongly criticised, but made up my

27*

mind to do it with the absolute certainty of its justness, and that time would sanction its wisdom." (¹⁵)

General Sherman sent a letter by flag of truce to General Hood, informing him that he would send those who wished to go South to Lovejoy's, with all their goods, and all the negroes who might desire to go with their old masters. General Hood protested against the measure. These his words: "It transcends in studied and ingenious cruelty all acts ever before brought to my attention in the dark history of war. In the name of God and humanity I protest, believing that you are expelling from their homes and firesides the wives and children of a brave people." (¹⁶)

Though thus protesting, General Hood consented to send wagons to receive the goods of the people.

In regard to the protest General Sherman made this reply: "You style the measure unprecedented, and appeal to the dark history of the war for a parallel. It is not unprecedented; for General Johnston himself very wisely and properly removed the families all the way from Dalton down, and I see no reason why Atlanta should be excepted.... You yourself burned dwelling-houses along your parapet, and I have seen to-day fifty houses which have been rendered uninhabitable because they stood in the way of your forts and men.... I say that it is a kindness to these families of Atlanta to remove them at once from scenes to which women and children should not be exposed.... I ask you not to appeal to a just God in such a sacrilegious manner. You, who, in the midst of peace and prosperity, have plunged a nation into war, dark and cruel, who dared and badgered us to battle, insulted our flag, seized our arsenals and forts that were left in the honorable custody of peaceful ordnance sergeants, seized and made 'prisoners of war' the garrisons sent to protect your people against negroes and Indians, long before any overt act was committed by the (to you) hated Lincoln Government; tried to force Kentucky and Missouri into rebellion, spite of themselves; falsified the vote of Louisiana; turned loose your privateers to plunder unarmed ships; expelled Union families by thousands, burned their houses, and declared by Act of your Congress the confiscation of all debts due Northern men for goods had and received. Talk thus to the marines, but not to me, who have seen these things, and who will this day make as much sacrifice for the peace and honor of the South as the best Southerners among you. If we must be enemies, let us be men, and fight it out as we propose to do, and not deal in hypocritical appeals to God and humanity. God will judge us in due time, and he will pronounce whether it be more human to fight with

REMOVING THE PEOPLE FROM ATLANTA.

From a Sketch made at the time.

FALL OF ATLANTA. 425

a town full of women and the families of a brave people at our back or to remove them in time to places of safety among their own friends and people." (")

The mayor and some of the councilmen of Atlanta appealed to General Sherman to revoke the order, setting forth the hardship and suffering that would follow its execution. General Sherman admitted that it would cause great suffering.

"I have," he said, "read your petition carefully, and give full credit for your statement of the distress that will be occasioned, and yet shall not revoke my orders, because they were not designed to meet the humanities

GENERAL SHERMAN'S QUARTERS.

of the case, but to prepare for future struggles, in which millions of good people outside of Atlanta have a deep interest. We must have peace, not only at Atlanta but in all America. To secure this we must stop the war that now desolates our once happy and favored country. To stop war we must defeat the rebel armies which are arrayed against the laws and Constitution that all must respect and obey. . . . You might as well appeal against a thunder-storm as against the terrible hardships of war. They are inevitable, and the only way the people of Atlanta can hope once more to live in peace and quiet at home is to stop the war, which can only be done by admitting that it began in error and is perpetuated in pride. We don't want your negroes, or your houses, or your lands, or anything you have, but we do want and will have a just obedience to the laws of the United States. . . . When peace comes, you may call on me for anything. Then will I share with you the cracker and watch with you to shield your homes and families against danger from any quarter."(¹⁸)

For ten days there was an armistice between the Union and Confederate armies, during which the people were packing their goods. General Sherman detailed wagons and men to assist them, and gave strict orders against pillaging, and the officers and men did their work very kindly and courteously, delivering them to the Confederate officers and soldiers detailed to receive them—thus mitigating in some degree the untold hardships and sufferings of the war.

NOTES TO CHAPTER XVI.

(¹) "Memoirs of Gen. W. T. Sherman," vol. ii., p. 85.
(²) Idem, p. 103.
(³) Idem, p. 104.
(⁴) Idem.
(⁵) J. W. Avery, "History of Georgia," p. 505.
(⁶) Correspondence of *Charleston Courier*, August 29, 1864.
(⁷) S. R. Watkins, "First Tennessee Regiment," p. 191.
(⁸) "Memoirs of Gen. W. T. Sherman," vol. ii., p. 105.
(⁹) Idem.
(¹⁰) Gen. J. B. Hood, "Advance and Retreat," p. 205.
(¹¹) Idem.
(¹²) S. R. Watkins, "First Tennessee Regiment," p. 199.
(¹³) *Richmond Examiner*, August 25, 1864.
(¹⁴) Idem, September 5th.
(¹⁵) "Memoirs of Gen. W. T. Sherman," vol. ii., p. 111.
(¹⁶) Gen. J. B. Hood, "Advance and Retreat," p. 280.
(¹⁷) "Memoirs of Gen. W. T. Sherman," vol. ii., p. 120.
(¹⁸) Idem, p. 126.

CHAPTER XVII.

CONFEDERATE RAIDS.

IN 1863 the energetic Confederate commander, Gen. John H. Morgan, crossed the Ohio River below Cincinnati, rode through Indiana and Ohio, but was captured and put in prison (see "Marching to Victory," p. 328). He had made his escape, and was once more in command of a large cavalry force in Virginia and East Tennessee. He was burning with desire to make another raid into his native State, Kentucky, to fill up his ranks with the hot-blooded young men who admired his achievements. General Buckner, in command of the Confederates in Kentucky, approved his plan.

General Morgan was near Abingdon, on the East Tennessee Railroad, when he learned that General Burbridge, commanding the Union cavalry at Mount Sterling, was moving east to the valley of the Big Sandy River, to join another body of troops, and that he was supposed to be on his way to destroy the salt-works and lead-mines in south-west Virginia. A portion of General Morgan's troops had no horses, but it was thought that the movement into Kentucky would not only supply them with horses, but that a great deal of mischief might be done before Burbridge could turn back, which he would be likely to do instead of pressing on to Virginia.

As the movement of Morgan was to be made across ranges of mountains, no cannon could be taken. He came to Pound Gap, in the Cumberland range, which was held by a handful of Union cavalry, who retreated, and who sent word to Burbridge. Morgan turned west, intending to reach Mount Sterling, and help himself to supplies from the Union storehouses in that town. His troops were not disciplined soldiers, but mostly new men who had joined him after his escape from prison, with the expectation of leading a wild, rollicking life, with opportunities of helping themselves to plunder. He made such long marches that his horses began to break down. He seized all that he could find, also all the food he could obtain from the farm-houses and barns. He reached Mount Sterling, broke open the bank in the town, and plundered

June 2, 1864.

it of sixty thousand dollars. His men burst open the stores, and helped themselves to whatever they liked, making no distinction between those who sympathized with the Union and those who favored the Confederacy.

General Burbridge learned of Morgan's movement, and started in pursuit, marching two hundred and thirty miles in ten days. He reached Mount Sterling in the early morning, and dashed upon the pickets. The main body of Confederates quickly sprang to their saddles, charged upon Burbridge's artillery, seized the guns, but were quickly driven in turn. It was a sharp engagement, soon over, the Confederates fleeing, with a loss of nearly five hundred men, most of whom were taken prisoners.

General Morgan was not in the engagement. He had taken the route to Lexington with one brigade. He reached the outskirts of that town at midnight, set several buildings on fire to light up the scene. The handful of Union troops in Lexington retreated to a fortification overlooking the town, while the seventeen hundred Confederates broke open the stores and houses of Union men. He obtained ten thousand dollars from the Branch Bank of Kentucky, attempted to burn a large number of freight cars, but was kept at bay by the artillery of the Union troops. Knowing that Burbridge would soon be upon him, Morgan hastened to Cynthiana, where he burned a portion of that town.([1])

The Union troops reached Lexington soon after the departure of Morgan and pressed on to overtake him. It was Sunday morning when Burbridge arrived at Cynthiana. He was delighted to learn that Morgan was waiting to give battle. He had not marched ninety miles in thirty hours([2]) to decline a contest after having brought the enemy to bay. He formed his lines, advanced, and opened fire, charging impetuously upon the Confederates, who, after a sharp engagement, broke and fled in confusion. A small portion of Morgan's old soldiers rallied around him, but the large part of his force—men who had joined him not to fight but to pillage—became panic-stricken, each man seeking his own safety. Morgan returned to Virginia with a small portion of his troops. Instead of retrieving his waning fortunes, he had lost the respect even of those who had been his friends, through the robberies committed by his men. His biographer says: "He suffered from envy, secret animosity, and detraction within his own command. Many faithful friends still surrounded him, many more lay in prison, but he began to meet with open enmity in his own camp. ... Reports of excesses committed in Kentucky had reached Richmond, and created much feeling."([3])

A commission was appointed by the Confederate Government to investigate the charges. The ill success that had attended him, and the appointment of a commission, preyed upon his proud spirit. His face was care-worn, and instead of the enthusiasm of former days, he became listless.(¹)

Quite likely he saw, as many saw, that the fortunes of the Confederacy were rapidly waning. "A conviction," wrote one of his officers, "was stealing upon the Confederate soldiers that the fiat had gone against us, and that no exercise of courage and fortitude could arrest the doom."(²)

During the last week in August, General Morgan, with sixteen hundred men, marched from Jonesborough, with the intention of driving General Gillem and a party of Union troops from Bull's Gap. There were not many Union troops in East Tennessee, and he hoped to drive them out. He reached the house of Mrs. Williams, at Greenville. She was loyal to the Union, and, mounting a horse, rode to the nearest Union pickets with the information that Morgan was at her house.(³) It was midnight when General Gillem started. He made a rapid march, and at daylight dashed upon Morgan's unsuspecting men, who, taken by surprise, fled in confusion. Morgan was killed in Mrs. Williams's garden while attempting to escape. With the death of this brave, energetic commander the Confederate cavalry which had given Sherman and Grant so much trouble in Kentucky and East Tennessee was scattered to the winds, and never reorganized.

GEN. A. J. SMITH.

While General Sherman was pushing towards Atlanta, General Forrest, with a large cavalry force, was endeavoring to destroy the railroads in his rear. General Sturgis, with a body of cavalry, went out from Memphis to meet him, but was defeated. Gen. A. J. Smith, with one division of the Sixteenth Corps and one of the Seventeenth, which had been loaned to General Banks for the expedition up Red River, returned to Memphis and moved to Tupelo. Forrest, emboldened by his victory over Sturgis, determined to attack Smith, but was defeated, with heavy loss. The Confederate commander was much chagrined, planned a bold movement—to dash into Memphis, capture the town, destroy the supplies, and by thus depriving Smith of the means of subsistence, compel him to evacuate Mississippi.(')

He selected fifteen hundred of his best men—not a force large enough to fight much of a battle; that was not his intention; he would avoid a battle, rather. Many of his troops were young men from Memphis, who were familiar with the streets of the city. It was to be a swift movement, and a surprise to the Union troops guarding the city.

Rain was falling when General Forrest started, but not minding the storm, he marched through the night. In the morning he found that his artillery horses were so broken down that he was compelled to leave two of his four cannon. He came to a small stream only sixty feet wide, but the water was overflowing its banks and he could not ford it. He was fertile in expedients, and set the men to making a strong cable of grape-vines, which was stretched across the stream. Some buildings were torn down, logs were floated to the spot, and a bridge constructed and held in place by the grape-vines.(*)

Aug. 18, 1864.

At nightfall he was within twenty-five miles of Memphis, meeting the scouts who had been in the city, and who informed him in regard to the location of the five thousand troops guarding the place, nearly all of whom were colored. The headquarters of General Washburne, in command of the Department, were on Union Street; those of General Hurlbut were at the Gayoso Hotel.

Aug. 20, 1864.

It was six o'clock Sunday morning when Forrest halted his command for a few moments' rest at Cone Creek, four miles distant from Memphis. He called his officers around him and gave them specific instructions. One company, under the command of Capt. W. H. Forrest, was to surprise the pickets and then ride straight to the Gayoso Hotel and seize the Union officers before they could leave their beds. Three regiments were to attack a small body of white troops encamped on the outskirts of the city. Another detachment was to ride to the Mississippi River and seize the steamboats. Still another detachment was to capture General Washburne. If the Union officers could be secured it would create such confusion that the Confederates might possibly have things their own way. To make sure that each officer understood just what he was to do, the troops were halted and Captain Anderson repeated the order. "They understand what they are to do," he said, and the column moved on.

Aug. 21, 1864.

"Who comes there?" It was the hail of the Union picket.

CONFEDERATE RAIDS. 431

"A detachment of the Twelfth Missouri Cavalry with Rebel prisoners," was the answer.

"Advance one!"(⁹)

Captain Forrest rode forward, and the next moment the unsuspecting picket was lying senseless upon the ground, felled by a blow upon his head with the butt-end of the officer's revolver. A moment later the Confederates were seizing the picket-guard. One only had time to fire his musket. The report came sharp and clear upon the morning air, bringing the second guard, nearer the city, to their feet. The Confederates dashed upon them, but were received with a volley. Instead of surprising the Union pickets, Forrest found them alert and the alarm rolling

FORREST'S CAVALRY IN MEMPHIS.

from camp to camp. He must act with decision. The bugles sounded the charge, and his men, forgetting the injunction to be silent, yelled as loud as they could, as they swept like a whirlwind into the city. Blinds were flung back, sashes raised, by men and women who leaped from their beds, and, though in undress, waved their handkerchiefs and night-dresses to their friends in the Confederate ranks.(¹⁰) The detachment detailed to seize the Union officers in the hotel reached the building, and several of the men, stooping in their saddles, rode into the halls. Others leaped from their horses and burst open the chamber doors; but General Hurlbut was not there. The detachment which was to capture General Washburne dashed upon his headquarters; but the one signal-gun, the volley following it, and the wild yell of the Confederates had awakened the entire city, and General Washburne had hastened to rally the troops, a portion of which ran into the State Female College and fired from the windows. Forrest saw that the Union troops would soon be cutting off his way of escape. His troops, welcomed by friends, had become in a measure disorganized. He had captured six hundred prisoners, but had lost a large number of his own men. He could stay no longer, and made a hasty retreat. The movement had resulted in failure. He could not in any event have held the city any length of time, for a superior force soon would have closed around him. Such a dash could have no appreciable effect, other than to break down horses and men by the long and hard riding.

From the beginning of the war, a large majority of the people living in the Shenandoah Valley gave their allegiance to the Confederate Government. With but few exceptions, the men old enough to bear arms were either to be found in the army or else were secretly aiding and assisting the Confederate commander. Over the whole of Northern Virginia ranged partisan commanders, with bands of men who one day might be seen at work on their farms, following the plough or gathering their harvests, but who, twenty-four hours later, at the call of their chief, would be riding miles away to fall upon a wagon-train loaded with supplies for the Union army, capturing and shooting stragglers from the ranks.

They were familiar with every foot of ground, every path-way leading into the mountain dells and secluded nooks. They could ride rapidly, at night as well as by day, over oft-frequented roads. Their work accomplished, they disappeared as suddenly as they came. Their operations were approved by the people, who were ever ready to give information of the movements of the Union wagon-trains, or of small bodies of troops that might be safely attacked.

We have seen General Hunter making a movement to Lynchburg, and from there retreating down the valley of the Kanawha. When at Lexington he burned mills and furnaces which had furnished supplies to the Confederates, besides large amounts of grain. Ex-Governor Letcher had issued a call to the people to become guerillas and do all the damage possible to the Union troops.

General Hunter regarded this act of ex-Governor Letcher as inviting the people to murder straggling Union soldiers. Governor Letcher was not holding any official position, but had advised the people to commit acts of violence against soldiers regularly enlisted in the service of the United States, whereupon General Hunter ordered the soldiers to burn his house. They were fired upon from the windows of the Military Institute at Lexington, for which he directed that it also should be burned.(11) The house of Mr. Anderson, near Buchanan, was burned by General Hunter, together with several others belonging to prominent citizens, one of whom (Mr. Boteler) was General Hunter's own cousin. The Union commander informed the people of the valley that he should hold them responsible for acts committed by guerillas, whom they countenanced.

We have seen General Early, after his failure to enter Washington, retreating across the Potomac River and making his way into the Shenandoah Valley, with large herds of cattle and horses which he had taken from the farmers in Maryland. He was at Strasburg, in a position to return to Richmond or to make a movement in some other direction.

July 24, 1864.

The Union troops confronting him were those commanded by General Crook, which we have seen retreating from Lynchburg down the Great Kanawha to the Ohio, and ascending that river to Wheeling, and then being transported east over the Baltimore and Ohio Railroad. Early had much the larger force, and seeing his opportunity, advanced rapidly from Strasburg. Crook had between three and four thousand men belonging to a large number of regiments, men who had been picked up from the hospitals and camps at Washington. They were a heterogeneous collection of undisciplined soldiers. When the Confederates attacked them they became panic-stricken, and ran as fast as they could from Kernstown through Winchester to Martinsburg. "They behaved in a most disgraceful manner, their officers in many instances leading them off and starting all kinds of lying reports tending to demoralize the whole command; and it was only owing to the steadiness and good conduct of the infantry which came with us from the Kanawha that the army was saved from utter annihilation," wrote General Hunter.(12) General Crook brought off all his artillery and trains. One artillery officer, becoming frightened, abandoned four cannon, but the infantry took hold of the guns and drew them till other horses were obtained. The Union loss in killed, wounded, and prisoners was not far from twelve hundred, while the Confederate loss was very light.

General Crook retreated to Sharpsburg, in Maryland, and encamped on the battle-field of Antietam. The cavalry under General Averill were stationed at Hagerstown. General Early advanced to Martinsburg, and once more destroyed the Baltimore and Ohio Railroad, which had been torn up at that point many times during the war.

General Early, having obtained so many horses and cattle and a large amount of supplies from Maryland, determined to add to his plunder by sending his cavalry into Pennsylvania. He had been with General Lee in the Gettysburg campaign, and was thoroughly acquainted with the country.

General McCausland, acting under General Early's directions, came to the Potomac at Clear Spring, above Williamsport, with two brigades and four cannon, accompanied by two divisions of infantry. To cover the movement, General Imboden and General Jackson advanced to Harper's Ferry, fording the Potomac to the Maryland side. General Vaughn crossed at Williamsport and advanced to Hagerstown. Quickly the news flew down the beautiful Cumberland Valley. From every telegraph station messages were flashed to Governor Curtin, at Harrisburg, and from there to Washington, calling for troops. The soldiers of Pennsylvania were in the armies, and there were few troops at hand to resist the advance of Early's army, except those which had fallen back from Kernstown. General Couch was at Chambersburg with about one hundred and fifty men. The farmers, with their horses and cattle, came riding through the town. General Couch sent the military stores to Harrisburg.

July 29, 1864.

General Averill's pickets rode into Hagerstown with the information that a body of Confederates—those under Vaughn—were crossing the Potomac at Williamsport, that another large body of cavalry and infantry farther up the river was pushing towards Chambersburg. General Averill loaded his supplies into the cars and started for Greencastle, which is twelve miles south of Chambersburg. Soon after the Union cavalry had left Hagerstown the Confederates dashed in, captured the train of cars, and burned it.

The troops under McCausland, twenty-nine hundred in number, were moving rapidly towards Chambersburg. At ten o'clock in the evening, when within two miles, they saw the flash of a cannon, and a shell came whirling through the air. Not knowing how large a force was confronting him, McCausland halted and waited for the morning. The cannon had been fired by Lieutenant McLean, who with sixty men had been detailed by General Couch to make a show of resistance, that the people might gain time in removing their goods. General Couch was in command of the Military Department of Pennsylvania, but he had less than three hundred available men to oppose McCausland.

The cocks were crowing in the farm-yards at three o'clock in the morning when McCausland planted his cannon, and without warning to the unoffending inhabitants, fired three shells into the town, followed by the advance of nine hundred of his men. He sent one of his soldiers to the Court-house to ring the bell, calling the citizens together, but the citizens did not come; whereupon McCausland sent Major Gilmore to arrest the leading men and bring them to the Court-house, where Captain Fitzhugh, McCausland's chief of staff, read a letter written by General Early, demanding one hundred thousand dollars in gold, or five hundred thousand in United States currency. If they did not pay it at once, General McCausland was directed "to lay the town in ashes."(¹⁰) General Early stated that he did this because the houses of three of the prominent citizens of Jefferson County, in Virginia, had been burned by General Hunter.

July 30, 1864.

"We have no gold, and probably there is not fifty thousand dollars in money in the town," said the citizens.

"I must have the money or I shall carry out my order," said McCausland, who went into the hotel and ordered the landlord to prepare a breakfast. While he was eating, the soldiers were breaking open the stores and helping themselves to whatever they liked, drinking themselves drunk with liquor, snatching watches from the pockets of the citizens, compelling them to give up their hats, boots, and shoes.

McCausland finished his breakfast, and as the five hundred thousand dollars had not been paid, ordered Major Gilmore to set the town on fire. Soldiers were detailed to execute the order, who broke open the houses, piled the furniture in heaps—beds, tables, chairs—and set them on fire, paying no heed to the pathetic prayers of old men and women, the entreaties of mothers with infants in their arms, or the crying of children. One of the soldiers, more tender-hearted than others, said, "I must obey orders," but others, whose brains were on fire with the liquor they had drunk, with fiendish laughter applied the torch to women's clothes hanging in the closets.(¹¹)

It was mid-forenoon when the great volume of flame and smoke rose to heaven—bursting out simultaneously from every part of the town. No picture can adequately portray the scene. Old men and women tottering through the streets, mothers pressing their babes to their breasts, with frightened children rending the air with their cries, clinging to them amid the suffocating smoke, going they knew not where; women fleeing with their clothes in their arms, rudely assaulted, the clothes taken from them and thrown into the flames; valued articles snatched from their hands by ruthless ruffians. In some instances men were halted, compelled to sit down and pull off their boots and hand them over to the Confederates.

The sick and infirm had to be carried to places of safety by the citizens, who could do nothing to save their homes. Some of the Confederate soldiers, moved by the terrible scene, kindly assisted; others looked on stolidly, or else gloried in the opportunity to help themselves to whatever they might choose to take. In a few cases, houses situated in the outskirts were spared by the owners paying a ransom. It was half-past ten

RUINS OF CHAMBERSBURG.

when a cavalryman came to tell McCausland that the Union cavalry was approaching, and it was time for him to be on the move. He called in the parties detailed to burn the town and rode rapidly away towards the west, crossing North Mountain and making all haste towards the Potomac, with Averill in pursuit.

General Averill has been much criticised for not reaching Chambersburg in season to have prevented its destruction. At Greencastle he was notified by telegrams from General Couch of the rapid advance of the Confederates towards Chambersburg. He was asleep beside a fence, near Greencastle, at four o'clock in the morning, when he was wakened by the telegraph operator. At the moment, the booming of cannon was heard in the direction of Chambersburg.(¹⁸) General Averill replied that he would be at Chambersburg in the morning. He did not start at once, or issue any orders for an immediate movement. When at last he took up the line of march, it was not directly towards Chambersburg, but eastward to Greenwood, whence he turned towards the west. The reason for this detour, eight miles out of the way, possibly may have been the fear that General Vaughn, with another body of Confederate cavalry, might also be advancing towards Chambersburg, and that were he to take the direct road, he might be caught between Vaughn and McCausland, and attacked in front and rear at the same moment. A bolder commander would have readily and joyfully improved the opportunity that presented itself to Averill; he was between McCausland and the Potomac; by cutting off his retreat, falling upon him, and driving him still farther into Pennsylvania, he would soon be surrounded by the rapidly gathering detachments under General Couch. It would seem that General Averill had little apprehension of the great opportunity that had come to him to strike an effective blow upon McCausland.

Sad and mournful the scene when he rode towards Chambersburg beneath the cloud ascending from the five hundred and thirty-seven buildings burned by the order of General Early. In the streets and fields stood two thousand homeless men and women, many of them reduced by the morning's work from competence and comfort to penury and want.

" For this act I alone am responsible, as the officers engaged in it were simply executing my orders, and had no discretion left them," is the frank, explicit avowal of General Early.(") He gave the order in retaliation for the houses burned and property destroyed in the Shenandoah Valley by the order of General Hunter.

The Union commanders in the Shenandoah Valley during 1862 and 1863 had refrained from destroying buildings. Nearly all the people in the valley were hostile to the Union. Their sympathies and acts were in favor of the Confederates. They gave aid and assistance to the guerillas, who were seemingly peaceful citizens during the day, but who at night would be in the saddle, pouncing upon Union wagon-trains, capturing stragglers from the ranks, or shooting their prisoners. When General Hunter succeeded to the command of the valley he determined to put an end to this mode of warfare, and issued a notice that guerillas, who were unorganized soldiers, belonging to no regiment in the Confederate service, would be summarily punished when arrested for depredation and murder. He also gave notice, as we have seen, that all who aided and assisted such irregular soldiers would be punished. He said: "The firing by guerillas into defenceless wagon-trains, and the assassination of soldiers, are practices not recognized by the laws of war of any civilized nation, nor are the persons engaged therein entitled to any other treatment than that done by the universal code of justice to pirates, murderers, and other outlaws."(") . . . He said: "Without the countenance given them by the Confederate residents of the valley they could not support themselves a week." He notified the people that for every train fired upon, or Union soldier wounded or assassinated by guerillas, the houses and other property of every secession sympathizer within a circuit of five miles should be burned. By his order he made the people responsible for the acts of the guerillas.

The increasing acts of barbarity on the part of the Confederates demanded redress. On May 22d, six Union soldiers were found strapped to a fence near Charlestown, having their throats cut from ear to ear.[14] It was to put a stop to such fiendish acts that General Hunter issued his order, which, however, never was literally executed, but many buildings were burned under it, which brought about the retaliatory act of General Early. No Confederate soldier had ever been robbed or injured by a citizen of Chambersburg. No Confederate wagon-train had been fired upon by the people of that town; while the people in the Shenandoah Valley, on the other hand, harbored, aided, and secreted the men who improved every opportunity that offered to capture or murder Union soldiers. The verdict of history, when all passion and prejudice have passed away, quite likely will place the ultimate responsibility for the destruction of Chambersburg upon those who aided and abetted the guerillas of the Shenandoah.

The burning of Chambersburg could have no appreciable effect upon the final outcome of the war. It was a deliberate act of vandalism on the part of General Early, who, though a quarter of a century has rolled away, still frankly accepts the responsibility, and justifies the act.[19]

NOTES TO CHAPTER XVII.

(1) Basil W. Duke, "History of Morgan's Cavalry," p. 526.
(2) Idem, p. 524.
(3) Idem, p. 530.
(4) Idem, p. 532.
(5) Idem, p. 529.
(6) Idem, p. 537.
(7) "Campaigns of Lieutenant-general Forrest," p. 534.
(8) Idem, p. 535.
(9) Idem, p. 539.
(10) Idem, p. 542.
(11) George E. Pond, "The Shenandoah Valley in 1864," p. 30.
(12) Hunter to Halleck, Unpublished War Records.
(13) Jacob Hake, "The Great Invasion," Appendix, p. 582.
(14) Idem, p. 582.
(15) T. R. Bard, quoted in "The Great Invasion," Appendix, p. 585.
(16) Gen. Jubal A. Early, "Memoirs of the Last Year of the War," p. 70.
(17) Maj.-gen. David Hunter's Order of May 24, 1864.
(18) Jacob Hake, "The Great Invasion," p. 597.
(19) Jubal A. Early, Address at Winchester, May, 1889.

CHAPTER XVIII.

POLITICAL AFFAIRS IN MIDSUMMER, 1864.

JEFFERSON DAVIS, in midwinter, 1864, was far-sighted enough to see that something must be done to counteract, if possible, the effect of the victories won by the Union troops at Vicksburg, Gettysburg, and Chattanooga. He saw that the armies of the Union were being largely reinforced; that the Government was putting forth all its energy to carry on the war. He knew that there was a large portion of the Democratic party in the Northern States opposing the war, and took measures to foster the discontent, bring about an uprising, if possible; also to prevent the re-election of Abraham Lincoln; to release the large number of Confederate prisoners on Johnson's Island, in Lake Erie, near Sandusky; at Camp Douglas, near Chicago; Camp Chase, at Columbus; and at Rock Island, Ill. If these could be released, and an uprising brought about at the same moment, it was hoped that the theatre of war might be transferred from Northern Georgia to Indiana, Illinois, and Ohio; and that out of the turmoil would come the breaking of the blockade either by France or England, or by both nations acting in concert; or that the iron-clad vessels building in England and France, and paid for with Confederate cotton, would suddenly make their appearance off Charleston and Wilmington, and scatter the blockading fleets, or possibly enter the harbor of New York, and lay that metropolis under contribution. Such the roseate hued picture of the possible outcome of a well-concerted plan of action. Even if this could not wholly be brought about, an influence might be exercised by judicious action which would result in the election of a successor to Abraham Lincoln who would enter into negotiations for peace.

These the words of Jefferson Davis: "Political developments at the North favored the adoption of some action that might influence public sentiment in the hostile section. The aspect of the Peace party was quite encouraging, and it seemed that the real issue to be decided in the Presidential election of that year was the continuance or cessation of the war. A commission of three persons eminent in position and intelligence was accordingly appointed to visit Canada, with a view to negotiate with such persons in the North as might be relied on to aid in the attainment of peace." (¹)

Had we been in Wilmington, N. C., we should have seen a steamer lying low in the water, painted white, with raking funnel and masts, loaded with cotton, its cabins crowded with passengers, and among them Mr. James P. Holcomb. It was ten o'clock, and the night dark, when the steamer made her way down the harbor, and out over the bar, avoiding the Union war-ships, shaping her course to Nassau, where Mr. Holcomb took passage on another steamer to Halifax.

March 1, 1864.

The steamer *Thistle*, built in England to run the blockade, left Wilmington with Jacob Thompson, Clement C. Clay, and W. W. Cleary on board, the three commissioners selected by Jefferson Davis to manage affairs in Canada, in connection with Mr. Holcomb, who was especially charged to defend some Confederate sailors who had been arrested in Halifax. Mr. Thompson was from Mississippi. He had been a member of Congress from 1839 to 1851. He owned a large number of slaves, and had used all his influence for the extension of slavery. The State of Mississippi had obtained a large amount of money by issuing bonds, but instead of meeting its obligations, repudiated them in 1857. Jefferson Davis and Jacob Thompson both advocated the dishonorable transaction. President Buchanan appointed Mr. Thompson Secretary of the Interior. Under his administration, in connection with John B. Floyd, Secretary of War, nearly one million dollars of Indian Trust Funds were stolen from the Treasury. Mr. Thompson knew all the circumstances of the transaction, but used his influence to protect the guilty parties. While holding the office of Secretary of the Interior, and drawing his salary, he was also acting, in January, 1861, as Commissioner from the Confederate States to North Carolina, to induce the Legislature of that State to secede from the Union. He was one of the few original conspirators who plotted the overthrow of the Government and the establishment of a slave power upon its ruins (" Drum-beat of the Nation," p. 29). The commissioners reached Halifax, and made their way overland to Montreal.

May 6, 1864.

Col. Thomas H. Hines, of the Ninth Kentucky Confederate Cavalry, who had been captured with Morgan in Ohio, in 1863, but who had escaped from prison, was commissioned by Mr. Seddon, Confederate Secretary of War, to make his way to Canada, to collect the Confederate soldiers there. He was to put himself in communication with the Sons of Liberty, and to do all in his power to induce them to organize and prepare themselves to aid the Confederates, and to employ the soldiers he might collect in "hostile operations." Colonel Hines was directed to observe "neutral obligations."

The Confederate Government was using the hospitality of England to construct a navy; with the connivance and knowledge of Louis Napoleon, Emperor of France, the Confederate Secretary of the Navy was having a fleet of iron-clads under construction in the ports of that country. The order of Mr. Seddon to Colonel Hines to collect Confederate soldiers who had made their way to Canada, arm them, and engage in hostile operations against the United States, was in itself a violation of neutral obligations. Were the Confederates to enlist as soldiers in Canada, without arming them, it would be a violation of international law, yet Captain Hines was commissioned not only to collect the Confederate soldiers, but to make a hostile attack from Canada upon the United States. The authority given by Mr. Seddon was supplemented by Jefferson Davis. "I hereby direct you," wrote the President of the Confederacy, "to proceed to Canada, there to carry out the instructions you have received from me verbally in such manner as shall seem most likely to conduce to the further interests of the Confederate States."(²)

Mr. Thompson was chief commissioner, and Captain Hines was to confer with him. The Confederate Government had commissioned all the parties, and would therefore be responsible for whatever they might do.

The secret society which was organized in the Western States early in the war as the "Mutual Protection Society," which was changed to the "Knights of the Golden Circle," again changed its name, and had become the "Sons of Liberty." Its members were bitterly opposed to the war. The calls of President Lincoln for more troops, and the ordering of the draft, made them more than ever determined and active in their disloyalty. They were in communication with the Confederates. "The object of the order was to aid and assist the Confederate Government, and restore the Union as it was before the war," as stated by one of its officers.(³)

The members were most numerous in Indiana, Illinois, and Missouri, but the organization extended eastward, and had many members in New York. A General Council of delegates held a secret session in New York on the anniversary of Washington's Birthday, who chose Mr. Clement L. Vallandigham Grand Commander.(⁴) In "Marching to Victory" (p. 162) we have seen that Mr. Vallandigham, member of Congress from Ohio, was arrested by General Burnside for treason, that he had been sent South by President Lincoln, but had made his way from Richmond to Bermuda, and thence to Canada. The

Feb. 22, 1864.

Democratic party of Ohio had nominated him for Governor, but the people of that State, in the fall of 1863, had defeated him by more than one hundred thousand majority, given for John Brough, a Democrat, who supported the war. Vallandigham was at Windsor, opposite Detroit, and in constant communication with the Sons of Liberty, also with Mr. Thompson, Mr. Clay, and Captain Hines, who were using every possible effort to inaugurate civil war in the Western States, and who indulged the belief that they could bring about a secession of those States, and the establishment of a North-western Confederacy. One of the leading Democratic newspapers of the West said: "The continuance of the war on the present terms is as certain to result in the independence of the seceded States as night and day are to follow each other. . . . The North-west does not propose to pay tribute, and, in case of the disrupture of the republic, will make her own terms. . . . She knows her capacity to make terms with whatever section she may treat with after its dissolution."([5])

In an interview between Mr. Thompson and Mr. Vallandigham, the Grand Commander of the Sons of Liberty said that the members of the order were only partially armed; that while the organization was not compact, it was controlled by efficient and determined men, and if provocation and opportunity combined, its members would defend their principles at any cost. He intended to return to Ohio, where he expected to be arrested, which would lead to a general uprising.([6])

Mr. Thompson supplied money, which was to be used in arming the Sons of Liberty. He wrote a letter to Richmond, informing the Confederate Government of what he was doing, and what he expected would be accomplished:

"Though intending this for a Western Confederacy, and demanding peace, if peace be not granted then it shall be war. There are some choice spirits enlisted in this enterprise, and all that is needed for success is unflinching nerve. It is agreed that Capt. T. Henry Hines shall command at Chicago and Capt. John B. Castleman at Rock Island. If a movement could be made by our troops into Kentucky and Missouri it would greatly facilitate matters in the West. . . . If Lee can hold his own in front of Richmond, and Johnston defeat Sherman in Georgia prior to the election, it seems probable that Lincoln would be defeated. It is not improbable that McClellan will be nominated by the War Democrats. His recent war speeches have broken him down with the Peace party, but in my opinion no Peace candidate can be elected unless disaster attend the Federal armies in Virginia and Georgia. In short, nothing but violence can terminate the war."([7])

If the Sons of Liberty or the Confederates in Canada thought that the military authorities of the United States did not know what was going on, they were mistaken. General Rosecrans was in command at St. Louis, and his provost marshal, Colonel Sanderson, knew that there were mysterious meetings at night in a room over a store. He knew who attended them, and what was said and done within the chamber by the Sons of Liberty, several of whom he caused to be arrested.

Colonel Carrington, in Indianapolis, knew all about secret meetings held by the Sons of Liberty in southern Indiana. In Missouri, Illinois, and Indiana, detectives employed by the Government were initiated into the order, attended the meetings, and learned the plan of the conspirators. The return of Mr. Vallandigham to Ohio, and his second arrest by the Government, was to be the signal for the general uprising. It was learned that John Morgan was to invade Kentucky.(*) It was expected that there would be simultaneous movements of the Confederate armies northward to intensify the excitement.

On March 4, 1865, the term of years for which Abraham Lincoln was elected President would expire. Although the day was a twelve-month distant, there were those who were forecasting the event, and planning for the election of his successor. There were men in the Republican party who earnestly advocated his election in 1860, but who now were opposed to his re-election; some of them because he was so slow, cautious, and conservative, and was not doing just what they thought he ought to do. They wanted generals to be placed in command of the armies who would act with more vigor than General Meade had exhibited after the battle of Gettysburg. They wanted the rebellion crushed out at once, and the lands of those who were in arms against the United States confiscated to the Government. On the other hand, there were those who opposed his re-election because he had gone so fast and so far. They said that he had no constitutional authority to issue the Proclamation of Emancipation. They denounced the employment of negroes as soldiers. Men who had solicited appointments to important positions, but who had not received them, manifested their resentment by opposing his election for a second term of years. Under another President they might obtain what they desired.

Among those who earnestly opposed Mr. Lincoln's re-election was Horace Greeley, editor of the *New York Tribune*, a paper which for a long period before the war had wielded a commanding influence, ever on the side of freedom. He was not always well balanced, and his political course was erratic. Before the outbreak of the war, when the conspirators were plotting for the overthrow of the Government, he said, "Wayward sisters, go in peace." If the majority of the people of a State wished to secede, he would allow them to do so. He had criticised many of the acts of President Lincoln, and was strenuously opposing his renomination.

One of the members of President Lincoln's Cabinet, Mr. Chase, Secretary of the Treasury, ardently desired to be President. He had always been opposed to slavery, and while a member of the Senate had battled manfully against the aggression of the slave-holders. He allowed his friends to present his name as a candidate, and a circular was issued by them which represented that it was impossible for the Republican party to re-elect Mr. Lincoln; that Mr. Chase possessed all the qualifications needed at such a crisis in the affairs of the nation. Mr. Chase was from Ohio, but the Legislature of that State passed resolutions indorsing Mr. Lincoln and advocating his re-election; whereupon Mr. Chase, seeing that there was no prospect of his being nominated, withdrew his name as a candidate.

The men who thought Mr. Lincoln was going too slow called a convention, which met at Cleveland, Ohio. About one hundred and fifty persons assembled, but they had not been elected by any constituent bodies as delegates; they only represented themselves. They issued a platform demanding that the rebellion be suppressed without a compromise, that the right of *habeas corpus*, which President Lincoln had suspended, should be respected, and that the lands of the slave-holders and all their property should be confiscated. They nominated General Fremont for President, and Gen. John C. Cochrane, of New York, for Vice-president. General Fremont wrote a letter three days later accepting the nomination, in which President Lincoln was charged with incapacity and want of fidelity to the Constitution. He declared that if the Republican convention, which was to meet at Baltimore the first week in June, were to nominate Mr. Lincoln, he ought not to be elected. Others of the Republican party thought that it would be better to select General Grant as candidate; but General Grant would not consent to such an arrangement.

May 31, 1864.

The Republican convention met in Baltimore. The temporary chairman was a white-haired man from Kentucky, Robert J. Breckinridge, who had received from college and university the honorable degrees of Doctor of Divinity and Doctor of Laws for his learning and eloquence. He was uncle to John C. Breckinridge, who had been voted for by the slave-holders in 1860, and who was a lieutenant-general in the Confederate army. Though many of his relatives and friends had given their sympathies to the Confederacy, he ardently loved

June 7, 1864.

the Union. "This nation shall not be destroyed," he said. "The only enduring and imperishable cement of all free institutions has been the blood of traitors. . . . We must use all power to exterminate the institution of slavery, which has raised the sword against the Union."

President Lincoln was almost unanimously renominated, and the convention declared that there should be no compromise with rebels in arms, and that the war should be prosecuted with the utmost possible vigor. Andrew Johnson, of Tennessee, was nominated for Vice-president.

From the beginning of the conflict, the Peace Democrats, as they called themselves, opposed the prosecution of the war. They denounced President Lincoln as a usurper and tyrant. The victories won by the soldiers of the Union gave them no pleasure, and they rejoiced whenever there was a defeat to the armies bearing the Stars and Stripes. Many Democrats who supported the President at the breaking out of the rebellion now opposed him, because he had given liberty to the slaves. In 1860 the Democratic party was divided, part voting for Breckinridge and part for Mr. Douglas; but it was to act now as a united party.

Those who opposed the war said that the South could not be conquered; that so brave a people as they had shown themselves to be never could be compelled to lay down their arms; that the thousands of men who had given up their lives on the battle-fields, who were dying in the hospitals, had suffered in vain; it was a crime against humanity to prolong a struggle which had cost so much blood and treasure, and brought ruin and desolation to so large a section of the country. "We must have peace at any price," they said.

The National Democratic Convention was to meet in Chicago July 4th. The committee which had matters in charge selected the anniversary of national independence, hoping that the choice of such a day would awaken enthusiasm, but their arrangements were unexpectedly thrown into confusion.

The Peace Democrats of south-western Ohio were in session at Dayton, when the door opened and Mr. Vallandigham, Grand Commander of the Sons of Liberty, entered. It was an unlooked-for event. He had come in the night from Canada. He was greeted with a yell of delight. He made a speech to the convention, and went on to his own home in Hamilton, where he made another speech. Quite likely Mr. Vallandigham was somewhat disappointed because a regiment of soldiers did not come with an order to arrest him a second time. Just what motive induced him to suddenly leave Canada and appear unheralded in Ohio is not known, but the Sons of Liberty were not quite ready

June 16, 1864.

for an uprising. The Confederate agents had not perfected their plans for the release of the Confederate prisoners. The Sons of Liberty were preparing clock-work machinery, to be placed on steamboats, which at a given time would strike a match and set the boat on fire.(⁹) Two boats had already been destroyed. They intended to destroy steamboats and railroads so that there could be no rapid concentration of Union troops. At a secret meeting in Chicago, it was agreed that the Confederate prisoners should be released, the arms in the arsenals at Chicago and Springfield, Ill., should be seized at the same moment, and that it should be done some time before August 16th; that the Confederate prisoners and the Sons of Liberty were to rendezvous at Louisville, New Albany, and Jeffersonville, on the Ohio, where they were to be joined by a Confederate force which would march to their assistance.(¹⁰) Vallandigham was to select the day on which the uprising was to take place. But there was consternation among the Sons of Liberty when, a day or two later, Judge Buillet, Dr. Kaulfus, and several other prominent Sons of Liberty were arrested and sent to Fort Lafayette, thus upsetting all their plans.

The arrival of Mr. Vallandigham and his election as delegate to the Chicago Convention was not anticipated by the leaders of the Democratic party, who feared that he might be a ruling spirit in the convention. The committee which had matters in charge saw that something must be done, for while Vallandigham and the Peace Democrats were in a fair way to control the convention, Grant was crossing the James to Petersburg, and Sherman making his way towards Atlanta, and hopes of the success of the party at the election in November were fading away. The members of the committee hastened to New York, and after consultation adjourned the meeting of the convention to August 29th. The reason given for the adjournment was that it was thought best to wait for possible events. One of the Democratic newspapers frankly said that it was best to wait and take advantage of any blunder that might be made, whereupon the Republican papers said that it was the first time in history that a political party, pretending to be loyal to the Constitution and the Union, could only hope for success from disaster to the armies of the Union.

Among the Confederates in Canada was Mr. George Sanders, of Kentucky, who sent a letter to Horace Greeley, editor of the *New York Tribune*, informing him that the Confederate agents in Canada were anxious to bring about peace. The editor of the *Tribune*, thinking that he might possibly render a great service to the country, wrote thus to President Lincoln: "I venture to remind you that our bleeding, bankrupt, almost dying country, longs for peace, shudders at the prospect of fresh conscriptions, of future wholesale devastations, and of rivers of human blood." Mr. Greeley asked that a safe-conduct be given to Mr. Clay, Mr. Holcomb, and Mr. Sanders to visit Washington to arrange a peace. Mr. Greeley did not know that he was being made a fool of by the Confederates; that they had no proposition; that Jefferson Davis never had conferred any authority upon them to negotiate a peace. President Lincoln was farther-sighted than Mr. Greeley. This the writing which he sent to the Confederates, and which was given them by Mr. John Hay, one of his private secretaries:

"To WHOM IT MAY CONCERN:

"Any proposition which embraces the restoration of peace, the integrity of the whole Union, and the abandonment of slavery, and which comes by and with an authority that can control the armies now at war against the United States, will be received and considered by the Executive Government of the United States, and will be met by liberal terms on substantial and collateral points; and the bearer or bearers thereof shall have safe-conduct both ways.
"ABRAHAM LINCOLN."

The Confederates did not want peace on any such terms, but an absolute independence. The commissioners did not go to Washington. The people of the South were not ready to accept peace on the terms offered by Mr. Lincoln. A Georgia newspaper said: "We may lose much by presenting a hostile front to the movements of the Peace Democracy. Live with them under the same Government we never will, but if they will use the ballot-box against Mr. Lincoln while we use the cartridge-box, each side will be a helper to the other, and both co-operate to accomplish the grandest work which this country and this continent has ever witnessed."(")

Five thousand Confederate prisoners were confined at Camp Douglas, near Chicago. The camp contained sixty acres, surrounded by a board fence fourteen feet high. The guard in the month of May was composed of two regiments of veteran soldiers. Many of the Confederates had served under Morgan. Some of them were from Texas—wild, reckless, and ever ready for adventure. The officer in command of the garrison allowed the Confederate officers to have, in some degree, control of the men, allowing them to serve out their food and distribute clothing and keep the records of the regiments. A writer says that the prison, in fact, was in charge of the prisoners.(¹²) Some of the prisoners, under parole, were allowed to visit their friends in the city. A new commander, Col. J. B. Sweet, was placed in charge of the prisoners, who changed the order of things. The Confederates had been allowed to write to their friends, and the letters went South by flag of truce at Petersburg. Colonel Sweet noticed that a great many letters were written. As they were unsealed, he noticed that some of them contained but a few lines, and that there would be large spaces on which nothing had been written. On a day in June he held one of the letters near a fire, when, lo and behold! the blank pages became written lines, and the officer read something about the Fourth of July, that there might possibly be an unexpected celebration in the camp. He kept his own counsel; but from day to day new prisoners were brought to the camp, who soon found out that it was expected a large number of people would come to the Democratic convention on July 4th from southern Illinois and Indiana, and that there was a literary society in Chicago which held secret meetings; that the members were in sympathy with the Confederates. The Confederate prisoners who revealed all this to the new-comers did not know that they were in conversation with Colonel Sweet's detectives; nor did the members of the literary society know that one of their new members was a detective in the service of the new commander of the camp. Many troops were passing through Chicago, some stopped there, and for the time being came under the command of an officer, who quietly reinforced the guard. The Fourth of July came, but as the Democratic convention had been adjourned, there were no arrivals of men from southern Indiana, Illinois, or Canada. The arrest of several leading members of the Sons of Liberty in Cincinnati, Louisville, and St. Louis, together with postponement of the convention, had disarranged the plans under way for the liberation of the prisoners.

During the month of August the Confederate agents in Canada and throughout the North-west were very busy. Mr. Thompson sent a large amount of money to Indiana and Illinois to trusty parties for the purchase of arms.(¹³)

A Confederate writer, who was one of the chief agents in the management of affairs, says: "Mr. Vallandigham's representatives were furnished means of transportation, and had ample time to make proper distribution, and explain to the more faithful and courageous county commanders why the rank and file should come to Chicago and resist any further attempts on the liberty of the citizens."(¹⁴)

Mr. Thompson, at Toronto, issued commissions to Captain Castleman and Captain Hines. They were to command the expeditions for the release of the prisoners, and were directed to take with them from Canada all such Confederate soldiers as were suited to aid in the perilous undertaking.

Aug. 24, 1864.

The leaders of the Sons of Liberty had visited Mr. Thompson in Canada, and all arrangements were made to liberate the prisoners while the Democratic convention was in session. The trains which rolled into Chicago on the 27th and 28th of August over the Michigan Central Railroad contained a large number of men whose faces were sunburned, who wore slouched hats, and who talked but little with the passengers. When they reached Chicago some of them went to the Richmond House and registered their names from various places, and acted as if they were strangers to each other. They were Confederate officers from Canada.([14])

A Confederate writer says: "Men commended to us by Mr. Vallandigham had been intrusted with the necessary funds for perfecting county organizations; arms had been purchased in the North by the aid of professed friends in New York; alliances offensive and defensive had been made with peace organizations, and though we were not misled by the sanguine promises of our friends, we were confident that with any sort of co-operation on their part success was possible. During the excitement that always attends a great political convention, increased as we supposed it would be by the spirit of opposition to the administration, we felt that we would be free to act unobserved, and that we could move with promptness and effect upon Camp Douglas. With five thousand prisoners there, and over seven thousand at Springfield, joined by the dissatisfied elements in Chicago and through Illinois, we believed that we would have a formidable force, which might be the nucleus of more important movements.... Arms were ready, and information had been conveyed to the prisoners of our intention. Chicago was thronged with people from all sections of the country, and among the vast crowd were many county officers of the secret organization on whom we relied for assistance." ([16])

Had we been guests at the Richmond House we should have seen men entering one of the rooms, when the door was carefully guarded, and every one who came to be admitted was closely scrutinized. It was a conference of the Confederate leaders with the leaders of the Sons of Liberty. It was shown that a large number of the Sons of Liberty had arrived, but that they had not been organized for action.

Aug. 28, 1864.

The trains brought a multitude of men from southern Indiana and Illinois. "As day after day passed," wrote an editor of one of the Chicago newspapers, "the crowd increased till the whole city seemed alive

29

with a motley crew of blear-eyed, whiskey-blotched vagabonds, the very excrescence and sweepings of the slums and sinks of all the cities of the nation. I sat at my window and saw the filthy stream of degraded humanity swagger along to the wigwam on the lake shore, and wondered how our city could be saved from burning and plunder, and our wives and daughters from a far more dreadful fate."('') They talked loudly about the convention, cursed Abraham Lincoln, and praised Vallandigham. They swaggered through the streets, lounged at the corners, drank a great deal of whiskey, and yelled with delight at the mention of the name of Jefferson Davis. Some of them went out towards Camp Douglas; but when they saw how many soldiers were guarding it, and how the cannon were placed pointing down all the avenues, to sweep them, if need be, by their fire, they turned away with scowls and frowns upon their faces.

The time came at length for holding the convention. Mr. Belmont, of New York, called the delegates to order. "Four years of misrule," he said, "by a sectional, fanatical, and corrupt party have brought our country to the verge of ruin. . . . The inevitable result of the re-election of Mr. Lincoln must be the utter disintegration of our whole political and social system, and bloodshed and anarchy, with the great problems of liberal progress and self-government jeopardized for generations to come." Mr. Hunt, who had once been Governor of New York, wanted an armistice that a convention of States might be called to amend the Constitution, to insure the perpetuation of slavery in the Southern States. He desired "to insure to each State the enjoyment of all its rights and the constitutional control of its domestic concerns." Governor Hunt and those who agreed with him were blind to the meaning of the great events of the hour; they did not see that the whole world was moving on to a loftier ideal of life.

Aug. 29, 1864.

The draft which President Lincoln had ordered was violently opposed by Mr. Long, of Ohio, member of Congress, who wanted a committee appointed to go to Washington and demand that the draft be postponed till the people could decide whether or not the war should go on.

Horatio Seymour, Governor of New York, was president of the convention. He said that the Republican party was responsible for the war. He had no word of censure for Jefferson Davis or any of the Confederates. He wanted the fighting suspended, and he arraigned President Lincoln for not consenting to an armistice. "The Administration," he said, "will not let the shedding of blood cease, even for a little time, to see if Christian charity or the wisdom of statesmanship may not work out a method to save our country. They will not listen to a proposal of peace which does not offer that which this Government has no right to ask. . . . We are resolved that the party which has made the history of our country, since its advent to power, seem like some unnatural and terrible dream shall be overthrown."

What was it that the Government, in his opinion, had no right to ask? This: the freedom of the slaves.

Men animated by lofty ideals, by high moral principle, when confronted by great moral questions and emergencies; men who are gifted with far-sightedness into coming years, who have the faculty of advancing, as it were, into those years and looking back upon the present, rarely make mistakes in statesmanship; but Horatio Seymour and the men composing the Chicago Democratic Convention were not thus endowed. They were blinded by prejudice, partisan zeal, and passion, and saw only a hated political party to be overthrown, and victorious armies which they desired should melt away. The Stars and Stripes, stained with the blood of dying heroes, awakened no enthusiasm in the convention. The aim, intention, and spirit of the members were thus expressed: "The Constitution has been disregarded in every part, and public liberty and private right alike trodden down, and the material prosperity of the country injured. Justice, humanity, liberty, and the public welfare demand that immediate efforts be made for a cessation of hostilities, with a view to an ultimate convention of all the States, that at the earliest practicable moment peace may be restored."

The resolutions were written by Mr. Vallandigham. The Peace Democrats had the making of the platform, but they had no candidate upon whom they could unite, and so it came about that General McClellan was nominated as candidate for the Presidency, and Mr. Pendleton, of Ohio, for Vice-president. General McClellan had been idolized by a portion of the soldiers of the Army of the Potomac. From the hour of his removal, in November, 1862, a portion of the Democratic party had selected him as the candidate who would be most likely to defeat Mr. Lincoln; but when his name was brought before the convention some of the members hissed their disapproval. "General McClellan," shouted Mr. Harris, delegate from Maryland, "is a tyrant! He it was who first initiated the policy by which our liberties were stricken down." He referred to the arrest of the members of the Legislature of Maryland by General McClellan. "He is the assassin of State rights, the usurper of liberty, and if nominated will be beaten as he was at Antietam," continued Mr. Harris.

"You have arraigned Lincoln," said Mr. Long, of Ohio, "for interfering with the freedom of speech, the freedom of elections and of arbitrary arrests, and yet you propose to nominate a man who has been guilty of the arrest of the Legislature of a sovereign State. He has suspended the writ of *habeas corpus* and helped to enforce the odious Emancipation Proclamation of Lincoln, the willing instrument of a corrupt and tyrannical administration."

While the convention was resolving that the war was a failure the Confederate flag—waving over Fort Morgan, at the entrance to the Bay of Mobile—was giving place to the Stars and Stripes, the troops of Sherman, with drums beating and colors flying, were marching into Atlanta, and the artillery of the Army of the Potomac was hurling a salute of shot and shell into the Confederate trenches at Petersburg.

Not a cheer went up from the convention when the news of the surrender of Fort Morgan was received, but there was a sinking of hope instead. It was a convention in which disaster to the Union armies would have been welcome news. More than this, while the convention was holding its sessions the Confederate officers commissioned by Jefferson Davis to bring about the outbreak in Chicago were counting their followers, and also the number of soldiers guarding the prisoners. The Confederate prisoners had organized themselves into companies, regiments, and brigades. After the war ended and there was no longer any need for secrecy they informed the Union officer who paroled them that it was their intention to leave the city.(¹⁸) They found, however, that a great many of the men who were cursing Abraham Lincoln and shouting for Vallandigham had no inclination to join in an attack upon veteran soldiers who had been in a score of battles. The Confederate officers had spies in every place —in the telegraph office and close by Colonel Sweet's headquarters. The Sons of Liberty outnumbered the soldiers two to one, but they were not organized. The Confederates could not hope to succeed without their aid. The convention adjourned, and the great crowd of Sons of Liberty, whose fare had been paid to Chicago by money from the Confederate treasury, through Mr. Thompson, left the city, together with the Confederates, who had registered at the hotels under assumed names.

The reception by the public of the doings of the convention was not what Horatio Seymour and Mr. Vallandigham, representing the two sections of the convention, expected. They thought that a majority of the people were weary of the war, and were ready to make peace on any terms, and that the name of General McClellan would awaken great enthusiasm. The resolutions demanded peace, but the candidate had been nominated for what he had done in carrying on the war. If it was right to begin the war to maintain the authority of the Constitution and the

Union, it was right to carry it on ; if it was wrong, then General McClellan's course of action was wrong. General Grant, General Rosecrans, and a large number of the generals, and many thousands of soldiers, had acted with the Democratic party, and the resolutions which had been accepted by only four dissenting votes were condemnatory of what they were doing to preserve the Union. They reflected that no cheer had been given when the news of the surrender of Fort Morgan was received ; that no hurrah rent the air when the telegraph brought the information that the Stars and Stripes were flying over Atlanta. The people saw that the action of the convention was hollow-hearted and insincere. The meaning of the resolutions was plain—peace on any terms which might be dictated by the Confederate Government; the end a divided country, the Constitution torn to tatters, the government of the people a failure.

General McClellan repudiated the resolutions but accepted the nomination. The false attitude of the Democratic party, together with the victories won by the armies of the Union, made the political defeat of General McClellan a foregone conclusion. Principles are priceless jewels ; men, individually or as a party, cannot deliberately and recklessly throw them away and maintain the respect of their fellow-men. A quarter of a century has gone by since the Democratic party cast aside its time-honored principles at Chicago through the machinations of Jefferson Davis and at the dictation of Mr. Vallandigham, but the time has not been sufficiently long for that party to wholly outgrow the blighting influence of its action in 1864.

NOTES TO CHAPTER XVIII.

([1]) Jefferson Davis, "Rise and Fall of the Confederate Government," vol. ii., p. 611.
([2]) Capt. T. Henry Hines, *Southern Bivouac*, December, 1886.
([3]) Green B. Smith, testimony reported in St. Louis *Democrat*, August 5, 1863.
([4]) F. G. Stidger, testimony reported in "Treason Trials at Indianapolis," p. 24.
([5]) Chicago *Times*, August 1, 1864.
([6]) Capt. T. Henry Hines, *Southern Bivouac*, January, 1887.
([7]) Thompson to Benjamin, unpublished Confederate State Papers.
([8]) Gen. H. B. Carrington to Author.
([9]) F. G. Stidger, testimony reported in "Treason Trials at Indianapolis," pp. 22–28.
([10]) William Clayton, testimony reported in "Treason Trials at Indianapolis," p. 41.
([11]) Atlanta *Register*, quoted in Chicago *Tribune*, June 21, 1864.
([12]) *Atlantic Monthly*, July, 1865, p. 109.
([13]) Capt. T. Henry Hines, *Southern Bivouac*, February, 1887.
([14]) Idem.
([15]) Idem.
([16]) Quoted in *Atlantic Monthly*, July, 1865.
([17]) Gov. William Bross, "Biographical Sketch of the late Gen. B. J. Sweet," p. 18.
([18]) Captain Thurley to Gov. William Bross, quoted in "Biographical Sketch of the late Gen. B. J. Sweet."

CHAPTER XIX.

SILENT FORCES.

IN the War of the Rebellion forces other than those in arms, marshalled upon the battle-field, were at work to bring about final defeat to the Confederates, ultimate victory to the armies of the Union. They were forces silent and unseen, never responding to *reveille* or roll-call, never keeping step with the drum-beat, never rending the air with volleys of musketry or the thunder of the cannonade. They marshalled themselves without waiting for orders from president or general. When Jefferson Davis and his fellow-conspirators planned to overthrow the Government of the people, they took no account of the silent powers that would come unbidden into the contest to work for the discomfiture and defeat of the Confederacy, or, if they saw them, they greatly under-estimated their strength and power.

Let us keep ever in mind the truth that the war was a conflict between two systems of labor; on one side, the labor of bondmen who could be bought and sold, who were only property—so many hundred dollars' worth of flesh, bone, muscle, and brains—valued in proportion to their ability to guide the plough, wield the hoe, or their deftness in picking cotton, stripping tobacco, waiting upon master or mistress, or to become mothers. However kind the master or mistress, however tender the relation between owner and slave, the commercial value overshadowed and controlled all other considerations. Financial distress, the taking away by death of master or mistress, brought the slave to the auction-block, side by side with the master's favorite horse, his oxen and pigs. The Confederacy was established on property ownership in human beings. The laws of the seceding States were framed to meet the needs of such a system of labor. Society constructed itself upon the system, and the political and domestic economy of the Confederacy was framed upon it for conducting the war. The opposing system was that of the free men who were their own masters, each individual exercising in his own way the endowment of powers which he had received from his Creator; free to go and come, to labor or rest, enjoy the fruits of his toil, to make the most of himself.

When the war began, the great planters of the South, and the conspirators who had brought about the conflict, declared, and not without reason, that slavery would be an element of strength to the Confederacy; that while the masters would do the fighting, the slaves would still do the ploughing, cultivating, producing, and harvesting; whereas every Union soldier called from the plough, harvest-field, or workshop would be a withdrawal of so much productive labor. It was a common sentiment throughout the seceding States that the slaves would supply all necessary productions for an army not only for defence, but for an invasion of the Northern

AGRICULTURAL INDUSTRY IN THE CONFEDERACY.

States. But an army or a community cannot live upon bread alone. The States of the Confederacy were agricultural but not industrial. They had no great manufactures, but were dependent upon the Northern States or foreign countries for implements used upon the plantations, utensils in the household, or the clothing worn alike by master, mistress, and slave. Before the outbreak of the war, a member of Congress from the Southern

States said: "You want Bibles, brooms, buckets, and books, and you go to the North; you want pens, ink, wafers, envelopes, and you go to the North; you want shoes, hats, handkerchiefs, umbrellas, pocket-knives, and you go to the North; you want furniture, crockery, glassware, pianos, and you go to the North; you want toys, school-books, fashionable apparel, machinery, medicines, tombstones, and a thousand other things, and you go North for them." The Southern States manufactured nothing because labor was not free; the Northern States manufactured every article called for by the ever-increasing wants of a progressive civilization. The absolute needs of the human race are few; its wants are an ever-increasing quantity, regulated only by man's ability to satisfy them. The slave needed only clothes of the coarsest material. He consumed corn, rice, molasses, sweet-potatoes, pea-nuts, and bacon. The cotton planters of South Carolina needed no machinery except the cotton-gin; the sugar planters of Louisiana none except the mill to press the juice from the sugar-cane. Slavery degraded free labor, and it wanted no machinery to supplant human muscles and so depress the value of slaves in the market. The records of the Patent Office accorded few inventions to the slave States, while in every machine-shop in the North, journeyman and apprentice, as they watched the movement of wheels and pinions doing the work of human hands, were ever thinking of some contrivance whereby production would be quickened and cheapened. The South, with all its natural wealth of iron and coal, purchased its machinery in the North. The engineers running the locomotives upon its railroads were from the North. Seeing only the needs of the world for cotton; believing that the millwheels of New England would soon cease to turn; that grass would grow in the streets of Boston and New York, Philadelphia and Chicago; that the thousands of wage-earners in the North would be clamoring only for bread; that England would send her fleets to break any blockade that might be established to obtain cotton for her starving millions—seeing only this aspect of political economy, the conspirators brought about the appeal to arms.

We have already seen how the railroads of the Confederacy were wearing out; that there were no mills where new rails could be rolled; that the Government was wholly dependent upon England for its supplies of arms; that through the enforcement of the blockade, the increasing watchfulness on the part of the sailors, it was becoming daily more difficult for vessels to run the blockade; but beyond all this, there were powerful forces at work to bring about the inevitable result—the overthrowing of a system of labor antagonistic to the welfare of the people and an advancing civilization. The Confederate Government at Richmond, through 1864, was laying its plans for a long continuance of the struggle. Jefferson Davis and the Confederate Congress did not comprehend how swift and powerful were the silent forces at work for their overthrow.

Just before the war began a gentleman living in Alabama made an inventory of his property and its valuation in gold. He owned eight hundred acres of land, twelve grown-up slaves, and eight slave children, who were not large enough to work, but which, like colts and young pigs, had a certain market value. This was the inventory:

Eight hundred acres of land	$8,000
Twelve slaves	14,000
Eight young slaves	4,000
Cattle and farming implements	1,000
Seven mules	1,050
One horse	200
	$28,200

He was accustomed to raise sixty bales of cotton per annum, which he sold for three thousand dollars. His wants were few, and his expenses did not exceed one thousand dollars per annum. His slaves were sure to increase in number, and he could look forward to a large and constantly increasing annual income through their labor. The war had changed the aspect of affairs. In midsummer, 1864, he had the same acreage of land, but his slaves had increased; he had twenty-four able-bodied men and women besides twenty slave children. The price of cotton had changed, as had the value of everything else. This was the valuation in Confederate money and in gold:

	Confederate Money.	Gold.
Eight hundred acres of land	$40,000	$1,143
Twenty-four slaves	96,000	2,742
Twenty slave children	30,000	860
Cattle and hogs	4,000	114
Farming implements	2,500	71
Horses and mules, none—all having been impressed by the Confederate Government.		
	$172,500	$4,930

The country had been divided into districts, and an impressing agent appointed in each district, who was ordered from time to time to take such property as was not actually necessary for the support of a family. The prices were fixed by two commissioners—one appointed by the State, and one by the Confederate Government. The commissioners met every month, and gave valuation upon the property taken, giving a certificate of the Government's indebtedness. If they suspected any property had been secreted, the premises were rigorously searched.(¹)

Before the outbreak of the Rebellion the conspirators never were tired of saying "Cotton is king; it rules the world;" but in 1864 this gentleman, owning eight hundred acres of land, was not allowed by law to

"COTTON IS KING !"—A COTTON SHED IN NEW ORLEANS.

plant more than three acres with cotton-seed. One of his neighbors has written the following account of the dealings of the Confederate Government with him:

"My friend has had all his horses impressed. He is allowed by law to plant only three acres of cotton. All his meat (bacon), above one-half the usual allowance for his negroes, has been impressed. All his cattle, except oxen actually used on his farm, and milch cows *actually* giving milk, and all other cattle except sucking calves, are impressed. He is unable to obtain more than half the iron requisite for his ploughshares. His negroes have not for four years had a single blanket, but for a substitute a loose spongy fabric of home-made cotton. One of these poor substitutes for blankets is given each year to every adult negro. The children have none. He and his immediate family have only such clothing as they make from the fabric produced on their own wheels and looms, introduced in 1861 and 1862. As they have no sheep, they have no wool for blankets or anything else. . . . His property is consumed by taxation, his servants are a burden ; he has abandoned the idea of educating his children. . . . His last carpet, being cut into pieces two yards long by one wide, has gone where all his blankets and most of his coverlets have gone to eke out the limited blankets of the soldiers."(²)

Taxation, the waste of war, the depreciation of the value of slaves through the want of a market, and the continued advance of the armies of the Union, the inability to construct and employ machinery to do the work of human hands, together, were depriving the people of the Confederacy of power to continue the contest. After General Sherman entered Atlanta there was but one machine-shop and one rolling-mill remaining in the Confederacy—that at Richmond, employed not in rolling rails or building locomotives, but in turning out cannon, shot, and shells. Every locomotive destroyed, every freight car worn out or burned, was so much loss of inanimate force which could not be replaced.

The wealth of the Confederacy consisted not of money, but of land and slaves, neither of which could be converted into gold. A planter might sell his slaves, but he would receive only promises to pay, issued by the Confederate Government. He was confronted by the question as to what he should do with them. Until November, 1861, the paper currency had been accepted at its face value, but when people saw that the armies of the Union were preparing for a great struggle it began to depreciate in value. The amounts required to buy one hundred dollars in gold were: December, 1861, $120; do., 1862, $300; do., 1863, $1900; do., 1864, $5000.

In 1864 the men who raised corn and wheat would not sell it to receive pay in the promises issued by the Government, which, as we have seen, became a despotism, and sent its impressing officers to seize whatever was needed, giving in return certificates of the Government's indebtedness. The owners of slaves refused to hire them to the Government, but impressing officers took them to build intrenchments, drive teams, and cook for the soldiers. The States had seceded that slavery might be established forever, and that under it the conspirators might retain political power; but now slavery was disappearing under the silent forces, and far-seeing men were looking forward to the hour when through the utter exhaustion of the material wealth of the country it would, with the Confederacy as a form of Government, go down before the continued victories of the armies under Grant and Sherman. Jefferson Davis and the members of his Cabinet, however, in midsummer of 1864, were not looking for any such result. The Democratic party of the North had raised the cry that there must be peace at any price, that the South would accept peace on reasonable terms. President Lincoln did not believe that Jefferson Davis would consent to a peace on any terms except the absolute independence of the

WEAVING IN THE CONFEDERACY.

Confederate States. To test the matter he permitted two gentlemen, Colonel Jacques and Mr. J. R. Gilmore, to visit Richmond to see on what terms the Confederate Government would enter into negotiations for peace.

"The war must go on," said Mr. Davis, "till the last of this generation falls in his tracks, and his children seize his musket and fight his battle, unless you acknowledge our right to self-government. We are not fighting for slavery; we are fighting for independence, and that or extermination we will have."

WEAVING IN THE NORTH.

"May we suggest that a general vote of the people of both sections be allowed to be taken upon the question, and let the majority settle it?" said one of the gentlemen.

"We seceded to rid ourselves of the rule of the majority, and this would subject us to it again."

"But the majority must rule in the end, either with ballots or bullets."

"I am not so sure of that. Neither current events nor history can show that the majority rules, or ever did rule. The contrary, I think, is true. The man who should go before the Southern people with such a proposition—with any proposition which implied that the North was to

THE POWER OF FREE LABOR.

have a voice in determining the domestic relations of the South, could not live here a day; he would be hanged to the first tree without judge or jury. Say to Mr. Lincoln that I shall at any time be pleased to receive proposals for peace on the basis of our independence. It will be useless to approach me on any other."(³)

It is not probable that the members of the Confederate Government, with the comforts to be found in Richmond, had any adequate comprehension of the rapid wasting of the resources of the country, or of the hardships of the people. There was not much suffering during the first two years of the war, but in 1864 the supply of boots, shoes, clothing, pins, needles, fine thread, and the countless articles in common use was exhausted. The blockade was so stringently enforced that not many vessels could enter the carefully guarded ports of Wilmington and Charleston, the only ones held by the Confederates east of the Mississippi after Farragut had compelled the surrender of the forts at the entrance of Mobile Bay.

A lady in Alabama has pictured the daily life of women who formerly lived daintily, with household slaves to minister to every want. She was on a large plantation in the interior of the State. "We were far," she wrote, "from the border States, remote from the seaboard. Our soldiers had to be fed and clothed; our home ones had to be fed and clothed. All clothing and provisions for the slaves had to be produced and manufactured at home. Leather had to be of our own tanning. The huge bales of kerseys, osnaburgs, and boxes of heavy brogan shoes, which had been shipped from the North to clothe and shoe the slaves, were things of the past."(⁴)

Leather was made from pig-skins, tanned in a trough with oak-bark. It was a great mortification for young ladies to wear pig-skin shoes.(⁵) As no shoe-blacking or polish could be had, each family made its own of soot and cotton-seed oil and flour paste. It was again the age of homespun articles of clothing, carding cotton by hand into rolls, spinning yarn, and weaving cloth in the household loom. For coloring the cloth a cask was partly filled with vinegar and water, into which were thrown old nails, bits of iron, old horseshoes, which made a mordant for setting the colors—garnet from the roots of the pine, blue from the indigo-plant, brown from the bark of butternut.

These her words: "I doubt very much if a fine sheet could have been found in any house in our settlement when the war closed. Perhaps there was not one in the blockaded South."(⁶)

Fine white pillow-shams were cut up and made into white waists. Bed-ticking, with its stripes of blue, was used for dress goods. This the picture of the system of labor upon which the Confederacy had been established: "If a negro was sick, a doctor who was already paid was called in all haste, as planters used to engage a doctor by the year at so much for each slave, whether large or small. One negro boy called 'Jim,' about eighteen years of age, was quite sick of a fever. His master and mistress had him brought from the 'quarters' over to the dwelling-yard, and placed in the cook's cabin, so that he might be given close attention. One or the other watched him day and night (for he was a very valuable boy), and gave him medicine. On Saturday his master had to go to the city, and he asked me to help his wife and daughter care for Jim, saying as he stepped into his

"SHEEP BEGAN TO MULTIPLY UPON THE GREEN MOUNTAINS OF VERMONT."

buggy, 'Now, be careful of him, and see to it that he lacks for nothing, for if he dies I've lost one thousand dollars good as gold.' "(⁷) Behind the tenderness that cared for Jim as a human being was his commercial value as a piece of property. This property was disappearing. Wherever the Union armies marched, the slaves abandoned master and mistress to become freemen. The area of slavery was rapidly diminishing. All the rice-growing lands of Georgia and South Carolina were overrun by Northern troops. The valley of the Mississippi from New Orleans to Memphis was once more beneath the Stars and Stripes. The great army of the north-west had wrenched Atlanta from the Confederacy. The railroads were worn out; locomotives broken down. Swiftly, in 1864, the silent forces incident to the system of labor on which the Confederacy had been established were weakening and undermining the power of Jefferson Davis to continue the struggle.

Far different was the efficacy of the silent forces in the Northern States. Knowledge is power; in freedom there is energy of action. The people of the North at the beginning of the war were unprepared for a conflict. The building of batteries on Morris Island and the firing upon Fort Sumter were a surprise. When they awoke to the sad reality that war had begun, they found that they must organize great armies and furnish every needful supply. Men left the plough, laid down trowel, hammer, and plane, to become soldiers. Instead of being producers they became consumers. They must be armed, equipped, and fed. Multifarious their wants. They must have not only boots, shoes, and clothing, but knapsacks, canteens, belts, swords, guns, pistols, cannon, cartridges, tents, wagons, harnesses— all the appliances of war. Jefferson Davis and the slave propagandists reasoned correctly, that a man taken from the farms and workshops of the Northern States would diminish the number of producers, but they did not comprehend the reproductive power of a free people. They did not forecast the ability of free labor to make good the loss. Forges began to flame, and millwheels whirled as never before. Manufacturers deprived of cotton changed their machinery, adapting it for spinning and weaving of woollens to supply the soldiers with clothing. Sheep began to multiply upon the green mountains of Vermont, the granite hills of New Hampshire, and the broad prairies of the West. Jefferson Davis, in his speech at Montgomery on the evening of his inauguration as Provisional President of the Confederacy, predicted that grass would grow in the streets of Boston and New York; but never in the history of the nation was there such a busy tramping of feet and rumbling of wheels. Inventive genius was contriving new machinery to do the work of human muscles. Reaping-machines had been in use before the war, but now their music was heard in every harvest-field. No longer was there the swinging of the scythe amid the clover-blooms, but the farmer was guiding his stalwart team, and the mowing-machine was cutting the fragrant grasses, while the farmers' sons were behind the trenches of Petersburg or holding the hill at Atlanta. Everywhere there was life, activity, and unparalleled energy. There were more trains upon the railroads. Louder than ever before was the ringing of the carpenters' axes in the ship-yards of the Merrimac, the Piscataqua, and along the shores of Maine. Never before were the builders of engines for steamships so busy; never so great the demand for locomotives and railroad cars. The harbors of New York and Boston were white with sails of vessels arriving from or departing to foreign shores. Agriculture, manufactures, commerce, alike felt the mighty energy of a great free people, animated by a lofty ideal—that, cost what it might, the Rebellion should be crushed, and that which had caused it swept from the country.

While organizing and supporting great armies, while calling more than two million young men to the field, the country began the construction of a railroad from the Atlantic to the Pacific, to bind the Union indissolubly together with the bands of commerce. While the thunder of the cannonade was reverberating from the Potomac to the James, the great white dome of the Capitol of the nation was rising in its beauty and glory. A free community, having unwavering faith in itself, in its government, in the righteousness of the cause for which it was fighting—having abiding confidence in the future destiny of the republic—astonished the world by its activity and power. The faith of the nation in itself was the powerful, unseen, and silent force which was bearing it on to final victory.

In another volume we shall see how at last the Confederacy suddenly disappeared as a bubble upon a swirling stream; how slavery, which brought about the war, was swept from the land, and how out of all the waste, the desolation, sorrow, and woe there began a new and greater life of the nation from the efforts put forth in Redeeming the Republic.

NOTES TO CHAPTER XIX.

(¹) G. S. Plumley, *Harper's Magazine*, August, 1864.
(²) Idem.
(³) J. W. Draper, "The Civil War in America," vol. iii., p. 474.
(⁴) Parthenia Antoinette Hayne, "A Blockaded Family," p. 15.
(⁵) Idem.
(⁶) Idem, p. 115.
(⁷) Idem.

INDEX.

(C, *Confederate;* U, *Union.*)

ABBOTT, Colonel (U.), 336.
Abbott, J. H., Sergeant (U.), 184.
Alabama Regiment (C.), the Thirty-second, 232; the Forty-eighth, 232.
Alden, Captain (U.), 383.
Alexander, Captain (U.), 280.
Ames's division (U.), 142, 146, 151, 178.
Anderson, Captain (U.), 430.
Anderson, Colonel (U.), 200.
Anderson, Colonel (C.), 398.
Anderson, General (C.), 95, 98, 100.
Anderson, Mr. (C.), 433.
Anderson, Robert, Major (U.), 34.
Anderson's corps (C.), 315.
Armand, Colonel (C.), 54.
Armstrong, Lieutenant (C.), 309.
Army of the Cumberland (U.), 199, 208, 215, 231, 254, 343, 405, 413.
Army of the James (U.), 140.
Army of the Ohio (U.), 199, 208, 215, 231, 236, 336, 405, 415.
Army of the Potomac (U.), 73, 97, 139, 199, 208, 374.
Army of the Tennessee (U.), 199, 208, 216, 231, 405, 413.
Atkinson, Sidney (U.), 151.
Audenreid, Major (U.), 13.
Augur, C. C., Gen. (U.), 283.
Averill, John T., Gen. (U.), 261, 267, 270, 433, 436.
Ayres's brigade (U.), 102, 122, 181.

BAILEY, JOSEPH, Colonel (U.), 62, 65.
Baird, Absalom, Gen. (U.), 416.
Baird's division (U.), 17, 416.
Baldwin, Captain (U.), 296.
Banks, N. P., Gen. (U.), 48, 53, 56, 58, 73, 112, 294.
Barlow, Francis C., Gen. (U.), 109, 116, 186, 189.

Barlow's division (U.), 104, 107, 116, 324, 327, 358.
Barry, General (U.), 240.
Bartlett's brigade (U.), 102, 181.
Barton's brigade (C.), 22, 140.
Bate, General (C.), 239, 244.
Bate's division (C.), 344, 347, 349.
Battery: Arnold's (U.), 109; Battery B. (U.), 56; the Chicago Mercantile (U.), 53; De Gress's (U.), 355; the Eighth Michigan (U.), 346, 354; the First Iowa (U.), 240; the First United States (U.), 56; the First Vermont (U.), 56; the Fourth United States (U.), 138; the Fourteenth Ohio (U.), 349; Hooper's (U.), 354; Klaus's (U.), 53; McKnight's (U.), 369; McMahon's (C.), 53; Metcalf's (U.), 119; Nims's (U.), 53, 57; the Ninth Indiana (U.), 56; Pennington's (U.), 274; Prescott's (U.), 416; Simonson's Indiana (U.), 244; the Tenth Massachusetts (U.), 186; the Twenty-fifth New York (U.), 56; Valvedere (C.), 57; William's Third Ohio (U.), 346, 354.
Battle's brigade (C.), 117.
Battles: Atlanta, 348; Atlanta, siege of, 401; Bermuda Hundred, 137; Cold Harbor, 178; Dallas, 240; Drewry's Bluff, 142; Dug Gap, 213; Ezra Church, 405; Fort Morgan, bombardment of, 386; Fort Pillow, 38; Fort Powell, bombardment of, 379, 397; Hanover, 157; Hawes's Store, 166; Jonesborough, 414; Kenesaw, 254; Louisa Court-house, 273; Monocacy River, 280; New Hope Church, 232; New Market, 262; North Anna, 161; Olustee, 22; Paducah, 37; Peach-tree Creek, 344; Petersburg, siege of, 324, 358; Pickett's Mill, 236; Piedmont, 266; Pleasant Hill, 58; Resaca, 214; Spottsylvania, 100; Totopotomoy, 177; Wilderness, 86.

INDEX.

Beard, Colonel (C.), 54.
Beauregard, P. G. T., Gen. (C.), 22, 38; at Weldon, 133; near Petersburg, 141; sends message to Jefferson Davis, 142; at Drewry's Bluff, 142, 145, 150; at Bermuda Hundred, 151; sends despatch to Bragg, 312, 328; sends a brigade to Wise, 314; sends telegrams to Lee, 319; sends troops to Petersburg, 324; advantage of position, 327; reasons for his view of Grant's movements, 331; credit due for holding Petersburg, 332; sends to Lee for troops, 373.
Beaver, Colonel (U.), 190.
Beckwith, General (U.), 200.
Bell's brigade (C.), 41.
Belmont, Mr. (U.), 450.
* Benedict's brigade (U.), 55.
Benning's division (C.), 91.
Bidwell's brigade (U.), 286.
Birney, General (U.), 117, 124, 186.
Birney's division (U.), 91, 104, 108, 110, 116, 124, 320, 324.
Blair, F. P., Gen. (U.), 208, 243, 351, 355, 405, 414.
Blair, Mr. (U.), 286.
Booth, L. F., Major (C.), 38, 41.
Bradford, Governor of Maryland (U.), 288.
Bradford, Major (C.), 41, 42.
Bragg, Braxton, Gen. (C.), 17, 73, 133, 203, 207, 312, 340.
Bray, Benjamin (U.), 150.
Breckinridge, John C., Gen. (C.), 158, 163, 262, 265, 267, 274, 444.
Breckinridge, Robert J. (U.), 444.
Breckinridge's division (C.), 190.
Breeze, Captain (U.), 48.
Brooks, Colonel (U.), 109.
Brooks, General (U.), 190.
Brooks's brigade (U.), 104, 108, 116, 139, 146, 148, 178, 182, 320.
Brough, John, Mr. (U.), 442.
Brown, Captain (U.), 280.
Brown, Colonel (U.), 109.
Brown, General (C.), 406.
Brown, Governor of Georgia (C.), 221, 258, 340.
Brown, Lieutenant (U.), 383.
Brown, Major (C.), 398.
Brown's brigade (U.), 116.
Bryan's brigade (C.), 182.
Buchanan, Admiral (C.), 384, 391, 394.
Buchanan, James, President (U.), 444.
Buchell's cavalry (C.), 56.
Buckner, Simon B., Gen. (C.), 427.
Buillet, Judge (C.), 446.

Burbridge, Stephen G., Gen. (U.), 427.
Burnham, General (U.), 183.
Burnside, Ambrose E., Maj.-gen. (U.), at Annapolis, 73; at Washington, 75; at the Wilderness, 86; at Spottsylvania, 121; at Ox Ford, 162; puts himself under Meade, 164; at Cold Harbor, 186, 190; at Petersburg, 322, 366, 370.
Butler, B. F., Gen. (U.), at Fortress Monroe, 73, 77; at City Point, 99, 103, 131, 137, 312; receives instructions from Grant, 133; at Bermuda Hundred, 138, 141; declines plan proposed by Smith and Gilmore, 141; at Drewry's Bluff, 142, 146, 150; withdraws to Bermuda Hundred, 151; sends troops to Grant, 178; at Petersburg, 370.
Butler, Mr. (C.), 48.
Butler's brigade, (C.), 166, 178, 273.
Butterfield's division (U.), 220, 232.
Byrd's brigade (U.), 336.
Byrnes, Colonel (U.), 190.

Cabell, Sergeant (C.), 264.
Cameron, General (U.), 55.
Cameron's brigade (U.), 254, 336.
Canby, General (U.), 112, 380.
Candy's brigade (U.), 232.
Canty's division (C.), 208, 212.
Carlin, General (U.), 416.
Carlin's division (U.), 415.
Carney, Joe, Lieutenant (C.), 222.
Carr, Billy (C.), 222.
Carrington, Colonel (U.), 443.
Carroll, General (U.), 122.
Carroll's brigade (U.), 110, 117.
Casement, Colonel (U.), 339.
Casey, David (U.), 193.
Casey, Mr. (C.), 48.
Castleman, John B., Capt. (C.), 442, 448.
Chambers, John C., Lieut.-col. (U.), 150.
Chapman's brigade (U.), 127.
Chase, Secretary (U.), 444.
Cheatham, B. F., Gen. (C.), 257, 405, 417.
Cheatham's corps (C.), 17, 343, 345, 347, 354, 357.
Churchill's division (C.), 56.
Clark, Adjutant-general (U.), 349.
Clay, Clement C. (C.), 440, 447.
Cleary, W. W. (C.), 440.
Cleburne's division (C.), 17, 236, 344, 347, 351, 354, 357, 416.
Clendennis, Colonel (U.), 278.
Clingman's brigade (C.), 149, 151, 181.
Cochrane, John C., Gen. (U.), 444.
Cole, Edwin (U.), 150.

INDEX.   471

Cole, William D. (U.), 150.
Collins, John, pilot (U.), 386.
Colquitt, General (C.), 22.
Colquitt's brigade (C.), 142, 146, 370.
Comstock, Colonel (U.), 98.
Confederacy, song of the, 1; object of the, 6; dealing in cotton, 47, 49; principle on which established, 454.
Connecticut Regiment (U.), the Seventh, 22; the Second, 182; the Eighteenth, 263; the Tenth, 324; First Artillery, 366.
Cooper, Adjutant-general (C.), 342.
Corse's brigade (C.), 142, 149, 151.
Couch, General (U.), 434.
Coulter's brigade (U.), 102.
Cox, General (U.), 215, 239, 254.
Cox's division (U.), 336, 340.
Craven, Captain (U.), 386.
Crawford's division (U.), 86, 102, 110, 158, 181, 327.
Crittenden's division (U.), 162, 181.
Crook, General (U.), 77, 260, 267, 269, 433.
Cruft's division (U.), 17.
Curtin, A. G., Governor of Pennsylvania (U.), 434.
Curtin's brigade (U.), 326.
Custer, George A., Gen. (U.), 25, 29, 178, 273.
Custer's brigade (U.), 126, 167, 178.
Custis, Mr. (C.), 128.
Cutler's division (U.), 102, 110, 158, 160, 181.

DAHLGREN, ULRICH, Col. (U.), 25, 29.
Daniel, General (C.), 118, 121.
Davies's brigade (U.), 126.
Davis, General (U.), 336, 405, 415.
Davis, Jefferson (C.), calls for more men, 4; sends orders to Beauregard, 134; at Drewry's Bluff, 142; appoints Johnston to command of army, 204; removes him, 340; favors movement of Wheeler at Atlanta, 406; views of political affairs, 439; orders to Colonel Hines, 441; does not comprehend powers at work to defeat the Confederacy, 454, 460.
Davis's division (U.), 17, 235.
Dayton, Mr., Minister to France (U.), 296.
De Bray's cavalry (C.), 53, 56.
De Gress, Captain (U.), 355.
Dearing, General (C.), 146, 316.
Delaware Regiment, the Second (U.), 116.
Denison's brigade (U.), 102.
Devin's brigade (U.), 126, 178, 182.
Dickey, Captain (U.), 54, 56.
Dodge, General (U.), 208, 236, 349, 414.
Dole, General (C.), 182.

Dole's brigade (C.), 110.
Donaldson, Commander (U.), 383.
Donaldson, General (U.), 200.
Douty, Jacob, Lieutenant (U.), 370.
Drayton, Captain (U.), 383, 385.
Duane, Major (U.), 315, 334.
Duckworth, Colonel (C.), 34.
Duffie, General (U.), 267, 270.
Dwight's brigade (U.), 55.

EARLY, JUBAL A., Gen. (C.), at the Wilderness, 93; at Spottsylvania, 100, 104, 107; at the Totopotomoy, 177; at Cold Harbor, 181; moving west, 268; at Lynchburg, 270, 274; moves towards Frederick, 278; at Monocacy River, 280; moving towards Washington, 282; reasons for giving up assault of Washington, 285; in Shenandoah Valley, 433, 437.
Echols, John, Gen. (C.), 262, 265.
Echols's division (C.), 277.
Edie, Lieutenant-colonel (U.), 415.
Egan's brigade (U.), 159, 324.
Ellet, General (U.), 50.
Elliott's brigade (C.), 370.
Emory, General (U.), 283.
Emory's division (U.), 55.
Epps, Dr., 137.
Este's brigade (U.), 416.
Evans's brigade (C.), 117.
Ewell, General (C.), 76, 82, 86, 100, 122, 124.

FARRAGUT, Admiral (U.), 302, 379.
Featherstone's division (C.), 254.
Fernald, Corporal (U.), 150.
Ferrero, General (U.), 370, 373.
Field, Colonel (C.), 222.
Field's division (C.), 102, 182, 328.
Finnegan, General (C.), 22.
Fish, John D., Capt. (U.), 119.
Fitzhugh, Captain (C.), 435.
Fitzpatrick, Thomas, Coxswain (U.), 390.
Floyd, John B. (C.), 440.
Force's brigade (U.), 346, 353.
Forrest, N. B., Gen. (C.), 13, 17, 30, 41, 43, 429.
Forts: Anderson, 34; Darling, 145; De Russey, 285; Donelson, 33; Gaines, 377; Morgan, 377, 452; Pillow, 38; Powell, 377; Powhatan, 137; Slocum, 285; Stevens, 285.
Foster, General (U.), 369.
Franklin, General (U.), 49, 53, 55.
Freeman, Martin (U.), 386.
Fremont, Charles, Gen. (U.), 444.
French, General (C.), 10.

Fullam, Mr. (C.), 309.
Fuller, General (U.), 349.
Fuller's division (U.), 348, 350, 355.

GARRARD, General (U.), 236, 248, 258, 401, 410, 413.
Garrard's division (U.), 335, 343.
Geary, General (U.), 216.
Geary's division (U.), 282, 343.
Georgia Regiment, the Sixty-sixth (C.), 350.
Getty's division (U.), 86, 182, 286.
Gherardi, Lieutenant (U.), 388.
Gibbon, General (U.), 186, 189.
Gibbon's division (U.), 104, 108, 110, 116, 324, 358.
Gibbs's brigade (U.), 126.
Gile, Captain (U.), 349.
Gillem, General (U.), 429.
Gillmore, Quincy A., Gen. (U.), 21, 133, 138, 141, 140, 312, 314.
Gilmor, Harry (C.), 288.
Gilmore, J. R., Mr. (U.), 460.
Gilmore, Major (C.), 435.
Goodman, Captain (C.), 41.
Gordon, James B., Gen. (C.), 92, 117, 128.
Gordon's division (C.), 117, 128, 181, 277, 280.
Gorringe, Captain (U.), 61.
Gould, Colonel (U.), 327.
Govan's brigade (C.), 415.
Gowin, William (U.), 310.
Gracie's brigade (C.), 141, 147, 370.
Graham, General (C.), 314.
Granberry, General (C.), 239.
Granberry's brigade (C.), 146.
Granger, Gordon, Gen. (U.), 380, 398.
Grant, Ulysses S., Gen. (U.), appointed Lieutenant general, 68; meets Meade at Brandy Station, 71; meets Sherman at Nashville, 72; views of military operations, 73, 199; at Fortress Monroe, 74, 133; at Germania Ford, 81; at the Wilderness, 85; at Spottsylvania, 97; directs military movements, 104; unfolds plan of campaign, 112; sends letter to General Halleck, 112; changes position of troops, 122; lays new plans, 153; movements criticised, 161; remarks on his position, 103; sends despatch to Halleck, 164; changes base of supplies, 165; orders Sheridan to move towards Mechanicsville, 166; moves towards Cold Harbor, 167; orders Butler to send troops, 178; orders assault at Cold Harbor, 186; remarks on the battle, 186; sends letters to General Lee, 196; views of the assault, 197; orders pontoons sent to the James, 198; directs Sigel to move up the Shenandoah, 260, 262; sends orders to Hunter, 266; directs Sheridan to move towards Lynchburg, 278; sends troops to Halleck, 278; sends Ord to Washington, 282; orders Emory to Washington, 283; difficulty of transferring army to Petersburg, 313, 314; issues orders to Butler, 316, 331; begins the siege of Petersburg, 334; plan of siege, 358; at Bailey's Creek, 369; sends Mott's division to Petersburg, 370; failure of plan at Petersburg, 374; hears of evacuation of Atlanta, 418.

Greeley, Horace (U.), 443, 446.
Greeley, Lieutenant-colonel (U.), 324.
Green, General (C.), 53, 56, 61.
Greene, Lieutenant (U.), 383.
Gregg, David McM., Gen. (U.), 273.
Gregg, General (U.), 167.
Gregg's brigade (C.), 91.
Gregg's cavalry (U.), 78, 99, 124.
Gregg's division (U.), 25, 126, 166, 182.
Griffin's division (U.), 102, 158, 181, 326, 333.
Grover's division (U.), 50.
Guthrie, Mr. (U.), 200.

HAGOOD's brigade (C.), 134, 137, 139.
Halleck, H. W., Gen. (U.), 47, 67, 73, 278.
Hallett, General (U.), 167.
Hampton, Wade, Gen. (C.), 108, 278.
Hampton's division (C.), 166, 361.
Hancock, W. S., Gen. (U.), commands second corps of Army of the Potomac, 76; at the Wilderness, 85, 86, 87, 91, 95; at Spottsylvania, 97, 104, 107, 110, 115, 117; marches towards the North Anna, 153; reaches it, 158; his position there, 162; at Cold Harbor, 184, 186; moves towards Petersburg, 315; receives message from Grant, 320; remarks on Smith's failure to attack, 323; reaches Bailey's Creek, 369.
Hardee, General (C.), 342, 344, 355, 414.
Hardee's corps (C.), 207, 214, 220, 221, 225, 235, 240, 244, 348, 347, 350, 355, 416.
Harris, Colonel (C.), 328.
Harris, Governor of Tennessee (C.), 30.
Harris, Mr. (C.), 451.
Harris's brigade (C.), 118.
Harrow's division (U.), 240, 348, 405.
Hascall's division (U.), 239.
Hawkins, Colonel (U.), 34.
Hawley's brigade (C.), 22.
Hay, John (U.), 447.
Hayes, Rutherford B., Col. (U.), 261.
Hazen's brigade (U.), 236.

INDEX.   473

Hazen's division (U.), 414.
Heckman, General (U.), 138, 140, 147, 149.
Heckman's brigade (U.), 138, 140, 146.
Heth's division (C.), 88, 91, 108, 120, 181, 369.
Hickenlooper, General (U.), 349.
Hicks, S. G., Col. (U.), 34, 37.
Hill, A. P., Gen. (C.), 76; at the Wilderness, 82, 85, 91, 93; at Spottsylvania, 117, 118; at Cold Harbor, 182; at Petersburg, 358, 361.
Hill, Captain (C.), 264.
Hill's corps (C.), 160, 190, 268, 315, 331.
Hindman's division (C.), 236.
Hines, Thomas H., Col. (C.), 440.
Hinks, General (U.), 137, 142, 146, 151, 316, 320.
Hoffman's brigade (U.), 160.
Hoke, General (C.), 134, 147.
Hoke's brigade (C.), 158, 163, 182.
Hoke's division (C.), 146, 149, 319, 370.
Holcombe, James P. (C.), 440, 447.
Hood, John B., Gen. (C.), at Resaca, 215, 220; at Cassville, 226; sends message to Johnson, 236; falls back to Zion's Church, 254; supersedes Johnston, 342; plan of battle at Atlanta, 343, 344; moves against McPherson, 347; in battle, 353, 354; at Atlanta, 401; discovers plan of Stoneman, 404; thinks Sherman is retreating, 413; orders troops to Jonesborough, 414; orders Hardee back to Atlanta, 415; collects his army at Lovejoy's Station, 421.
Hood's corps (C.), 207, 214, 221, 225, 232, 235.
Hooker, General (U.), 94, 207, 208, 215, 225, 231, 235, 254, 405.
Hovey's division (U.), 215.
Howard, O. O., Gen. (U.), 138, 208, 215, 232, 235, 254, 405.
Humphreys, General (U.), 85, 92, 102, 120, 125.
Hunt, General (U.), 334.
Hunt, Mr. (U.), 450.
Hunter, General (U.), succeeds Sigel, 260; at Staunton, 267; decides to march to Lynchburg, 268; retreats down Kanawha Valley, 270, 274, 432; moves east from Wheeling, 286.
Hunter, Senator (C.), 140.
Hunter's brigade (U.), 182.
Hunton, General (C.), 146.
Hurlburt, Stephen A., Gen. (U.), 13, 430.

ILLINOIS REGIMENT (U.), the Eighth Cavalry, 278, 280, 284; the Twelfth, 356; the Twentieth, 346; the Thirtieth, 346; the Thirty-first, 346; the Forty-fifth, 346; the Fifty-fifth, 356; the Sixty-fourth, 349, 350, 352; the Sixty-sixth, 356; the Sixty-seventh, 53; the One Hundred and Seventh, 356; the One Hundred and Eleventh, 356.
Imboden, J. D., Gen. (C.), 263, 265, 267, 270, 277, 434.
Indiana Regiment (U.), the Forty-ninth, 57; the Sixty-seventh, 53.
Iowa Regiment, the Fourteenth (U.), 57.

JACKSON, General (C.), 434.
Jackson, Stonewall, Gen. (C.), 85, 125, 200, 260.
Jacques, Colonel (U.), 460.
Jenkins, Captain (U.), 383.
Jenkins, General (C.), 261.
Johnson, Andrew (U.), 445.
Johnson, Bradley T., Gen. (C.), 277.
Johnson, Edward, Major-gen. (C.), 117, 122.
Johnson, General (C.), 278, 282, 406.
Johnson's (Bushrod) brigade (C.), 139, 149, 151.
Johnson's division (C.), 102, 110, 116, 118, 324, 358, 370.
Johnson's division (U.), 236, 239.
Johnston, Captain (C.), 394.
Johnston, Joseph E., Gen. (C.), at Dalton, 17, 73, 199, 209; at the Wilderness, 92; appointed commander of army, 204; neglects to guard Snake Creek Gap, 209; withdraws to Resaca, 211; orders artillery to open fire, 216; orders troops to Calhoun, 219; retreats from Resaca, 221; orders troops to concentrate at Cassville, 225; consults with officers, 226; sends message to General Jackson, 231; describes battle of New Hope Church, 232; moves south-west, 235; remarks on battle of Pickett's Mill, 239; moving towards Lost Mountain, 243; at Pine Mountain, 244; at Kenesaw, 248; in battle, 254; abandons Marietta, 258; builds new fortifications, 335; retreats across the Chattahoochee, 340; superseded by Hood, 342.
Johnston, R. D., Gen. (C.), 121.
Johnston's (R. D.) brigade (C.), 117.
Jones, Colonel (C.), 232.
Jones, William E., Gen. (C.), 261, 266.
Jouett, Lieutenant (U.), 388, 389.
Judah, Henry M., Gen. (U.), 215.

KAULFUS, Dr. (C.), 446.
Kautz, General (U.), 134, 137, 140, 142, 146, 151, 314, 316, 320, 361.
Keith, Lawrence M., Col. (C.), 181.
Kell, Mr. (C.), 304, 307.

Kemper, General (C.), 153.
Kentucky Regiment, the Nineteenth (U.), 53.
Kershaw's brigade (C.), 102, 118, 158, 181.
Kershaw's division (C.), 328, 331, 369.
Kilpatrick, Judson, Gen. (U.), 25, 29, 215, 219, 406, 409.
Kinney, John C., Lieut. (U.), 389.
Kitching's brigade (U.), 122, 123, 124.
Knights of the Golden Circle, 441.
Knowles, Quartermaster (U.), 386.

LAIRD, Captain (U.), 349, 352.
Lamson, John (U.), 390.
Landram, General (U.), 53.
Lane's brigade (C.), 117, 120.
Le Roy, Commander (U.), 383.
Ledlie's division (U.), 327, 370, 373.
Lee, Fitz-Hugh, Gen. (C.), 125, 273, 362.
Lee, General (U.), 53.
Lee, Joe P., Capt. (C.), 222.
Lee, Robert E., Gen. (C.), constancy of army to, 6; near Richmond, 25; sends flag of truce to General Meade, 29; condition of his army, 73, 76; at the Wilderness, 82; at Spottsylvania, 98, 107, 118, 153; transfers troops to Richmond, 103; loss at Spottsylvania, 116, 124; changes position of troops, 121, 122; learns of General Stuart's death, 131; receives troops from Beauregard, 152; at Hanover Junction, 157; at the North Anna, 161; at Cold Harbor, 178; replies to Grant's letters, 196; orders Breckinridge to come to his assistance, 266; learns of Jones's defeat at Piedmont, 267; sends Early west, 268; sends Hampton and Fitz-Hugh Lee to resist Sheridan, 273; design in sending Early west, 274; learns of Grant's movement, 315; position of his army, 319, 331; tries to discover Grant's position, 331; directions to Hill at Petersburg, 358; sends Mahone against Kautz and Wilson, 362; strengthens fortifications at Petersburg, 374.
Lee, S. D., Gen. (C.), 340, 405, 414.
Lee, W. H. F., Gen. (C.), 331, 361, 370.
Lee's (Fitz-Hugh) division (C.), 99, 166, 181.
Leggett's division (U.), 346, 348, 351, 355.
Letcher, John, Governor of Virginia (C.), 267, 432.
Lewis, John E. (U.), 193.
Lewis's brigade (C.), 414, 416.
Liddell, General (C.), 58.
Lieb, Captain (U.), 280.
Lincoln, Abraham, calls for more men, 3; orders expedition to Jacksonville, 21; appoints Grant Lieutenant-general, 68; at Washington, 75; meets troops at Washington, 283; at Fort Stevens, 285; receives news of evacuation of Atlanta, 418; criticism of, 443, 445, 450; renominated, 445; letter to Confederate commissioners, 447; sends men to confer with Davis, 460.
Llewellyn, Mr. (C.), 308.
Logan, John A., Gen. (U.), at Resaca, 208, 215, 219; at Pickett's Mill, 236; at Dallas, 240; at Kenesaw, 254; at Atlanta, 346; takes McPherson's place, 352; cheers Fifteenth Corps, 356; at Ezra Church, 405; at Jonesborough, 414.
Long, Mr. (C.), 450.
Longstreet, James, Gen. (C.), 18, 76, 82, 86, 182.
Longstreet's corps (C.), 268.
Loring, General (C.), 10, 18, 251, 405.
Loring's division (C.), 405.
Louisiana Regiment (C.), Crescent, 54; the Eighteenth, 54; the Twenty-eighth, 54.
Lovell, General (C.), 342.

MAHONE's division (C.), 108, 358, 362, 370.
Maine Regiment (U.), the Fifth, 118; the Ninth, 149; the Sixteenth, 101; the Twentieth, 102.
Maitland, Mr. (U.), 61.
Mallory, Mr. (C.), 128.
Malloy's brigade (U.), 346, 348, 355.
Maney's division (C.), 344, 347, 351, 354, 357.
Manigault's brigade (C.), 355.
Marchand, Captain (U.), 383.
Marine Brigade (U.), 50.
Martin's cavalry (C.), 219.
Martindale's division (U.), 178, 182, 185, 320.
Maryland brigade (U.), 124.
Maryland Regiment (U.), the Eleventh, 280; the Third Regiment of Potomac Home Guards, 280.
Massachusetts Regiment (U.), the Twelfth, 102; the Thirteenth, 101; the Eighteenth, 102; the Twenty-third, 148; the Twenty-fourth, 263; the Twenty-fifth, 151, 193, 196; the Twenty-seventh, 140; the Twenty-eighth, 369; the Thirty-fourth, 266; the Thirty-ninth, 101; the Fifty-seventh, 325.
McCann, Lieutenant (U.), 383.
McCausland, General (C.), 268, 270, 282, 284, 434.
McClellan, George B., Gen. (U.), 67, 167, 173, 313, 451.
McCook, Daniel, Gen. (U.), 281, 402.
McCulloch's brigade (C.), 41.

INDEX. 475

McGevney, Colonel (C.), 222.
McGowan, General (C.), 121.
McGowan's brigade (C.), 118.
McLaughlin, Colonel (C.), 264.
McLean, Lieutenant (U.), 434.
McLean's brigade (U.), 236, 239.
McMillan's brigade (U.), 55.
McPherson, James B., Gen. (U.), commands Sixteenth Corps in attack on Meridian, 13; commands Army of Tennessee, 199; at Snake Creek Gap, 209, 211; at Resaca, 214; at Cassville, 225; at Pickett's Mill, 235; at New Hope, 240; at Kenesaw, 244, 254; approaches Atlanta, 340, 343; moves against the city, 344; killed, 351.
Meade, George G., Gen. (U.), consents to raid on Libby Prison, 25; receives message from Lee, 29; meets Grant, 71; at the Wilderness, 85, 88, 92; at Spottsylvania, 97, 103, 108; order to Wright, 118; disagreement with Sheridan, 124; at Cold Harbor, 164, 167, 181; issues congratulatory order to Sixth Corps, 184; sends order to Hancock, 316; assumes command at Petersburg, 324; preparations for assault, 328; order to attack, 332; orders movement of Second Corps, 358; consents to mine at Petersburg, 366; objects to colored troops leading assault, 370; orders withdrawal of troops, 374.
Memminger, Mr. (C.), 128.
Mercer's brigade (C.), 207.
Merritt's brigade (U.), 178.
Merritt's division (U.), 25, 99, 125.
Metcalf, Lieutenant (U.), 119.
Michigan Regiment (U.), the First, 102; the Fifth, 274; the Sixteenth, 102; the Twenty-sixth, 116; the Twenty-seventh, 196; the Forty-eighth, 369.
Miles, Nelson A., Gen. (U.), 369.
Miles's brigade (U.), 109, 116, 190.
Mink, Captain (U.), 160.
Minnesota Regiment, the First (U.), 282.
Missouri Regiment (U.), the Sixth, 356; the Twelfth, 216; the Eighteenth, 349, 350; the Twenty-fourth, 57.
Mitchell, John (U.), 196.
Montgomery, Colonel (C.), 22.
Moor, Colonel (U.), 263.
Moore, Governor of Alabama (C.), 377.
Moore's brigade (U.), 416.
Morgan, John H., Gen. (C.), 424, 443.
Morgan's division (U.), 416.
Morrell's brigade (U.), 348.
Morris, H. O., Col. (U.), 190.

Mott's division (U.), 91, 104, 110, 115, 117, 358, 370.
Mouton's division (C.), 53.
Mower's brigade (U.), 56.
Mullany, Commander (U.), 384, 391.
Mulligan, Colonel (U.), 277.
Munson, Colonel (U.), 346.
Mutual Protection Society, 441.

NAPOLEON, LOUIS, Emperor of France, 47, 441.
Navy (U.), 9.
Neill, General (U.), 182.
Neill's brigade (U.), 110.
Neill's division (U.), 328.
New Hampshire Regiment, the Fifth (U.), 190.
New Jersey Regiment, the Ninth (U.), 140, 148.
New York Regiment (U.), the Twenty-first, 118; the Forty-fourth, 102, 111; the Fifty-first, 280; the Sixty-first, 116; the Sixty-fourth, 116; the Sixty-sixth, 116; the Seventy-third, 369; the Eighty-third, 102; the Ninety-seventh, 102; the One Hundredth, 281; the One Hundred and Fourth, 101; the One Hundred and Twelfth, 149; the One Hundred and Twenty-first, 118.
Newspapers the New York Tribune, 443, 446.
Newton's division (U.), 216, 239, 343.
Nields, Ensign (U.), 389.
Noble, Colonel (C.), 54.
Northrop, Colonel (C.), 131.

OHIO MILITIA (U.), the One Hundred and Forty-ninth, 280; the One Hundred and Fifty-ninth, 280.
Ohio Regiment (U.), the Seventh, 232; the Twentieth, 352, 354; the Twenty-seventh, 349, 352; the Thirty-ninth, 349, 352; the Forty-eighth, 53; the Fifty-seventh, 356; the Sixty-third, 349; the Seventy-eighth, 352, 356; the Eighty-first, 349, 356; the Eighty-third, 53, 54; the Ninety-sixth, 53; the One Hundred and Third, 339; the One Hundred and Twenty-third, 263.
O'Neil, Lieutenant (U.), 34.
O'Neill, Captain (U.), 196.
Ord, Edward O., Gen. (U.), 282.
Osterhaus, General (U.), 216, 240.
Ould, Mr. (C.), 140.
Owen's brigade (C.), 117.

PAGE, R. L., Gen. (C.), 399.

Page's Artillery (C.), 117.
Palmer, John M., Gen. (U.), 17, 208, 235, 254, 257.
Palmer's division (U.), 343.
Parson's division (C.), 56.
Patrick, General (U.), 123.
Paul, Colonel (C.), 373.
Peace Democrats, 3, 5, 489, 442, 445, 447, 451.
Pegram's brigade (C.), 92, 117.
Pendleton, Mr. (U.), 451.
Pennington, Captain (U.), 274.
Pennsylvania Regiment (U.), the Eleventh, 102; the Sixteenth, 284; the Forty-eighth, 366, 370; the Fifty-third, 116; the Eighty-first, 116; the Eighty-third, 102; the Eighty-eighth, 102; the Ninetieth, 102; the Ninety-fifth, 118; the Ninety-sixth, 118; the Ninety-ninth, 369; the One Hundred and Seventh, 360; the One Hundred and Eighteenth, 102; the One Hundred and Fortieth, 116; the One Hundred and Forty-fifth, 116; the One Hundred and Forty-eighth, 116, 190; the One Hundred and Eighty-third, 116, 369.
Perrin, General (C.), 118, 121.
Perrin's brigade (C.), 118.
Peterkin, Rev. Mr., 131.
Pickett, General (C.), 133, 137.
Pickett's division (C.), 102, 153, 163, 182.
Pierce's brigade (U.), 159.
Pleasants, Colonel (U.), 366, 370.
Polignac, General (C.), 50, 56.
Polk, Leonidas, Gen. (C.), 10, 17, 208, 214, 219, 221, 225, 235, 244.
Porter, David D., Admiral (U.), 48, 58, 65.
Potter's division (U.), 120, 163, 181, 325, 373.
Prestman, Colonel (C.), 335, 342.
Preston, Colonel (C.), 5.
Price, Edwin, Coxswain (U.), 390.

RAMSEUR, General (C.), 118, 121.
Ramseur's brigade (C.), 118.
Ramseur's division (C.), 277, 280, 284.
Ransom, Robert, Gen. (C.), 141, 146.
Ransom, T. E. G., Gen. (U.), 53, 414.
Ransom's division (C.), 147.
Raum, Colonel (U.), 406.
Rawson's brigade (C.), 370, 373.
Raymond, Captain (U.), 150, 351.
Red River Expedition, 44.
Rees, Henry, Sergeant (U.), 370.
Reese, Captain (U.), 219.
Reilly's brigade (U.), 254.
Rice, James C., Gen. (U.), 111, 160.
Rickett's division (U.), 86, 182, 278, 280, 281.

Robinson's division (U.), 86, 102.
Rodes, General (C.), 118.
Rodes's division (C.), 93, 102, 110, 117, 181, 277, 280.
Rosecrans, General (U.), 443.
Rosser's brigade (C.), 273.
Rousseau, General (U.), 401.
Russell's brigade (U.), 110, 111, 118.
Russell's division (U.), 166, 182, 185.

SANDERS, GEORGE (C.), 446.
Sanderson, Colonel (U.), 443.
Scales's brigade (C.), 120.
Schneider, Edward (U.), 325.
Schofield, General (U.), at Knoxville, 18; commands Army of Ohio, 199; moves towards Resaca, 208, 214, 219; at Cassville, 225; near Dallas, 231, 235; near Lost Mountain, 244; at Kenesaw, 254; crosses the Chattahoochee, 336; approaches Atlanta, 340, 345; attacks, 349; receives order from Sherman, 356; at Rough and Ready, 415.
Scott, Winfield S., Gen. (U.), 67.
Scott's brigade (U.), 346, 352, 354.
Scribner's brigade (U.), 236, 239.
Seddon, Secretary (C.), 4, 440.
Sedgwick, General (U.), 76, 85, 93, 95, 103, 104.
Semmes, Raphael, Capt. (C.), 288.
Sewell, Joe (C.), 222.
Seymour, Horatio (U.), 450, 452.
Seymour, Truman, Gen. (U.), 21, 25.
Seymour's brigade (U.), 92, 93.
Shaler's brigade (U.), 92, 93.
Shaw's brigade (U.), 56.
Shepley, General (U.), 41.
Sheridan, Philip H., Gen. (U.), made commander of cavalry, 74; moving towards the Wilderness, 78; reaches it, 86; at Spottsylvania, 99, 103; at the North Anna, 165; moves towards Cold Harbor, 167; at Cold Harbor, 178, 181; disagreement with Meade, 124; orders to division commanders, 128; moves towards Lynchburg, 273; at Bailey's Creek, 369.
Sherman, William T., Gen. (U.), at Vicksburg, 10, 13, 14; escapes capture at Decatur, 13; at Memphis, 48; meets Grant at Nashville, 72; plan of campaign, 199; gives orders to McPherson and Hooker, 209; views of McPherson's course, 211; at Dug Gap, 213; at Resaca, 215; orders troops to cross Lay's Ferry, 219; at Cassville, 225. organizes an engineer corps,

228; moves against Johnston's flank, 231; at New Hope Church, 232; moves northeast, 235; at Pickett's Mill, 236; at Dallas, 240; advances towards Lost Mountain, 244, 248; at Kenesaw, 254; enters Marietta, 258; compels Johnston to fall back, 335, 340; learns that Hood has superseded Johnston, 343; consults with McPherson at Atlanta, 348; appoints Logan to take McPherson's place, 352; sends orders to Schofield, 356; plan of action at Atlanta, 401; favors plan to release prisoners at Andersonville, 402; begins siege of Atlanta, 405; pleased with action of Kilpatrick, 409; sends despatch to Halleck, 410; hears of evacuation of Atlanta, 418; enters Atlanta, 421; sends letter to Hood, 422; removes people of Atlanta, 425.

Ships: Alabama (C.), 47, 288; Ariel (U.), 294; Black Hawk (U.), 48; Brilliant (U.), 291; Brooklyn (U.), 383; Chastelaine (U.), 295; Chickasaw (U.), 384; Conrad (U.), 310; Constitution (A.), 294; Couronne (F.), 304; Courser (U.), 291; Cowslip (U.), 384; Cricket (U.), 61; Deerhound (B.), 304, 308, 309; Eastport (U.), 61; Gaines (C.), 378, Galena, (U.), 384; Golden Eagle (U.), 295; Golden Rule (U.), 295; Guerriere (B.), 295; Hartford (U.), 379, 383; Harvest Home (U.), 290, Hatteras (U.), 294, 301; Hindman (U.), 61, 66; Itasca (U.), 379, 383; Juliet (U.), 61; Kearsarge (U.), 293, 296, 301; Kennebec (U.), 383, Lackawanna (U.), 383; Lexington (U.), 58, 65; Manhattan (U.), 384; Metacomet (U.), 383; Monongahela (U.), 383; Morgan (C.), 378, Neosho (U.), 66; New Era (U.), 41, Ocmulgee (U.), 290, Octorora (U.), 379, 383; Olive Branch (U.), 41, Olive Jane (U.), 295; Oneida (U.), 384; Osage (U.), 58, 61; Ossipee (U.), 383; Palmetto (U.), 295; Parker Cooke (U.), 293; Pawpaw (U.), 34; Piosta (U.), 34; Port Royal (U.), 383; Richmond (U.), 383; San Jacinto (U.), 299; Selma (C.), 378; Seminole (U.), 383; Starlight (U.), 280; Sumter (C.), 290, 293; Tecumseh (U.), 380, 384; Tennessee (C.), 378; Thistle (C.), 440; Tonawanda (U.), 290, 292; Tuscaloosa (C.), 310; Vanderbilt (U.), 295; Wales (U.), 293; Winnebago (U.), 384; Wyoming (U.), 296.

Shirk, Lieutenant (U.), 34.
Sickel, Colonel (U.), 261.
Sigel, General (U.), 77, 260, 262, 265, 277, 284.
Skip, Colonel (U.), 263.
Sleeper, Captain (U.), 186.
Slocum, General (U.), 417.
Smith, A. J., Gen. (U.), 429.
Smith, Colonel (C.), 265.
Smith, E. Kirby, Gen. (C.), 50, 58, 340.
Smith, G. W., Gen. (C.), 343.
Smith, General (U.), 314, 316, 319.
Smith, Giles A., Gen. (U.), 216, 346, 348, 350, 352, 355.
Smith, John E., Gen. (U.), 251, 254, 406.
Smith, Morgan L., Gen. (U.), 240, 405.
Smith, William F., Gen. (U.), 133, 138, 141, 146, 148, 178, 182, 186, 189.
Smith, William Sooy, Gen. (U.), 13, 17.
Smith's (A. J.) division (U.), 48.
Smith's cavalry (C.), 38.
Smith's (Morgan L.) division (U.), 348, 354, 356.
Smythe's brigade (U.), 109, 116
Sons of Liberty, 440, 441, 445, 448.
Sprague's division (U.), 348.
Stahl, General (U.), 277.
Stanley, General (U.), 405, 413, 415.
Stanley's division (U.), 216, 239, 343.
Stanton, Edwin M. (U.), 67, 71.
Steele, Captain (U.), 349.
Steele, General (U.), 48, 50.
Stevens, Captain (U.), 394.
Stevenson, General (C.), 214, 216, 220.
Stewart, General (C.), 342, 347, 405, 414, 416.
Stewart's corps (C.), 343, 344.
Stewart's division (C.), 216, 232.
Stone, Colonel (U.), 54.
Stoneman, General (U.), 402.
Stoneman's division (U.), 214, 236, 240.
Strong, Commander (U.), 383, 391.
Strong, Inspector-general (U.), 349.
Stuart, Brigadier-general (C.), 86, 99, 122, 124, 128, 131.
Stuart's brigade (C.), 117.
Sturgis, General (U.), 429.
Sweeney's division (U.), 219, 348, 356.
Sweet, J. B., Col. (U.), 448.
Sweitzer's brigade (U.), 102, 181, 184.

Taylor, Colonel (U.), 240.
Taylor, Richard, Gen. (C.), 50, 53, 56, 58, 204.
Tennessee Regiment, the One Hundred and Fifty-fourth (C.), 222.
Terry, General (U.), 324.
Terry's brigade (U.), 117.
Terry's division (U.), 145, 146, 149, 152.
Texas Regiment, the Seventeenth (C.), 54
Thoburn, Colonel (U.), 264.
Thomas, C. R., Mr. (U.), 280.
Thomas, George H., Gen. (U.), commands

INDEX.

Army of Cumberland at Chattanooga, 17, 199; at Ringgold, 208; at Resaca, 215; at Cassville, 225; near Dallas, 231; near Kenesaw, 235, 244; at Peach-tree Creek, 340, 343, 345; at Atlanta, 348; at Shoal Creek Church, 413; sends order to Stanley, 415; hears of evacuation of Atlanta, 418.
Thomas's brigade (C.), 120.
Thompson, Jacob (C.), 440, 442, 448.
Thompson, N. P., Gen. (C.), 34, 37.
Thompson, Orderly (U.), 349, 351.
Torbert, General (U.), 178.
Torbert's division (U.), 166, 178, 273.
Turchin's brigade (U.), 18.
Turner's division (U.), 146, 149.
Tyler, General (U.), 124, 278, 281.
Tyler's brigade (U.), 101, 122.

UPTON, Colonel (U.), 119.
Upton's brigade (U.), 110, 118, 122, 182.

VALLANDIGHAM, CLEMENT L. (C.), 441, 445, 448, 451.
Vance's brigade (U.), 53, 54, 55.
Vanderbilt, Mr. (U.), 294.
Vaughn, General (C.), 434.
Veatch's division (U.), 216.
Vermont Regiment, the Tenth (U.), 280, 281.
Virginia Regiment, the Sixty-second (C.), 265.

WADSWORTH's division (U.), 86, 88, 102.
Walcott, General (U.), 354.
Walcott's brigade (U.), 240.
Walker, Colonel (C.), 54.
Walker, General (C.), 121, 350.
Walker's brigade (U.), 117.
Walker's division (C.), 50, 53, 56, 219, 343, 347, 349, 352, 357.
Wallace, Lew., Gen. (U.), 278, 281.
Wallace, Sergeant (U.), 150.
Walthall's division (C.), 405.
War Democrats, 442.
Ward's division (U.), 343.
Warren, General (U.), 76, 85, 88, 93, 95, 109, 153, 158, 161, 186, 190, 315, 328, 331, 333.
Washburne, E. B., Mr., M. C. (U.), 68, 93,111.

Washburne, General (U.), 430.
Webb, General (U.), 122.
Webb's brigade (U.), 110.
Weber, General (U.), 277.
Webster, Daniel, 299.
Weitzel, General (U.), 146, 147, 149.
Welles, Colonel (U.), 349, 355.
Welles, Lieutenant (U.), 384.
Wharton, General (C.), 262, 265.
Wheaton, General (U.), 286.
Wheaton's division (U.), 118.
Wheeler, General (C.), 347, 348.
Wheeler, Lieutenant (U.), 150.
Wheeler's cavalry (C.), 207, 239, 248, 406.
White, Colonel (U.), 261.
Whiting, General (C.), 142, 146, 151.
Whitney, General (C.), 134.
Wilcox's division (U.), 120, 181, 327, 373.
Wilcox's division (C.), 88, 91, 369.
Wilkes, Rear-admiral (U.), 296.
Williams, Captain (U.), 354.
Williams, Lieutenant-colonel (C.), 308.
Williams, Mrs. (U.), 429.
Williams's division (U.), 214, 216, 232, 343.
Wilson's cavalry (U.), 78, 99, 124, 126, 164, 315, 361.
Winslow, John A., Capt. (U.), 299, 301, 385.
Wisconsin Regiment (U.), the Twelfth, 346; the Thirteenth, 346; the Twenty-third, 53.
Wise, Colonel (C.), 265.
Wise, General (C.), 312, 319, 370.
Wise's brigade (C.), 142, 146.
Wofford's brigade (C.), 182.
Wood's division (U.), 216, 236, 239, 343, 345, 348, 356.
Woods, C. R., Gen. (U.), 216.
Wrangelin's brigade (U.), 351.
Wright, Colonel (U.), 244.
Wright, Horatio G., Gen. (U.), 104, 109, 118, 122, 182, 186, 189, 285.
Wright's division (U.), 56, 86, 92.

YORK's brigade (C.), 117.
Young's brigade (C.), 273.

ZETLICH, Ensign (U.), 389.

THE END.

www.ingramcontent.com/pod-product-compliance
Lightning Source LLC
Chambersburg PA
CBHW021422300426
44114CB00010B/609